THE LITERATURE OF FO

THE LITERATURE OF FOOD

AN INTRODUCTION FROM 1830 TO PRESENT

Nicola Humble

BLOOMSBURY ACADEMIC

LONDON • NEW YORK • OXFORD • NEW DELHI • SYDNEY

BLOOMSBURY ACADEMIC
Bloomsbury Publishing Plc
50 Bedford Square, London, WC1B 3DP, UK

BLOOMSBURY, BLOOMSBURY ACADEMIC and the Diana logo are
trademarks of Bloomsbury Publishing Plc

First published in Great Britain 2020

Cover design by Sharon Mah
Cover image: © shutterstock

A catalogue record for this book is available from the British Library.

Library of Congress Control Number: 2019949342

ISBN: HB: 978-0-8578-5455-1
       PB: 978-0-8578-5456-8
       ePDF: 978-1-4725-2151-4
       ePub: 978-0-8578-5475-9

Typeset by Integra Software Services Pvt. Ltd.
Printed and bound in Great Britain

To find out more about our authors and books visit www.bloomsbury.com
and sign up for our newsletters.

CONTENTS

LIST OF IMAGES

PERMISSIONS DETAILS

Images

1. Alexis Soyer's model soup boiler, from *Illustrated London News*, 17 April 1847. In the public domain.
2. A costermonger depicted in *London Labour and the London Poor* (1851), by Henry Mayhew (London: Dover Publications, 1968). Illustration by Henry Mayhew. Image in the public domain.
3. The young David Copperfield buying beer on his birthday, from *David Copperfield* (1850), by Charles Dickens. (Harmondsworth: Penguin, 1985) Image in the public domain.
4. Frontispiece for *A Book of Mediterranean Food* by Elizabeth David *c.* 1950 (litho), Minton, John (1917–57) / Private Collection / The Stapleton Collection / Bridgeman Images.
5. Badger's house from Kenneth Graham's *The Wind in the Willows* (1908). Reprinted with permission from The Estate of E. H. Shephard.
6. The tedium of daily cooking, from Peg Bracken's *The I Still Hate to Cook Book* (1966). Copyright © 1966 by Hilary Knight. Reprinted with permission of the artist.
7. The Mock Turtle from *Alice in Wonderland* (1865) by Lewis Carroll. Image in the public domain.
8. Tom Kitten trussed up ready for the pie in *The Tale of Samuel Whiskers* (1908) by Beatrix Potter. Image in the public domain.
9. Illustrations by Lane Smith, copyright © 1992 by Lane Smith; from *The Stinky Cheese Man: And Other Fairly Stupid Tales* by Jon Scieszka. Used by permission of Viking. Children's Books, an imprint of Penguin Young Readers Group, a division of Penguin Random. House LLC. All rights reserved.
10. The final image of *Egg Drop* (2004) by Mini Grey. Reprinted with permission from Penguin Random House.
11. Roman food in Kes Gray and Chris Mould, *Vesuvius Poovius* (2003). Reproduced by permission of Hodder Children's Books, an imprint of Hachette Children's Books, Carmelite House, 50 Victoria Embankment, London imprint, EC4Y 0DZ.

Text

Extract from *Collected Poems* by Sylvia Plath. Reproduced with the permission of Faber and Faber Ltd., and HarperCollins.

Extracts from *The Waste Land* and *Collected Poems 1909–1962* by T.S. Eliot. Reproduced with Permission from Faber and Faber Ltd.

ACKNOWLEDGEMENTS

As books tend to, this has taken considerably longer to write than originally envisaged. This expanded time scale has meant that I have worked with a number of editorial teams at Berg and then Bloomsbury. For their vision, encouragement and forbearance I owe a great debt to Louise Butler, Jennifer Schmidt, Miriam Cantwell, Sophie Hodgson, Molly Beck and Lucy Carroll. The anonymous original reviewers of the proposal and three readers of the manuscript offered a great deal of extremely helpful advice which has contributed greatly to the range and ambition of the finished book.

Colleagues at the University of Roehampton provided feedback and support throughout the writing of *The Literature of Food*. Laura Peters very generously read the entire manuscript and made some very thoughtful suggestions; she also offered tremendous support in her capacity as Head of Department. Alison Waller's ideas about the structure of the children's literature chapter were invaluable. For their interest and advice, I am very grateful also to Louise Lee, Lisa Sainsbury, Jane Kingsley-Smith, Kate Teltscher, Clare McManus, Ian Haywood, Sarah Turvey, Cathy Wells Cole, Jenny Hartley, Susan Matthews and Simon Edwards. Students on my 'Literature of Food' courses contributed in many ways with their insights and interest. All of my research students have inspired me with their enthusiasm and engagement: I owe particular thanks, for inspirational conversations on the topic of this book, to Ellie Reed, Erica Gillingham, Emily Wilde and Stephanie Riley.

The many friends with whom I have shared discussions on food and literature over the years have made an incalculable contribution to my thinking on the subject. They include: Caroline Ash, Jenny Bell, Tracy Anderson, Katrina Chapman, Frances Child, James Davidson, Ruth Edwards, Matthew Fox, Charlotte Higgins, Tara Lamont, Andrew Manson, Judith Murray, Ciarán O'Meara, Liz Pickard, Sophie Popham, Caroline Rudkin, Paula Thompson, Frances Wilson. For support above and beyond, I owe a particular debt to Caroline Rudkin and Tara Lamont.

Above all, I must thank my family. My parents, Brian and Patricia Humble; my sisters, Rachel and Julia Humble; my stepchildren Ben and Anna Priestman and their partners Yasmin Ahmed and Chris Hoolihan; and most of all, my husband Martin Priestman and our son Luke have all maintained their interest and encouragement to the bitter end. I am more grateful than I can say.

INTRODUCTION: FOOD AS CHIMERA – STRANGENESS AND THE EVERYDAY

One of my early reading memories is of a seemingly innocuous passage in Arthur Ransome's *Swallows and Amazons* (1930) where Susan, the boring domestic sister, discusses methods of cooking eggs with one of those handy farmer's wives who pop up so conveniently in middle-class children's adventure stories of the first half of the twentieth century. Susan professes that her "'best'" eggs are buttered eggs. The farmer's wife expresses surprise: "'most folk are best at boiled.'" "'Oh, well, I don't count boiled,'" says Susan (2011: 21). That exchange stayed with me for years. I'm sure I couldn't quote much of the rest of *Swallows and Amazons*, so why was this so memorable? At first, I think, it was the mysterious buttered eggs (scrambled, it turns out), also the competence of Susan talking to the farmer's wife as an equal – and competence of course is one of the pleasures of Ransome's books ('better drowned than duffers'). I was also intrigued by what it meant to not count boiled: in the idea of a sort of cooking too elementary to count as cooking. What interests me now is also the question of memorableness. What snagged me in this food passage, that it should be remembered whole, while the various scenes of sailing and imagined adventures in Ransome's oeuvre have blurred into one? What are the particular effects and pleasures of accounts of cooking and eating? And what should we make of the way in which this shared egg-knowledge – linking Susan and the farmer's wife, but also Susan and my various reading selves – seems to push beyond the boundaries of the text? The passage, like all textual food-moments, throws up many more questions: what does it say about Susan that she has a 'best' form of egg preparation? What is the novel telling us about feminine enculturation? How do Susan's culinary interest and skill, apparently so fundamental to her characterization, speak to her assigned role as 'Mate' which designates her as second-in-command of the boat but also as wife-in-training? It was questions like these which formed my starting point in thinking about the literature of food: how do we read textual food, and how do those readings intersect with the many complexities of real-world food culture?

The subject of this book is the literature of food considered in its broadest aspect – that is, food within conventionally literary texts – novels, poems and essays – and also within cookbooks, food memoirs and food journalism. It considers food in texts from the 1830s to the present; the dominant focus is British and North American literature, though authors from Europe and further afield (Mexico, the West Indies, Australia) are also discussed. The purpose of this range is to explore difference: to begin to consider the multifarious ways in which food both works and plays within texts, and the variety of functions – ideological, mimetic, symbolic, structural, affective – which it serves. Consequently, there is no neat narrative structure: a trot through food in literature from the early nineteenth to the twenty-first century would have been simple to write, but it would have missed many of the most interesting ways in which food appears in literary texts, and the very different forms of narrative work it performs. Instead, I have adopted a series of different overarching approaches, circling round the topic of food to approach it from various angles: the first section addresses food literature from an historical perspective, the second considers form and genre, and the book is framed by chapters on affect. I follow Elspeth Probyn in seeing a 'rhizomatic logic' to the multiple branchings, connections and intertwinings of the areas into which we are led by a study of food and eating.[1] So, certain issues, authors and texts reappear in different places and contexts throughout the book, nodal points in a web of interconnections. The authorial 'nodes' at the centre of the literary food canon here constructed include Gaskell, Dickens, Alexis Soyer, Isabella Beeton, Woolf, Joyce, Lawrence, Beckett, Orwell, M. F. K. Fisher, Elizabeth David, Margaret Atwood, Norah Ephron, Nigel Slater, Lewis Carroll, Roald Dahl, and Richmal Crompton: a profoundly heterogeneous set of writers linked by an intense engagement with food as object, idea and process. In a branching discussion which approaches these nodal authors from multiple critical and theoretical perspectives, I offer a series of provocations which open up ways of reading the food-rich text. In this key respect, my project differs from the recent study of food and literature co-authored by Tigner and Carruth (2018) and edited collection by Shahani (2018): both offer a fascinating series of case studies of different themes and periods, but the topics and texts discussed remain discrete; the rhizomatic logic of my approach, in contrast, allows for the tracing of multiple, previously unexplored, points of connection between different authors, genres, themes and forms.[2] Also central to my purposes is the contention that we should take cookbooks and other practical food writings seriously as objects worthy of detailed textual analysis; where most other works on the literature of food tend to deploy such texts mainly as context for the discussion of works of fiction, I afford them equal weight, exploring the many formal and thematic intersections between canonical, popular and extra-literary texts. Throughout, the primary logic of my approach has been to think about what happens to texts and readings when we allow food to attain prominence. The 'literature of food' as I define it is not merely 'books about food', but 'texts in which food has power'.

One of my most fundamental contentions is that not all textual food is the same. Food, as I will demonstrate, functions very differently in different genres and at different historical moments. My second contention is that food is often strikingly disruptive of the processes of the texts in which it is located. Even within the realist novel, where it has an 'official' function as part of the 'reality effect', food, as Alice discovers, will not meekly lie down. The food in many novels leaps further off the page than it should, claiming our attention, refusing to remain in the background. It pushes towards the real, or the symbolic, or the merely strange. This is why fictional food is often so memorable, but why it also offers a challenge to the 'protocols of reading' on which realism depends (Freedgood 2006: 1). Much realist food, even within realist texts, is not 'realist' at all.

The food within cookbooks has an apparently opposite function to the food in realist novels: its role is to suggest the possibility of its escape from the text, and its potentiality to become real, at your hands, in your mouth. Yet in many of the descriptions of food in cookbooks, the reverse happens, as the food seems to recede into the past of memory, fugitive, ghostly, fundamentally unrepeatable. Similar paradoxes beset the food in modernist literature, in fantasy, in poetry, in children's literature. Even in our lived experience we repeatedly and wilfully misread food – its social function, its imaginative components, its role in our lives – and underestimate its complexity. Food is always paradoxical – both absolutely ordinary yet also strange and fugitive. It appears odder, I suggest, the longer we look at it. In most of our cultural representations we treat food as a *thing* – a fixed, solid, immutable object to be represented in still lives, in the illustrations in cookbooks, in advertisements, in the descriptions in fiction. But food is not really (or not only) an object: it is a process. We grow or purchase, prepare and cook it, consume it, chew it, swallow and digest it; it becomes part of our bodies or the energy that moves them, and we excrete the waste. This is one of the most fundamental aspects of our existence: we do this or else we die. And yet in our constant hankering after the object status of food we wilfully side-line these processes, shying away from the sight – even the thought – of food denatured by chewing, or rotting, often disgusted even by the remains of a meal, the crumbs and shells and egg-smeared plates. The problem of having our cake and eating it is a genuine one, at the heart of what, culturally, we understand and what we ignore about food.

Food as an object of study is over-saturated with meaning, full to dripping with associations and histories and practices and prohibitions and feelings and memories. One challenge this offers to analysis is suggested by Elaine Freedgood in *The Ideas in Things*, when she describes her approach to the 'things' of the novel as essentially metonymic: 'Metaphor defines and stabilizes; metonymy keeps on going, in any and all directions. It threatens: to disrupt categories, to open up too many possibilities, to expose things hidden' (14). Food threatens instability by the myriad ways in which it opens up meaning. It refuses to be contained by neat disciplinary boundaries or approaches, always forging more connections, raising more questions: about the politics of gender, class and race; about production and consumption and their powers and disempowerments; about materialism, ritual and the everyday; about how we read objects and how we read processes; about desire and disgust; about bodies. The protocols and debates and grounding assumptions associated with these questions do not mesh neatly to make up a seamless field of study: the interdisciplinary terrain opened up by food is a bumpy one.

The second critical problem with food lies in its intractable materiality, its utter familiarity, the sense that it is somehow superficial – even silly.[3] Food obtrudes: it threatens to disrupt the post-structuralist, post-Freudian, post-modernist theoretical orthodoxies into which literary studies has settled, the agreement that when we talk about texts, we talk only about representations, that even what we define as real can only be apprehended through the veils of metaphor. One solution to this conundrum lies in Michel de Certeau's conception of the ordinary as those things that theory and disciplines have excluded as outside their fields of study precisely in order to define those fields.[4] The ordinary, by definition, is the class of things at which we do not look.[5] Food, a matter of necessity, of familiar practice, of the everyday, is a key exemplar of this category (though it is also, in other guises, an exemplar of the luxury). This formulation allows us to conceive of the embarrassment of the real not as posing a block to investigation, but as an artefact of the boundary-formation of disciplines and theoretical territories, something it is possible to move beyond. In particular, I take my lead from Margaret Visser's anthropology of everyday life, and her grounding assertion that 'the extent to which we take everyday objects for granted is the precise extent to which they govern and inform our lives' (1989: 11). Another model I have borne in mind is the idea, advanced by Alison and Jessica Hayes-Conroy, of a 'visceral politics' which would 'develop a means to specify the links between the materialities of food and ideologies of food and eating' (2008: 461). Throughout, I have sought particularly to bring textual analysis into contact with historical enquiry – both the cultural history which shares with literary criticism a post-structuralist scepticism of what we can know outside representation, and the social and economic history which remains confident that there is such a thing as a potato and that its presence and absence have had real historical consequences.

The historical section of the book begins with hunger: the central, irreducible aspect of any politics of food. It focuses on two historical moments when the experience of food scarcity emerges as a dominant concern in literary texts as in political debates: the 1840s and '50s in the British Isles, and the 1930s and '40s in Britain, Europe and America. Looking at essays, journalism, memoirs and cookbooks alongside poetry and fiction, it examines the use of the potato as a figure of absence in discourses of hunger, and the alternative culinary trope of hotchpotch which speaks of the random, ambulatory street-food culture of the mid-century city. While the hungry poor represent both abjection and threat in nineteenth-century accounts of hunger, the twentieth-century hungers produced by the Depression and the Second World War are represented as both global and existential: hunger is no longer that of the Other, but an emblem of the essential human condition. Chapter 2 moves from lack to plenty, examining the representation of the ritual of the dinner in fiction and practical food texts, from the rumbustious grotesque realism of Thackeray in the 1830s, through the mid-century fiction of Dickens and Gaskell to the high-realist abstractions of George Eliot and Henry James, and the exemplary modernist re-castings of Virginia Woolf's dinners. The meal is examined as trope, symbol and plot device, its shifting patterns of representation related to changing social practice. Chapter 3 shifts focus from the brilliantly lit table to the servants who stand back in the shadows, considering the central role played by food culture in the dissimulations, mistrust and elaborate power dynamics at the heart of the relationships between mistresses, masters and servants across the period 1830–1950. The fourth historical chapter considers the gendering of narrative form, voice and readership in food texts across the whole historical period of the study, by way of an examination of the figures of the chef, the gourmet, the bachelor, the culinary refusnik and the mother.

The second section of the book focuses on form, starting with Chapter 5, which makes the case for a distinctively modernist food literature. It begins by examining the multiple formal and connotative functions of fruit and meat in the texts of literary modernism, considers the experimental food literature of the early twentieth century, and ends with an examination of the distinctive tropes shared between this literature and 'official' modernist texts. The next chapter considers the specific functions of food in children's literature from Victorian to contemporary picture books under three rubrics: foods as textual objects, food as play, and the spectre of being food. It argues that food plays distinctive roles in texts for children and young adults: as a conduit to fantasy, as a mode of enculturation into contemporary gender roles and a site of resistance to those norms, and as a psychic space where dark adult impulses towards children are vented. Chapter 7 considers the recipe as literary form, examines some key cases of texts which take the recipe (too) seriously, looks at novels and memoirs which include recipes as part of their graphic texture, considers the construction of identity in African American food memoirs, and examines the paradoxes of memory and recreation at the heart of the recipe form.

The beginning and end of the book consider affect: the ways in which textual food entwines with primal emotional drives. The hungers of Chapter 1 are both historically grounded and matters of the visceral individual body. The final chapter explores food disgust in relation to four distinctive literary modes already addressed in earlier parts of the book. Engaging with various models of disgust drawn from literary and psychoanalytic theory, from anthropology, social history and the cognitive sciences, the chapter examines the varied uses to which this mode of affect is put in the engagements with food in modernist literature, the memoir, feminist fiction, and children's literature.

Food is everywhere in texts, as in life. Every chapter of this study could have expanded to book-length, while the number of food-related topics I did not address could have formed the subject of another monograph. I do not, for example, except in passing, consider taste as a social concept, the semiotics of food, immigrant food, the ecology of food, food and sexuality, food in drama, queer food, obesity, or self-starvation. My greatest challenge has been knowing when to stop.

CHAPTER 1
THE POLITICS OF FOOD: HUNGER

The politics of food is a huge and multi-faceted topic, embracing questions of how food is produced, allocated, distributed and consumed locally, nationally and globally. It includes issues as diverse as state food control and subsidies, food justice, the economic case for vegetarianism, disease prevention, the adulteration of food, anorexia, obesity and starvation. As an academic topic, it 'belongs' to disciplines as various as sociology, anthropology, gender studies, media studies, history, geography and political economics, operating on their boundaries and frequently troubling their grounding disciplinary assumptions. And yet the politics of food is also radically simple: too little food; too much food; the wrong food. It seems ethically appropriate to begin this study of the literature of food not with excess or anxiety but with the stark absolutes of hunger and starvation. Treatments of hunger in literary studies have traditionally tended to take one of two approaches: an analysis of hunger as metaphor, or a focus on the topic of self-starvation (usually understood as rebellion and creative act).[1] While the tropic element of hunger will form a significant part of my analysis, I want also to locate it within a specifically material context, thinking of it not simply as an abstract lack but as an element of particular food cultures and politics. In recent years there has begun to be an increased literary-critical focus on hunger as historically contingent, particularly in nineteenth-century studies.[2] My approach is distinctive in its interest in the *different* ways in which hunger is understood and constructed in particular historical circumstances. To that end, this chapter will focus on two historical moments in which hunger and its effects come to the fore in people's lives and in literary accounts: the 1840s and early 1850s in the British Isles, and the 1930s and '40s in Europe, America and Britain. My interest is in the particularities of the response to and the construction of hunger in texts, including novels, reportage, journalism and cookbooks belonging to these two moments, roughly a century apart.

Hunger in the 1840s and '50s

Two specific hungers befell the population of the British Isles in the mid-nineteenth century: the 'Hungry Forties' endured by the industrial north of England, and the Irish Great Famine of 1845–52. The term 'Hungry Forties' is a coinage of the early twentieth century, but discourses about hunger were a dominant feature of contemporary debates about economic distress.[3] The hunger of the first half of the 1840s was felt across the country, but most deeply in the industrial north, where periods of trade difficulties led manufacturers to reduce hours and lay off workers. The industrial working class, cut off from the land for a generation, were unable to produce their own food and were uniquely vulnerable to shifts in availability caused by poor harvests and alterations in trade agreements, while the price of bread was kept artificially high by the Corn Laws, which protected British agricultural landowners by imposing high tariffs on imported wheat. The Irish Famine began in the middle of the decade, with a blight (*Phytophthora infestans*) hitting the potato which had been the principal food of most of the Irish peasantry since the mid-eighteenth century. The reasons for this mono-culture are complex and much debated among historians but come down in essence to the management of Irish land and agriculture in the interests of absentee English landowners, who turned much of the country over to the grazing of beef cattle for export to England, leaving only small plots of inferior soil to the peasantry. Another factor in the particularly devastating effect on Ireland of the potato blight, which affected much of Europe in 1845, is the lack of genetic diversity in the Irish potato. Whatever the reasons, the result was absolute catastrophe: between a quarter and a third of the total crop was lost in 1845, and three-quarters in 1846. The first deaths from starvation were recorded that autumn.[4] Exact figures for the number who died in the Great Hunger are not possible: 'accurate accounts are impossible in a world where corpses littered the road sides unburied', but modern historical consensus puts it at about a million, with at least another million emigrating (Morash 1995: 3). Deaths resulting from the Famine included illnesses induced by malnutrition and those caused by the mass movement of the population into workhouses and to the vicinity of soup kitchens.

From the first, the hunger of the 1840s is understood as political, both in its causes and in its proximate and likely long-term effects. Hunger had already been placed clearly on the political agenda by the Chartist campaign for universal male suffrage and Parliamentary reform that had begun in the late 1830s. Although the movement was ostensibly focused on political rather than social reform, the underlying drive behind its demands was the alleviation of the dire poverty of the working class which formed the majority of its membership. Chartism, according to radical Methodist preacher Joseph Rayner Stephens, was 'a knife and fork, a bread and cheese question' (1838: 7). Articles, stories, poems and songs in Chartist newspapers return frequently to the issue, with the threat of starvation shown as an ever-present reality. 'A Simple Story', published in 1840 in *The English Chartist Circular*, is the tale of Joe, an apprentice, whose employer and co-workers, discovering that his family is starving, give him first their own meals, and then a portion of their wages. The story announces its aim to demonstrate 'the patient endurance of misery, the real benevolence of heart, and generosity of action' of the poor, as shown by the actions of the co-workers and of Joe himself, who immediately runs off with the small portion of food to share it with his siblings (Haywood 1995: 41). At the end of the story, however, the sentimental portrait of mutual aid is superseded by an impulse towards raw naturalism:

> Should any readers of the CIRCULAR desire to know where poor Joe now is, or what has become of him, we regret to add that he died about three years after the

incident occurred, which is related above, from a want of sufficient nourishment, the condition of two many of the working classes. It was said by the neighbours that he died in a decline.' (45)

Thomas Cooper, one of the most prolific of the Chartist writers, offered a similarly bleak conclusion in his 'Merrie England – No More!', in which half-starved characters emerge from a crowd to tell their stories: the mother unable to feed her baby; the father of an adolescent boy who had almost taken the army recruiting officer's shilling after three months resistance, because he 'felt almost pined to death' and the officer gave him breakfast (Haywood 1995: 55). The former is offered momentary aid by the neighbours who share morsels of food, but when her husband returns with the news that they have been refused relief and must enter the workhouse, the only comfort these friends, also 'the children of misery', can offer is 'reflections drawn from despair' of the fact that 'they would not have to starve long, for life, with all its miseries, would soon be over' (57). Although apparently antithetical, the swings between the themes of mutual aid and renunciation to death offer readers a single political philosophy: the workers can depend on no-one but each other, and they have nothing to lose.

For Tory Radical Thomas Carlyle, the desperate hunger of the poor is a sign of the failures of the laissez-faire economic policies of the Whig ascendancy. His 1843 *Past and Present* sets up an extended contrast between the charitable social structures of the medieval age, centred on the monastery, and the horrors of contemporary society, with its Poor Laws and workhouses. In the first part, 'Midas', he rails against the latter state of affairs, singling out for extended comment a case heard at Stockport Assizes two years earlier: 'a Mother and a Father are arraigned and found guilty of poisoning three of their children to defraud a "burial-society" of some 3l. 8s. due on the death of each child':

> The Stockport Mother and Father think and hint: Our poor little starveling Tom, who cries all day for victuals, who will see only evil and not good in this world: if he were to be out of misery at once; he well dead, and the rest of us perhaps kept alive? It is thought, and hinted: at last it is done. And now Tom being killed, and all spent and eaten, is it poor little starveling Jack that must go, or poor little starveling Will? – What a committee of ways and means! (Carlyle 1899: 4)

The crime of these parents is uniquely personal, imagined in its slow formulation and committal, but also representative: the 'apex' of the enormous mountain of absolute want and by no means the only case of its type: 'the authorities, it is whispered, hint that perhaps the case is not solitary, that perhaps you had better not probe further into that department of things' (4). Their crime of killing their children for food edges very close to the spectre of cannibalism, which, as Gurney has shown, is frequently evoked in discourses on poverty in this decade: 'gothic melodramatic tropes [...] were [...] a general feature of the highly charged atmosphere of the early 1840s, when it was feared that workers were eating carrion or even each other in order to avoid starvation' (2009: 102). In his earlier *Chartism* (1839), published in the year of the first petition to Parliament, Carlyle had deployed the abject hunger of the poor as argumentative weapon wielded against both the government and the Chartist leaders. He sees it as his role to speak *for* the suffering masses: 'these wild inarticulate souls, struggling there, with inarticulate uproar, like dumb creatures in pain, unable to speak what is in them!' (1971: 155). This trope of the voiceless people he returns to repeatedly through this and other works, wilfully ignoring the fact that Chartism was an essentially *textual* movement, with its own newspapers, songs, poetry, fiction and political publications, in which its members expressed precisely their political, social and economic aims and ideas. The trope of the dumb, suffering, *animal* masses casts the poor as figures of absolute abjection, and therefore as objects of pity more than fear. The spectre of their hunger works in precisely the same way: 'the widow picking nettles for her children's dinner' (163); the English workman reduced to the condition of the Irish – 'to scarcity of third-rate potatoes for thirty weeks yearly' (173); the Scotch farm-labourers who raise cows but 'taste no milk, can procure no milk' (173) are figures of pathos rather than threat. The Chartist demand for parliamentary representation he sees as a trick played upon the workers by deceitful leaders: 'the expectant millions have sat at a feast of the Barmecide; been bidden fill themselves with the imagination of meat' (217). Like the beggar of the *Arabian Nights*, given empty dishes by the Sultan and bidden to eat, the poor are cozened into agitating for the chimerical vote rather than the solid reality of food. The text circles around the fearful spectacle of violence, but continually displaces it: it is the reflected image of the French Revolution, or the petty violence accompanying the delivery of the Chartist petition to Parliament which 'breaks out into brickbats, cheap pikes, and even into sputterings of conflagration', or the potential violence – a 'Berserkir rage' – deep in the Saxon British heart, which we must be careful not to awaken. By insisting on the abject nature of the masses, their threatening ire can be explained away: they are misled, they are mad, and – crucially – they are radically undernourished and therefore weak. The hunger of the poor is threat but also opportunity: there is still time for reform. For Friedrich Engels, the hunger of the English urban poor suggests a very different political outcome. In *The Condition of the Working Class in England* (1844), written during a two-year stay in Manchester, Engels, the son of a wealthy German industrialist, recorded his forays into the slums of the city and the economic and political conclusions he draws from what he sees. He argues that the English bourgeoisie refuse to acknowledge the starvation of the poor, citing the fact that

> during my residence in England, at least twenty or thirty persons have died of simple starvation under the most revolting circumstances, and a jury has rarely been found possessed of the courage to speak the plain truth in the matter. Let the testimony of the witnesses be never so clear and unequivocal, the bourgeoisie, from which the jury is selected, always finds some backdoor through which to escape the frightful verdict, death from starvation. (1844: 38)

'The bourgeoisie', he declares, 'dare not speak the truth in these cases, for it would speak its own condemnation'. The unspeakable hungers Engels documents were, of course, to become a foundational element in Marxist thinking, which sees the interests of the capitalist and the worker as fundamentally opposed, with the only solution being the seizure of the means of production by the working class: no rapprochement is possible.

Hunger and its political implications haunt the early Victorian novel, in which scenes of unconsumable or unreachable plenty and excess are juxtaposed with almost rhythmic regularity with accounts of starvation, want and denial. One of the earliest concerted novelistic responses to the English mass food deprivation of the 1840s was Elizabeth Gaskell's *Mary Barton* (1848).[5] Subtitled *A Tale of Manchester Life*, it locates itself, like Engel's text, in the contemporary life of this centre of chaotically rapid industrial expansion, focusing on the experiences of factory worker John Barton and his daughter Mary. The novel begins in a rare moment of leisure for its working-class characters, when Barton and his family meet unexpectedly with their friends the Wilsons as they walk in fields close to the city on a half-day spring holiday. The meal to which the Bartons entertain their friends after this excursion casts a glow of loss over the rest of the novel. The description of their combined kitchen and sitting room (the 'house-place') emphasizes its conveniences and grace-notes: it is 'tolerably large', glowing by the light of fire and candle, its windows dressed with checked curtains, geraniums on the sill. A large cupboard is full of crockery and glass, proudly displayed with the doors open; a bright green-and-red 'japanned' tea tray catches the light. Taking great pride in treating her friends, Mrs Barton instructs her daughter to go and buy eggs and ham: "'a pound and a half, Mary. And get it cumberland ham, for Wilson comes from there-away, and it will have a relish of home with it he'll like'" (1848: 49–51). The meal of fried eggs and ham is served with tea ('warmed' with rum) and bread: a luxurious version of a traditional working-class high tea. It is the last moment in the novel that shopping for, cooking or eating food is described without anxiety. It is also the last moment that we see food situated into any sort of cultural meaning other than the basic binary division of plenty and lack: the nicety of Cumberland ham, chosen for its associative, mnemonic qualities for their guest, is a luxury the text soon moves beyond. Mrs Barton dies that night, late in pregnancy, and 'one of the good influences over John Barton's life' (58) is lost. Gaskell's narrative purpose, as she sets it out in her preface, is to represent to the middle class she assumes to be her readers the situation and feelings of industrial workers, whose 'belief of the injustice and unkindness which they endure from their fellow-creatures, taints which might be resignation to God's will' (37). She is careful to temper any statement of the resentment of men like John Barton with elaborate explanations of all the things they do not fully understand about the economic circumstances of their employers, but, as many critics have noted, the emotional evidence of the narrative (in the first half, at least) is firmly on the side of the workers. Immediately after the account of Mrs Barton's death the novel begins an examination of John Barton's state of mind, tracking forward two or three years after his wife's death, and then back to the death of his son years earlier. In these paragraphs Barton is represented as a test case ('Among these few was John Barton'), an exemplar of the bitter attitudes of the workers towards the employers they see still affluent in times of want, but also as a feeling, suffering individual, 'bewildered' by his fate but willing to 'bear and endure much without complaining' if only he 'could … also see that his employers were bearing their share' (59). The careful, even-handed recognition that the workman may not see all of the story is undermined with detailed examples from Barton's own life, beginning with the bald sentence summing up his early history: 'his parents had suffered, his mother had died from an absolute want of the necessaries of life'. When his young son catches scarlet fever, the doctor tells him that his life depends on 'good nourishment'; recently put out of work and unable to obtain more credit, or even to find the opportunity to steal, Barton finds himself outside the doors of a shop:

> Hungry himself, almost to an animal pitch of ravenousness, but with the bodily pain swallowed up in an anxiety for his little sinking lad, he stood at one of the shop windows where all edible luxuries are displayed: haunches of venison, Stilton cheeses, moulds of jelly – all appetising sights to the common passer by. And out of this shop came Mrs Hunter! She crossed to her carriage, followed by the shopman loaded with purchases for a party. The door was quickly slammed to, and she drove away; and Barton returned home with a bitter spirit of wrath in his heart, to see his only boy a corpse! (60–1)

The sight of the wife of the factory owner who has turned him off, still able to purchase frivolous luxuries while his child dies for want of nourishing food carries such empathetic weight for the reader that the protestations of the justice of the employer's perspective ring hollow. Such emotive narrative juxtaposition is deployed most strikingly in the chapters which follow the burning of Carson's mill, an accident which the owners find fortuitous because 'the mills were merely worked to keep the machinery, human and metal, in some kind of order for better times' (95), and which allows them the opportunity to refit the factory using the insurance money. Newly leisured, they can spend time with their families, enjoying relaxed breakfasts, becoming more acquainted with their accomplished daughters. In the homes of their workers, however, 'many a penny that would have gone little way enough in oatmeal or potatoes, bought opium to still the hungry little ones, and make them forget their uneasiness in heavy troubled sleep' (96). Reduced to almost nothing, like the other laid-off factory hands, Barton and Wilson nonetheless take it upon themselves to offer charity to the family of a fellow worker, Davenport, who lies sick in a cellar. Barton pawns his coat and only pocket handkerchief to buy bread and meat and coals for a fire to warm the wet, fetid cellar in which the family reside, while Wilson makes his way through elegant streets to the home of Carson, the manufacturer, to ask for an 'Infirmary order' to get Davenport admitted into a fever ward for treatment. Carson – unthinking, if not actively cruel – refuses, claiming to need all the inpatient orders for potential factory accidents (although the factory is closed), but offers an outpatient order for the following Monday – too late to help Davenport, who dies shortly after Wilson returns to the cellar. When Wilson arrives at Carson's house we are offered one of very few glimpses into the conventional territory of the Victorian novel – the middle-class home – as we witness the Carson family at breakfast and their servants gossiping in the kitchen. As Wilson waits in the kitchen he is overwhelmed by the smells of the cooking food:

Meanwhile, the servants bustled to and fro; an out-door man-servant came in for orders and sat down near Wilson; the cook broiled steaks, and the kitchen-maid toasted bread, and boiled eggs.

The coffee steamed upon the fire, and altogether the odours were so mixed and appetizing, that Wilson began to yearn for food to break his fast, which had lasted since dinner the day before. If the servants had known this, they would have willingly given him meat and bread in abundance; but they were like the rest of us, and not feeling hunger themselves, forgot it was possible another might. So Wilson's craving turned to sickness while they chattered on. (106)

The extreme hunger experienced by the Davenport family is a matter of binary absolutes: the small children rolling on the filthy floor cry pitifully for bread, reduced to a near-animal state, while their mother is so 'clemmed' that she cannot eat at all; what Wilson experiences is an intense hunger that is not yet starvation. He is still capable of appetite, of responding to the smells and imagined flavours of the food being prepared in the kitchen: his is a gustatory response to food, though it turns to sickness when not met. The difference between hunger and starvation – the first a voracious unsatisfied appetite, the second the state of body weakened beyond appetites – is a crucial distinction in many narratives of want.

Two primal emotions animate the graphic accounts of deprivation and starvation in *Mary Barton*: pity and fear. The abject suffering of the poor is represented in terms designed to elicit strong feelings of sorrow, with the plight of small children and the desperation of their parents particularly lingered upon. Gaskell had lost her own infant son to scarlet fever shortly before beginning writing the book (her first) as what seems to have been a form of therapy. But the intense sympathy the text evokes for the suffering poor is counterbalanced by an equally powerful fear of the potential revolutionary power of the masses if pushed too far. She ends her preface, dated October 1848, with a guarded reference to the potential of want spilling over into the revolutionary form it had recently taken in a number of European nations. The fear of revolution, or at least violent revolt, serves as counterweight to the pity of suffering in virtually all middle-class responses to the hunger of the 1840s: for every pitiable Oliver Twist there is a fearsome Bill Sykes. Charlotte Brontë's *Shirley* (1849), distinctly less radical than *Mary Barton*, sets its imagined industrial uprising a generation earlier, with the Luddite riots of 1811–12, but has clearly in mind the parallels with the Chartist agitation of the 1830s and '40s. The suffering of the workers is more distantly handled, the sympathies less finely balanced. The 'distress' of the period is described in terms of crises of international trade and the progress of industrial technology rather than as a matter of individual suffering, with a sense that these forces are too large for any effective intervention:

As to the sufferers, whose sole inheritance was labour, and who had lost that inheritance – who could not get wages, and consequently could not get bread – they were left to suffer on; perhaps inevitably left: it would not do to stop the progress of invention, to damage science by discouraging its improvements; the war could not be terminated; efficient relief could not be raised: there was no help then; so the unemployed underwent their destiny – ate the bread and drank the waters of affliction. (1974: 62)

The *actual* hunger of the workers slips very easily into a metaphorized form in Brontë's prose. The narrative evinces some sympathy for the suffering masses but focusses much more closely on the interests of the mill owner, Louis Moore, whose livelihood they threaten with their riots. At the end of the novel the trade situation changes, and Moore, having finally 'seen the necessity of doing good', plans for an expansion of his mill which will see the whole rural Yorkshire valley turned into a mill village 'with lines of cottages and rows of cottage-gardens'; his business expansion glossed as an act of charity: 'the houseless, the starving, the unemployed shall come to Hollow's Mill from far and near' (597–8). The charitable or economic initiatives of the wealthy are the only agents of effective change in the novel; the political energy of the poor dissipating itself in pointless violence.

Potato and soup

Writers slip easily into metaphor when addressing the hunger of the English poor in the 1840s, but it is a subject straightforwardly – indeed, obsessively – figurable in text. The Irish Famine, in contrast, has seemed to largely resist figuration. For Christopher Morash's *Writing the Irish Famine*, the Famine itself is essentially indeterminate – 'there were no framing texts; there is no ceremonial beginning, no ceremonial ending' – there had been other famines, and it is only in the mid-1850s, he argues, when it is named as a complete finished event, that the Great Famine could be distinguished from earlier endemic food shortages (1995: 3). Commenting on the paucity of contemporary literary and historical accounts of the Famine in his *Heathcliff and the Great Hunger*, Terry Eagleton suggests that the event challenged signification in its enormity: 'the Famine was apparently nonsignifying, then, not only because it figures ideologically as a brute act of nature, but also because it threatens to burst through the bounds of representation as surely as Auschwitz did for Theodor Adorno' (1995: 12). The Famine in Eagleton's account unmakes meaning: 'Culture is the surplus we have over stark need and a social order shorn of that creative surplus can no longer make history at all [...] the modern period in Ireland flows from an origin which is also an end, an abyss into which one quarter of the population disappears' (14). He persuasively argues that the silencing effect of the Famine is due to the shameful sense of abjection it left in its wake:

> Ireland's disaster was a kind of inverted image of European turmoil, one in which you suffer rather than create, which strips culture to the poor forked Beckettian creature and which, in threatening to slip below the level of meaning itself, offers to deny you even the meagre consolations of tragedy. What lingers on, in such contaminated remnants of the epoch as the language itself, would seem less

tragedy than the very different culture of shame. During the Famine, starving families boarded themselves into their cabins, so that their deaths might go decently unviewed. After the event there were villages which could still speak Irish but didn't; it was considered bad luck. (12)

In fact, as both Eagleton and Morash acknowledge, there *were* contemporary texts which depicted the Famine: William Carleton's *The Black Prophet* (1847), written before it became clear that the Famine was more than a blight, but which proved prescient in its looking back to earlier famine years; Anthony Trollope's 1859 novel *Castle Richmond*, in which the Famine forms the background to a love story and murder mystery; and the work of a number of poets. These included James Clarence Mangan and Richard D'Alton Williams, University wits whose poetry changed absolutely in response to the enormity of the Famine, and Jane Francesca Elgee (later to be the mother of Oscar Wilde), who rejected her Unionist background to write impassioned, fiercely nationalist Famine poetry under the pen name 'Speranza'. Later critics have offered some revision to the 'myth of silence', looking closely at these and other textual responses to the Famine, with Melissa Fegan, author of one of the most significant reappraisals, including chapters on historiography, travel writing and political polemic.[6] The case she mounts for the existence of a body of Famine literature is persuasive but Morash's statement that 'the literature of the Famine […] exists as a series of tangents to the elusive event itself' continues to apply (1995: 187). Fegan demonstrates a series of strategies by which writers separated themselves from the stark immediacy of the suffering with which they were surrounded: travel writers and intellectuals, casting the Famine victim as living skeleton – absolute, abject Other – make no attempt to speak with or for any individual sufferer: '[t]here could be no dialogue with the Famine victim. Famine for the traveller was a purely visual phenomenon, with little or no linguistic contamination' (2002: 95); poets, whatever their 'differences of background, tradition, class, gender, and even style', adopt 'an epic, exhortatory, apocalyptic tone which represented an idealistic escape from the harsh choices they were faced with in reality' (8). Speranza despite offering some of the most strikingly visceral descriptions ('the corpses that were buried without coffins, and the men and women that walked the roads more like corpses than living creatures, spectres and skeletons at once, the little children out of whose sunken eyes the very tears were dried, and over whose bare little bones the hideous fur of famine had begun to grow; the cholera cart, with its load of helpless, huddled humanity' (*Dublin Review* April 1865)) writes from the viewpoint of an outsider: 'much of her most powerful Famine poetry registers the surprise of a naïve but interested onlooker' (Fegan 2002: 177). This is the case with most other Famine poets also, who depict the starvation, illness and death as spectacle rather than experience. Famine is determinedly othered, even in the case of writers who were themselves victims: the fact that Mangan died of starvation was denied by his associates, an indication of the shame and survivors' guilt which Eagleton highlights (Fegan 2002: 167). Much of the shame associated with the Famine, at the time and later, is a product of its abjection. Where English writers fear the potentially violent power of the hungry, Irish nationalist writers express shame at the inverse: the lives wasted through starvation that could have been more gloriously expended in rebellion against the colonizing powers. So, in 'Hand in Hand', Richard D'Alton Williams exhorts his starving countrymen to 'bravely stand for our lives and land, / And prove that men have souls!', while Speranza, in 'France in '93: A Lesson from Foreign History', compares the unarmed famished of Ireland with the armed famished of France who sate their hunger with 'Wild Justice', rather than 'wail[ing] and wait[ing]', and in 'The Exodus' bemoans the loss to death and emigration of 'A million a decade' when instead the nation 'could triumph while mourning the brave, / Dead for all that was holy and just' (Morash 1989: 234; 226; 220). There had, in fact, been an attempt at rebellion early in the Famine – the Young Irelander rising of July 1848, in which rebels, inspired by revolutions on the Continent, besieged a unit of the Irish Constabulary in a farmhouse in Ballingarry, South Tipperary. The failure of the rebellion (they were routed by police reinforcements) led to the breaking up of the Young Irelanders, with their leaders transported, and to a pronounced reduction of sympathy for the plight of the Famine-stricken Irish in England. The English press parodied the rising as 'the Battle of Widow McCormack's cabbage patch', reducing failure to farce. It is notable that the mention of food should serve as comic dismissal even in the midst of starvation. This sense of food itself as somehow petty and bathetic is one that is found surprisingly often in Famine writings – even in later historiographical and critical analysis. It is notable, for instance, how little either Morash or Eagleton discusses food itself: there are no entries for 'hunger', 'food' or 'potato' in Morash's index, and for both texts there is a sense that, in the face of the absolute nature of the famine – the disease, horrors and deaths – food itself becomes unspeakable. Food in its intractable material reality seems somehow disreputable, embarrassingly trivial, and so is elided, replaced by metaphors, unrepresented. While discourses of hunger dwell on the meagre, unwholesome, repetitive diet of the poor, those of starvation often shy away from any mention of the absent food.

Two foods, however, do figure the famine: the potatoes whose rotting caused it and the soup which was the meagre form of charitable resistance to it. The potato, along with alcohol, looms large in English representations of the Irish long before the Great Famine. Peter Gurney notes the fallout from the statement in the early 1840s of Corn Law protectionist Robert Bullock Marsham, the Warden of Merton College, Oxford, that although English workers could not buy bread they at least 'rejoiced in potatoes' (*Times* 25 Jan 1843: 5). The hapless Marsham earned himself the nickname 'Potato Dick'; William Cobden, one of the leaders of the Anti-Corn Law League poured scorn on the notion that potatoes could possibly equal wheat, in a speech to the House of Commons, describing the shift from the latter to the former as a descent 'in the scale of physical comfort'; while Carlyle quotes the phrase as part of warning of the dire revolutionary consequences that might result from the Corn Laws: 'when [...] five millions, as is insolently said, "rejoice in potatoes", there are various things that must be begun, let them end where they can' (Gurney 2009: 99; Carlyle 1899: 166). The animus of the English establishment towards the potato has much to do with its association with Ireland. Gurney cites a cartoon in the radical populist weekly *The Struggle*, Feb 1843, entitled 'Rejoicing in Potatoes', in which the mother of a potato-eating family bemoans that 'we are become a sort of English Irish' (115). In Ireland itself, the lowliness of the potato led some British officials to conclude that

> the famine was a sign of divine displeasure with the potato, and a golden opportunity for the Irish to shift to a less barbarous form of nourishment. In a kind of dietary determinism, a less lowly food would produce a more civilized, and hence less politically belligerent people. What scandalized these commentators was the apparent bovine contentment of the Irish with their humdrum, socially unaspiring existence; and since growing potatoes involved little labour, it confirmed them in their endemic indolence. (Eagleton 1995: 16)

As Colin Spencer notes, it had taken a long time for the potato to be considered acceptable food at all: throughout the eighteenth century there is considerable suspicion, with Lancashire (closest to Ireland) unusual in its early adoption of the tuber (2002: 226–7).[7] Lying behind the English disgust at the potato as staple food seems to be a concept of land use and landscape as well as ideas about the relative nutritional value of wheat and the tuber: the wide wheat-growing fields of England produced by the enclosure of agricultural land in the eighteenth century are imaginatively contrasted with the Irish landscape, sub-divided into tiny peasant farms, with small muddy potato patches. (The largely absentee Anglo-Irish landowners leased their lands to middlemen, who sub-divided it into as many plots as possible to maximise rents: the majority of tenant farms in the mid-1840s were smaller than 15 acres, with a quarter less than 2 acres, meaning that the potato was the only possible staple crop.) The dominant food stuff makes the landscape in a form considered to reflect national character. The potato is a speaking absence in Irish Famine poetry, rarely mentioned even in metaphoric terms. Instead, the reference is to the land itself, its fertility blighted or else misappropriated to the use of the British: so in James Clarence Mangan's religiously quietist poem 'The Famine' 'a blight fell on the land - / The soil, heaven-blasted, yielded food no more', while Denis Florence Mac Carthy's 'A Mystery' depicts a land rich in wheat and pasturage, its bounty stolen by the 'harpy hands' of the invaders: 'They are dying! They are dying! Where the golden corn is growing, / They are dying! They are dying! Where the crowded herds are lowing'. The latter ends with a striking reversal in which the image of the fertile land is turned on its head:

> Is this all our destiny below,
> That our bodies, as they rot,
> May fertilise the spot
> Where the harvests of the stranger grow? (Morash 1989: 132; 190–1)

A rare exception to this potato absence is a poem by Speranza, written considerably after the events of the Great Famine: 'A Lament for the Potato A.D. 1739'. Subtitled 'From the Irish', it professes to be a translation of a poem dating from the earlier famine, in which the potato crop was destroyed by a severe frost and 400,000 starved. Employing an archaic idiom – 'Woe to Lorc's ancient kingdom'; 'Well I mind me of the cosherings' – it places the lost potato in the context of feasting and halls, and 'seven sorts of wine': not the food of poverty but of a benign, legendary feudalism, where 'the people' and 'their Chief' eat together, and the potato is at the centre of a traditional and desirable cuisine:

> Yet was ever the Potato our old, familiar dish,
>   And the best of all sauces with the beeves and the fish. (Morash 1989: 227)[8]

It seems that it is only through the multiple displacements of translation from Irish, of a famine a hundred years distant, rendered in conscious archaisms that the potato can be reclaimed as anything other than shameful.

If the potato figured what Carlyle calls 'Irish-ism' (the reduction of the indigenous British to the condition of the Irish immigrant), soup is understood as the mode of rescue both for and from this lowly condition. Many pages in British newspaper columns, letter to editors and chapters in cookbooks are devoted to the virtues of soup and its ability to save the poor from material distress and from their own debased habits. Soup kitchens had existed for decades, particularly in London, organized by private charitable concerns and often run by and for immigrant communities, but it was in the 1840s that soup and its distribution became a matter of national public debate (Cowen 2006: 117).[9] Alexis Soyer, the celebrated chef of the Reform club, started a correspondence in *The Times* in

Figure 1 *Alexis Soyer's model soup boiler.*

February 1847, with a plan for large-scale model soup kitchens to be opened in London and Dublin, and a subscription list for donations, which he headed with a personal contribution of £30. He received sufficient subscriptions to take to an iron foundry his plans for a new kind of soup-boiler, which he calculated might feed more than twenty thousand people. A week later a second letter was published, in which he gave detailed recipes for two soups suitable to be made in enormous quantities and distributed by charitable organisations (Langley 1987: 32). The recipes are deliberately made as cheaply as possible, to make the case that vast numbers of people can be fed affordably: the first 'receipt' uses one ounce of dripping, a quarter of a pound of beef, two onions, and sundry vegetable peelings and offcuts to 2 gallons of water; it is thickened with half a pound of flour and half a pound of pearl barley. The second recipe, which he claims is even cheaper, contains practical instructions for mass cooking: 100 gallons can be made at a time in a suitably large container, using a 'piece of board in the shape of a cricket-bat' for the purpose of stirring. Soyer's public interventions appeared at the time when the British Government was finally realizing that they needed to provide food directly to the starving Irish: Soyer was invited to take his model soup-kitchen to Dublin, where his records showed that the kitchen served a million meals in under five months. For the Irish, soup kitchens were by no means a straightforwardly benign institution: for nationalists, the need for the people to accept this meagre charity from the Government whose inactions and pillage they blamed for the crisis was the ultimate humiliation. Young Ireland leader John Mitchel, in a letter he wrote to the prime minister after being charged with sedition, described the opening of Soyer's soup kitchen as a low point in Irish history:

> We three criminals, my Lord, who are to appear to-day in the Court of Queen's bench, were spectators of that soup-kitchen scene; and I believe we all felt it with one thought – that this day we had surely touched the lowest point – that Ireland and the Irish *could* sink no further; and that she must not see such another Easter Monday, though she should die for it. (*United Irishman* 15 April 1848: 152)

Thirty years later, another witness described the soup kitchens as a scene from hell: 'Around these boilers on the roadside there daily moaned and shrieked and fought and scuffed crowds, of gaunt, cadaverous creatures that once had been men and women made in the images of God'. The horror of the famine is transferred to the soup kitchen: the making visible of the starving people almost more terrible than the fact of their desperation:

> I once thought – ay, and often bitterly said, in public and in private – that never, never would our people recover the shameful humiliation of that brutal public soup-boiler scheme. I frequently stood and watched the scene till tears blinded me and I almost choked with grief and passion. It was heart-breaking, almost maddening to see; but help for it there was none. (Sullivan 1877: 62)

For Denis Florence Mac Carthy soup is 'the fat fluid of the slave', doled out by the rulers denoted with bitter irony as 'kindly', while 'our corn filled the manger / Of the war-horse of the stranger!' (Morash 1989: 190–2). The nationalist anger directed at government soup kitchens is about the shame of having to accept charity from imperialist oppressors; there was also pervasive suspicion about the soup kitchens run independently by church groups, particularly those run by Protestant Evangelicals. It was widely believed that such groups provided soup only in exchange for religious instruction with the aim of conversion. For many years afterwards, people who were believed to have 'taken the soup' were ostracized.[10]

In the rest of the British Isles, soup continued to be associated with charitable endeavours beyond the 1840s, as indicated by Isabella Beeton's recipe for 'Useful Soup for Benevolent Purposes': considerably more generous than Soyer's receipts (with 4 lbs of cheap meat, bones, 6 leeks, a number of vegetables each by the half pound, 1/2 pint of beer and 4 lbs of rice or barley to 10 gallons of water), this recipe is notable because it is one of very few to which Beeton, usually so distant, appends a personal note:

> The above recipe was used in the winter of 1858 by the Editress, who made, each week, in her copper, 8 or 9 gallons of this soup, for distribution amongst about a dozen families of the village near which she lives. The cost, as will be seen, was not great; but she has reason to believe that it was very much liked, and gave to the members of those families, a dish of warm, comforting food, in place of the cold meat and piece of bread which form, with too many cottagers, their usual meal, when, with a little more knowledge of the 'cooking' art, they might have, for less expense, a warm dish every day. (1989: 85)

(The use of a copper – a large vessel in which clothes were boiled – is a common feature in charitable recipes for soup, with little concern ever demonstrated about how to remove traces of soap before putting it to this new purpose.) Soyer, Beeton and other food writers see soup as food for the poor in two senses – it is food suitable to be made in large quantities and distributed *en masse*, but it is also, they suggest, the sort of food that the poor should be making for themselves. Soyer's statement that 'vegetables are not sufficiently appreciated, or used to the greatest advantage by the industrious classes' (Langley 1987: 32), and Beeton's about their general lack of culinary knowledge typify contemporary discourses about food and the poor. In his *Shilling Cookery for the People* (1854), Soyer elaborates on his theme: in a lengthy passage on the 'General Ignorance of the Poor in Cooking', the narrator demonstrates the titular proposition with an account of an impromptu cooking lesson delivered to an elderly woman: beginning with a statement of the current cheapness and nutritional benefits of ox cheeks, she notes that 'frequently on my visits to the abodes of the poor [...] I have seen this article of food completely spoiled'.[11] She enquires of an old woman into the cooking methods employed: "'But, my dear woman," I inquired, "how long do you cook it?" "Ah!" she replied, "sometimes as long as an hour, and boiling it like the very deuce all the time, till the water will not stand it any longer." "And pray," I asked, "what do you do with the water?"

"Faith, there is no water left, only black muck at the bottom of the pot, which I throw away," was her reply'. She offers to come and show her how to cook the dish properly, but the old woman has no more money, so her eager instructress pledges to buy her the ox cheek, leaving her a sixpence to purchase sand to scour the muck off the pot. The next day she returns for the lesson and shows the old woman how to simmer the meat slowly, yielding a broth to be served with bread as well as the tender ox cheek. Taking her leave she is entreated to stay and have "'a drop of the "crature"'", which she identifies as 'blue ruin', that is, tainted gin, clearly bought with the remains of the donated sixpence (Langley 1987: 61–2). The passage encapsulates the keynotes of middle-class attitudes towards the food of the poor: the primary problem is not availability or affordability of food, but lack of skills and knowledge leading to wastefulness (the boiling away and throwing out of the majority of the nutrients of the dish), and a feckless spending of what resources they have on luxuries (so Gaskell notes that the houses of the factory workers are crammed full of furniture bought when times are good). These attitudes are not only class prejudices designed to lessen middle-class guilt: in particular, it is demonstrably the case that the agrarian 'revolution' of the eighteenth century had the effect of cutting off the British peasantry from the land, while the industrialization which followed created instead a mass urban working class, largely severed from local food traditions and reliant on market forces to supply all food stuffs. In comparison with Continental Europe, which retained dominant rural peasant economies until well into the twentieth century, the British urban working class of the nineteenth century was profoundly de-skilled in culinary terms, and alienated from its food history (Spencer 2002: 246). Soup, eaten for centuries as 'pottage', and on the continent still one of the fundamental items of nourishment, is an index of that loss. Even the rural cottagers, shorn of their land by the enclosures movement and employed as day labourers by increasingly distant tenant farmers, or as piece workers for industrial concerns, had no time to grow food for themselves, little land on which to do so, and often not enough money to pay for fuel for cooking. It is from this class of desperately poor rural workers that most of the servants employed in middle-class homes were drawn: an explanation of the common complaint of servant girls unable to cook, as in Eliza Acton's comment that 'the inability of servants to prepare delicately and well even a little broth [...] is often painfully evident' (1993: 21). The lack of means and skill to prepare the basic hot foods which had nourished their ancestors for centuries speaks of a working class alienated not only from its own labour but from its most fundamental birthright.

Nothing and hotchpotch

The tendency to nothing represented by the potato and the random hotchpotch of the soup are the two key modes of representation deployed by writers of the mid-century in their representation of the food of the poor. The first trope is dominant in Engels's taxonomy of the meagre diets of urban workers at different pay levels, in which he traces the ways in which the average diet declines as income lessens:

The better paid workers, especially those in whose families every member is able to earn something, have good food as long as this state of things last; meat daily and bacon and cheese for supper. Where wages are less, meat is used only two or three times a week, and the proportion of bread and potatoes increases. Descending gradually, we find the animal food reduced to a small piece of bacon cut up with the potatoes; lower still, even this disappears, and there remain only bread, cheese, porridge, and potatoes, until on the lowest round of the ladder, among the Irish, potatoes form the sole food. (84)

But even the lowest level in Engels's scale of consumption – that of the potato-eating Irish – assumes employment: without that, the worker 'is wholly at the mercy of accident, and eats what is given him, what he can beg or steal. And, if he gets nothing, he simply starves […]. In these cases, all sorts of devices are used; potato parings, vegetable refuse, and rotten vegetables are eaten for want of other food, and everything greedily gathered up which may possibly contain an atom of nourishment' (84). The decline Engels maps from inadequate food to a subsistence diet to begging and finally to the eating of refuse is traced in fictional form in Charlotte Brontë's *Jane Eyre:* fleeing from Mr Rochester, Jane flings herself on the mercy of the maternal nature of the heath, consuming her meagre bounty:

Nature seemed to me benign and good; I thought she loved me, outcast as I was; and I, who from man could anticipate only mistrust, rejection, insult, clung to her with filial fondness. To-night, at least, I would be her guest, as I was her child: my mother would lodge me without money and without price. I had one morsel of bread yet: the remnant of a roll I had bought in a town we passed through at noon with a stray penny – my last coin. I saw ripe bilberries gleaming here and there, like jet beads in the heath: I gathered a handful and ate them with the bread. My hunger, sharp before, was, if not satisfied, appeased by this hermit's meal. (1987: 350)

Nature, kinder than men, is not, however, sufficient and the next day she walks to a village, longs for a cake of bread from a bakery but is unable to bring herself to barter for it with her gloves or handkerchief. Desperate for solitude, but forced to remain in the vicinity of food, she wanders for hours around the village, hunger by now an insistent presence of mythic intensity: 'the vulture, hunger […] sank beak and talons in my side' (354). All pride now forgotten she returns to the bakery and tries to barter, with no success. Towards evening she begs a piece of bread from a farmer who is eating his supper of bread and cheese on his doorstep; he gives it to her, she assumes, precisely because he does not think she really needs it: 'I imagine he did not think I was a beggar, but only an eccentric sort of lady, who had taken a fancy to his brown loaf' (355). At her lowest, she is finally reduced to refuse, asking a little girl outside a cottage for the 'mess of cold porridge' she is about to throw into the pig trough. The crust of cold, dried porridge, unappealingly retaining the shape of the pot from which it was scoured, of no interest even to the pig, represents the abject condition to which she has so quickly sunk; the fact that this ultimate food is porridge takes us back to Lowood school and the burnt porridge which 'is almost as bad as rotten potatoes; famine itself soon sickens over it' (78). Charlotte Brontë's fiction (like her sister's *Wuthering Heights*) is essentially starved: food is meagre at the best of times, and protagonists seem to live mostly on will power (*Villette*'s Lucy Snowe surviving mainly on coffee and passive aggression). In *Jane Eyre* this is particularly the case, with Jane's hunger both a matter of deprivation (most notably that of Lowood where Mr Brocklehurst insists on starving the 'vile bodies' of the children in order to feed their immortal souls) and a metaphor for her burning desire for liberty.

The alternate trope of random, heterogeneous mixture to depict the food culture of the poor is notably deployed in journalist Henry Mayhew's *London Labour and the London Poor*, a collection of the results of his extensive study of and interviews with the poor who thronged the streets of the capital. Beginning as a series of articles in the *Morning Chronicle*, the material was published in three volumes in 1851.[12] The food he details is street food, cooked in one of the many outlets that thronged the streets of the city: chop houses, taprooms and beer shops, eating houses, cookshops and pudding shops; or by street hawkers with barrows and stalls selling everything from chestnuts to fish and chips. Many of his interview subjects are themselves street sellers, and he uncovers a vast, complex network of food supply involving costermongers (the keepers of cheap market stalls and of barrows selling raw vegetables, meat and fish), hot and cooked food sellers of all varieties, and the large group of people involved in the collection and reselling of the food refuse discarded by those above them in the social scale. The distinct and elaborate culture of the costermongers is given detailed attention, including their language, the slang used for weights and measures, the particular cries employed by barrow sellers on their rounds, their nicknames, conveyances, donkeys, gambling and entertainment. The tricks employed to make the best of the goods are carefully explicated: oranges boiled to make them swell; cheap apples shined up and mixed in with dearer ones; strawberry containers filled with cabbage leaves with only a few of the fruit on top; nuts baked to look ripe; dead eels mixed with live ones; old herrings made to look bright and fresh by employing candle light to glance off the scales. Where Engels's account is an expression of outrage, determined to open the eyes of the reader to a poverty they choose not to see, Mayhew's, although often moving, is motivated more by an intense curiosity. The details he uncovers are mesmerizing in their particularity, painting a picture of a food culture based not on a traditional cycle of food production, preserving and home preparation, but a dramatically varied one drawn from a multitude of different influences. Pea-soup, hot eels, pickled whelks, fried fish, baked potatoes, boiled sheep's trotters, ham sandwiches, hot green peas, plum duff, chelsea buns, muffins and crumpets: all these and many more items are sold by hawkers specializing in a single food-stuff. Traditional fare dating back to the Elizabethan period is still available – a few gingerbread sellers remain, and milk sellers in St James's Park milk their cows to order – but this is a food culture in constant flux, with new practices and tastes continually emerging, so Mayhew notes that the street selling of coffee and tea has replaced 'saloop' in the last twenty years, and that the selling of ham sandwiches had

Figure 2 *The Coster Boy and Girl Tossing the Pieman in Henry Mayhew's* London Labour and the London Poor *(1851).*

been unknown until eleven years previously.[13] Many of the sellers are immigrants – the costermongers 'appear to be a distinct race – perhaps, originally, of Irish extraction' (Quennell 1969: 30); others are more recent arrivals from Ireland, or Jews from Eastern Europe. His food sellers do not just cater to the poor – many of these wares are purchased by all classes – but their narratives of their customers and of their own eating practices offer a picture of a diverse, ambulatory eating culture, in which conventional meal times and nutritional needs are disregarded in favour of quick, hot, immediately satisfying food. The emphasis is on cheap protein and filling carbohydrates, with a considerable taste for sweet indulgences and for stimulants. So he notes of the average costermonger's diet that they 'breakfast at a coffee stall', spending 1d. on a small cup of coffee and 'two "thin" (that is to say two thin slices of bread and butter)'; for dinner buy what they call 'block ornaments' – 'the small, dark-coloured pieces of meat exposed on the cheap butcher's blocks', which they have cooked in a tap-room; or a meat-pie; and in the evening eat saveloys with a pint of beer (Mayhew 1968: 52). The young, in particular, eat in a ramshackle, grazing manner: a youthful pickpocket declares that he 'spend[s] the chief part of [his] money on pudding'; while the coster-boys, who are 'very fond of good living', indulge themselves by spending much of their income on cakes and nuts, manage 'a relish' of herrings or bacon for breakfast, and pass between them news of the eating-houses whose plum-duff contains the most fruit so that they can plan their routes around a chance of the delicacy. The eight-year-old watercress girl is more abstemious, despite going without dinner and only eating two sparse meals a day ('"Mother gives me two slices of bread and butter and a cup of tea for breakfast, and then I go until tea, and has the same"'), she saves her money rather than spending it on sweet things: '"it's like a child to care for sugar-sticks, and not like one who's got a living and vittals to earn"' (Quennell 1967: 123; 83–4; 95). The particulars of his subject's choices in food and drink are a fundamental aspect of Mayhew's enquiry, giving precise character to the tribes and the individuals whose lives he elucidates. The city whose street life he attempts to map is one fundamentally made up of the buying, selling, preparing and getting of food; its sounds the cries of street sellers and rumbling of barrows, its scents and sights those of markets, stalls, shops and itinerant sellers. The marked contradictions of Mayhew's food-city with its plenty juxtaposed with stark need, its luxuries both cheap and exotic (puddings and pies, tea and coffee, pineapples and ices) and its hungry food sellers are also echoed in a number of novels of the mid-century: most strikingly, perhaps, in Dickens's *David Copperfield* (1850), where the young David's traumatic experiences as a child worker parallel in many particulars the lives of the young costermongers and apprentices interviewed by Mayhew. In a section of the novel which draws very closely on Dickens' own boyhood experiences of being forced to work in a blacking factory for some months while his father was incarcerated in a debtors' jail, ten-year-old David is sent by his unkind step-father to work as 'a little labouring hind' at Murdstone and Grinby's warehouse in Blackfriars. Living in lodgings with the feckless Micawbers, but providing his food for himself, David has for his 'own exclusive breakfast' 'a penny loaf, and a pennyworth of milk', and keeps 'another small loaf and a modicum of cheese on a particular shelf of a particular cupboard, to make [his] supper on when [he] came back at night' (1985a: 214). The issue of the food he purchases for himself in the course of the working day occupies several pages: an account imbued with deep anxiety, shame and sense of betrayal. This passage bears very close similarities to the 'autobiographical fragment' which Dickens vouchsafed to his friend John Foster, and which the latter included verbatim in his *Life of Charles Dickens* (1872–4), and is notable for an intense preoccupation with the attitudes of the people who encounter the child David, and a powerful sense that he must have cut a very extraordinary figure in his attempts to live 'life on [his] own account' (208). His chief difficulty is in the proper disposition of the remainder of his six or seven shillings wages a week: he is 'so young and childish, and so little qualified […] to undertake the charge of [his] own existence', that he is frequently tempted in the mornings by the stale pastry sold at half-price by pastrycooks, and leaves himself no money for dinner. He then either goes without, or buys a roll or a slice of pudding. His precise detailing of the qualities of the puddings at two rival pudding shops bears very close resemblance to the accounts of the pudding-connoisseurship of Mayhew's costerboys:

> One was in a court close to St Martin's Church – at the back of the church, – which is now removed altogether. The pudding at that shop was made of currants, and was rather a special pudding, but was dear, twopennyworth not being larger than a pennyworth of more ordinary pudding. A good shop for the latter was in the Strand – somewhere in that part which has been rebuilt since. It was a stout pale pudding, heavy and flabby, and with great flat raisins in it, stuck in whole at wide distances apart. It came up hot at about my time every day, and many a day did I dine off it. (215)

Figure 3 *The young David Copperfield buying beer on his birthday.*

As did the costerboys, David sees puddings as a matter of urban geography, ranging far and wide to obtain the best specimens. The locations of the puddings are given precisely enough that we could retrace his footsteps, though the rapidly changing nature of the city has put the actual puddings beyond the reach of the reader and the adult David. The child consumer, responsible for purchasing his own sustenance, is a figure of anxiety in both texts: free to indulge his immediate impulses he becomes a victim of his own desires for sweetness and satiation. With food cut free from the home and from maternal control, it threatens to become a matter of self-indulgence rather than nurture. Shorn of the traditional meal structure and the behavioural codes of the table, the urban eating experience threatens degradation. The shame that David associates with his street eating is very much to do with his sense of having been forcibly de-classed: his most painful memories are of the moments when, having saved his money, he attempts to eat at more salubrious establishments:

> Once, I remember carrying my own bread (which I had brought from home in the morning) under my arm, wrapped in a piece of paper, like a book, and going to a famous alamode beef-house near Drury Lane, and ordering a 'small plate' of that delicacy to eat with it. What the waiter thought of such a strange little apparition coming in all alone I don't know; but I can see him now, staring at me as I ate my dinner, and bringing up the other waiter to look. I gave him a halfpenny for himself, and I wish he hadn't taken it. (215)

The fear of being a spectacle to the waiter is a class-based anxiety: a similar incident has occurred earlier at an inn, when David is being taken by stage-coach to school. David imputes his visibility as a consumer on the London streets to his childish size and appearance, but as Mayhew's account makes clear, many thousands of children find themselves in similar circumstances. Dickens himself is well aware of this fact: his novels are full of lone children surviving independently, from Oliver Twist, to Jo the crossing-sweeper in *Bleak House*, to Jenny Wren the dolls' dressmaker, caring for her drunkard father in *Our Mutual Friend*. It is his attempts to behave like a gentleman – a status he feels slipping inexorably way from him – that he believes render him visible: his being singled out as 'the little gent' by the workmen at the factory is reported with some pride, and he is at pains to explain that though he was 'perfectly familiar' with the other boys (Mick Walker and 'Mealy Potatoes' – so called for his pale complexion) his 'conduct and manners were different enough from theirs to place a space between [them]' (218). The primary horror David experiences in his new circumstances, the 'secret agony of [his] soul' (210) is his placement in companionship with these boys: far worse than being singled out as visible on the streets would be the horror of being indistinguishable from them. His efforts to rise above pudding and to 'dine regularly and handsomely' are a rebellion against his circumstances, a fundamental assertion of self. For David, as for Mayhew, the foods of the urban scene function as much as spectacles as consumables: at his half hour tea break, when he lacked the money for coffee and a slice of bread and butter, he would instead indulge in food tourism: 'I used to look at a venison shop in

Fleet Street; or I have strolled, at such a time, as far as Covent Garden Market and stared at the pineapples' (215).[14] The exotic foods of the wealthy, displayed in shop windows or on market stalls, form part of the entertainment culture of the street, at one with the jugglers and acrobats and peep-show exhibitors. The figure of the hungry poor staring through the glass at unreachable food is an oft-used device in the mid-Victorian novel: John Barton staring at the window full of 'edible luxuries', Jane Eyre peering into the bakery, the ragged figures gazing into shop windows who Nicholas Nickelby sees from the coach bringing him into London: 'pale and pinched-up faces hovered about the windows where was tempting food, hungry eyes wandered over the profusion guarded by one thin sheet of brittle glass – an iron wall to them' (1978: 489). Just as the food of the wealthy is spectacle to the poor, so are the poor themselves and their idiosyncratic, sparse and public eating a spectacle to novelists, journalists, economists and their readers: their act of looking simultaneously an attempt to assuage guilt and an indulgence of curiosity.

As social conditions improved in the second half of the nineteenth century, hunger became less dominant as a textual trope. Individual hungers are still represented – the ravenous need of the escaped convict Magwitch in *Great Expectations* (1861), the fulfilling of which results in Pip's eventual enrichment; Maggie Tulliver's hunger in George Eliot's *The Mill on the Floss* (1860), when she runs away to become queen of the gypsies; but with a few notable exceptions (Eliot's *Romola* (1861), which details the Florentine famine of the 1490s, is a striking example), the hungers of the British novel from the 1860s to the 1890s are more metaphorical than actual. Even those texts whose central subject matter is the lives of the poor do not present hunger as a major concern.[15] In Hardy's 1895 study of exclusionary poverty, *Jude the Obscure*, for example, the hunger is metaphoric: the hearts and souls of Jude Fawley and Sue Brideshead are hungry for unachievable freedoms; Arabella Donn's sexual desire for Jude is expressed in 'a curiously low, hungry tone of latent sensuousness' (44), the characters are trapped by their social circumstances, but actual food is not in short supply. Hunger again becomes a central literary trope only in the 1930s, when worldwide economic depression makes it once more a widespread concern.

Hunger in the 1930s and '40s

The Great Depression began with the collapse of the stock markets in the United States in the autumn of 1929. The effects were felt worldwide, with world gross domestic product falling by about 15 percent between 1929 and 1932 and international trade dropping by more than half. Some economies began to recover in the mid-1930s, but many were still suffering the effects of the Depression at the start of the Second World War. At its height, a quarter of the working-age population was unemployed in America and up to a third in other nations (Frank and Bernanke 2007: 98). Crop prices fell by about 60 per cent, devastating rural areas, while construction ground to a standstill in many countries. Heavy industry (and therefore the cities dependent on it) declined sharply, and the consequent steep reduction in the demand for fuel had a devastating effect on mining and logging. In Britain the effects of the Depression were experienced disproportionately by the industrial north: in some urban areas of the northeast unemployment reached 70 percent in the early 1930s. A series of hunger marches attempted to bring the plight of the unemployed to the attention of the rest of the nation, which had suffered much more lightly. Many economic historians argue that it was the rearmament programmes undertaken by European nations in the latter part of the 1930s, and in America in the early 1940s, which led to their ultimate recovery from the Depression. Unemployment declined sharply, and was ended by military deployment as countries entered the war. However, the effect of six years of conflict was severe food shortages in almost all nations, with mass hunger for displaced people across Europe during and after the conflict, while deliberate policies of starvation of prisoners were employed by the Nazis and the Japanese. Literary accounts of hunger in these decades skew markedly to the documentary and naturalistic, a tendency supported by organizations such as the Federal Writers' Project in America, which funded writers during the Depression, commissioning ethnographies and local histories (and whose participants included John Steinbeck, Saul Bellow and Richard Wright[16]), and the Left Book Club in Britain, which sought to educate its members on contemporary social and political issues and international affairs, and which published one of the major contributions to the literature of hunger: George Orwell's 1937 work of shocking documentary realism *The Road to Wigan Pier*.

Orwell's reportage is the twentieth-century equivalent of that of proto-sociologists like Engels and Mayhew; but where they and others like them (Dickens included) conducted their interviews as clear outsiders to the life of the streets, Orwell indulged in a species of disguise, living as and among the people whose lives he was investigating, experiencing their poverty and desperation at first hand. In *Down and Out in Paris and London* (1933), Orwell gives an account of his experiences living as a tramp in London and as a *plongeur* (dish-washer) working in Parisian restaurants. In contrast to the case studies of the Victorians, his account of hunger is a deeply personal one, noting the erosion of moral certainties and sense of self that results from the constant gnawing, demeaning experience of chronic lack of food:

> You discover what it is like to be hungry. With bread and margarine in your belly you go out and look into the shop windows. Everywhere there is food insulting you in huge, wasteful piles; whole dead pigs, baskets of hot loaves, great yellow blocks of butter, strings of sausages, mountains of potatoes, vast Gruyere cheeses like grindstones. A snivelling self-pity comes over you at the sight of so much food. You plan to grab a loaf and run, swallowing it before they catch you; and you refrain, from pure funk. [...] You discover that a man who has gone even a week on bread and margarine is not a man anymore, only a belly with a few accessory organs. (Orwell 2013: 14–15)

The unreachable mounds of food that confront John Barton as he stares into the shop window are luxuries, 'appetising sights to the common passer by', while the 'wasteful piles' by which Orwell's hungry persona is assailed are 'insulting' in their plenitude: their description does not tempt, but affront: the dairy products made monstrous by their excessive quantity; the meat proclaiming its status as corpse without the aesthetic disguise of butchery. The description does nothing to beguile the imaginative appetite of the reader; instead we recoil. A few years later, Orwell undertook another work of reportage, *The Road to Wigan Pier* (1937), an investigation of the extreme poverty of the industrial north of England. He began the book with a lengthy pen portrait of his experience living in the Brookers' 'tripe shop and lodging-house' in an unspecified Northern city. The lodgers – mechanics, commercial travellers, old-age pensioners – sleep crammed into shared rooms: Orwell's room, the original drawing room, contains four beds in among the wreckage of the furniture from the house's previous incarnation. The keynote of his claustrophobic account of the conditions in this house is disgust, communicated in lingering descriptions of sights, smells and physical sensations, and – particularly – though the disturbing juxtaposition of food and dirt. The house is used in such a way that the 'proper' separation of different bodily functions is not observed: the dingy storeroom off the kitchen-living-room where the tripe is kept is partly blocked by a sofa on which 'Mrs Brooker, our landlady, lay permanently ill, festooned in grimy blankets', wiping her mouth on strips of newspaper which litter the floor in slimy balls; the fire is blocked by a line of damp washing, and in the middle of the room is the table at which the family and lodgers eat (1989a: 5). The kitchen table is itself a landscape of disgust:

> I never saw this table completely uncovered, but I saw its various wrappings at different times. At the bottom there was a layer of old newspapers stained by Worcester Sauce; above that a sheet of sticky white oil-cloth; above that a green serge cloth; above that a coarse linen cloth, never changed and seldom taken off. Generally the crumbs from breakfast were still on the table at supper. I used to get to know individual crumbs by sight and watch their progress up and down the table from day to day. (5)

The passive pose Orwell strikes in relation to the table's unpleasant state (not even troubling to brush the crumbs aside himself) is in part a function of the narrative persona he adopts throughout the book, in which he describes the conditions of northern working-class life by experiencing it himself; but it is also demonstrative of his wider argument about the ways in which poverty grinds down its subjects to a state of acquiescence: 'A thousand influences constantly press a working-man down into a *passive* rôle. He does not act, he is acted upon' (44). The first chapter is a masterpiece in the development of a slow, creeping miasma of disgust, so that by the time the reader reaches the end they feel thoroughly begrimed. From the sticky layers of the table cloths, we are taken into the shop next door, and briefly introduced to the tripe which is the Brookers' main item of sale: 'there was a slab on which lay the great white folds of tripe, and the grey flocculent stuff known as "black tripe", and the ghostly translucent feet of pigs, ready boiled'. The tripe is a thing of gothic horror, its form monstrous, its secret storage location a place of darkness and decay. A characteristic taste of the north (usually served boiled with onions in a white sauce), it is already an alien substance for Orwell's largely southern middle-class readership. The fact that tripe is stomach lining makes it singularly appropriate for Orwell's purposes in describing a situation in which the act of eating has to be performed in the face of continual disgust. The disgust occasioned by the tripe is to do with its physical form, its colours, its age and the conditions of its storage. No one is seen eating the tripe – the Brookers largely fail to sell it and they do not offer it to their lodgers or eat it themselves. Orwell at first assumes this is because it is too expensive, but later concludes that it was 'because we knew too much about it' (6). The slang meaning of tripe as nonsense or rubbish also reverberates: the tripe occupies a place at the limits of consumption, a symbolic boundary of horror, of that which cannot be eaten, but which casts a shadow over all that is eaten in the house. The other shadow is cast by Mr Brooker's 'peculiarly intimate, lingering manner of handling things' with his permanently dirty hands (5). His contaminating touch is tracked through the description of the domestic tasks he carries out with glacial speed: 'carrying a full chamber-pot which he gripped with his thumb well over the rim' (10) then, immediately after, peeling potatoes in filthy water, his 'hatred of this "bloody women's work", as he called it, fermenting inside him, a kind of bitter juice'. Mr Brooker's slow-moving mind, like his hands, works like the cow's stomach which is his trade: he chews his 'grievances like a cud' (10), the bitter ferment of his resentments another symbolic link to the untouchable horror of the tripe. The actual food that the lodgers are offered carries both the literal taint of the thumb and the figurative taint of the tripe:

> The meals at the Brooker's house were uniformly disgusting. For breakfast you got two rashers of bacon and a pale fried egg, and bread-and-butter which had often been cut overnight and always had thumb-marks on it. However tactfully I tried, I could never induce Mr Brooker to let me cut my own bread-and-butter; he would hand it to me slice by slice, each slice gripped firmly under that broad black thumb. For dinner there were generally those threepenny steak puddings which are sold ready-made in tins – these were part of the stock of the shop, I think – and boiled potatoes and rice pudding. For tea there was more bread-and-butter and frayed looking sweet cakes which were probably bought as 'stales' from the baker. For supper there was the pale flabby Lancashire cheese and biscuits. The Brookers never called these biscuits biscuits. They always referred to them reverently as 'cream crackers' – Have another cream cracker, Mr Reilly. You'll like a cream cracker with your cheese' – thus glozing over the fact that there was only cheese for supper.

The food is uniformly pale and flabby – like the tripe. Like the world outside, it is monochrome: without variation, starved of colour and vitamins. The Brookers' language is as flat and colourless as their fare: the borrowed verbiage of commercial products and advertising, like the ersatz language of the advertising posters ('"QT Sauce Keep Hubby Smiling"', '"Kiddies clamour for their Breakfast Crisps"') despised by Gordon

Comstock in *Keep the Aspidistra Flying* (1936), the novel Orwell had just completed before beginning his journey north (1989b: 5). Orwell's prose is an ever-tightening net: we are trapped by disgust, never allowed to forget the dirt contaminating the food and its precise nature and origins: the human waste expelled into chamber pots in over-crowded smelly rooms, disposed of daily by a man trapped in a life of demeaning circularity and petty exploitation, transferred to their shared food by a hand both abject and controlling. The final straw for Orwell is the morning when an unemptied chamberpot remains under the breakfast table throughout the meal. He allows us to exit the scene with a final political coda: that 'it is no use saying that people like the Brookers are just disgusting and trying to put them out of mind. For they exist in tens and hundreds of thousands; they are one of the characteristic by-products of the modern world' (14). It is necessary – 'a kind of duty' – to 'see and smell such places now and again, especially smell them, lest you forget that they exist'. The smelling – that is, a visceral imaginative inhabiting – of such scenes is particularly important because it forces us into the experience. We are not allowed the relatively safe journalistic distance of the Victorian observations of the poor: we are trapped with the Brookers and their exploited, underfed guests in the long, laborious, smelly, slimy horror of their days.

Orwell begins with this enforced experience of quotidian disgust in order to rub the reader's nose up against the realities of the experiences of the northern poor; later chapters are focused on statistics as well as experiences: on the particular details of the miners' wages which so many in the south imagine to be generous, the exact dimensions of back-to-back houses, tables of unemployment benefits, a break-down of the budget of individual poor families. The book is divided into two parts: the first the result of Orwell's personal investigation into the conditions in the north of England, the second his analysis of the problem and his testing of solutions, particularly socialism. This latter part of the book was felt to be deeply problematic by his publisher, Victor Gollanz, who thought Orwell's very personal comments on why most 'decent' people dislike the 'crank' presence in socialist groups – the 'fruit-juice drinker, nudist, sandal-wearer, sex-maniac, Quaker, "Nature Cure" quack, pacifist and feminist' (161) – highly likely to offend the typical reader of his Left Book Club publications. More successful than the rather splenetic revelations of Orwell's prejudices (he was also strongly homophobic) are the passages in this second section in which he discusses visceral class antagonism as a physical response: the middle classes absolutely separated from the working class by different standards of cleanliness and opportunities for bathing. His aim is not just to see the working class from the middle-class viewpoint, but also the latter from the point of view of the former: 'there is much in middle-class life that looks sickly and debilitating when you see it from a working-class angle' (107). Food culture is one of his most effective means of mapping that class divide. The Victorian public debate about appropriate food for the poor is reinvigorated in the newspapers of the 1930s, with debates about the Means Test – what Orwell describes as 'a disgusting public wrangle about the minimum weekly sum on which a human being could keep alive' (87). He cites as exemplar a letter to the New Statesman from someone who claimed to be feeding themselves on 3 shillings 11 and a half-penny a week (with no allowance for fuel as the correspondent claimed he ate all his food raw). Orwell fully acknowledges the dietic sense of the list of food, especially when compared with the diet of a miner's family he had cited earlier, but makes the crucial point that more is at stake in our dietary choices than the best nutritional decisions: 'The basis of their diet [...] is white bread and margarine, corned beef, sugared tea and potatoes – an appalling diet. Would it not be better if they spent more money on wholesome things like oranges and wholemeal bread or if they even, like the writer of the New Statesman letter, saved on fuel and ate their carrots raw? Yes, it would, but the point is that no ordinary human being is ever going to do such a thing' (88). In a passage of extraordinary empathy he explains the diet of the typical unemployed family as a matter of comfort, familiarity, and tiny treats:

> When you are unemployed, which is to say when you are underfed, harassed, bored, and miserable, you don't *want* to eat dull, wholesome food. You want something a little bit 'tasty'. There is always some cheaply pleasant thing to tempt you. Let's have three pennorth of chips! run out and buy us a twopenny ice-cream! Put the kettle on and we'll all have a nice cup of tea! *That* is how your mind works when you are at the PAC level. White bread-and-marg. and sugared tea don't nourish you to any extent, but they are *nicer* (at least most people think so) than brown bread-and-dripping and cold water. Unemployment is an endless misery that has got to be constantly palliated, and especially with tea, the Englishman's opium. A cup of tea or even an asprin is much better as a temporary stimulant than a crust of brown bread. (88–9)

The sense of shared experience in the imagined voices, of the comforts of family and of small indulgences is striking. Unlike Elizabeth Gaskell worrying about the profligacy with which the factory workers spend their wages in good times, Orwell requires us to think our way into the experience of the unemployed worker, to identify with the psychological and bodily needs which outweigh the exercise of sheer rationality. Rather than the pity and fear of the Victorian observations of the hungry poor, his text produces a visceral, bodily connection via shared experiences of disgust, emptiness and a desire for comfort.

Another thirties' work of reportage also begins in a boarding house. Christopher Isherwood's *Goodbye to Berlin* (1939) records 'his' experiences in Germany in the early 1930s, observing the effects of economic collapse and the rise of the Nazis. Isherwood's account is ostensibly closer to memoir than Orwell's journalism-cum-sociology, but like Orwell he minimizes the personal element of his narrative while being bodily present in the scenes and incidents he describes. The position of consciously detached observer is established in the famous opening statement that 'I am a camera with its shutter open, quite passive, recording, not thinking': among the many aspects of bohemian Weimar Germany that Isherwood's camera-self records is the culture's relationship with food (1940: 13). The Berlin he inhabits is one where everyone is selling what little they have – often themselves. The erstwhile-respectable Frl. Shroeder whose boarding house is a central location, once 'went to the Baltic for her summer holidays and kept a maid to do the housework' (15) but now fills her house with disreputable boarders, including prostitutes, waiters and music-hall performers, cleans it herself, and sleeps on a broken-springed sofa in the living room, through which guests have to walk to reach the bathroom. Throughout much of the linked narratives that make up the text, hunger is intermittent and partial rather than all-consuming: these people have survived 'the War and the Inflation' (the period of hyper-inflation from 1921 to the start of 1924, when the currency became essentially worthless), and as the narrative begins are at the start of the Great Depression. At this point their diets are meagre and peculiar rather than desperate: many seem to survive chiefly on coffee and cigarettes, and the infamous Sally Bowles claims a diet as consciously eccentric as herself:

> 'Would you like a Prairie Oyster?' She produced glasses, eggs and a bottle of Worcester sauce from the boot-cupboard under the dismantled washstand: 'I practically live on them'. Dexterously, she broke the eggs into the glasses, added the sauce and stirred the mixture with the end of a fountain-pen: 'They're about all I can afford'. (51)

Christopher, whose means of support are ambiguous, but include his income from giving English lessons, makes little mention of personal poverty, but sometime after 1931 leaves Frl. Shroeder's house to stay in a working-class district in the home of Otto Nowak, a youth he has met that summer staying on Ruegen Island. Otto has been the companion of Peter, an Englishman of Christopher's age and class, and the narrative makes it clear that the relationship is a sexual one, despite the fact that Otto himself is much more interested in girls: their relationship is essentially that of rent boy and client. Christopher is an unwilling confidante of both parties; after the summer and the collapse of the relationship, he plans to return to Berlin. The next story starts with him visiting Otto's family and then moving, for unexplained reasons, into their 'leaky, stuffy little flat' (194), sharing a room with Otto. There is no indication of any intimate relationship between the two of them, though, as Isherwood's later biographical works make clear, his sojourn in Berlin was largely motivated by the opportunities it afforded for sexual encounters with young men (and despite the fact that Otto is given to performing naked handstands to show off his muscles). In the Nowak's flat, shared with Otto's parents and his sisters and brother, Christopher lives as one of the family, eating meals which rely heavily on bread and margarine and potatoes (usually fried in margarine) in the damp-stained living room with its 'big table, six chairs, a sideboard and two large double-beds', the room 'so full of furniture that you had to squeeze into it sideways' (162). Christopher's contributions as a paying guest allow the family to afford better food than they otherwise would: on his first night Frau Nowak serves 'an immense meal of lung hash, black bread, malt coffee and boiled potatoes', her sense of reckless extravagance indicated by the fact that she 'had prepared enough potatoes for a dozen people' (172). The lung hash, like the tripe of *The Road to Wigan Pier*, is heavily symbolic, as Frau Nowak is a consumptive, who spends her nights coughing up blood; her removal to a sanatorium ends Christopher's time with the family. The most extreme depiction of hunger and its necessities appears close to the end of the book, but is set not in the 1930s, but a decade earlier during the last years of the war, as retold by one of Christopher's pupils, a young engineer: when resources were so limited that people stole the carriage upholstery of trains to make into clothes, food was so hard to obtain that 'farmers and butchers were omnipotent. Their slightest whim had to be gratified, if you wanted vegetables or meat' (292). His family knew of a butcher who always had meat to sell, but he would only do so if his 'peculiar sexual perversion' was fulfilled:

> His greatest erotic pleasures was to pinch and slap the cheeks of a sensitive, well-bred girl or woman. The possibility of thus humiliating a lady like Frau Krampf excited him enormously: unless he was allowed to realise his fantasy, he refused, absolutely, to do business. So, every Sunday, Krampf's mother would travel out to the village with her children, and patiently offer her cheeks to be slapped and pinched, in exchange for some cutlets or a steak. (292)

The 'meat' of the mother's body – with a deliberate ambiguity about which 'cheeks' are involved – functions as a direct exchange for the meat with which she will feed her family. Unlike Orwell, Isherwood does not set out to offer a detailed account of the economic and social circumstances of the people among whom he lives: these facts are presented to us slant, without comment or affect: the outrage that Orwell's work seeks to elicit is missing here: the effect, rather is of a growing sense of inevitability, as the pieces of the jigsaw slot together to reveal the coming to pass of the history we already know. In the penultimate section, 'The Landauers', the narrative moves back in time to 1930 to tell the story of Christopher's acquaintance with a wealthy Jewish family, traced from his employment as English tutor to their daughter, Natalia, to his later friendship with her sophisticated worldly cousin, Bernhard. The latter's disappearance and death at the hands of the Nazis are revealed to Christopher in an overheard conversation in a cellar restaurant shortly before he leaves Berlin in 1933. The conversation takes the form almost of a play, all speech and stage directions, with no indication of Isherwood's emotional response. Two business men – 'undoubtedly prosperous, technically Aryan, and politically neutral' – discuss travel and the price of food, which they agree is 'dear everywhere' (281), before moving their gossip on to the confiscation of Jewish businesses, and Bernhard's murder, all the while one of them, 'fat and sleek' punctuates the conversation by picking at his teeth:

> 'Bernhard?' said the Austrian. 'Let's see – he's the son, isn't he?'
> 'I wouldn't know …' The fat man dislodged a tiny fragment of meat with the point of his toothpick. Holding it up to the light, he regarded it thoughtfully.
> 'I think he's the son', said the Austrian. 'Or maybe the nephew … No, I think he's the son.'
> 'Whatever he is', the fat man flicked the scrap of meat on to his plate with a gesture of distaste: 'He's dead.' (281)

The fat man's distaste is for the detritus he worms from between his teeth rather than for Bernhard's murder: the two are figures from the Expressionism of George Grosz or

Max Beckmann, monsters of complacency, their grotesquery a function of their well-fed self-satisfaction. For two more pages as Isherwood listens in silence they ruminate on the concentration camps and the horrors to come, the fat man belching the while, until at last, 'his digestion working well again' (283) he settles back in 'the right after-dinner mood' to hear his friend's joke about 'the Jew and the Goy girl with the wooden leg'. In a time and place when food is dreary, meagre and repetitive for the majority of people, those who will profit from the mounting horror can be recognized by their over-fed bodies and their access to meat.

The Second World War produced an enormous quantity of food literature, much of it issued by or to the specifications of Government agencies, designed to reconcile populations to food shortages and rationing. This is particularly the case in Britain, where the Ministry of Food advertisements appeared daily in newspapers and magazines, exhorting the public not to waste food, to save fuel and to make the most of easily grown vegetables like potatoes and carrots. Their Food Facts columns, which appeared in all of the daily papers and the *Radio Times*, offered recipes and hints about wartime cooking, with injunctions to cut out and keep the material (advice which seems to have been widely followed judging by the frequency with which such cuttings appear saved between the pages of second-hand wartime cookbooks). The Kitchen Front radio programme was broadcast for fifteen minutes every day after the morning news, a mixture of hints and tips, recipes (often from listeners) and medical advice about a healthy diet. Independent food writers largely fell in with the official line, writing cheery books full of encouragement about the usefulness of the various dried foods being sent from America as part of the Lend-Lease scheme, and suggestions for often bizarre ingredient substitutions (these included dried milk powder instead of sugar and butter, raw grated turnips instead of pepper, ground rice instead of fish and carrots instead of almost everything, from tomatoes to apricots).[17] The keynote was upbeat, cheerful compliance; remarkably few food writers broke ranks: complaining or talking about the hungry realities of wartime food was deeply unpatriotic. One of the most striking aspects of war-time food literature was the universality of its focus: the intense class-consciousness of the 1930s had been left behind, and a strong sense of trans-class unity was the dominant note. Fictional representations of the food situation in wartime Britain tend to be less sanguine. Many detail the various manipulations people could deploy to supplement their rations, and a number demonstrate gross personal selfishness rather than the upbeat 'kitchen front' spirit of official propaganda. Remarkably few, however, show involvement with the black market, which as recent historical research has shown, was in fact extensive (Roodhouse: 2013). A striking exception is Nancy Mitford's *The Pursuit of Love* (1945) in which the aristocratic Alconleighs struggle with the rations, their long-standing cook unable to make the meat ration stretch more than a couple of days: she is '"the kind of cook who is quite good at a cut off the joint and two veg., but she simply hasn't an idea of how to make up delicious foreign oddments out of bits of nothing"' (1986: 136). Luckily, it turns out that the raffish Spaniard brought home from a prisoner-of-war camp by the narrator's absentee mother, The Bolter, is a professional cook and is soon installed in the kitchen, working wonders:

He was more than a first class cook, he had an extraordinary talent for organization, and soon, I suspect, became king of the local black market. There was no nonsense about foreign dishes made out of little bits of nothing at all; succulent birds, beasts, and crustaceans appeared at every meal, the vegetables ran with extravagant sauces, the puddings were obviously based upon real ice-cream. (138)

In a novel which seeks to rewrite the Nazi sympathies and political treachery of her family members as light social comedy, Mitford clearly feels a bit of black-marketeering is neither here nor there. Rations become irrelevant – the monstrously selfish Bolter can indulge her habit of putting her cigarette out in the sugar bowl secure in the knowledge that Juan will provide from his Aladdin's-cave store-cupboard. In Elizabeth Bowen's *The Heat of the Day* (1949) protagonist Stella Rodney accompanies her lover Robert Kelway on a visit to his family home. 'Holme Dean' emerges as a sort of gothic stronghold of toxic middle-class respectability, figured by its plenitude of solid furniture and particularly by its tea-table, over which Robert's mother presides, witch-like. A marked contrast is drawn between the war-time food experiences of Stella, existing in a state of hectic freedom in Blitz-torn London, free of the old social and moral frameworks, eating mostly in restaurants, and the solidly respectable Kelways with their traditional culinary rituals and their accommodation of the 'realities of the home front' (1962: 111). These realities are particularly demonstrated in 'the butter arrangements': 'each one of the family had his or her own ration placed before his or her own plate in a differently coloured china shell. Today was the delusive opening of the rationing week; the results of intemperance, as the week drew on, would be to be judged' (111). The mimsy 'fanciful' fairness of the china shells makes Stella feel herself to be 'seedy, shady', but it is Mrs Kelway and Holme Dean – 'a man-eating house' (257) – that the novel ultimately blames for the fact that Robert is, in actuality, a Nazi spy, driven to embrace the ideology in reaction to the loss of caste of his sex, trained to espionage by the loving mutual surveillance of the middle-class family in which 'their private hours [...] were spent in nerving themselves for inevitable family confrontations such as meal-times, and in working on to their faces the required expression of having nothing to hide' (256). Robert's profoundly anti-establishment impulses are prefigured in the tea-time scene when he helps himself to a thick coating of plum jam, shocking his young nephew who asks if they are able to eat that way in London. His response – '"Black market", said Robert out of the corner of his mouth' (111) – and suggestion that they will have to visit him in prison are jocular, but his deliberate flouting of the codes of wartime food politics hints at his political betrayal.

The war-time food situation in the United States was by no means as dire as in Britain (where extreme hunger was only alleviated by the supplies sent by America from 1941 onwards), but rationing was introduced in 1942 following the attack on Pearl Harbour and America's entry into the war. An early literary response was M. F. K. Fisher's *How to Cook A Wolf* (1942). Fisher is commonly acknowledged as one of the greatest of American food writers, an experimental prose stylist who turned the study of food into a meditation on all aspects of culture. In a series of short essays, she offers thoughts on propositions and problems derived from food shortages including 'How to Distribute

Your Virtue' (what to do with small amounts of rationed ingredients) and 'How to Boil Water' (the benefits and techniques of soup making). In keeping with her philosophy of food as centrally connected to all aspects of experience, she addresses the issues that bedevilled many women in those years: loneliness, sleepless nights, how to endure blackouts, 'how to comfort sorrow'. The most striking essays address how to deal with moments of extreme food poverty: in 'How to Keep Alive' she considers those 'times when helpful hints about turning off the gas when not in use are foolish, because the gas has been turned off permanently [...] and you don't care about knowing the trick of keeping bread fresh by putting a cut apple in the box because you don't have any bread and certainly not an apple' (1991: 240). Her solution, detailed at considerable length, is to borrow fifty cents, which will 'last you from three days to a week, depending on how luxurious your tastes are' (240), and deploy it on ground whole-grain wheat cereal, fifteen cent's worth of ground beef ('if you choose to be Lucullan') and a selection of vegetables – 'it does not matter if they be slightly battered: you will wash them and grind them into an odorous but unrecognizable sludge' (241). The sludge will be achieved with the loan of a food mill, the resultant mass cooked with water over a borrowed stove until it attains a pap-like consistency. Desperately unappealing, this mixture – 'like stiff cold mush, and a rather unpleasant murky brown-gray in color' – is 'strictly for hunger'. It is very similar to the various 'panadas' Soyer recommended for the poor a hundred years earlier. The difference is not in the ingredients or methods, but in the attitude expressed towards them. Where Soyer attempted to make his foods for the poor sound as appetizing as possible, stressing that he had fed them to aristocratic admirers with much success, Fisher emphasizes the dire straits to which one must be reduced in order to turn to such food, and the spirit of fortitude required to get through them: 'if you had to choose between it and hunger, with its inevitable aftermath of fatigue and bad teeth and dull hair and wrinkles you would eat it three times a day as long as the emergency lasted and perhaps even derive a certain esthetic satisfaction from your own good sense, if not from the food itself' (242–3). Her guiding assumption in recommending the sludge is that the emergency is temporary. In a later essay, 'How to Be Cheerful Though Starving' she turns to a more permanent lack: 'the problem of having the wolf camp with apparent permanency on your doorstep' (252–3). The solution she offers is fairly whimsical: a philosophical attitude towards lack can be adopted if it is shared and addressed with grace. Her example is couched in story, as is so often the case: she recalls a woman she once knew, who lived alone, spending 'no more than fifty dollars a year on what she ate' (255), periodically sharing her strange, magical food with acquaintances. 'Sue', an unknown artist, lived in 'a little weatherbeaten house on a big weatherbeaten cliff', the smelly, candle-lit house stuffed, 'like all dwellings of old lonely people', with 'a thousand relics of the fuller years'. Like 'the Lolly Willowes of the Laguna'[18], Sue gathers 'sea-spinach and pink ice-plant' by moonlight along the cliff tops, and serves salads of bruised herbs picked from the weeds around her shack:

> There was the common bowl of rice (or potatoes which Sue had probably stolen the night before from some patch up the canyon). There was tea, always. There

was, occasionally, a fresh egg, which also was stolen, no doubt, and which Sue always put in the teapot to heat through and then broke over the biggest dish of food. (255)

Like the elderly spinster Alice in *Mary Barton*, Sue lives off the land, treasuring its meagre bounty and sharing it willingly. Just as Alice, retaining the knowledge of her rural ancestors, collecting nettles and herbs, drying them and preparing health-giving drinks for her neighbours, represents one last gasp of pre-industrial knowledge and culture, so Sue's way of life, as Fisher notes in one of her copious annotations of the text for the 1951 edition, is no longer possible: 'For long now the cliffs have been covered in villas, and the wild herbs have vanished. I still taste and smell them in my memory, and feel the close-packed cold beads of the ice-plant's leaves and petals' (255). As a solution to food poverty Sue's narrative exists at the boundary of possibility, its fugitive atmosphere of the strange and magical an indication that Fisher is well aware that survival at this level is tenuous at best.

Some of the most extreme food shortages during the Second World War occurred in Europe. This was particularly the case, of course, as a result of the policies of starvation employed in the Nazi death camps and in forced hunger marches: Auschwitz '*is* hunger', says Primo Levi in his extraordinary memoir, *If This Is a Man* (1958): 'we ourselves are hunger, living hunger' (1988: 80). Bread, and sometimes thin soup, which swells the stomach grotesquely are the only foods in the camp. The prisoners wake to frantic activity, desperate to be ready for the day's first distribution of food: 'Some, bestially, urinate while they run to save time, because within five minutes begins the distribution of bread, of bread-Brot-Broid-chleb-pain-lechem-keynér, of the holy grey slab which seems gigantic in your neighbour's hand, and in your own hand so small it makes you cry' (45). Bread is also their 'only money', a currency in the brief moment between distribution and consumption. They are haunted by the memory of food, particularly food uneaten: seventeen-year-old Sigi 'talks endlessly about some marriage luncheon and remembers with genuine regret that he failed to finish his third plate of bean soup', while Levi recalls the dish of spaghetti he had just cooked and started to eat at the sorting-camp 'when we suddenly heard the news that we would leave for here the following day; and we were eating it (it was so good, yellow, filling), and we stopped, fools, stupid as we were – if only we had known!' (80). The terror and grief of the announcement of their dispatch to Auschwitz are as nothing, seen from his present moment, compared to the fact of solid, nourishing food left uneaten. In the camp, their lives have shrunk to nothing but food and its absence. He imagines, briefly, other futures where he might have access to food: 'And if it happened again …' only to dismiss the thought: 'Absurd. If there is one thing sure in this world it is certainly this: that will not happen to us a second time'. A bowl of spaghetti is an unimaginable future: they are trapped in an eternal present made up only of hunger.[19]

The hunger of the death camps was deliberate, planned. Other starvations were a side-effect rather than a weapon of war. At least 20 million people are estimated to have died during the war of starvation and associated disease, as many as died in the combat (Ellis 1993: 253–4). Immediately after the war whole populations were on the brink of starvation. This was particularly the case for the millions of displaced people who wandered Europe in the aftermath of the war, their cities and livelihoods destroyed. Their hunger and deaths are not much represented either in literature or in historical accounts, as Lizzie Collingham notes in *The Taste of War: World War Two and the Battle for Food*, quoting a cynical newspaper editor to explain 'why many of those who died of hunger during the Second World War are largely forgotten today':

> Death by famine lacks drama. Bloody death, the deaths of many by slaughter as in riots or bombings is in itself blood-bestirring; it excites you, it prints indelible images on the mind. But death by famine, a vast slow dispirited noiseless apathy, offers none of that. Horrid though it may be to say, multitudinous death from this cause … regarded without emotion as a spectacle is, until the crows get at it, the rats and kites and dogs and vultures, very dull. (2012: 1)

One exception to this lack of representation is the work of Samuel Beckett. Beckett spent the war years in France and worked for the resistance during the German occupation. The tramp-like figures who walk the empty landscapes of his novels and many of his plays have been persuasively seen as representing not just the dispossessed of Ireland but also the displaced persons of post-war Europe.[20] The asymptotic tendency towards zero (always approaching close to death and cessation, never quite getting there), which becomes the dominant element of Beckett's work from 1945 onwards, makes hunger a natural subject for him. In *Molloy* (1950), the first of the prose works in which he develops this aesthetic of impoverishment and subtraction, the protagonist, losing his sense of self and language, is nevertheless compelled to go on towards something he cannot fully remember. The self whose journey he is recalling has to keep moving, although his body no longer functions adequately, attempting to manoeuver his bicycle while carrying the crutches he needs to walk (2003: 13). His body's machine has ceased to work effectively, to the extent that food has become difficult to consume. When he is arrested (for reasons unknown, but he believes for his 'deplorable' physical posture), a woman who may be a social worker gives him some food: 'She was holding out to me, on an odd saucer, a mug full of a greyish concoction which must have been green tea with saccharine and powdered milk. Nor was that all, for between mug and saucer a thick slab of dry bread was precariously lodged' (23–4). The food is impossible for him to consume, but he is not able to refuse it: 'Against the charitable gesture there is no defence, that I know of. You sink your head, you put your hands all trembling and twined together and you say, Thank you, thank you lady, thank you kind lady. To him who has nothing it is forbidden not to relish filth' (24). A short time later, he regrets his rejection of the food: 'I thought of the food I had refused. I took a pebble from my pocket and sucked it. It was smooth, from having been sucked so long, by me, and beaten by the storm. A little pebble in your mouth, round and smooth, appeases, soothes, makes you forget your hunger, forget your thirst' (26). Like the protagonist of Knut Hansum's *Hunger*, chewing splinters of wood, Molloy distracts his stomach with a form of eating which is not eating.[21] The stone as a palliative for hunger has fairytale associations, as in the traditional European folk tale of 'Stone Soup', in which a traveller tricks passers-by into providing the ingredients for his meal by inviting them to supply mere garnishes for the delicious magical pot of stone soup he is preparing. Cold, hard, nearly eternal, undissolvable by human action – regardless of Molloy's belief that the action of his sucking has shaped it – the stone is a counterpart to the soft, frail, failing bodies of Beckett's people. The stone or rather stones, since Molloy has many, are not merely substitutes for food, they also replace relationships. Beckett's characters harbour powerful feelings for inanimate objects: emotions which are oddly touching but also emblematic of their profound alienation. Molloy is deeply attached to a mysterious little silver object which he has stolen from a woman with whom he had a sexual relationship: he describes it at fascinated length as something like a miniature sawhorse and is entirely unable to comprehend its purpose, but takes it now and then from his pocket and 'gaze[s] upon it, with an astonished and affectionate gaze' (63). The most likely identity of this object, I believe, is a Georgian knife rest – an attribution made more likely by the fact that he stole it at the same time as some 'massive teaspoons'. A defunct relic of an earlier model of table manners, the knife rest (if such it is) speaks to the artificial impositions of culture on the base material fact of eating, just as the sucking stones represent Molloy's attempt to move beyond the gross necessity of consumption altogether. He eats when necessary only under compulsion, claiming to have the appetite of 'a thrush':

> But the little I did eat I devoured with a voracity usually attributed to heavy eaters, and wrongly, for heavy eaters as a rule eat ponderously and with method, that follows from the very notion of heavy eating. Whereas I flung myself at the mess, gulped down the half or the quarter of it in two mouthfuls without chewing (with what would I have chewed?), then pushed it from me with loathing. One would have thought I ate to live! (53–4)

In Beckett's poetics of negation eating is a hateful activity that prolongs the unpleasant act of living, but one that it is not possible to entirely escape. Their bodies chain his subjects to existence, and yet remain a source of continual fascinated self-examination. The sucking stones allow Malloy to satisfy his oral urges without needing to actually take in sustenance. Their importance to him is indicated by the extraordinary six-page mental meander in which he describes the complicated system of the distribution and re-distribution of sixteen stones among his various pockets in order to ensure that each receives an equal share of sucking. The solution to this conundrum is simultaneously obsessively important to him and utterly irrelevant: 'the solution to which I rallied in the end was to throw away all the stones but one, which I kept now in one pocket, now in another, and which of course I soon lost, or threw away, or gave away, or swallowed' (74). The stones anchor him to the world, to the urges and drives of the body, but they are also as close to nothing as Beckett's characters are allowed to get: detritus, picked up from the sea shore, as easily discarded as swallowed, leaving only a fugitive taste of salt.

Historical end points are always arbitrary. As rationing in Britain tailed off in the early 1950s, and the welfare state swung into action, hunger ceased to be such an immediate concern for most of the population. This was not always the case, though, for the many immigrants from the West Indies who arrived in the years after the British Nationality Act of 1948, which gave citizenship and right of settlement to all people living in British colonies in an attempt to fill shortages in the labour market. Sam Selvon's *The Lonely Londoners* (1956) details the disappointing experience of a loosely associated group of Caribbean men who arrive in London expecting jobs and welcome only to find themselves excluded from employment and accommodation by racism. Living hand to mouth in ramshackle rooms they learn to navigate the city, inserting themselves into its districts and culture and at the same time remaking it.

> Before Jamaicans start to invade Brit'n, it was hell of a thing to pick up a piece of saltfish anywhere, or to get a thing like pepper sauce or dasheen or even garlic. It had a continental shop in one of the back street in Soho, and that was the only place in the whole of London that you could pick up a piece of fish. But now, papa! Shop all about start to take in stocks of foodstuffs what West Indians like, and today is no trouble at all to get saltfish and rice. (2006: 63)

With all other aspects of their lives utterly changed, their own food culture is one of the few things they have left to cling to. Tanty, an elderly relative of one of the 'boys' who has come to join him, uninvited, is a marker for the ways in which West Indian food stuffs and culinary and social practices begin to infiltrate the city: she and her fellow women treat the local food shop as a social hub 'just as if they in the market-place back home'; she persuades the shop keeper to give credit, and unlike native housewives gets away with choosing her own goods from the market stalls rather than accepting the rotten ones from the back. Nostalgia for home is almost always wrapped up in thoughts of food: Moses, the closest thing to a central consciousness for the novel, is always wondering why the others don't give up and return home. Talking to a greedy friend about what he would do with a pools win, he imagines for him a glorious return: "'But Big City, you only have mouth, man. I sure if you win all that money you head straight back for Trinidad to eat a breadfruit and saltfish and go Maracas Bay to bathe in the sea." (86); his fantasy of his own return is very similar, composed of sun and sleep under a tree and a fish broth by the sea.

The predominant experience for many is hunger: one man, Cap, exists by sponging off his friends and women, and periodically skipping out on his lodgings, rent unpaid. He manages periods of lack by sleeping through them: 'If he have money, he would get up in the morning. If not, he would sleep all day, for to get up would mean hustling a meal' (30). Hustling food is the order of the day: Cap, gifted with 'the sort of voice that would melt butter in the winter', is good at latching on to newcomers and spinning 'the hardluck story' (30). The food metaphors appear frequently, speaking to an underlying current of hunger. Ambitious Bart, who is always tense with the fear that one of the others will try and borrow from him, has his pride and his economic means eaten away by the experience of the city: 'a few door slam in Bart's face, a few English people give him the old diplomacy, and Bart boil down and come like one of the boys' (47), a reduction that leads to his 'train[ing] himself to liv[ing] only on tea for weeks', before inuring himself to all shame and becoming precisely the sort of scrounger he reviled in others: '[w]hen Bart go round by Moses Moses would say "Take a plate from the cupboard and hit a pigfoot and rice," and though the way he say it is no invitation, Bart lost to all intonation of voice' (48–9). Towards the end of the novel, two similar extended episodes dramatize both the marked differences in cultural food practices and attitudes of the immigrants to those of their hosts, and the desperation produced by their prolonged hunger. Galahad, who we first encounter just off the boat train in the opening pages of the novel, a cocky young man determined to take his adopted city by storm, is brought down to earth in a bitter winter when all the boys lose their jobs:

> That particular winter, things was so bad with him that he had was to try and catch a pigeon in the park to eat. It does have a lot of them flying about, and the people does feed them with bits of bread. Sometimes they get so much bread that they pick and choosing, and Galahad watching them with envy. In this country, people prefer to see man starve than a cat or dog wanting something to eat. (117)

The marked contrast between native British attitudes to animals and to (black) people legitimizes Galahad's social transgressions – both the stealing of a publically 'owned' creature and the unlicensed killing. Nonetheless, his denunciation by an old woman who witnesses the snatch sends him into a spiral of shame and self-doubt. Galahad's desire to catch a pigeon is not presented as simply a random act of desperation: it is imbedded in his memory of familial and cultural foodways – specifically, his father's similar snatches back home. The idea of eating pigeon is assigned to cultural rather than rawly nutritional categorizations: Galahad has a cooking method in mind – he is going to roast it – and he ends up sharing it with Moses, his guilt and anxiety forgotten as he savours the dish:

> 'Is a long time I ain't eat pigeon, boy', Galahad say.
> 'Pigeon meat really sweet', Moses say.
> In about an hour they was eating pigeon and rice. Galahad sucking the bones and smacking his lips.' (119)

A later episode reprises the theme of catching and killing birds for food. Cap, who for most of the novel seems to survive on no visible means of support, one day notices the seagulls flying above his attic room. That evening, lying weak with hunger on his bed, he remembers them:

> Cap lay there thinking about big meals at Chinese and Indian restaurants, and remembering the times when fortune favour him and his belly full so he didn't have to worry about food. And while he was in this meditation, the seagulls started to fly across his mind. (130)

The account of his trials and errors and final success in catching one oscillates between comedy and high drama. The description of his killing and preparing and cooking the bird is omitted – we move from his holding down the bird under his blanket to the fact that for two weeks 'he lessen he seagull population in London evening after evening' (132). As with Galahad's pigeon, the seagull is understood in terms of existing food culture: in this case, not the traditions of his Caribbean home, but those of China and India, renowned for making use of a much wider range of ingredients, and associated by him with celebratory feasts in the recently opened restaurants of these other immigrant groups. The meals he produces from his catches are described in culinary terms which evoke formal dinners and chefly innovation as well as nutrition: '[t]he menu had him looking well, he eat seagull in all manner and fashion' (132). These scenes of killing for food represent the ingenuity of the West Indian immigrants, their willingness to fend for themselves, to use all that the country offers, untrammelled by the apparently arbitrary food rules within which its native population operates. Despite the doors closed to them with hostile 'diplomacy', they possess a resilience and active agency: they will survive despite their hunger.

Hunger is both an abstract, trans-historical force and an event with specific historical lineaments and particular patterns of narrative representation. With the exception of Chartist accounts, the hungers of the 1840s are represented as happening to others and are understood largely as spectacle. The hunger of the mid-twentieth century is shown as that of all humanity, with the reader required to imaginatively partake in it. These later hungers produce little fear: the hungry poor are no longer seen as figures of revolutionary potential. Hunger is both more global and more personal. Shared by almost all these representations of hunger is a sense that it is only part of a system of food distribution, the flip side of which is plenty. The next chapter will examine one aspect of this plenitude in a consideration of the dinner party, and the central performative role it plays in the fiction of the nineteenth and early twentieth centuries.

CHAPTER 2
THE DIFFICULT DINNER PARTY: FOOD AS PERFORMANCE IN NINETEENTH- AND EARLY TWENTIETH-CENTURY FICTION

The subject of this chapter is crucially not only the dinner party, but also its difficulty. The dinner party is the place where numerous complexities of food culture collide – issues of etiquette, the form of the meal, the order of courses, mode of service, innovation versus tradition, alcohol and its social rituals, questions of the make-up of the party, invitations, conversation, modes of behaviour, let alone table settings, crockery, cutlery, decoration, and so on. The semiotics of even the simplest meal are extraordinarily involved, as Margaret Visser has shown (1989; 1992). In considering some of the many and various ways in which the dinner party appears in the fiction of the nineteenth and early twentieth centuries and the changes in both its representation and its narrative function I am interested in how novelists write the dinner party, but also in how we might read it. In both cases the same issue arises: the dinner party is such an elaborate concatenation of ritual, social pressures and culinary complexities that it is over-significatory. It brims with too much meaning, too many possibilities. In this it emblematizes some of the myriad problems of reading food, which is always both replete with symbolic possibility and resolutely, obdurately physical. Almost all of the authors considered here are revisited elsewhere in the book: the focus here is not on their food writing *per se* but on the centrality of dinner scenes in their work, on the logic and significance of those scenes, and on a mapping of the shifts in the use of the dinner as a fictive device across the period.

Victorian dinners

It is hard to think of a Victorian novel that does not contain a dinner party. In the works of Dickens, Gaskell, Eliot, Trollope and Thackeray, of Wilkie Collins and Charlotte M. Yonge, we find the same scenario replayed repeatedly: David and Dora Copperfield's first dinner party in their new married home, the old-fashioned dinner with Mr Holbrook that leaves the genteel Cranford ladies all a-twitter about how to eat their peas, the clerical dinners of Barchester, the many meals that mark Becky Sharp's social ascent. Even in a novel as starved as *Jane Eyre* we have the dinner Mr Rochester throws for Blanche Ingram (though Jane is notably not invited and eats alone in her room). How are we to read these set-pieces? Until recently most critical accounts have regarded them as simply what realism does: part of the richly delineated social background whereby it renders itself apparently three-dimensional, in what Roland Barthes calls 'the reality effect' (1989: 148). In such an account, these scenes of dinner are so prevalent precisely because they are ordinary, part of the 'ambivalent generosity' with which realism 'provides its readers with lots of objects and details that do not demand interpretation' (Freedgood 2006: 100).[1] Highly conventional occasions for which all the rules are known, they enable the reader to do his work in bringing to life the world of the book through a comfortable process of recognition. But there is a problem with this model: far from being an ordinary assimilated ritual, the dinner party, for the Victorian middle class, was both strange and awkward.

Previously a feature of upper-class society, in the course of the nineteenth century the dinner party became an increasingly important element of middle-class life, one of the key means of bolstering, consolidating and advancing social status.[2] So crucial was it that by the mid-century household and advice manuals simply assume that a significant portion of the monthly income will automatically be set aside for the purposes of entertaining. Isabella Beeton's hefty chapter on 'Dinners and Dining' in her 1861 *Household Management* interweaves its rather bleak weekly plans for 'plain family dinners' (with their good-housekeeperly logic of re-using the Sunday joint in subsequent meals) with altogether different dinner party menus for six, eight, ten, twelve and eighteen persons. These are arranged on a monthly basis, with a number of different examples each month, particularly for the smaller parties. She gives eighty-two such menus in total, not including the grander plans for a game dinner for thirty and a ball supper for sixty. While we might see these last as dream-fodder for her socially ambitious readers, the sheer number and detail of the less ambitious menus are a strong indication that regular dinner parties were of some importance to Beeton's middle-class readership. This state of affairs was a fairly recent evolution: in the early years of the nineteenth century formal entertaining was largely restricted to the aristocracy and gentry, with the middle classes adhering to more casual and intimate forms of entertaining. As the middle class grew in social and economic importance, and as it became largely urban, its social behaviour became increasingly codified, elaborate and formal. Where a small businessman in the 1830s, working from his home, might have given fairly impromptu dinners to close friends and family, his equivalent in the 1870s, working from an office in a city, would have welcomed existing and potential professional associates to his home with as much splendour and ritual as he could muster, clear in his understanding that such events contributed to his professional success. It would have been equally apparent to his wife that a reputation as a good hostess was crucial to her family's social status. We find the moment of transition marked in Alexis Soyer's *The Modern Housewife* of 1849. Soyer, the chef of the Reform Club, was, as discussed previously, a flamboyant highly public figure, and an extremely successful self-publicist. Alongside organizing soup kitchens and inventing numerous kitchen gadgets, he produced a succession of cookbooks, each geared to a particular social group. *The Modern Housewife* spoke to the middle-class woman, employing the conceit that it was a series of letters exchanged between two friends, Mrs B. ('Hortense') and Mrs L. ('Eloise'). Mrs B., who is acclaimed 'the Model Housekeeper' by all who witness her domestic management, shares her domestic and culinary secrets with her less experienced friend. Mrs B. has previously been 'in business' with her husband, running a shop from their home, but has now clearly moved up in the world ('we thought as much of five pounds then as we do now of twenty') and entertains in a much more formal style (Langley 1987: 38). Her description of their current mode of entertaining is prefaced with a counter example: the poorly managed dinner she had attended at the home of a city acquaintance of her husband in the previous week. The occasion is criticized not for the lack of grandeur or expense, both being plentiful, but the lack of effective management: insufficient servants for the formality of the service, food too heavy and abundant, the hot dishes turning cold during the time taken to serve them, the long pauses between courses. Her account of her own procedure is used by Soyer to demonstrate a careful balance between show and effectiveness. She invites twelve guests although her table will accommodate more, because she has plates for that number; she chooses those dishes that are easiest to carve and easy for the cook to prepare. Despite recommending simplicity the account of the dinner is extraordinary in its detail, covering such intricacies as the number of lights on the table and the number to remove in order to have dimmer light for the dessert course; the width of her dining table; every detail of the table setting; the distribution of condiments between table and sideboard; the minutiae of serving, conversation, drinking and wiping of hands; and the tricky question of when the ladies should withdraw and when the gentlemen should join them. The highly detailed account is deemed necessary by Soyer because every item is potentially open to contestation. The B.s remove the cloth from the table for dessert in the traditional manner, but Mrs B.'s explanation suggests that this is not the invariable current practice ('Mr B. says he likes to see the mahogany, for when he asks a City friend to come and put his feet under his mahogany, it looks rather foolish if he never sees it.' (52)); they use napkins and rose water despite understanding this to be a rather un-English habit (Soyer is often at pains to introduce small items of European sophistication); and at Christmas they observe the 'city custom' of a loving cup – a shared cup of punch in which each gentleman in turn drinks the health of the lady on his left. The rituals of drinking are in particular flux at this point in the mid-century: the older custom whereby women drink wine only if 'challenged' to do so by a gentleman is still observed by the B.s, but the meal is begun by the serving of champagne to all. A great deal of attention is given to the problematics of serving the food. The B.s employ a mode of service known as 'à la français', in which all of the food for each 'grand course' is placed on the table at once, with the host carving and people helping themselves and their neighbours from the dishes closest to them. So Mrs B. has the soup and the fish on the table to start, which are then replaced by the roasts and other main course dishes. Service à la français was replaced in the course of the nineteenth century by a new mode of formal service, à la Russe, in which no food is left on the table, and each separate small course is handed to diners by servants. The introduction of this form of service to Paris in the 1830s was credited to the Russian Prince Kourakin and by the 1880s it had become the dominant mode, but what is crucial is that for the intervening fifty years no one was quite sure which form to use. Each had advantages and disadvantages: for the very wealthy the older mode allowed them to show off their fine china and silver plate serving dishes, but the newer form allowed for display in the greater number of servants it deployed. It also had the advantage of keeping the food hotter. For the middle classes the requirement for greater numbers of servants was more problematic, but most felt the need to incorporate the new fashion to some extent. The result was that for half a century almost everyone who entertained at all adopted their own compromise between the two systems. (Mrs B remarks that at her friend's dinner there were not enough servants to pass the dishes, but that it was too formal for any diner to dare pass them themselves; her own compromise is to have the food on the table in the old style, with her husband and a male guest carving, but to have sufficient hired-in servants to pass the food to the guests.) My interpretation of the confused complexity of Victorian dining habits differs from that of Judith Flanders, who argues in *The Victorian House* that the multitudinous and shifting rules governing entertaining were not problematic for the vast majority of middle-class Victorians: 'what was done, or not done, was never permanently fixed, but at any one time most people in a single group had a clear idea of what was expected at that level, and had books and magazines to instruct them if they were hoping to move on to the next' (2004: 253). Her account of the life of the dining room, however, rings with the bemusement of individual Victorians about the constantly changing patterns of dining behaviour and etiquette and it is to be noted that even those helpful books and magazines very frequently disagreed about the correct procedure. Flanders's somewhat benign interpretation is that the function of the elaborately codified rules of social engagement was to allow for social mobility, whereas one might equally argue that their complexity was to patrol the boundaries within the middle class. In practice, of course, class markers work both ways simultaneously, allowing some people in and keeping others out. The crucial point is that the dinner, until the late Victorian period, was a source of intense social anxiety as well as a ritual of major cultural importance. This further suggests that contemporary readers, encountering elaborate dinner-scenes in novels, were unlikely to assign those accounts to the uninterpretable, non-symbolic 'background', but instead to consider them elements to be actively read.[3]

Early Victorian literary dinners

We gain a sense of both the newness and the ubiquity of the habits of dinner giving among the aspirant middle classes from the peculiar intensity with which William Makepeace Thackeray dwells on the topic in his works of the 1840s. In his *Book of Snobs* (1848), a series of satirical squibs directed at various pretensions of modern life, he singles out 'Dinner-giving Snobs' with particular glee:

> For instance, suppose you, in the middle rank of life, accustomed to Mutton, roast on Tuesday, cold on Wednesday, hashed on Thursday, etc, with small means and a small establishment, choose to waste the former and set the latter topsy-turvy

by giving entertainments unnaturally costly – you come into the Dinner-giving Snob class at once. Suppose you get in cheap-made dishes from the pastrycook's, and hire a couple of greengrocers, or carpet-beaters, to figure as footmen, dismissing honest Molly, who waits on common days, and bedizening your table (ordinarily ornamented with willow-pattern crockery) with twopenny-halfpenny Birmingham plate. Suppose you pretend to be richer and grander than you ought to be – you are a Dinner-giving Snob. And oh, how I tremble to think how many and many a one will read this! (1879: 79)

Thackeray sees the dinner-giving snob as contemptible in his pretensions but recognizes that the type is becoming so common as to be scarcely containable within the category of eccentricity that encompasses the rest of his Snobs. In condemning this increasingly common behaviour he is aware that he is fighting a rear-guard action, as the dinner party comes to seem an increasingly indispensable part of the lives of the middle classes. The act of dinner giving or dinner attending as an attempt – often failed – at social advancement is a trope in many of his early short works of journalism and social satire: key examples include the comic novella 'A Little Dinner at Timmins's' in which the protagonists are ruined by their attempts at grand entertaining, and a cod-journalistic piece, 'A Dinner in the City', written in the persona of Mr Spectator. The latter is a biting account of a public dinner in the City of London, its excesses of pomp, self-importance and rich food dwelled on in emetic detail. In a satirical tone thinly masquerading as excitement the piece describes the receipt of the coveted invitation to 'dine with the Worshipful Company of Bellows-Menders, at their splendid Hall in Marrow-pudding Lane' (1993: 187; 189). The event functions as a parody of the annual Lord Mayor's banquet, the menu of which has been bathetically compared at the opening of the article with 'the Homeric poems' (187). This banquet was renowned for one dish – turtle soup – and it is this dish that Mr Spec contemplates with wonder: 'The last year's paper had a bill of fare commencing with "four hundred tureens of turtle, each containing five pints" … "Fancy two thousand pints of turtle, my love," I have often said to Mrs Spec, "in a vast silver tank, smoking fragrantly, with lovely green islands of calipash and calipee floating about – why, my dear, if it had been invented in the time of Vitellius he would have bathed in it!"' (187). At this point the turtle soup is a somewhat shifting signifier: the classical gloss, the exotic description, the technical terms (calipash is the gelatinous green fat attached to the upper shell of the animal and calipee the yellowish fat that attached to the lower; considered the choicest parts of the dish they were cut into small squares which floated on the surface of the soup): all could mark this description as the approval it professes to be, but the sheer volume of the soup begins to tip it towards a sense of excess and gluttony which is fully borne out in the description of the soup served at the actual dinner. Turtle soup was extremely expensive – Mrs Beeton, writing a decade later, puts the cost at one guinea a quart. Made from giant green sea turtles imported alive from the tropics, it was really a dish for large public entertainments with professional chefs and enough guests to consume the meat before it could go off. Its expense and relative rarity meant that an invitation to such a gathering had high status and was much sought-after. But what

Thackeray chiefly sees in the dinner is its pretension: the over-weaning self-importance of the City magnates aping aristocratic manners and forms. The turtle soup becomes an index of their smugness and their greed, and also of their lack of the elegance and taste to which they lay claim. The exoticism of this first description, the choice morsels of turtle floating in a sea-like soup that resembles the distant realm from which they come, is replaced a few pages later with an account of the serving of 'this broth of the City' and its consumption by one Mr Spec's table-neighbours:

> There was a gentleman near us – a very lean old Bellows-Mender indeed, who had three platefuls. His old hands trembled, and his plate quivered with excitement, as he asked again and again. That old man is not destined to eat much more of the green fat of this life. As he took it, he shook all over like the jelly in the dish opposite to him. He gasped out a quick laugh once or twice to his neighbour, when his two or three old tusks showed, still standing up in those jaws which had swallowed such a deal of calipash. He winked at the waiters, knowing them from former banquets. (192–3)

The description is grotesque: the body of the old man food-like in its quivering, the tusk-teeth making his mouth repellent. The desperation of his greedy desire for the soup renders the pleasure of the other guests also suspect. Like much of Thackeray's work, the passage teeters back and forth in its moral judgements and sympathies: the old man's greed is tempered by the humane acknowledgement that he will not taste many more turtle soups, and by the extension of the pleasure of the green fat to encompass others of life's delights; but his familiarity with the waiters, and particularly his matey acknowledgement of them, suggests an irredeemable vulgarity. All the potential elegance and sophistication of the dinner are finally removed in the description of the general scene:

> Conversation, rapid and befitting the place and occasion, went on all round. 'Waiter, where's the turtle fins?' – Gobble, gobble. [...] These year pease have no taste. Hobble-goobleobble. [...] 'Waiter, three 'Ocks, mind your manners!' [...] Hobble-obbl-gooble-gob-gob-gob. A steam of meats, a flare of candles, a rushing to and fro of waiters, a careless clinking of glass and steel, a dizzy mist of gluttony, out of which I see my old friend of the turtle-soup making terrific play among the pease, his knife darting down his throat. (194)

Far from elegant table talk, the shouted demands and complaints vie with the viscerally represented sounds of mastication. The scene dissolves into a miasmic haze of smells and steam and noise, overwhelmed by the rich food and the competing sensations it teeters on the brink of nausea. Language fails the reeling Mr Spec, who has to wait until the next day to pose his question to his friend: 'what can be the meaning of a ceremony so costly, so uncomfortable, so unsavoury, so unwholesome as this?' (198). It is a question which has long preoccupied readers of Thackeray – what are we to make of such a dinner – what does it mean? In 'Oysters and Brown Stout', George Orwell, commenting that Thackeray writes about food 'more often even than Dickens, and more accurately' suggests that the author is never himself certain where he stands: 'He cannot make up his mind whether the raffish upper class or the money-grabbing middle class is more objectionable. [...] the characteristic flavour of Thackeray is the flavour of burlesque, of a world where no one is good and nothing is serious' (1968: 301). It is a moral ambivalence that is perhaps most fully manifested in what is commonly acknowledged as his masterpiece: *Vanity Fair* (1848). In this 'novel without a hero' the reader is torn between condemning and admiring Becky Sharp's relentless campaign of social advancement – much of which is conducted on the field of the dinner party. Newly launched on the world and staying at the home of her school friend Amelia she 'sets her cap' at Amelia's fat and clumsy brother Jos, who has just returned from India.[4] The first of many dinner party scenes is a family affair, at which is served a fine turbot which Mr Sedley, a stock-broker, has bought home with him from Billingsgate market, and a curry – a pillau – in honour of Jos, who stuffs his mouth with it 'his face quite red with the delightful exercise of gobbling' (1985: 61).[5] Hoping to flatter him with her intense interest in all things Indian, Becky tries the curry, claiming it excellent, while 'suffering tortures from the cayenne pepper' (61). To relieve her pain, Jos suggests she should try a chilli, and watches with delight as she bites into what she expects from the name and appearance to be something cool, fresh and green. The accounts of food in *Vanity Fair* are as startling and insidious as that chilli. Dishes are idiosyncratic and particular – prawns for breakfast in Brighton, tartines for breakfast in France. Food weaves its way into the texture of life and language in unexpected ways: the gentle Dobbin is paid for at school in groceries ('the representative of so many pounds of tea, candles, sugar, mottle-soap, plums ... and other commodities' (77)); while the saying 'fine words butter no parsnips' becomes the hook for an elaborate disquisition on the ways in which skilful social players can butter up their marks with flattering words, by way of a reference to Alexis Soyer and his ingenious ways with a soup (226). Food never recedes into the background in this novel – it is in the spotlight, recognized as a key element in the elaborate games of manipulation played by the inhabitants of the social zoo. When Becky secures a post as governess in the home of Sir Pitt Crawley she bitterly congratulates herself that she will at least be among '*gentlefolks*, and not with vulgar city people' (103); Sir Pitt, who she mistakes for a servant, and who dines in the kitchen with the charwoman on boiled tripe and onions which he fishes himself from a saucepan, therefore comes as something of a shock. Taken by Sir Pitt to his family home, Queens' Crawley, she dines the first evening with his timid second wife and daughters and his son Mr Pitt Crawley. The dinner, described by Becky in a sardonic letter to her friend Amelia, is a masterpiece of social and physical discomfort and competing notions of correct behaviour:

'The sideboard was covered with glistening old plate – old cups, both gold and silver; old salvers and cruet-stands, like Rundell and Bridge's shop. Everything on the table was in silver too, and two footmen, with red hair and canary-coloured liveries, stood on either side of the sideboard.

Mr Crawley said a long grace, and Sir Pitt said Amen, and the great silver dish-covers were removed.

"What have we for dinner, Betsy?" said the Baronet.

"Mutton broth, I believe, Sir Pitt," answered Lady Crawley.

"*Mouton aux navet*," added the Butler gravely (pronounce, if you please, moutongonavvy); "and the soup is *potage de mouton à l'Ecossaise*. The side-dishes contain *pommes de terre au naturel*, and *choufleur à l'eau*". (113)

The sly jokes about menu French and English food plain to the point of aggression are exacerbated by the argument between the determinedly blunt-spoken Sir Pitt and his buttoned-up son as to whether it is correct to refer to the soup as 'potage' or as 'Scotch broth'. Sir Pitt robustly compounds his offences against gentility by quizzing the Butler as to the particular animal they are eating, when it was killed, and where the other parts of the carcass had ended up. Sir Pitt's absolute confidence in his social place, surrounded by the relics of generations of his ancestors, means he need have no truck with the niceties with which the more socially insecure protect or consolidate their positions. His gold and silver plate speaks for him – the food itself need not: "'Mutton's mutton'", he decisively asserts. Thackeray significantly refuses to assign notions of good taste or elegance to any social level in the new food culture he observes with such mesmerized intensity. In its assertive materiality his food always at least teeters on the edge of vulgarity. It is food to be eaten, not looked at; its robust, lingering smells and the noisy greed with which it is consumed evoking discomfort as much as pleasure in his readers.[6]

Mid-Victorian literary dinners

Although Soyer and Thackeray have very different agendas, these texts of the 1840s share a strong sense of the difficulty of the dinner – of its high stakes and its many and various pitfalls. The dinner party continues to be of intense interest for mid-Victorian novelists, with the textual pleasure lying often in its virtual impossibility – in the inevitability of failure. This is certainly the case with Dickens, for whom the dinner is a multivalent event, speaking of social climbing and artificiality but also of the idealized virtues of home. There are several dinner party scenes in *David Copperfield* (1850), which in each case play off the yawning gap between the social rules for such occasions and the achieved reality. The reader is asked to feel pleasure – not simply pleasure at failure, though that is part of it, but pleasure at the ways in which the failure cuts through social pretensions and facades. The first married dinner party given by David and Dora is an informal affair: a spontaneously arranged 'little dinner to Traddles'. David's retrospective account makes it clear that he understands that one of the key objectives of the occasion is display – of his home and, most crucially, of his wife: 'I could not have wished for a prettier little wife at the opposite end of the table' (1985a: 708). The rest of the scene consists in the steady revelation of all the ways in which the event fails to live up to even the most basic standards of entertaining. The room is very small even without a guest in it, and David is concerned that Traddles is 'so hemmed in by the pagoda and the guitar case, and Dora's flower painting, and my writing-table' that he doesn't have room to use his knife and fork. There are multiple affronts to the notion of gracious, or even decent, living: 'the skirmishing plates upon the floor', Dora's dog walking around on the table 'putting his foot in the salt or the melted butter', and 'the disreputable appearance of the castors, which were all at sixes and sevens, and looked drunk'. The drunken castors echo the drunken servant whom they had had the misfortune to employ, who ran up bills at the public-house in Dora's name. If the dining arrangements are lacking, the food is even more so. The boiled mutton is mostly raw and apparently comes from a deformed sheep and the oysters Dora has proudly procured are unopened and unopenable as they have neither the means nor the knowledge to deal with them. The scene, like so many in Dickens, teeters on the edge of realism, its anarchic table reminiscent of the final scene of *Through the Looking Glass*, where diners and dinner change places, 'several of the guests … lying down in the dishes' while 'the soup ladle was walking up the table to Alice, and signing to her to get out of its way' (1968: 277); as with Carroll's scene, the anarchy is both joyfully ludic and discomforting. David and Dora play at keeping house – and play at adulthood – in their tiny room which, full of Dora's toys, more resembles a playroom than a dining room. When Dora requests that David think of her as his 'child-wife' she is asking permission to remain in this state of play, without the responsibilities of having to take her domestic role seriously. Her only success on this occasion is not what she does but what she is – when she undertakes the quintessentially feminine act of pouring tea, she does so not as a woman but as a child acting womanliness: 'By and by she made tea for us; which it was so pretty to see her do, as if she was busying herself with a set of doll's tea-things, that I was not particular about the quality of the beverage' (710). The double performativity of her enactment of this iconic femininity works to make quotidian domesticity strangely impossible. David's much-desired domestic comfort is beyond reach and in its place is only the charming image of Dora's failed enactment of womanliness.[7]

While the dinners in *David Copperfield* are an index, chiefly, of David's tentative and inadequate attempts to gain the gravitas and status that will allow him full entry into society, the many dinners in *Our Mutual Friend* (1864–5) reveal the hollow forms and hypocrisy of that society. This novel, Dickens's last completed work, offers a social satire more biting than in many of his earlier novels. The institution of dinner is one of the key carriers of this tone, with the endless social round of the rich and powerful being represented in the repeated, interchangeable dinners thrown by the social-climbing Veneerings and the prosperous, smugly philistine Podsnap. We meet the former in the second chapter of the novel, where they are described as 'bran-new people in a bran-new house in a bran-new quarter of London' (1918: 20). The mystery of the Veneering's 'new-ness' is expiated on throughout the novel, particularly in the puzzled thoughts of Twemlow, in whose life the 'ever-swelling difficulty' is 'the insoluble question whether he was Veneering's oldest friend, or newest friend' (21). We first encounter Twemlow in the context of a description of the Veneerings' furniture:

> There was an innocent piece of dinner-furniture that went upon easy castors and was kept over a livery stable-yard in Duke Street, Saint James's, when not in use, to whom the Veneerings were a source of blind confusion. The name of this article was Twemlow. Being first cousin to Lord Snigsworth, he was in frequent requisition, and at many houses might be said to represent the dining-table in its normal state. Mr and Mrs Veneering, for example, arranging a dinner, habitually started with Twemlow, and then put leaves in him, or added guests to him. (20)

The Veneerings and those many others they represent in caricatured form use decayed aristocrats such as Twemlow (whose address in a mews in Saint James tells us everything about both his impoverishment and his clinging on to social status) as rungs in their social climb. His presence at their dinners is as fundamental as the table: people can be invited to meet him, or invited because they know him. Twemlow, and those similarly situated such as the monstrously flirtatious Lady Tippins, is to be met with at virtually every social occasion in the novel, bored and confused, props rather than actors, but a fundamental part of the scene. Meals in Dickens are never incidental, and the many dinners in the novel are described with an extraordinary amount of detail, but where the food in a novel like *David Copperfield* is alive in its idiosyncratic particularity, the details of the food are absolutely not the point of these dinners. The absence of description of the food itself is marked: it appears generically: Twemlow is 'revived by soup' and is 'appealed to, at the fish stage of the banquet, by Veneering' (24). Food appears as courses, not specific dishes. We are told that it is good – 'the Veneering dinners are excellent dinners – or new people wouldn't come' (25) but not what it is. This withholding of gustatory detail is one of many devices that keeps us from identifying with the Veneerings and their ilk – we cannot share their sensory, bodily sensations so they remain caricatures. The detail in the description of the first Veneering dinner is devoted not to the food but to the elaborate staging and performance of the occasion. We see it at one remove, reflected in 'the great looking-glass above the sideboard' (24), first the table, with Veneering's shiny new silver crest in the form of a camel (discovered – or invented – for him by the Herald's College), with a further 'caravan of camels' – we presume also of silver – bearing fruit, flowers and salt, then the assembled company, described with satiric detail. The 'dinner' is not the food, it is the people: their presence, with its confirmation of Veneering's status, their interactions, their implicit approval. These dinners are not singular: the point is their repeatability, the fact that these people will come again, or invite the Veneerings elsewhere. The dinners *are* Society: their emptiness and ritualized repetition are absolutely the point, which is why the novel gives us so many of them, all virtually the same. The pace of the dinner-giving increases exponentially when Veneering decides to run for Parliament, and the redoubtable Lady Tippins advertises him and his 'dinners out of the Arabian nights' (293) all over town until she succeeds in 'bringing him in' as candidate, the dinners variously his hustings and his supporters' reward. The other Society dinners we witness are those hosted by the Podsnaps. Where the Veneerings are 'bran-new', Mr Podsnap is well established – 'Mr Podsnap was well to do, and stood very high in Mr Podsnap's opinion' (155). Unlike the shiny, varnished surfaces of the

Veneering's life, Podsnap's environment is marked by its solidity, as typified by his table settings:

> Hideous solidity was the characteristic of the Podsnap plate. Everything was made to look as heavy as it could, and to take up as much room as possible. Everything said boastfully, 'Here you have as much of me in my ugliness as if I were only lead; but I am so many ounces of precious metal worth so much an ounce; – wouldn't you like to melt me down?' […] All the big silver spoons and forks widened the mouths of the company expressly for the purpose of thrusting the sentiment down their throats with every morsel they ate. (158)

Where dinners for the Veneerings are the key means of social advancement, for the Podsnaps they are a tedious but essential duty of status and they feel much relieved when various 'friends of their soul' invited to celebrate their daughter's eighteenth birthday are unable to attend and can be crossed off their list of obligations. The food remains undescribed, but the fact that the 'lesser friends of their soul' invited to come to the after-dinner entertainment 'had a claim to be invited to come and take a haunch of mutton vapour-bath at half-past nine' (158) tells us all we need to know. The fugitive presence of the mutton casts a sickly pall over the scene: food as atmosphere rather than pleasure. It is notable that the concept of taste is introduced in this passage in which lingering odours stand in for actual food. The aesthetic of taste, as so often in the literature of food, substitutes curiously for the physical sensation. 'The Podsnap establishment', we are assured, had nothing in common with that of the Veneerings: 'Mr Podsnap could tolerate taste in a mushroom man who stood in need of that sort of thing, but was far above it himself' (158). Taste, one commonly accepted arbiter of class, is rejected by Popsnap in favour of the assured solidity of his inherited respectability and importance (with the physical dimension of taste transferred metaphorically in the imagining of Veneering as food). This would suggest that the Veneering's establishment epitomizes tastefulness, but the novel's initial summative judgement – 'what was observable in the furniture, was observable in the Veneerings – the surface smelt a little too much of the workshop and was a trifle sticky' (20) – is never revoked. Claims to both taste and class are undermined by the deployment of visceral sense associations – the fatty reek of mutton, the stickiness of varnish. The manipulation of readerly distaste works to remove the grounds on which social superiority seeks to establish itself.

Attendance at dinners is as rote as the giving of them for the members of Society: 'Mr Podsnap went out to dinner, and to dinner, and yet to dinner, arm in arm with Mrs Podsnap' (301); 'Lady Tippins lives in a chronic state of invitation to dine with the Veneerings, and in a chronic state of inflammation arising from the dinners' (724). Nearly all of the seventy-plus references to dinner in the novel are occasions of this sort, empty rituals in which personality is reduced to caricature and social intercourse to a form of puppetry. But a few other meals form a counterpoint to social dining – meals in which fellowship and pleasure are central. Two dinners at Greenwich are significant for their informality and enjoyment, and also for their intimate secrecy. The first occurs when Bella Wilfer, visiting home during her lengthy stay with the wealthy Boffins, hands her 'poor dear struggling shabby little Pa' (379) a purse and demands that he buy himself a new suit and take 'this lovely woman' out to dinner. Their adventure is described in terms of bubbling satisfaction, their pleasure paradoxically rendered in the very paucity of language to describe it:

> The little expedition down the river was delightful, and the little room overlooking the river into which they were shown for dinner was delightful. Everything was delightful. The park was delightful, the punch was delightful, the dishes of fish were delightful, the wine was delightful.' (374–5)

Dickens frames the scene as one of secrecy and anonymity, a rare pleasure seized from the daily round; yet a trip to Greenwich to eat a whitebait dinner at one of the hostelries on the river was such a fashionable activity that all the members of the Cabinet would decamp to Greenwich for an annual feast of whitebait washed down with champagne. For the rest of the year the dinners were particularly popular with artists and writers, including Dickens himself. The small fish were so numerous in the upper reaches of the Thames in July and August that contemporary accounts describe the river boiling with them. There was some debate as to their brief season, as they were believed to be a distinct, previously unknown species of fish – one that was so numerous in the Thames because it thrived on the river's pollutants. (It was only towards the end of the century that scientists proved conclusively that they were the young of a number of different fish species) (Davidson 1999: 846). The dish of fried whitebait was exclusive to Greenwich and its environs because it was believed that the flavour of the dish began to deteriorate within an hour of their being landed. A dinner at Greenwich, then, occupies a locus that is both fashionable and bohemian, simultaneously public and private; Greenwich is a liminal space both within and outside the city, the river carrying whiffs of the sea and a world beyond. The whitebait and the 'watersouchy soup' which preceded it (a mixture of many species of fish) break the rules of the highly conventional order of courses; they are manifestly closer to the natural world, to the raw state. Decades before the evolution of restaurants in London, this is also a rare opportunity for a respectable young woman to dine in public, and it is one Bella takes full advantage of, performing her role as 'lovely woman' to the utmost. Bella and Pa return to Greenwich with her new husband John Rokesmith for her secret wedding dinner, where again the food and the setting are rendered with affectionate hyperbole, as Bella's exuberant charm spills over into the text:

> What a dinner! Specimens of all the fishes that swim in the sea, surely had swam their way to it, as if samples of the fishes of divers colours that made a speech in the Arabian nights (quite a ministerial explanation in respect of cloudiness), and then jumped out of the frying-pan were not to be recognised, it was only because they had all become of one hue by being cooked in batter among the whitebait. And the dishes being seasoned with Bliss – an article which they are sometimes out of, at

Greenwich – were of perfect flavour, and the golden drinks had been bottled in the golden age and hoarding up their sparkles ever since. (780)

In both cases the pleasure of the dinners is in their representing an escape from social rules, from the oppression of the Wilfer home and Mrs Wilfer, in the substitution of a private dining room in a public inn for the domestic table. The ships they watch on the river, around which Bella spins elaborate stories, represent escape and – like the fishes – exoticism: in their informality and secrecy, in their invitations to dressing-up and role-play, in the quirky particularity of their menus, these dinners are sites of play, the antithesis of the stuffy, social-climbing politicking of the novel's many other dinners, whose emptiness they highlight.

The social encoding of the dinner ritual is one of its key interests for Dickens's close contemporary Elizabeth Gaskell: the dinners on which she expends most detail are those in which two divergent sets of expectation about behaviour and etiquette clash. In one of her major 'industrial' novels *North and South* (1854–5) southerner Margaret Hale attends a dinner at the home of Mr Thornton, a Northern manufacturer. Her sickly mother, unable to attend the party, has enjoined her to 'notice the dinner well', eager to hear 'how they manage these things in Milton'. She is particularly intrigued about the second course – 'look what they have instead of game' (1986b: 213). The condescension underlying her whimsical interest (we have already been told she is 'curiously amused' by the invitation) is made manifest by the reference to game – her assumption is that this luxury is unavailable to the Thorntons because they live in a city and not the rural environment to which the Hales are used, but of course game also carries the connotations of aristocratic connections and the expensive leisure of shooting parties and the assumption that the Thorntons lack any such associations (198). So instructed, the reader 'looks' with the same intensity as Margaret at the Thornton dinner:

Mrs Hale would have been more than interested, – she would have been astonished, if she had seen the sumptuousness of the dinner-table and its appointments. Margaret, with her London cultivated taste, felt the number of delicacies to be oppressive; one half of the quantity would have been enough, and the effect lighter and more elegant. But it was one of Mrs Thornton's rigorous laws of hospitality, that of each separate dainty enough should be provided for all the guests to partake, if they felt inclined. Careless to abstemiousness in her daily habits, it was part of her pride to set a feast before such of her guests as cared for it. Her son shared this feeling. He had never known – though he might have imagined, and had the capability to relish – any kind of society but that which depended on an exchange of superb meals: and even now, though he was denying himself the personal expenditure of an unnecessary sixpence, and had more than once regretted that the invitations for this dinner had been sent out, still, as it was to be, he was glad to see the old magnificence of preparation. (213)

Mrs Hale's first assumption – that the food will be inadequate – is confounded, but the Thornton's dinner appears to fail on the more rarefied grounds of taste: there is too much, it is too lavish, in its abundance it lacks 'elegance'. But Margaret is nothing so simple as an authorial mouthpiece: the moral movement of the novel is to correct her southern snobberies about the north and the simplicities of her judgements. We, along with Margaret, are given an alternative geographical centre from which to judge, and the 'cultivated taste' of London is not allowed to remain the only standard. Margaret's snobbish attitude towards the Thorntons has already been established in her reaction to the dinner invitation and her conversation about it with the young factory girl she has befriended. In response to Bessy declaring that the Thorntons are 'th' first folk in Milton', she teasingly challenges her about whether the Hales are not themselves the 'first folk' (199). Bessy's answer makes explicit the grounds on which status is judged in the industrial north – 'yo' see, they thinken a deal o 'money here; and I reckon yo've not getten much'. Margaret, perhaps released from good taste in her conversation with a social inferior, is equally explicit about the grounds of her own snobbery:

> 'No', said Margaret, 'that's very true. But we are educated people, and have lived among educated people. Is there anything so wonderful, in our being asked out to dinner by a man who owns himself inferior to my father by coming to him to be instructed? I don't mean to blame Mr Thornton. Few drapers' assistants, as he was once, could have made themselves what he is.' (199–200)

Although many of Gaskell's readers might be expected to share Margaret's snobbery, or at least recognize its hegemonic status, her bald utterance of it is exposing. The gradual revelation of the motives of Mrs Thornton and her son in their lavish entertaining (pride, but also generosity) works to open up other possible codes of behaviour and to offer them to us as at least equally valid to Margaret's own. The use of food metaphors is significant, with Margaret's 'taste' balanced by Mr Thornton's 'relish'. The concept of good taste is not allowed to have the final word in assigning value to a social act, and it is notable that Mr Thornton's understanding of his mother's approach to the hosting of a dinner party is mediated through his comprehension of this act as a crucial element in the maintenance of his social world. We see a very similar tension between different understandings of the social rules of the dinner in *Cranford*, published in volume form the year before *North and South*. In this collection of short episodes in the life of a provincial backwater, the ladies of the small town have established their own elaborate codes of behaviour which effect a compromise between their gentility and their relative poverty. 'Elegant economy' is the agreed form, and Gaskell cracks the code for us in the first chapter, which details 'Our Society': 'we none of us spoke of money, because that subject savoured of commerce and trade, and though some might be poor, we were all aristocratic' (1986a: 41). This elegant economy means that the food served at entertainments can be legitimately meagre: 'it was considered "vulgar" (a tremendous word in Cranford) to give anything expensive in the way of eatable or drinkable, at the evening entertainments. Wafer bread-and-butter and sponge-biscuits were all that the Honourable Mrs Jamiseson gave; and she was sister-in-law to the late Earl of Glenmire' (42). It also means that the ladies give very few dinners, preferring tea and supper as more economical meals; consequently, when some of their number are invited to dine with 'an old bachelor' it is an occasion of some excitement. The bachelor in question, Mr Holbrook, had long ago been a suitor of Miss Matty's, but had been refused by her father and sister. Now in his seventies, he still represents a fugitive romance to the women. The narrator, Mary Smith, much younger than the other women, describes the visit with the subdued irony to which she subjects all of the events of Cranford. Mr Holbrook, a self-defined yeoman rather than gentleman, is proud of his traditional ways, which particularly manifest in the arrangement of his kitchen and the conduct of his meals. His dinner menu is markedly old-fashioned, with the (savoury) pudding served before the meat, and far from apologizing for it, as Mary Smith expects, he asserts his contempt for the 'new-fangled':

'My housekeeper will have these in her new fashion; or else I tell her, that when I was a young man, we used to keep strictly to my father's rule, "No broth, no ball; no ball, no beef"; and always began dinner with broth. Then we had suet puddings, boiled in the broth with the beef; and then the meat itself. If we did not sup our broth, we had no ball, which we liked a deal better; and the beef came last of all, and only those had it who had done justice to the broth and the ball. Now folks begin with sweet things and turn their dinners topsy-turvey. (74)'

The 'sweet things' to which Mr Holbrook objects are the more expensive delicacies of the meal, notably the meat, not actually sweet foods. His gustatory standards stem from a pre-industrial economy, when food is carefully husbanded rather than being part of a system of display and excess. Once again, Gaskell brings conflicting codes of dining into collision: Mr Holbrook's old-fashioned ways include his forks – 'two-pronged, black handled' – which make it impossible for the ladies to scoop up the green peas served with the ducks. Miss Matty picks them up one by one on the prongs of her fork, while Miss Pole gives up altogether. Only Mary Smith is flexible enough to substitute one system of manners for another:

I looked at my host: the peas were going wholesale into his capacious mouth, shovelled up by his large round-ended knife. I saw, I imitated, I survived! My friends, in spite of my precedent, could not muster up courage enough to do an ungenteel thing; and if Mr Holbrook had not been so heartily hungry, he would probably have seen that the good peas went away almost untouched. (74–5)

The fact that Mr Holbrook's spoon-like knife is round-ended means that by putting it in her mouth, Mary Smith is not in danger of cutting herself – one of the original reasons behind the interdiction; but this taboo is, as with all codes of manners, about far more than the safety or hygiene that might have been its original justification.[8] The fork, in particular, signals civilization, its adoption in Britain and Europe in the seventeenth century marking a dividing line between medieval gustatory modes and a new refinement and elaboration.[9] Mr Holbrook's adherence to older modes, as with his assertion of his yeoman status, positions him as separate from the codes of gentility by which the Cranford ladies are constrained. He is outside the logic of the Victorian class system, unable to be placed by the categories he determinedly predates. Mary Smith 'survives' the experience by reference to an element of the genteel code that the other ladies seem to forget: that a guest should follow the lead set by the host. Mary Smith's observation of Mr Holbrook's practice is arguably more correct than the rigid adherence to their own modes adopted by the others. The Darwinian language in which she announces her successful modification of her behaviour is both a joke by Gaskell and a proleptic recognition of the fate of the Cranford ladies – they and their kind will not survive as they are unable to adapt to the modern world.

The early to mid-Victorian texts discussed so far share an understanding of the dinner as primarily a social performance – the home is carefully constructed as a stage set complete with props and actors in order to perform domestic harmony and social respectability.[10] The occasions are even scripted, with advice manuals giving hints as to how to guide the conversation before, during and after dinner. Isabella Beeton encourages the 'introduction of any particular new book, curiosity of art or article of vertu' to 'pleasantly engage the attention of the company'; and example of such articles is given by Soyer's Mrs B. in the form of her husband's loving cup: 'Mr B. bought the cup at a sale, and it is stated to have been drunk out of by Henry the Eighth: this of itself is a subject of conversation, and draws out the talents and conversational powers of our guests, and one in which ladies can join, as there is hardly one of our sex who has not read Miss Strickland's "Queens of England"' (Beeton 1989: 12; Langley 1987: 53–4). The hostess is imagined in such descriptions as a theatrical director, carefully positioning props and eliciting the best possible performances from the assembled players. Where the novels differ from the manuals is chiefly in their rather gleeful understanding that however carefully orchestrated these events are they will invariably fall short in some particular. The idea of the dinner party as performance is one that continues to be foregrounded in the realist novels of the later nineteenth century, but with the difference that these scenes are depicted with far less attention to the material presence of the food. Those detailed accounts of preparing, displaying and even eating particular dishes begin to be replaced by more abstract accounts of meals.

Late Victorian literary dinners

We can mark the transition particularly in the work of George Eliot. In contrast to the assertive particularity of the food of Thackeray or Dickens, the many dinner parties in Eliot's late great realist novels are notable for their *lack* of material description – it is very hard to imagine what her characters actually eat, at least in formal settings. As Thad Logan notes, 'detail for Eliot comes dangerously close to figuring a deeply suspect sensuality. [...] Eliot's realism is not, in any case, a matter of the representation of material objects' (2001: 216–7). This is certainly true of *Middlemarch* (1871–2) and

Daniel Deronda (1876), in which food tends to be represented only generically, if at all.[11] The narrator breaks into the account of the rural splendours of the setting for the archery competition in *Daniel Deronda* to announce that "I am not concerned to tell of the food that was eaten in that green refectory"; instead, the reader is instructed to imagine: "it will be understood that the food and champagne were of the best" (1986: 185–6). The refusal to dwell on the particularities of this excellent food is part of an elaborate irony, whereby she adopts the insouciance of that aristocratic society "where no one makes an invidious display of anything in particular, and the advantages of the world are taken with that high-bred depreciation which follows from being accustomed to them" in order to refuse the reader the opportunity of identifying with the values of that society through any sort of sensual appreciation of its luxuries. In her earlier fiction, set in rural locations, Eliot represents food frequently and specifically: the "'nice bit o' cold pudding i' the safe'" which Mrs Poyser directs Hetty to eat for her supper in *Adam Bede* (1859); the jam puff over which Tom and Maggie quarrel in *The Mill on the Floss* (1860); the detailed account of the culinary and housekeeping traditions of the Dodson women in the same novel (1977: 143). But when the themes of poverty and rurality are left behind, so too are the specific accounts of food. In both *Middlemarch* and *Daniel Deronda*, the dinner party has a structural rather than a descriptive narrative function, allowing separate social circles to interlock. In these notoriously bipartite novels it also serves as a link between otherwise divided narrative foci: in *Middlemarch* Dorothea tends to encounter Lydgate mainly at dinner parties; the same is true in *Daniel Deronda*, where although Gwendolyn and Daniel first see each other in the more public surroundings of the German casino, they only actually meet considerably later in the novel at a dinner. Gwendolyn has asked to be introduced on the former occasion but Daniel has evaded the request; the acquaintance that can be avoided in public must of necessity be accepted in the semi-private forum of the dinner party. The giving of dinners is a key trope in *Middlemarch*. Lydgate's initial extravagance in his disastrous course of living beyond his means is the purchase of a dinner-service; Mr Vincy devotes much time and money to hosting dinners to consolidate his social status and promote his political ambitions; Dorothea first meets her future husband Casaubon in the second chapter of the novel, at a dinner given by her uncle, where she is misled by his serious demeanour and resemblance to the portrait of Locke to finding him more fascinating than the other men present. For Eliot's purposes, one of the most intriguing elements of the dinner party is the table talk. Dorothea finds her uncle's worldly chat about his acquaintance with Wordsworth and Southey banal, and Mr Casaubon's self-righteous high-mindedness (he has no time for such popular reading) appealing in contrast, while the reader feels exactly the opposite, finding Casaubon's inability to make small talk boorish. The dinner table is a place of failed understanding and misapprehensions: Dorothea thinks that Sir James Chettam, the local landowner, is interested in her sister, and despises him for his red-whiskered hearty English appearance, while Sir James, thinking himself adroitly paying court to Dorothea, has no idea that she does not return his feelings: 'He thought it probable that Miss Brooke liked him, and manners must be very marked indeed before they cease to be interpreted by preconceptions either confident or distrustful' (1985: 43).

Dorothea finds Casaubon handsome and distinguished, while all her sister Celia can see is his 'two white moles with hairs on them' (42). Dorothea is attracted to Casaubon as a serious man who will allow her to exercise her intellect – a misapprehension for which she will repent for much of the rest of the novel, while Sir James, well aware of his own intellectual failings, would welcome 'the prospect of a wife to whom he could say "What shall we do?" about this or that; who could help her husband out with reasons' (43). Of the meal itself, the only mention is the soup, in the first sentence of the chapter, over which the conversation begins. It is not just the food that is absent from the narrative – there is no mention of the table, the chairs, even the servants. The dinner ritual itself is profoundly uninteresting to Eliot: it functions in her later fiction only as the locus of sustained group conversation. In *Daniel Deronda*, Gwendolyn's conversational style means that her first great social success is intimately tied up with the possibility of social failure: invited to Quetcham Hall, one of the grandest houses in the district, she is unable to conquer her sense of superiority sufficiently to refrain from speaking satirically to her hostess. Eliot takes great delight in tracing the minutiae of assumptions and suspicions in the minds of each as they engage in apparently superficial social chit-chat, but the humour is tempered with the awareness of how close Gwendolyn comes to forfeiting her social position through her carelessness. The surface triviality of the dinner party, like its talk, overlays a more fundamental significance to the ritual. In this sense, the dinner party functions as a microcosm of Eliot's realism itself: an arena in which the smallest of small talk and most trivial aspects of behaviour add up to significant revelations of character and motivation of plot.

For Henry James, also, the dinner party – usually grand – is both a set-piece event and one in which it is difficult to discern any particularities of the food. Dinners are frequent occurrences in almost all of his novels and stories: long accounts in which almost the only element described is the conversation. Typical is a lengthy dinner-set chapter in *The Siege of London* (1883) in which the material particulars of the meal receive only the following description: 'It was a copious and well-ordered banquet, but as Waterville looked up and down the table he wondered whether some of its elements might not be a little dull' (1963: 71). The absence of material description is as purposeful as Eliot's: James's reworking of the realist tradition moves it towards material abstraction.[12] In his works food appears more often as metaphor than fact: in *The Portrait of a Lady* (1881) Ralph Touchett, returning to his father's house in Winchester Square, closed up out of season, lingers in the darkened dining-room where 'there was a ghostly presence as of dinners long since digested, of table-talk that had lost its actuality'; in *What Maisie Knew* (1897) Maisie's stepfather describes her schoolroom as 'dull as a cold dinner' and in the opening pages of James's first novel, *Roderick Hudson* (1875) wealthy young Rowland Mallet self-deprecatingly represents his proposed visit to Rome in an elaborate culinary metaphor: '"It is still lotus-eating, only you sit down at table, and the lotuses are served up on rococo china"' (1947: 148; 1984: 64; 1981: 27). Later in this novel Mallet hosts a dinner in honour of his protégée, sculptor Roderick Hudson. The description of this dinner and its planning occupies a chapter of the novel: 'it was small', we are told, 'but Rowland had meant that it should be very agreeably composed' (88). In a novel intimately concerned with art – both the looking at it and the making of it – the word 'composed' carries a freight of meaning. It quickly becomes apparent that the 'agreeably composed' nature of the dinner refers not to the food but to the company he will assemble. A potted history of his relationship with each of the four guests follows, with the initiatory moment of dinner itself subsumed into a description of the last, a young woman with whom Rowland fancies himself in love:

> It seemed to Rowland a sort of foreshadowing of matrimony to see Augusta Blanchard standing gracefully on his hearth-rug and blooming behind the central bouquet at his circular dinner-table. (93)

The description of the actual dinner is accorded precisely two words – it is 'very prosperous' (93). As in Eliot, these evasions are marked. But where Eliot's omissions of the material details of food seem often part of an irony directed at her characters (as when in *Felix Holt* (1866), she remarks that the rich, in their large houses need 'know nothing of […] vulgar details' such as the 'brothy odours' that linger in small houses after a meal) (1913: 262), in the case of James one suspects that he himself shares with his characters the notion that to discuss food in too much detail is vulgar. This sense of the vulgarity of the material and particularly of the bodily is both a class and a literary sensibility in James: the omission of such details as much about a break with the rambunctious realism of Dickens and Thackeray as an adherence to the social codes of polite society.

The same codes of polite disinterest about food operate in the work of James's contemporary Edith Wharton, but in her case the narrative function of the silences is much more overt. In *The House of Mirth* (1905), the beautiful, orphaned Lily Bart navigates New York high society during her marriageable years, torn between her aim of capturing a wealthy husband and her vague yearnings for something more. Lily travels between one society house party and the next, welcomed for her beauty but required to earn her bread and butter by helping her hostesses with the writing of invitations and dinner cards. There is little discussion, though, of the planning of menus: one of the absolute requirements of social place, as Lily has learned from her mother, is that 'whatever it cost, one must have a good cook' (2012: 34). To be anxious about the food one was serving would suggest a falling away from this standard and a lack of confidence in one's own taste. However, unlike those of James, Wharton's text does not straightforwardly adopt the codes of insouciant disregard that characterize the attitudes to food among Lily's elevated social set: instead, she presents the luxury of not talking – or thinking – about food as one of the many social privileges that Lily risks losing through her lack of complete dedication to the marriage game. Her parents, also, had teetered on the edge of high society: her mother, dedicated to 'living as though one were much richer than one's bank book denoted' (34), devoting her energies to social appearance and spectacle; her father working himself into the ground but failing to keep up with his wife's expenditure. Theirs was 'a house in which no one ever dined at home unless there was company' (32), but the scene in which Mr Bart announces his financial ruin takes place at the luncheon-table, as Lily and her mother eat up the left-overs from the previous night's dinner: left-overs precisely designated as *chaufroix* and cold salmon, *marrons glacés* (now melting) and candied cherries – it being 'one of Mrs Bart's few economies to consume in private the expensive remnants of her hospitality' (35). People who need to eat up leftovers are forced to lower themselves to quotidian details they might wish to rise above. Throughout the first half of the book, the moments in which food has to be thought about in detail constitute places where Lily's ideals of luxury are challenged. The first dinner we witness is described retrospectively, the meal itself having been passed over in silence in the initial description of Lily's time at the Trenors' house party. The meal is present only in Lily's later recollections, where her primary concern is with the function of the dinner as social stage:

> Mrs Trenor, true to her simple principle of making her married friends happy, had placed Selden and Mrs Dorset next to each other at dinner; but in obedience to the time-honoured traditions of the match-maker, she had separated Lily and Mr Gryce, sending in the former with George Dorset, while Mr Gryce was coupled with Gwen Van Osburgh. (62)

The codes of propriety and respectability in this social set have advanced to the point that married women have considerable licence to conduct flirtations and even affairs as long as they retain deniability while the unmarried need to maintain strict propriety: hence the two codes under which Mrs Trenor operates – acting simultaneously as chaperone and pander. Physically separated from her latest marriage target, Lily is free to 'read' the dinner on our behalf, taking in the flirtations, tensions and jealousies, but also – unlike James – the food and the diners' responses to it:

> George Dorset's talk did not interfere with the range of his neighbour's thoughts. He was a mournful dyspeptic, intent on finding out the deleterious ingredients of every dish and diverted from this care only by the sound of his wife's voice. On this occasion, however, Mrs Dorset took no part in the general conversation. She sat talking in low murmurs with Selden, and turning a contemptuous and denuded shoulder toward her host, who, far from resenting his exclusion, plunged into the excesses of the menu with the joyous irresponsibility of a free man. To Mr Dorset, however, his wife's attitude was a subject of such evident concern that, when he was not scraping the sauce from his fish, or scooping moist bread-crumbs from the interior of his roll, he sat straining his thin neck for a glimpse of her between the lights. (62)

As Lily surveys her fellow guests with a satiric eye it becomes apparent that it is only the men who are seen in any relationship to the food: from dyspeptic George Dorset, who spends the rest of the meal treating Lily to a 'prolonged denunciation of other people's cooks, with a supplementary tirade on the toxic qualities of melted butter' (65), to the host Gus Trenor, 'with his heavy carnivorous head sunk between his shoulders, as he preyed on a jellied plover' (63) and 'young Silverton, who had meant to live on proof-reading and write an epic, and who now lived on his friends and had become critical of truffles' (64). The women, instead, compete with the food for attention: Mrs Trenor 'suggestive, with her glaring good-looks, of a jeweller's window lit by electricity' (63), 'Carry Fisher, with her shoulders, her eyes, her divorces, her general air of embodying a "spicy paragraph"' (64). In this world, men get to consume the products of their wealth while women focus on turning themselves into something to be consumed. This and similar descriptions of dinners in the first part of the novel toy with food in the same desultory manner as do most of its wealthy characters, but the apparent textual insouciance is actually very specific to this elevated social circle. Those outside its rarefied walls are fascinated by all that goes on inside – including the luxurious excesses of the food. Lily's 'fatally poor and dingy' friend Gerty Farish, invited to the wedding of one of the circle, is naively excited by it: '"Isn't everything beautifully done?" she pursued, as they entered the drawing-room assigned to the display of Miss Van Osburgh's bridal spoils. "I always say no one does things better than cousin Grace! Did you ever taste anything more delicious than that mousse of lobster with champagne sauce?"' (103), while Lily's aunt, wealthy but socially retired, nonetheless pours over the details of the entertainments she does not attend: '"I think it was odd, their serving melons before the consommé: a wedding breakfast should always begin with consommé"' (125). Being forced to discuss culinary particulars is one of the many elements of her existence that Lily finds tedious. Part of her tiresome duties, living with this aunt, is to endure lengthy discussions as to all the minute details of her own infrequent dinner parties: 'Mrs Peniston's rare entertainments were preceded by days of heart-rending vacillation as to every detail of the feast, from the seating of the guests to the pattern of the tablecloth' (143). Lily's reluctance to pay such attention has multiple causes: her quailing from the 'society' marriage she has been trained to seek, her taste for the luxurious and pleasurable, and her 'modern' sense that social life should appear easy and unaffected rather than effortful. In the later part of the novel the main characters travel to Europe, where food suddenly becomes speakable – and much spoken about – for the members of Lily's set. This is because the dinners they give and attend are no longer the private dinner parties of New York and its environs, but meals at fashionable French restaurants. In such venues, it was newly acceptable for women to dine in public. Chef Georges Auguste Escoffier, one of the key figures behind this cultural development, noted that one of the main reasons for the popularity of the new hotels built in the 1880s and '90s was that 'they allow of being observed, since they are so eminently adapted to the exhibiting of magnificent dresses' (1957: xi).[13] It is exactly for this function of being observed – and of observing others – that the smart set in Wharton's novel frequent the public dining establishments of the south of France. A scene in which Selden meets a group of his acquaintances outside the casino in Monte Carlo defines the subtle social codes underlying this new form of culinary culture: the right attitude to be struck is that one knows where the best food is to be found, but does not demonstrate any ill-bred over-interest in it. Having opinions about food and the excellence of chefs and restaurants is a new form of cultural cachet. Food can be legitimately thought about once one is not oneself responsible for providing it, though the interest in it must be of the order of distanced cultural appreciation rather than urgent desire. But the grand dinner thrown later at the most fashionable restaurant is notable – in Selden's disenchanted eyes – for the 'stupid costliness of the food and the showy dullness of the talk' (251). The novel's expensive, elaborate society dinners, at which the real dish served up is the women, reveal a society hollow at the core, eaten away to nothing but its surface.

Modernist dinners

Although the dinner party is a fundamental device of nineteenth-century realism, it is not one of the elements of the realist tradition rejected by modernism. Dinners play a prominent role in the fiction of James Joyce: (the Misses Morstan's dinner-dance at the centre of 'The Dead' (1914); the Christmas dinner near the beginning of *A Portrait of the Artist as a Young Man* (1916) during which the family and friends of Stephen Dedalus come close to blows over the death of Parnell); E. M. Forster (the dinner at the Bertoloni pension at the start of *A Room with a View* (1908) during which the Emersons offer to exchange rooms with Lucy Honeychurch and her cousin; the all-female dinner party-cum-discussion club in *Howard's End* (1910)); and, particularly, Virginia Woolf. Woolf's novels are full of dinners: the bleak Sunday meal with his tutor and his family to which Jacob is rudely late in *Jacob's Room* (1922); in *Mrs Dalloway* (1925) Peter Walsh's surreal vision of everyone in London going out to dinner; and the meal from which Lady Brunton excludes wives. Probably the most famous of all modernist dinner parties appears in *To the Lighthouse* (1927) when the Ramsay family and their summer guests sit down to a simple three course meal, of soup followed by a *Boeuf en Daube* and then fruit. The meal is determinedly modern, belonging to a new genre of food that had emerged following the First World War. The new food culture was characterized by much shorter meals with fewer courses; simpler food, often influenced by the peasant and bourgeois food traditions of southern Europe; and an increasing bohemianism of manners and protocol which led to a relaxation of rules about service, a greater informality in the placing of food on the table, and the beginning of a preference for earthenware serving dishes rather than inherited plate. One of the main influences behind this new food culture was X Marcel Boulestin, a French émigré whose *Simple French Cooking for English Homes* (1923) had created a taste for French bourgeois domestic food as opposed to the *haute cuisine* of the grand restaurants and hotels frequented by the pre-war wealthy of the likes of Wharton's characters. The Bloomsbury group had been some of earliest adopters of Boulestin's food and culinary precepts, and Mrs Ramsay's meal might have come from the pages of his books. It is striking, therefore, that Woolf does not represent the meal as in any way modern. The *Boeuf en Daube* comes, we are told, from an old French recipe of Mrs Ramsay's grandmother's, allowing the un-Englishness and the fashionable bohemian daring represented by the great brown earthenware pot with its 'exquisite scent of olives and oil and juice', its 'shiny walls and its confusion of savoury brown and yellow meats, and its bay leaves and its wine' to be more fully owned by Mrs Ramsay and more completely represent her (1992a: 135). The dish and the meal she orchestrates around it stand in the novel for the power of female creativity and a sort of social witchery, which is contrasted with the arid intellectualism of her philosopher husband and his life-long quest to get to R in the string of reasoning he imagines as an alphabet. (Though the novel is also, of course, aware of the paradox of Mrs Ramsay's creativity being represented by a thing she did not personally create – the daube is earlier described as 'Mildred's [the cook's] masterpiece' (108).) The dinner is felt by Mrs Ramsay to be not an established social occasion which will run smoothly according to its protocols and rituals, but an imaginative construct which she has to control through act of will: 'Nothing seemed to have merged', she thinks as she looks at the people gathered around her table, 'They all sat separate. And the whole of the effort of merging and flowing and creating rested on her' (113). It is in this context of merging and flowing that the *Bouef en Daube* gains part of its meaning, its savoury confusion a triumph of the desired melding. The structure of the meal in this exemplary modernist retelling flows and reforms, in eddies of conversation and bleeding of narrative perspectives one into another. As Mrs Ramsay marshals her guests and assigns them their seats, she looks 'at all the plates making white circles' (112) on the table and wonders what she has done with her life.[14] Lily Briscoe, the artist, watches her and thinks how old she looks, and then, as Mrs Ramsay turns to William Bankes, that she – wrongly – pities him, failing to understand that he has his work. This leads Lily to remember her own work, and she moves a salt cellar to a new part of the tablecloth to remind her of the solution she has just found to the composition of her picture. Charles Tansley, a young philosopher always awkwardly conscious of his humble beginnings, bitterly condemns 'the rot these people wanted him to talk' (116) as he listens to the small talk of Mrs Ramsay and William Bankes about the post, while Lily Briscoe observes his table manners as indicative of his past, 'his plate swept clean [...] as if [...] he were determined to make sure of his meals' (115). William Bankes talks to Mrs Ramsay of old mutual friends then considers how much he would rather be eating alone and free to pursue his botanical studies. Mrs Ramsay worries as Mr Ramsay has become furious because Augustus Carmichael, the opium-addicted poet, has asked for another bowl of soup and Mr Ramsay 'loathed people eating when he had finished' (129). The thoughts and feelings and responses and observations of the assembled company flit back and forth across the table, now inwardly directed, now focussed on their neighbours, while at the same time they fidget with the table settings, observe or fail to observe various codes of etiquette and eat. They also talk about the food. One marked feature of the new food culture of the post-war years was the introduction of a new code of table talk which made it now acceptable – indeed, positively desirable – to discuss the food you were eating. When *Vanity Fair*'s Sir Pitt Crawley enters into his conversational dissection of the animal they are eating – and announces his plans for the killing of the little black pig which is now fat almost to busting because 'Miss Sharp adores pork' (114) – he is gleefully contravening any number of codes interdicting the discussion of food and its preparation over the dinner table. Virtually unique to Britain, and a feature of the increased gentility of the nineteenth century, these strictures are consciously dismantled after the First World War. 'Do not be afraid to talk about food', declared Boulestin, 'Food which is worth eating is worth discussing. And there is the occult power of words which somehow develop its qualities' (1923: 1). Woolf's characters are by no means afraid to talk of food. Greedy Mr Bankes briefly lays down his knife to declare the daube a triumph, then he and Mrs Ramsay plunge into a delighted dissection of the abominations of English cookery in comparison to the delights of the French: 'It is putting cabbages in water. It is roasting meat until it is like leather. It is cutting off the delicious skins of vegetables …. And the waste, said Mrs Ramsay. A whole French family could live on what an English cook throws away' (136). Mr Bankes's greed is not treated by the text in the same way as the greed of Thackeray's Jos Smedley, which is an index of the weakness and self-indulgence of his character. The idea of culinary greed has become more socially acceptable, carrying connotations of epicurism rather than indiscriminate stuffing, its social acceptability underlined by the presence of cookbooks like Mrs Philip Martineau's *Caviar to Candy* (1927) (with its titular focus on the luxurious titbit) or Nancy Shaw's 1936 *Food for the Greedy*. The greed that in *The House of Mirth* is an index of the social and sexual rapaciousness of the male characters is in Woolf's text an endearing facet of personality: though it is noticeable that it is only the male characters who publically enthuse about the food and who take second helpings. Like Wharton, Woolf is very conscious of the gender implications of the dinner ritual. Mrs Ramsay has solicitously taken 'the whole of the other sex under her protection' (10) and requires that her daughters and other women do likewise, so that Lily feels the intense moral pressure of Mrs Ramsay's desire that she should 'go to the help of the young man opposite': to make conversation that will allow Charles Tansley to 'expose and relieve the thigh bones, the ribs, of his vanity, of his urgent desire to assert himself' (123). Having briefly toyed with the delicious prospect of doing no such thing and leaving Tansley to founder in the mires of his ambition and social inadequacy she finally succumbs, the power of Mrs Ramsay's social vision having prevailed: 'of course for the hundred and fiftieth time Lily Briscoe had to renounce the experiment – what happens if one is not nice to that young man there – and be nice' (124).

In *A Room of One's Own* (1929), Woolf explicitly relates the institution of the formal meal to gender politics in her account, in the opening pages, of two meals eaten at 'Oxbridge' colleges in the course of one day. This leisurely yet urgent exploration of the material and mental conditions necessary for a woman to become an author begins with Woolf turned away from one of the college libraries and then proceeds with her welcome into another part of the same (male) college for luncheon. Before describing that meal, she explicitly grounds it in a fictional tradition, contemplating the turn away from the material taken by the realist fiction of the recent past:

> It is a curious fact that novelists have a way of making us believe that luncheon parties are invariably memorable for something very witty that was said, or for something very wise that was done. But they seldom spare a word for what was eaten. It is part of the novelist's convention not to mention soup and salmon and ducklings, as if soup and salmon and ducklings were of no importance whatsoever, as if nobody ever smoked a cigar or drank a glass of wine. (1992b: 12–13)

The literary tradition from which she determinedly separates herself is that late nineteenth-century realism of Eliot and James for whom the quotidian materiality of actual descriptions of food seems to undermine the novel form's potential for elevated intellectuality. Woolf herself will 'take the liberty to defy that convention', describing the food with a conspicuously greedy delight, itemizing the 'soles, sunk in a deep dish, over which the college cook had spread a counterpane of the whitest cream, save that it was branded here and there with brown spots like the spots on the flanks of a doe', the partridges, 'with all their retinue of sauces and salads, the sharp and the sweet, their potatoes, thin as coins but not so hard; their sprouts, foliate as rosebuds but more succulent', and finally 'a confection which rose all sugar from the waves' (13). Her insistence on the crucial importance of the precise details of the meal might seem to have something in common with the assertively material early Victorian realism of Dickens and Thackeray, but her project is different. Material detail for Woolf is not its own reward, not a means of fully realizing a social milieu, but a route to interiority:

Meanwhile the wineglasses had flushed yellow and flushed crimson; had been emptied; had been filled. And thus by degrees was lit, half-way down the spine, which is the seat of the soul, not that hard little electric light which we call brilliance, as it pops in and out upon our lips, but the more profound, subtle and subterranean glow which is the rich yellow flame of rational intercourse. No need to hurry. No need to sparkle. No need to be anybody but oneself. We are all going to heaven and Vandyke is of the company. (13–14)

The rational intercourse produced by the excellent meal is the condition for social belonging – in this instance, of the exclusive 'Oxbridge' club – but more importantly for the freedom of thought Woolf sees as the prerequisite for the writing life. The social and intellectual excellence thus produced is notably not the quick, glib wit of the fine-dining smart set of Wharton's novel: Woolf's ideal dining produces not a more effective social performance but a stronger sense of the grounding of identity – 'no need to be anyone but oneself'. This ideal luncheon is contrasted with the dinner she is served on the same day, this time in a women's college. The fictional Fernham is a thinly disguised version of the late Victorian foundations existing on the outskirts of Oxford and Cambridge, only partially members of the universities, and without the ancient endowments and well-stocked wine cellars of the male colleges. Woolf and the reader find themselves suddenly and disconcertingly plunged into this meal, as she breaks off a meandering imagining of the Fernham garden formless in a spring dusk to confront the reality of the college dining hall:

All was dim, yet intense too, as if the scarf which the dusk had flung over the garden were torn asunder by star or sword – the flash of some terrible reality leaping, as its way is, out of the heart of the spring. For youth –
Here was my soup. Dinner was being served in the great dining-hall. Far from being spring it was in fact an evening in October. Everybody was assembled in

the big dining-room. Dinner was ready. Here was the soup. It was a plain gravy soup. There was nothing to stir the fancy in that. One could have seen through the transparent liquid any pattern that there might have been on the plate itself. But there was no pattern. The plate was plain. (21)

The plainness of the soup and the plate and the prose slam the door on the imagination, their everyday ordinariness curtailing the possibility of something beyond. The soup is followed by beef and greens and potatoes, 'a homely trinity, suggesting the rumps of cattle in a muddy market, and sprouts curled and yellow at the edges, and bargaining and cheapening and women with string bags on Monday morning' (22), then prunes and custard, then cheese and biscuits. Rather than the lyrical heights of the description of the luncheon, the prose here damns with bitter irony: 'it is the nature of biscuits to be dry and these were biscuits to the core'; 'prunes ... are an uncharitable vegetable (fruit they are not), stringy as a miser's heart and exuding a fluid such as might run in miser's veins who have denied themselves wine and water for eighty years and yet not given to the poor'. There is 'nothing to stir the fancy' in this neo-Victorian meal, yet it is notable that it is in this passage rather than the preceding one that the figurative language leads us away from the food itself towards other imagined scenes – the dreary market, the diet of coal miners, the miser's heart. The good food – Edwardian classics well executed rather than the up-to-the-minute bohemianism of the Boeuf en Daube – turns reflection inwards, while the poor food, denying any bodily need but basic sustenance, leads the imagination outward, away from the self, into discomforting contemplations of the pinched inadequacies of contemporary life. Where for Dickens or Gaskell food figures shared experiences and an outward movement of sympathies, for Woolf's modernist project food functions most effectively as a means of allowing the self to know itself more fully.

The dinner sits at the heart of the novel: a gathering point for disparate characters, a locus for conversation, a stage for the performance of domestic values and social status, a ripe opportunity for humour and social satire. Its form and function, though, change dramatically across the period surveyed, materialism giving way to abstraction, performativity to interiority, display to studied informality. In all of these accounts of dinners, others lurk around the edges of the scene: the waiters who are winked at in Thackeray's 'Dinner in the City', the drunken servant in *David Copperfield*, the cook Mabel whose 'masterpiece' the daube really is. The next chapter will look squarely at these shadowy figures and think about the functions the servant performs in the homes and the narratives of the novel.

CHAPTER 3
KITCHEN POLITICS: THE COMING AND GOING OF THE BRITISH SERVANT

This chapter will consider the relationships between domestic service and food culture in Britain, examining the ways in which the identity of the middle classes is formed and reformed by their relationship to servants, from the moment in the nineteenth century when bourgeois status became absolutely defined by the employment of servants, to the 'Servant Problem' which so preoccupied the middle-class women of the interwar years, through to the immediate post-war years and the development of servant-replacing technology.[1] These large issues will be addressed specifically in terms of their significant relationship to food practices and particularly to the question of the kitchen and its management and occupation.

1830–1913: Problematic servants

By the middle of the nineteenth century middle-class status in Britain had become defined by one factor above all: the keeping of servants. With industrialization and the growing urbanization that accompanied it, the middle class of the early Victorian decades was rapidly expanding and becoming more affluent. Families that a generation earlier would have had one or two servants now employed at least three times that number. The increase was led by a number of factors: the fashion for large families among the affluent, the pervasive dirt of industrialized towns and cities[2], and – above all – the code of genteel leisure that required that the mistress of the house should not perform physical labour. Those who did not employ servants were not middle class: as John Burnett notes, 'at the end of the century Seebohm Rowntree, in his study of poverty in York, drew the upper limit of the working classes at "the servant keeping class", because to keep one "skivvy" in the kitchen as surely announced middle-class membership as the possession of a cottage piano indicated the "respectability" of a working man' (1974: 136). Where a mistress in previous generations would have worked alongside her servants, the new model of bourgeois gentility required her to take a hands-off approach – or at least, to give the appearance of doing so.[3] The mistress of an aristocratic establishment would have housekeepers and butlers and even stewards to manage the work of the lower servants, but in most middle-class homes the ostensibly idle mistress would need to undertake this task herself. Guides like Isabella Beeton's *Household Management* (1861) took as their primary purpose her instruction in this work of control, and key among their objectives was that labour – that of the servants, and particularly that of the mistress – should be invisible. The ideal was that the house should appear to run itself, the work done by unseen hands. So she notes that 'the footman is expected to rise early, in order to get through all his dirty work before the family are stirring', while the cook is instructed that 'the cleaning of the kitchen, pantry, passages, and kitchen stairs must always be over before breakfast, so that it may not interfere with the other business of the day. Everything should be ready, and the whole house should wear a comfortable aspect when the heads of the house and members of the family make an appearance' (1989: 965; 42). In practice, many middle-class women needed to perform a significant proportion of their domestic tasks themselves: it is notable that of the female domestic servants listed in the 1851 census, two-thirds of them are maids-of-all-work, the sole domestic workers in a household. The maid-of-all-work was employed by those at the bottom economic limit of the middle class: clerks, and what Beeton calls 'small tradesmen' (their income levels estimated by Samuel and Sarah Adams's *The Complete Servant* in 1825 as £100 a year and by Beeton in 1861 as between £150 and £200 a year). It is this lowest economic rung of the middle class that was by far the most populous: the average middle-class income in 1867 was £154 per annum (Crouzet 2013: 40). It is only at the income level of £500 a year that Beeton believes her readers will be able to afford a cook: below that the mistress would almost certainly be performing some culinary tasks alongside her maid.[4] Elizabeth Gaskell's *Cranford* (1853) demonstrates both the social fiction of the idle mistress and the ways in which it might be connived at and maintained: when Mrs Forrester, in her 'baby-house of a dwelling', gives a tea party, all her guests, some much more affluent, act as if the maid getting the tea tray out from under the sofa is a perfectly normal occurrence, and they accept the charade that the mistress has no idea what cakes will be served 'though she knew, and we knew, and she knew that we knew, and we knew that she knew we knew, that she had been busy all the morning making tea-bread and sponge cakes' (1986a: 41). The elaborate double-think exposed by Gaskell is a central element of the discourse of the household manual: Beeton's main text does not directly acknowledge that even the employer of a single maid-of-all-work will have to perform domestic tasks, but buried in the list of this servant's duties is a suggestion that she might generally be assisted by the mistress or daughter of the house with the beds, and that the lady of house often 'takes charge of' dusting and straightening the drawing room while the servant does the rough work (1989: 1002). The crucial point for such texts is in the framing of this labour: in 'assisting' and 'taking charge' the mistress's work is remade as kindness or supervision. Similarly, the chapter on the Mistress at the start of *Household Management* declares that 'it is desirable, unless an experienced and confidential housekeeper be kept, that the mistress should herself purchase all provisions and stores needed for the house' – a task that is framed not as labour but as sensible vigilance, of a part with the injunction to keep a careful check on the housekeeper's accounts (6).

Kitchen problems

Like Gaskell's Mrs Forrester, the Victorian novel engages itself much more actively in the affairs of the kitchen than the polite ideology of domesticity might approve. Kitchens themselves, as well as the tasks performed in them, are places of considerable interest to a number of texts. In Emily Brontë's *Wuthering Heights* (1847), the kitchen is the centre of life at the Heights. It is a complex space, in need of elaborate explanation at the very start of the novel. When Lockwood, the southern narrator, enters the house for the first time, he is at pains to describe the curious living arrangements of its inhabitants:

> One stop brought us into the family sitting-room, without any introductory lobby or passage: they call it here 'the house' pre-eminently. It includes kitchen and parlour, generally; but I believe at Wuthering Heights the kitchen is forced to retreat altogether into another quarter: at least I distinguished a chatter of tongues, and a clatter of culinary utensils, deep within; and I observed no signs of roasting, boiling, or baking, about the huge fireplace; nor any glitter of copper saucepans and tin cullenders on the walls. One end, indeed, reflected splendidly both light and heat from ranks of immense pewter dishes, interspersed with silver jugs and tankards, towering row after row, on a vast oak dresser, to the very roof. The latter had never been under-drawn: its entire anatomy lay bare to an inquiring eye, except where a frame of wood laden with oatcakes and clusters of legs of beef, mutton, and ham, concealed it. (1993: 4–5)

The room is both kitchen and not-kitchen: it has the dresser and the serving dishes and the home-prepared store food, but not the noise and activity of the kitchen-proper. The difficulty Lockwood has in accounting for it demonstrates the fact that life in the house is in a state of flux between two modes: the ancient rural traditions still observed elsewhere where the kitchen and parlour are one, and the modern genteel practice which separates the act of food preparation from the life of the family.[5] The local tradition that names the kitchen 'the house' evokes a way of life in which the primal pleasures of the hearth are still available to all. Wuthering Heights is inhabited in a way that is much more awkward: the employers and their servants are neither archaically convivial nor genteelly separate, but something uncomfortably in between. There are a number of scenes in the novel in which the existence of the two kitchens and the symbolic meaning of each are of considerable importance: discovering Cathy's diary the night he stays at Wuthering Heights, Lockwood reads of 'an awful Sunday', soon after the death of her father, when her brother and his new wife, ensconced in their 'paradise on the hearth', tyrannize over the child Catherine and Heathcliff, who are removed forcibly from the den they have made in the arch of the dresser and 'hurled […] into the back-kitchen', where the irascible servant Joseph assures them '"owd Nick" would fetch us as sure as we were living' (18–19). Both kitchens have fires, but in the back-kitchen the fire is separated off from the rest of the room by 'two benches, shaped in sections of a circle [which] nearly enclosed the hearth' (26): these high-backed settles facilitate the dramatic scene in which Heathcliff, lying unseen on a bench behind them, overhears Cathy telling Nelly that it would degrade her to marry him. Like Catherine's ancient box-bed, the settles create a womb-like room within a room; they corral the heat of the fire and cast the rest of the room into cold dimness. Throughout the novel this room functions more as a stage for familial drama than a functional space: Nelly hides the infant Hareton in a kitchen cupboard to try to protect him from his father's drunken rage; and it is the scene of Isabella's final melodramatic escape from the house, running from the violent Heathcliff, who is hurling dinner knives at her, knocking over Hareton 'who was hanging a litter of puppies from a chair-back' (157) in the kitchen doorway. This kitchen is only infrequently seen in terms of its primary function as a place in which servants prepare food. When Lockwood first visits the Heights and is attacked by a pack of dogs, he is rescued by an almost comedically apposite servant: 'a lusty dame, with tucked-up gown, bare arms, and fire-flushed cheeks, [who] rushed into the midst of us flourishing a frying-pan: and used that weapon, and her tongue, to such purpose, that the storm subsided magically' (7). For Lockwood, who applies the standards of the genteel world, this as-yet-unnamed servant is 'an inhabitant of the kitchen', but as the rest of the novel makes clear, it is not just servants who inhabit this kitchen.

Wuthering Heights is a house in which it is impossible to live genteelly, as Isabella discovers soon after her disastrous marriage to Heathcliff. Informed by Hindley that there is no lady's maid to help her, she is forced to enter the dark recesses of the kitchen alone where she finds the servant Joseph, 'bending over the fire, peering into a large pan that swung above it':

> I conjectured that this preparation was probably for our supper, and, being hungry, I resolved it should be eatable; so, crying out sharply, 'I'll make the porridge!' I removed the vessel out of his reach, and proceeded to take off my hat and riding-habit. 'Mr Earnshaw,' I continued, 'directs me to wait upon myself: I will. I'm not going to act the lady among you, for fear I should starve.' (122)

Isabella, for whom cooking in the past has only been 'merry fun', makes 'a rough mess' of the porridge, and is roundly castigated by Joseph who predicts that 'they'll be naught but lumps as big as my neive'. There is no parlour in which she can escape the repellant sight of young Hareton slavering as he sucks milk directly from the jug, and not even a bedroom to which she can retire. By the end of the novel the house is reduced to nothing but the kitchen: with all of the characters either dead or moved away, most of the house will be shut up, with Joseph as caretaker living only in the kitchen, the rest left 'for the use of such ghosts as choose to inhabit it' (288). It is not clear whether the territory of Joseph and the lad who will perhaps be hired to keep him company will encompass the 'house' as well as the back kitchen: the ambiguous nomenclature of these two spaces continues to the very end of the book. In Thrushcross Grange, the other house at the centre of the novel, by contrast, the distinction between the genteel and the servant spaces of the house is very clear: the Grange has a fully staffed 'kitchen wing' (140), and its inhabitants have a marked sense of class distinctions. This is displayed most dramatically when Heathcliff returns from his long disappearance and Edgar Linton does not want Catherine, now his wife, to meet her returned companion in the parlour, considering the kitchen a more suitable place for him: 'the whole household need not witness the sight of your welcoming a runaway servant as a brother' (82). Parodying his dismissal, Cathy asks Nelly to set two tables: one for herself and Heathcliff as 'the lower orders' and one for Edgar and Isabella as 'gentry'. Despite placing herself as Heathcliff's equal in notional 'lowness', Cathy has proclaimed herself unable to sit in the kitchen: the radical instability of class identity to which she is gesturing belongs specifically to the world of the Heights. The Earnshaw family is an ancient one, but more of the yeomanly than the genteel class; Hindley is master of the house but also a drunken hermit; Cathy is both wild gypsy and elegant young lady; Heathcliff's position is the most anomalous: variously orphan, gypsy, and wealthy self-made man, favoured adopted son and lowly servant. Nelly, though officially a servant, grows up with the Earnshaw children and sees Hindley in particular as her playmate as well as her employer. The boundaries between servant and employer are as unclearly designated as the identity, name and usage of the kitchen.

A very similar outdated, yeomanly kitchen arrangement is depicted in Elizabeth Gaskell's *Cranford* in the chapter entitled 'A Visit to an Old Bachelor', when some of the ageing Cranford spinsters pay a visit, along with youthful narrator Mary Smith, to the rural home of Mr Holbrook, who had long ago made an offer for the hand of Miss Matty. Like Lockwood, Mary Smith stumbles over herself in naming the room that both is and is not the kitchen:

> When he and I went in, we found that dinner was nearly ready in the kitchen, – for so I suppose the room ought to be called, as there were oak dressers and cupboards all round, all over by the side of the fire-place, and only a small turkey carpet in the middle of the flag-floor. The room might have been easily made into a handsome dark-oak dining-parlour, by removing the oven, and a few other appurtenances of a kitchen, which were evidently never used; the real cooking place being at some distance. (1986a: 39)

Caught, like Wuthering Heights, between two ways of living, the erstwhile kitchen retains the large fire, the oven and the dressers, but not the mess and noise and smells of a working kitchen. Like the Earnshaws, Mr Holbrook belongs to an older class than the gentry: his house does have a parlour, but it is an uncomfortable and ugly recent innovation – 'not at all pretty, or pleasant, or home-like' – and the ladies choose instead to spend the visit in the room in which their host usually relaxes: the farm counting-house, with its large desk from which he pays his labourers their weekly wage as his ancestors had done before him. Served by a 'respectable' housekeeper and a servant girl, Mr Holbrook forges his own way of life, combining the traditional practices of his forebears with his own pleasures and indulgences. Although themselves in thrall to the expectations of gentility, the Cranford ladies feel the nostalgic appeal of the ancient farmhouse practices which mingle work and leisure.

Intrusive and deceitful servants

Even the most biddable servants in Victorian fiction are notable for their intrusiveness. Mr Holbrook's unnamed housekeeper is described only in terms of her respectability and modesty, yet (as discussed in Chapter 2) seeks to impose her will over her employers' culinary tastes; Miss Matty's paragon of a maid servant Martha takes it upon herself to interfere in her mistress's life to the extent that she marries and takes a house with the apparently chief intention of being able to offer Miss Matty a home when she loses her money; and Peggotty, the devoted servant of the widowed Clara Copperfield, advises her against marrying Mr Murdstone and is denounced for her trouble. At the start of *David Copperfield* (1850) Peggotty lives on terms of considerable intimacy with David and his mother, sharing their two parlours, and 'quite [their] companion, when her work is done and [they] are alone' (1985a: 62). Indeed, it is Peggotty who is apparently the authority figure: one of David's first impressions is 'a sense that we were both a little afraid of Peggotty, and submitted ourselves in most things to her direction' (65). Before David's infantile idyll is disrupted by the arrival of his cruel stepfather, Peggotty shares the maternal role with Clara, distinguished from her in David's imagination by one key trope: Peggotty is a creature of food. She is not just the source of it, mistress of kitchen and storeroom, but compounded of it: the first description of the central objects of David's early consciousness renders Peggotty's body as food, her 'cheeks and arms so hard and red that I wondered the birds didn't peck her in preference to apples' (61), her forefinger, roughened by needlework, appears to him 'like a pocket nutmeg-grater' (61) and she refers to herself proudly as a 'Yarmouth Bloater' (78).[6] In psychoanalytic terms, an infantile desire to consume the mother's body is a common feature of the childhood imagination: the fact that this desire appears to be transferred to Peggotty, with his actual mother rendered more as fellow child, suggests the extent to which Peggotty usurps the maternal role.

Servantly control in the novel is most often exercised via the medium of food. When David first lives alone in lodgings he assays a couple of dinner parties as a sign of his new adult independence. For the first, an impromptu supper for his school friend Steerforth and some Oxford friends of his, David is persuaded by his manipulative landlady, Mrs Crupp, to purchase most of the food from the pastry cook, so that she can 'concentrate her mind on the potatoes' (418), and to hire two incompetent young people of her acquaintance to serve the food. Though not precisely a servant, the landlady's habitual location in 'the depths of the earth' (416) and her role as provider of food place her in a similar category in the novel's expectations, though Mrs Crupp herself makes it clear that she considers actual service beneath her status: 'in the first place, of course it was well known she couldn't be expected to wait' (418). She devotes considerable energies to defrauding David – a fact which the David of this date appears not to notice, though his narrating self makes it plain to the reader – reducing the mock-turtle-soup makings he purchases ('which I have since seen reason to believe would have sufficed for fifteen people' (418)) to '"rather a tight fit"' for four (419), and showing discomfort at the fact that two of the ordered bottles of wine were missing. The shadow of the handy young man is frequently to be observed outside the room 'with a bottle at its mouth' (419), while the 'young gal' lurks outside the room, spying on the guests and 'several times retire[s] upon the plates (with which she ha[s] carefully paved the floor), and [does] a great deal of destruction' (420). Not having learned from this social failure David tries entertaining again a few weeks later. His culinary preparations on this occasion are more economical: 'I did not repeat my former extensive preparations. I merely provided a pair of soles, a small leg of mutton, and a pigeon-pie' (471). Mrs Crupp only agrees to cook on condition that he dine out for the next fortnight. He re-hires the 'young gal' (on the agreement that when not serving she withdraw to the landing so that the guests cannot hear her sniffing), but not the handy young man, in consequence of having since met him in the Strand 'in a waistcoat remarkably like one of mine, which had been missing since the former occasion' (472). Despite David's careful planning, everything that could go wrong with the cooking does so: the joint prepared by the drunken Mrs Crupp is covered in ash and nearly raw, the 'young gal' spills the gravy down the stairs, and the pigeon-pie is delusive: 'the crust being like a disappointing head, phrenologically speaking: full of lumps and bumps, with nothing particular underneath' (474). David is entirely passive in the face of these calamities: left only to suppositions about what has occurred in the foreign territory of the kitchen: 'I suppose – I never ventured to inquire, but I suppose – that Mrs. Crupp, after frying the soles, was taken ill' (473). His impotence in the face of those who prepare his food is to continue throughout the novel. The meal on this occasion is saved when Mr Micawber has the ingenious idea of taking the cooking out of the hands of the servants altogether: the assembled company slice the raw mutton and devil it themselves over a gridiron:

What with the novelty of this cookery, the excellence of it, the bustle of it, the frequent standing up to look after it, the frequent sitting down to dispose of it as the crisp slices came off the gridiron hot and hot, the being so busy, so flushed with the fire, so amused, and in the midst of such a tempting noise and savour, we reduced the leg of mutton to the bone. (474–5)

This is food enriched by a virtuous circle of need, desire and production – they prepare it exactly as they want it; they eat it the moment it is cooked – 'hot and hot' – a rarity in a society where food has to be transported by servants a considerable distance between kitchen and dining room; their appetites are enriched by the activity and by the savour of the food as it cooks. The informality and the unusualness of the occasion transform labour into play. David, who has until now been 'liv[ing] principally on Dora and coffee' (471), finds 'miraculously' (475) that he can eat again. The fact that the relaxed pleasure of the meal has everything to do with the absence of those uncomfortable servants is made clear by the sudden appearance of Littimer, confidential manservant of Steerforth. The party is instantly abashed, with David reduced to 'a mere infant at the head of my own table' as Littimer gravely hands round the food and clears the table: 'All this was done in a perfect manner [...] yet his very elbows [...] seemed to teem with the expression of his fixed opinion that I was very young' (476). Littimer, intimidating as he is, appears an exception to the rule of incompetent, deceitful servants, but from our first introduction to him seven chapters earlier, it has been clear that he is not all he seems. 'Seems', in fact, is the significant word, as the narrator hints very heavily that the servant's respectability is a matter of delusory surfaces: he was 'in appearance a pattern of respectability'; 'it would have been next to impossible to suspect him of anything wrong, he was so thoroughly respectable' (356): hints which come to fruition much later in the novel, with the revelation of this paragon's role in the sexual ruination of Little Em'ly.

The series of servants employed by David and Dora in their new married home are similarly deceitful, thieving, lazy and incompetent. The absurdities of their 'Ordeal of Servants' are meticulously traced in the chapter devoted to 'Our Housekeeping', in which their naive delight at finding themselves alone together 'no one to please but one another' (701) is undermined by the iniquities of their employees. The first is Mary Anne Paragon 'whose nature was represented to us, when we engaged her, as being feebly expressed in her name' (701), but who drinks, steals the tea-spoons and hides her cousin in the coal-hole when he deserts from the Life-Guards. She is replaced by Mrs Kidgerbury, 'the oldest inhabitant of Kentish Town [...] who went out charing, but was too feeble to execute her conceptions of that art', and then by an amiable 'treasure' who breaks most of their belongings by falling up and down stairs. The earliest servants have names and are accorded physical descriptions, but the later ones decline, after some briefly memorable 'Incapables' into 'an average equality of failure' (707), not even distinguishable by their particular inadequacies and crimes. Most comical, because most transgressive, are those servants whose actions claim equality with their employers: the drunk who runs up bills at the public house in Dora's name; the 'young person of genteel appearance, who went to Greenwich Fair in Dora's bonnet' (707). Like the handy young man parading the Strand in David's waistcoat, the servant who can 'pass' by donning the clothes of their employer suggests the worrying lack of essential difference between those who are served and those who do the serving. This anxiety about servants passing is to be found in many household manuals: Beeton reports it as a general concern of 'Society' that 'the introduction of cheap silks and cotton, and, still more recently, those ambiguous "materials" and tweeds, have removed the landmarks between the mistress and her maid, and between the master and his man' (1989: 961), while Samuel and Sarah Adams, authors of *The Complete Servant* of 1825, advise their servant-readers to 'dress as becomes your station, if you desire to please your employers', noting firmly that 'the happiness of society arises from each of us keeping in our station, and being contented with it' (23). The pattern of disastrous servants in *David Copperfield* is presented as essentially comic, but its root cause – the failure of both Dora and David as household managers – is viewed with less levity. It is the cause of the first 'little quarrel' (702) of their married life, when Dora quails at the prospect of asking Mary Anne to serve their dinner at a regular hour. Her inadequacies as a domestic manager – and David's inability to manage her – are presented as the ultimate reasons for their being cheated and defrauded by their servants: 'we felt our inexperience, and we were unable to help ourselves' (702). This too tallies very precisely with the discourse of the household manual, where the character and diligence of servants are seen primarily as a function of the mistress's effective control, with Beeton, in particular, suggesting that she gets the servants she deserves: 'just in proportion as she performs her duties intelligently and thoroughly, so will her domestics follow in her path' (1989: 1). Domestics 'invariably partake somewhat of their mistress's character' (2), so the most effective method of judging potential servants is to closely observe 'the appearance of the lady and the state of her house', since 'negligence and want of cleanliness in her and her household generally, will naturally lead you to the conclusion, that her servant has suffered from the influence of the bad example' (7).

Middle-class anxieties about the untrustworthiness and intrusiveness of servants increase markedly towards the middle of the century. The Adamses, despite writing largely *for* servants and from the servants 'perspective (their Preface charts their claimed rise from footboy to house-steward and maid-of-all-work to housekeeper respectively), take for granted a small degree of immorality among the servant classes, but consider it something that employers can stamp out by taking a firm line: 'never keep servants, however excellent they may be in their stations, whom you know to be guilty of immorality' (18). By 1861, and despite the very high standards implied by her meticulously detailed outlining of domestic roles and duties, Beeton seems to regard the likelihood of petty immorality on the servants' part as pretty high, given their 'many temptations' (1989: 23), and simply offers the reader strategies to circumvent it. The subject of the potential immorality of servants appears a number of times throughout her text, and is addressed very early in the first chapter: instructing the mistress on her duties in the interviewing of previous employers of potential servants, she makes clear that the servant's morality – rather than efficiency – is the fundamental concern: 'Your first questions should be relative to the honesty and general morality of her former servant; and if no objection is stated in that respect her other qualifications are then to be ascertained' (7). The very first duty of her Housekeeper is surveillance over the other servants: she should be 'constantly on the watch to detect any wrong-doing on the part of any of the domestics' (21). It may be the case that servants became less trustworthy as their numbers dramatically increased, as more and more young untrained servants were employed by inexperienced employers, and as the social gulf between employers and employees narrowed, but there is little clear evidence of this. What does seem clear is that there is a significant upswing of mistrust on the part of their employers, coupled with a fatalism that leads them, like David Copperfield, to accept a certain degree of petty theft as an inevitable consequence of employing servants at all.[7] Both the petty criminality and the fatalism are detailed in Mayhew's *London Labour and the London Poor* (1851). In the second volume, a section entitled 'Of the Buyers of Kitchen-Stuff, Grease, and Dripping' details the door-to-door trade in kitchen waste and the numerous opportunities it afforded for petty thievery: women calling at the kitchen door would offer to buy 'kitchen-stuff', usually dripping, which would then be sold on to the poor as a substitute for butter:

> In this traffic was frequently mixed up a good deal of pilfering, directly or indirectly. Silver spoons were thus disposed of. Candles, purposely broken and crushed, were often part of the grease; in the dripping, butter occasionally added to the weight; in the 'stock' (the remains of meat boiled down for the making of soup) were sometimes portions of excellent meat fresh from the joint which had been carved at table; and among the broken bread, might be frequently seen small loaves, unbroken. (1968: vol II, 111)

Mayhew notably sets the trade in the recent past, claiming that there has recently 'been a considerable change', as the end-purchasers are no longer itinerant street sellers, but 'proprietors of rag and bottle and marine-store shops'. As a result, he argues that the trade has become 'more open and regular': 'the cook's perquisites are in many cases sold under the inspection of the mistress, according to agreement; or taken to the shop by the cook or some fellow-servant'. His interpretation that the new regularity of the trade has resulted in greater honesty is challenged, however, by one of his informants: 'One of these shopkeepers told me that in this trading, as far as his own opinion went, there was as much trickery as ever, and that many gentlefolk quietly made up their minds to submit to it, while others, he said, "kept the house in hot water" by resisting it.' What we see represented in accounts such as Mayhew's, in Beeton's assumptions and in the depictions of domestics in *David Copperfield*, is the development in the 1850s and '60s of a middle-class culture of anxiety, suspicion and mistrust of the servants with whom they share their homes.[8]

Watchers from the kitchen

The anxieties about servants represented in these depictions of deceit, incompetence, intrusiveness and encroachment are brought dramatically to the fore in the sensation novels of the 1860s. In the novels of writers such as Wilkie Collins and Mary Elizabeth Braddon, festering middle-class anxiety about servants comes to a head, their readers' paranoia stoked with portrayals of servants as blackmailers, impersonators and spies. In Braddon's second novel, *Aurora Floyd* (1863), she fuels the mistrust of her readers with a portrait of servants as spies, infringing on the privacy of their employers:

> Remember this, husbands and wives, fathers and sons, mothers and daughters, brothers and sisters, when you quarrel. *Your servants enjoy the fun.* [...] Your servants listen at your doors, and repeat your spiteful speeches in the kitchen, and watch you while they wait at table, and understand every sarcasm, every innuendo, every look, as well as those at whom the cruel glances and stinging words are aimed. They understand your sulky silence, your studied and overacted politeness. The most polished form your hate and anger can take is as transparent to those household spies as if you threw knives at each other, or pelted your enemy with the side-dishes and vegetables, after the fashion of disputants in a pantomime. Nothing that is done in the parlour is lost upon these quiet, well-behaved watchers from the kitchen. They laugh at you; nay, worse, they pity you. (1996: 177–8)

The passage is notable for a number of reasons: it is addressed directly to the reader, stating in naked terms the nature of their paranoia and the justifications for it. The home is understood as a performative space, in which familial as well as social relationships are 'acted' for an unwanted audience of watchful servants. The metaphor of the public spaces of the home as a stage is developed in many earlier Victorian texts; what is striking in Braddon's formulation is that the audience is not the guests invited to a carefully rehearsed dinner, but the 'watchers from the kitchen', their back-stage space flipped to front-of-house. These servants are spies, eavesdropping, mocking, and patronizingly pitying their employers, but it is striking that the truly bad behaviour – the cruelty, anger, hatred and spite – is assigned by Braddon to her middle-class reader, with the Victorian domestic idyll rendered as a continual war zone. Servants are rarely the primary villains in sensation novels, instead acting as agents of the central antagonists, or deriving personal gain from spying and blackmailing the perpetrators of larger crimes. Just as the authors of household manuals see the mistress as the creator of the character of the servants, so sensation novelists write servants as indices of the characters of their employers: insinuating, over-subtle employers have sly, manipulative servants; cruel masters employ cruel servants.

Like its literary descendant, the detective story, the sensation novel exploits the investigative and the plot potential of individuals who can shift seamlessly between background and foreground. Servants move unnoticed and unregarded through the domestic spaces of these texts, gathering intelligence which is used in the interest of the plots of both protagonists and antagonists, as well as to advance their own schemes. But they function also, most strikingly, as agents of readerly investigation, their accounts filling in the gaps in the mysteries of the narrative. So, one of the many first-person accounts that make up the complicated narrative structure of Wilkie Collins's *The Woman in White* is that of Hester Pinhoe, cook to the villainous Count Foscoe; another that of Mrs Michaelson, the housekeeper of his accomplice Sir Percival. The purely domestic insights offered in these accounts contain crucial information for the plot: Sir Percival's insistence on dismissing almost all of his servants – 'I mean to have this house clear of a pack of useless people by this time tomorrow' (1985: 396) – is a strong clue to the reader that he is planning actions that must not be witnessed. The fact that the one servant he retains is the viciously stupid and cruel Margaret Porcher – dismissed even by the benign Mrs Michelson as 'the most unintelligent servant in the house' (396) – hints, through association, at his own iniquities; but the strongest clue of all to confirm the reader's mounting suspicions is his intention of managing with far fewer servants than his rank demands. It is particularly the dismissal of the cook which bemuses his housekeeper: "'Who is to do the cooking, Sir Percival, while you are staying here?'" His response – "'What do I want with a cook if I don't mean to give any dinner-parties?'" – indicates a suspicious willingness to live with a standard of domestic help dramatically below his social status as a baronet. Count Foscoe is rendered suspect, for directly contrary reasons: not a disregard for culinary niceties, but an over-indulgence in them. In the account of Hester Pinhoe, 'taken down from her own statement' as a result of her illiteracy, she records her being hired as 'plain cook' by the Count and Countess the previous summer. Given the grandeur of their titles the domestic set-up is oddly sparse, with only Hester and 'a girl to do the housemaid's work' (420); the mistress she finds to be 'a hard one, if ever there was a hard one yet', but the Count is 'not a bad master – he had a monstrous civil tongue of his own, and a jolly, easy, coaxing way with him' (422). This coaxing he devotes particularly to inducing the cook to make pastries for him:

'"What are you making there? A nice tart for dinner? Much crust, if you please – much crisp crust, my dear, that melts and crumbles deliciously in the mouth." That was his way. He was past sixty, and fond of pastry. Just think of that!' (423)

This taste is noted as strange also by Marion Halcombe (one of the protagonists and investigator of the crimes being plotted against her half-sister Laura): 'We were all at lunch, in the room with the new French windows that open into the verandah, and the Count (who devours pastry as I have never yet seen it devoured by any human beings but girls at boarding-schools) had just amused us by asking gravely for his fourth tart' (246). Comically foreign, grotesquely flirtatious, outside the English social and class system, Foscoe is also othered through this apparently strongly gendered and childish taste for tarts. His taste in food, like his fondness for white mice as pets, works to wrong-foot the reader and those against whom he plots, rendering him so ridiculous that he is not taken seriously. The minute domestic details of these servantly observations form a key layer in the accretions of evidence and misdirection which the text and reader together scour for clues.

The servant's perspective is entered into most fully in Collins's *No Name* (1863), when the novel's protagonist adopts the role. After the sudden deaths of their highly respectable parents, Norah and Magdalen Vanstone discover that they had been unmarried at the times of their births, and married only recently after the death of their father's first wife – an act which has rendered his will invalid and disinherited his daughters in favour of a distant cousin. Magdalen's unconventional response is to embark on a campaign of disguise and espionage with the intention of marrying the sickly cousin under a false name and re-inheriting their fortune on his death. The marriage achieved, and her husband dead, she has still to reckon with the suspicions of his housekeeper, Mrs Lecount, who persuaded him to leave his money elsewhere. In order to find evidence to overturn the will, Magdalen becomes a parlourmaid in the home of its executor, Admiral Bartram. To accomplish this feat, she first embarks on a course of training from her own maid, Louisa, whereby, whenever they are alone, Magdalen waits on her. Magdalen is already established as a gifted actress, but the narrative's logic of how her maid will be able to pass as her employer for the purpose of the hiring interview relies on that nagging contemporary anxiety that the only difference between employer and employee is dress: as Magdalen assures Louisa, '"A lady is a woman who wears a silk gown and has a sense of her own importance. I shall put the gown on your back, and the sense in your head"' (1992: 453). Magdalen is several times discovered spying in her new position, and each time her curiosity is treated by her seniors and employers as natural in a servant. The role of parlourmaid is presented as an ideal one for the would-be-spy: on her first evening, Magdalen uncovers one deception when she observes her employer secretly feeding the richest dishes she serves him to his dogs, in order not to offend the cook by returning them uneaten. But the text plays with readerly expectations by denying Magdalen the crucial revelation she seeks: the Admiral reveals the information about the will to his nephew at a dinner where Magdalen has been waiting on them – but he waits to do so until she is out of the room. The reader, instead, is placed in the role of eavesdropping parlourmaid, privy to a shocking reversal which renders pointless Magdalen's entire charade.

Men in the kitchen

Admiral Bartram's essential good nature is revealed in his concern for the cook's feelings, and in his indulgence of the drunken episodes of his loyal old servant, Mazey. It is in this context of benignity that the reader is asked to regard his absolute insistence on 'youth and good looks' (451) in his servant girls. It is a taste shared by the text itself, as expressed in a strikingly libidinous description of Magdalen dressing for the first time in her uniform:

> In this servant's costume – in the plain gown fastening high round her neck, in the neat little white cap at the back of her head – in this simple dress, to the eyes of all men, not linendrapers, at once the most modest and the most alluring that a woman can wear, the sad changes which mental suffering had wrought in her beauty almost disappeared from view. In the evening costume of a lady; with her bosom uncovered, with her figure armed, rather than dressed, in unpliable silk – the admiral might have passed her by without notice in his own drawing-room. In the evening costume of a servant, no admirer of beauty could have looked at her once, and not have turned to look at her for the second time. (460)

The trope of servantly invisibility is overturned here by the invocation of a specifically masculine gaze: the costume renders the servant's body visible in precisely that situation in which she is conventionally invisible – the public drawing room. The servant's costume is arousing precisely because of its modesty, its contrast with the battle-ready silk armour of the marriage-seeking middle-class woman. The servant is alluring, by this logic, because she is not trying to be. Most striking is the assumption that all men (except those who draw an income from dressing women) will understand and share the erotic appeal of the servant's appearance. Sensation fiction, like most extremely popular cultural forms, reflects unshielded the prejudices, fears and fantasies of the audience it seeks. If it shows us the anxieties servants provoked in their middle-class employers, it also reflects the considerable role they played as erotic spectacles.

The servant is one of the most common stock figures of the nineteenth-century pornographic imagination. Famous exemplars include the diaries in which poet and barrister Arthur Munby and servant Hannah Cullwick both record and construct their eccentric relationship, and the exhaustive 4,000-page anonymous 'memoir' of sexual adventuring, *My Secret Life*. Munby had both an academic and a sexual fascination with working women and servant girls, who he interviewed, sketched and photographed. His relationship with Hannah, a maid-of-all-work who he met in 1854, fetishized their class differences and the roughest elements of her working life: she called him 'Massa', made herself as dirty as possible and wrote a detailed account of her daily labour for his perusal. They married in secret in 1873, but she lived with him as a servant rather than a wife, except on trips to Europe, where she 'performed' as his wife in public. Munby is remarkable among his contemporaries not for his sexual interest in servants, which seems to have been commonplace, but for the record he kept of this interest, and the curious intensity with which Hannah performed abjection for his delectation.[9] Appearing in eleven volumes from about 1888, *My Secret Life* claims to detail the sexual experiences of the pseudonymous 'Walter' from his earliest recollections to old age. Walter's earliest sexual experiences had all been with servants, and his account clarifies a number of key reasons for their erotic appeal to men of his class: they are working class, and so the social rules that limit the contact 'respectable' men can have with women of their own class do not apply; they are less likely to be diseased than the prostitutes on the street; and unlike those prostitutes, they are more likely to be grateful for male attention, particularly that of a gentleman: 'they all took to cock on the quiet, and were proud of having a gentleman to cover them. Such was the opinion of men in my class of life and of my age.'[10] But the simplest reason for their eroticization is perhaps the most shocking: they are convenient – just there, in the kitchen, within easy grasp. The spice in his seductions of the maids and cooks employed by first his mother and then his wife lies particularly in the ways in which his sexual transgressions challenge the realm of the domestic: 'It was more exciting now than ever to see a woman bolt downstairs directly she had been fucked, to cook potatoes' (II, 415). In a class and at a time when the woman who cooks one's food is absolutely distinct from the woman (officially) in one's bed, there is a powerful transgressive pleasure in linking sex with the activity of the kitchen.

My Secret Life dramatizes a gendered double-think around the sexuality of servants which is echoed in virtually every discourse in which they appear: the masculine gaze views the servant as intrinsically sexually available; the female employer considers any departure from the standards of middle-class sexual probity grounds for immediate dismissal but is unwilling to police the sexuality of her servants – or, indeed, of her sons and husband. So Mayhew, in discussing the sexually active servants he categorizes as 'clandestine prostitutes' (whether or not they charge money for sex)[11] who 'often give themselves up to the sons [of their employers], or to the policeman on the beat, or to soldiers in the Parks; or else to shopmen, whom they may meet in the streets' concludes that:

> Female servants are far from being a virtuous class. They are badly educated and are not well looked after by their mistresses as a rule, although every dereliction from the paths of propriety by them will be visited with the heaviest displeasure, and most frequently be followed by dismissal of the most summary description, without the usual month's warning, to which so much importance is usually attached by both employer and employed.' (1968: IV, 257)

The Victorian novel addresses these issues in veiled terms – for instance, the concern about the risk posed to servants by the men of the household is almost always re-shaped into a more palatable concern about the risk from men of their own class. But a pervasive anxiety emerges particularly in a concern to police the presence of men in the kitchen. In *David Copperfield* Miss Murdstone is 'constantly haunted by a suspicion that the servants had a man secreted somewhere on the premises', and spends her time 'div[ing] into the coal-cellar at the most untimely hours, and scarcely ever opened the door of a dark cupboard without clapping it to again, in the belief that she had got him' (1985a: 98). In

Cranford, an intense concern about the sexuality of servants is localized very specifically on the kitchen. Continually anxious about her pretty maid Fanny's 'lovers', Miss Matty forbids her to have followers, but, as narrator Mary Smith reports with wide-eyed faux-naivety: 'a vision of a man seemed to haunt the kitchen':

> Fanny assured me that it was all fancy; or else I should have said myself that I had seen a man's coat-tails whisk into the scullery once, when I went on an errand into the store-room at night; and another evening, when, our watches having stopped, I went to look at the clock, there was a very odd appearance, singularly like a young man squeezed up between the clock and the back of the open kitchen door: and I thought Fanny snatched up the candle very hastily, so as to throw the shadow on the clock-face, while she very positively told me the time half an hour too early, as we found out afterwards by the church-clock. But I did not add to Miss Matty's anxieties by naming my suspicions, especially as Fanny said to me, the next day, that it was such a queer kitchen for having odd shadows about it, she really was almost afraid to stay; 'for you know, miss,' she added, 'I don't see a creature from six o'clock tea, till Missus rings the bell for prayers at ten.' (Gaskell 1986a: 65)

It is clear that both Fanny and Mary protest too much: as with the issue of Miss Betty Barker's baking, Cranford as both town and narrative is a matter of knowing things and not saying them. The reader is clearly invited to interpret the queer shadows as Fanny's 'followers', but to assume a fairly benign interpretation of their presence. Yet a hint that Fanny's story is more like that of one of Walter's servants is dangled in the sly opening clause of the next paragraph – 'However, it so fell out that Fanny had to leave'. Victorian servants 'have to' leave, rather than actively choosing to, only when summarily dismissed: the assumed reason being pregnancy. Just like the multiple servants who leave the employ of Walter's mother and wife because he has impregnated them, Fanny is the one who will pay the price for her sexual indiscretions. The prose has no-one actively dismissing her – her having to leave in such circumstances is simply inevitable. With the cloaking equivocation of that 'however', which separates the leaving from its assumed cause, Mary also is able to apparently not know what it is she is telling us. The sexualizing of the kitchen is not resolved with the departure of Fanny. Her replacement is Martha, 'a rough, honest-looking, country-girl' (65), but even Martha has her pick of followers – 'many a one has as much as offered to keep company with me' – and she is keen not to waste her opportunities. She too sees the possibilities of the kitchen:

> Many a girl as I know would have 'em unbeknownst to missus; but I've given my word, and I'll stick to it; or else this is just the house for missus never to be the wiser if they did come: and it's such a capable kitchen – there's such good dark corners in it – I'd be bound to hide anyone. (79)

Even after Martha's dating privileges have been established (she is allowed one steady follower), kitchens remain worryingly at risk of male incursions: when rumours of a spate of burglaries circulate, the ladies think one of their own has been targeted: 'Mrs Jamieson's house had really been attacked; at least there were men's footsteps to be seen on the flower-borders, underneath the kitchen windows, "where nae men should be"' (92).

The men who haunt the kitchens in Victorian narratives are intruding on a space that has only recently been defined as exclusively for servants. The yeomanly kitchen of Wuthering Heights rarely belongs only to its servants (Nelly Dean recalls with pleasure the Christmas Eve she had the kitchen to herself and is able to enjoy her solitude and give 'due inward applause to every object' of her care: 'the shining kitchen utensils, the polished clock, [...] the speckless purity of my particular care – the scoured and well-swept floor' (1993: 96–7)). But when employers or guests enter the properly ordered Victorian kitchen, they need an excuse to do so, hence Mary Smith's careful justification of her entering the kitchen (on an errand to the store room, or to see the clock when their watches had stopped). As the end of the century approaches, this division of space starts to break down again, with the kitchen gradually ceasing to be conceived of as a separate realm. In narratives of the turn of the century we see increasing breaches of the divide. One example is *The Diary of a Nobody* (1892) by George and Weedon Grossmith, in which considerable humour is derived from the social missteps of city clerk Charles Pooter as he attempts to establish his status in a world where he is on a parity of income with the tradespeople whom he tries to send to the back door. Like Miss Matty in her reduced circumstances, Pooter and his wife Carrie have only one maid-of-all-work (with a char-woman for 'the rough'), but the power dynamics between servants and employers are markedly different. The first diary entry notes that he has directed his 'intimate friends' to always use the open side-entrance, so as not to disturb the servant; when he reprimands Sarah about her habit of shaking the breakfast crumbs over the floor, she answers 'very rudely: "Oh, you are always complaining"' (1892: 81). Space within the home is losing its clear demarcation: when Sarah asks for extra time off he allows it because he wants access to the kitchen himself: 'I gave her permission, thinking it would be more comfortable to sit with Gowing in the kitchen than in the cold drawing-room' (125). Pooter here anticipates the gradual middle-class reoccupation of the kitchen which is to be a feature of the domestic culture of the next half century.

1914–1945: The servant problem

Domestic service remained the largest form of employment for women in England until the First World War, though the sheer numbers employed in middle-class homes had begun to reduce at the end of the nineteenth century, as employers began to limit the size of their families. With the coming of the First World War the employment situation for working-class women changed, as they were now able to find work in munitions factories and in other occupations previously gendered male. In the interwar years, although some returned to domestic service, many more forms of employment for women became available – work in shops, in factories and particularly clerical work in offices. The result is what quickly became known as 'The Servant Problem', as would-be employers found that those still willing to enter domestic service were now in a position to pick and choose, or else were untrained, slow and unwilling. The effects began to be felt immediately after the war, and by the early 1950s only 1 per cent of middle-class households still employed live-in servants. The Servant Problem was not simply a matter of fewer servants available, but also the wages they could command and the duties they were willing to undertake. In the increasingly democratic climate that followed the war, the working classes were no longer so willing to accept service as their lot; while the middle classes, as a result of economic recession and heavily increased taxation, were no longer so able to pay for it. The expectations of potential servants had altered so significantly as to completely change the nature of the relationship between mistress and maid. Employers found themselves required to propitiate and coax their servants, rather than simply issue orders, and lived in fear of the cook or maid 'giving notice'. All this makes for rich comedy in the hands of novelists such as E. M. Delafield and short story writers like Richmal Crompton: the former's Provincial Lady spends a great deal of time in anxious interviews with her cook and futile letters to Registry Offices in an attempt to find new servants, while William's domestic depredations cause his long-suffering mother endless problems with her servants. Delafield's Provincial Lady details the minutiae of her life as an ordinary middle-class housewife over four volumes published between 1930 and 1940; in later volumes the protagonist becomes an author and brings her brand of distrait common-sense to bear on publishing parties, book tours to America, and war-work, but it is in the first volume that she taps most precisely into the blend of exasperation, anxiety and resentment which came to dominate the relationship between middle-class women and their servants. The issue emerges immediately, with the Provincial Lady's first diary entry ending with the ominous statement that 'Cook says there is something wrong with the range' (1991: 3). The entry of the next day details the fall-out:

> Nov 8th: Robert has looked at the range and says nothing wrong whatever. Makes unoriginal suggestions about pulling out dampers. Cook very angry, and will probably give notice. Try to propitiate her by saying that we are going to Bournemouth for Robin's half-term, and that will give the household a rest. Cook replies austerely that they will take the opportunity to do some extra cleaning. Wish I could believe this was true. (3)

The passage sets up the power differential as clearly in the cook's favour: she is unafraid to express her anger, she refuses to be mollified and she dictates the pattern of labour within the household rather than waiting for orders. Her employer is fearful of her servant's moods and craven in the face of them, mistrustful, but passive. The styling of the servant as 'Cook' marks a distinct shift from the Victorian period: Nelly and Zilla, Martha, Fanny and Peggotty are all responsible for the cooking, but none of them are afforded the title. The generic Victorian female servant is a maid, while her generic interwar equivalent is a cook: a conceptual promotion that is part of a general cultural mood of propitiation. The Provincial Lady worries about having to talk to the cook, and tries to avoid all direct confrontation; ordering the day's food is a fraught negotiation, with much stonewalling and hand wringing: 'Cook unhelpful and suggests cold beef and beetroot. I say Yes, excellent, unless perhaps roast chicken and bread sauce even better? Cook talks about the oven. Compromise in the end on cutlets and mashed potatoes' (30). The servants frequently give notice and much of the narrative's comedy involves the great difficulty of finding suitable replacements. When Ethel, the house-parlourmaid, gives notice, and 'Cook says this is so unsettling, she thinks she had better go too', 'despair invades' her (40). Numerous registry offices yield nothing but 'mythical' house-parlourmaids, while in the meantime Ethel is courted by affluent potential employers: 'opulent motor-cars constantly dash up to front door, containing applicants for her services' (41). The position Ethel holds is itself an indication of the Servant Problem – being a combination of the Victorian roles of house maid and parlour maid. Other desperate employers at Registry Officers are heard seeking 'cook-generals' – a role which is in essence a face-saving promotion for the erstwhile 'maid-of-all-work', though with considerably more restrictions as to the work that the maid will perform. One of the chief dissatisfactions the Provincial Lady expresses is with the food her various cooks produce. Early in the first volume they are served burnt porridge, which her husband insists she complain about. Her literary reference to *Jane Eyre* does not distract him and she is forced to confront the cook, who responds with 'expressions of astonishment and incredulity' (15). Incidents with stale sponge cake and arguments about picnic fare follow. It is only when (in *The Provincial Lady Goes Further*) this cook is due to leave that she indulges in an 'absolute[ly] unprecedented display of talent and industry', sending up 'hitherto undreamed-of triumphs of cookery, evidently determined to show us what we are losing' (1991: 147). Poor cooking is seen not as a function of inadequate training or lack of talent, but as a wilful power play on the part of the servant. The craven response of the employer to these newly empowered servants is one the reader is assumed to share: 'servants, in truth, make cowards of us all' (97). At the start of the final volume, *The Provincial Lady in Wartime* (1940) the protagonist still manages to retain a cook and two maids, though one maid soon leaves for war-work. The Provincial Lady herself, having installed an aunt to manage the house, servants and evacuees, leaves to do her own bit – in a canteen. The ludicrousness of this occupation for one with no experience of cooking is highlighted by the fact that she cannot tell her own cook what she has been doing: 'do not care to mention Canteen which would not impress Cook, who knows the extent of my domestic capabilities, in the very least' (1991: 460). It is at this moment that a clear shift in the text's ideology of the domestic takes place. Cook is forced to take a holiday on her uncle's farm, and a temporary cook is employed, from whom the Provincial Lady plans to take lessons in cookery. This intention leads her into thoughts of the post-war future:

Indulge in long and quite unprofitable fantasy of myself preparing and cooking very superior meals for (equally superior) succession of Paying Guests, at the end of the war. Just as I have achieved a really remarkable dinner of which the principal features are lobster à l'Américaine and grapes in spun sugar, Winnie comes in to say that the grocer has called for orders please'm and Mrs Vallence says to say that we're all right except for a packet of cornflour and half-a-dozen of eggs for the cakes if that'll be alright. (473)

The glamorous future involves earning money from cooking; the prosaic present involves the tedium of having to deal with servants and tradesmen. The ideological barrage of the new domestic discourses in which cooking is marketed to the middle classes as creative and fulfilling has finally convinced even the Provincial Lady of the greater freedom and stylishness of the life without servants which will, in any case, be inevitable after the war. The much-anticipated cooking lessons begin with instruction in how rabbits 'ought to be got ready, which', according to the cook, 'is a thing many ladies never have any idea of whatever' (473). After a 'gory and unpleasant interlude' which has her 'wishing from the bottom of [her] heart that [she] had taken Aunt Blanche's advice' ['to have nothing to do with rabbits'], she is congratulated by Mrs Vallence for having 'now done The Worst Job in All Cooking'. The power shift from the earlier volumes is marked: the cook (who is by no means a trained chef, merely the ex-kitchen maid of Lady Frobisher) is now named and seen as a respected authority, whose praise gives the Provincial Lady self-respect. Cooking is re-imagined as a necessary, complex and arcane art, rather than a set of lowly tasks.

Attitudes to servants and the politics of service and of domestic space shift similarly throughout the interwar and post-war period in Richmal Crompton's William stories. Starting in 1919 with 'Rice Mould' (first published in *Home Magazine*) and ending with the posthumous publication of *William the Lawless* in 1970, she depicts the devastation wrought on the lives of his family and village by genius of anarchy William Brown. While William remains always 11, the world in which he lives changes as the decades pass, offering a microcosmic picture of shifts in middle-class cultural mores and lifestyle. In the 1922 'A Question of Grammar', the kitchen is very much the domain of the servants; by 1932 in 'The New Neighbour' (*William the Pirate*), Mrs Brown is 'taking advantage of the cook's afternoon out to make a cake' (1954: 109). In the wartime *William Does His Bit* (1940) the family still have a cook, but in *William Carries On*, published two years later, the fact that 'his mother was "managing" without a cook' appears to William one of the major advantages of the war (1988: 97). By 1952 in *William and the Tramp*, Mrs Brown has only her 'daily', Mrs Peters, and the relationship between them is very different from that between Cook and Mrs Brown's earlier incarnations. At the opening of 'William and the Haunted Cottage', he returns home to find 'his mother busy with preparations for a cake at the table and Mrs Peters standing in the middle of the room, one hand on a broom handle and the other on her hip. Her long thin face was lengthened to its fullest extent and she was obviously labouring under some strong emotion' (1956: 145–6). While Mrs Brown distractedly mixes the cake, adding too many eggs without beating and being forced to scrap the mixture and start again, Mrs Peters complains about having to walk through the woods past a 'haunted' cottage to reach the Brown's house, and announces her intention of resigning: "'I may 'ave me faults, but no one's ever bin able to throw in me face as I've not done me week out. I'll do me week out, then I'll make other arrangements. I don't mind fer meself, but I've got me nerves an' me feet to study, so – well, that's 'ow it is'" (148). Self-employed, and able to dictate the terms of her employment, the daily is named by the text and addressed by Mrs Brown with the same formality accorded to the latter (though she herself throws Mrs Brown the very occasional 'mum'). She speaks to her employer as an equal – 'that's all you know' (146) and is notably unapologetic about her sudden decision to leave. Mrs Brown, to whose part all the cooking clearly now falls, works while her employee stands and talks, notably not using the broom she clutches. The scene ends with Mrs Brown 'sitting down despairingly at the kitchen table among the ruins of her cake'.

A striking feature of Crompton's early stories is a number of battles – both psychological and literal – between William and servants. These early stories display the preoccupation with class that typified the inter-war period: many of William's adventures involve him crossing class boundaries to befriend – or be tricked by – tramps, mount friendly battles with 'village children', and engage with Cockney infants sent to the country by charitable organizations. In 'William Below Stairs', a story from the first collection, *Just William* (1922), the comedy of class is put centre stage when William finds himself working as a servant. Feeling underappreciated, he runs away from home, but soon tires, and knocks on the door of a large house where he is greeted by the butler who mistakes him for 'the new Boots' (1991a: 61). He is sent to the kitchen and put to work cleaning knives and blacking shoes – tasks which he performs with insouciant lack of attention while creating his customary havoc and impressing the kitchen maid with his wild loquacity. The servants are stock comedic figures, their speech caricatured and their attitudes to 'the master' and his guests highly conventional. William's fight with the pompous butler, involving shoe blacking in the face and a chase through the house and round the dining room table, is pure slapstick, but underlying the story is a serious concern to absolutely rule out any genuine mis-assignment of William's class. His rescue and punishment combined come in the form of 'a pal of the master's' with whom the latter is dining in the room into which William and the butler erupt: this man, earlier conceded by the comically patronizing butler to be a 'decent-lookin' bloke' (70), is William's father. Ending on the moment of horrified recognition between father and son, the story leaves the reader to imagine the embarrassment of the former and dismay of the latter; the class-confusion enjoyably transgressive but safely temporary. In 'A Question of Grammar', another story from the same collection, William indulges in yet more war with servants. On the strength of his wilful misunderstanding of the rules of double negatives, William invites a horde of his friends to an impromptu party when his parents are away for the day. Seeing the disreputable gang approaching the house, armed with 'sticks and stones and old tins from the ditch' (124) and headed by William with a trumpet, the cook bars the door against them, but they "'storm her ole castle'" (125), trampling the garden, breaking the drawing room window and locking Cook in the coal cellar. Importantly, the cook is not a passive victim of this aggression: 'The house was full of shouting and yelling, of running to and fro of small boys mingled with subterranean murmurs of cook's rage. Cook was uttering horrible imprecations and hurling lumps of coal at the door. She was Irish and longed to return to the fray' (128). Having secured themselves unimpeded access to the cook's territory, the boys raid the larder:

> Ginger seized the remnants of a cold ham and picked the bone, George with great gusto drank a whole jar of cream, William and Douglas between them ate a gooseberry pie, Henry ate a whole currant cake. Each foraged for himself. They ate two bowls of cold vegetables, a joint of cold beef, two pots of honey, three dozen oranges, three loaves and two pots of dripping. They experimented upon lard, onions and raw sausages. They left the larder a place of gaping emptiness. Meanwhile cook's voice, growing hoarser and hoarser as the result of the inhalation of coal dust and exhalation of imprecations, still arose from the depths and still the door of the coal-cellar shook and rattled. (129)

The narrative pleasure produced by this scene has to do partly with the abandonment of all of the social rules governing the consumption of food – where, in what order, combination and quantity – and partly to do with the successful routing of an enemy. The pleasurable anarchy the boys enjoy is predicated on the absence of adults – it is notable that the moment William's family returns, the carnivalesque interlude is over. In this logic, the servants don't count as adults, as indicated by the cook's eagerness to join battle on the children's terms. It is significant that the weapons of choice are items of food – when Jane, the maid, returns from a date with her 'young man', she is pelted with lard and 'a shower of onions, the ham bone, and a few potatoes' (131) – and that the narrative lingers on the dirt and mess the boys import into the house, destroying the work of the servants. Crompton's William books were initially directed at an adult readership: the comedic enjoyment of this story is grounded, I would suggest, in a latent hostility towards servants which the wild scenes of plundered larder and food as missiles allow expression. There are many such scenes in other stories, particularly the earlier ones: in the first-ever William story, 'Rice-Mould', he engages in debate with a sarcastic family cook about whether she will provide cream blancmange for his elder sibling's party. He plans to steal the blancmange to give to the little girl next door to compensate for the hated rice mould that constitutes her own pudding, and, managing to get himself shut in the larder, glories in the fact that he has 'scored off cook!' (1995: 31). Scoring off cook is something off a trope in the British children's texts of the early twentieth century, with the unstable domestic labour situation transmuted into representations of children at war with cooks and a new licence for them to trespass on the realm of the kitchen. In E. Nesbit's *The Phoenix and the Carpet* (1904) the chapter entitled 'The Queen Cook' sees the children acting out hostility towards the cook, who has already threatened to resign because of their behaviour, with a series of bad deeds and mishaps. In faux-naive tones the narrator 'ask[s] you to believe that they didn't do all the things on purpose which so annoyed the cook during the following week', while conceding that 'I daresay the things would not have happened if the cook had been a favourite', but the text then records a week's worth of incursions in diary form, the day-by-day listing offering the reader the pleasure of anticipating each new challenge to the cook's authority and the order of her realm:

> *Monday*. – Liquorice put on to boil with aniseed balls in a saucepan. Anthea did this, because she thought it would be good for the Lamb's cough. The whole thing forgotten, and bottom of saucepan burned out. It was the little saucepan lined with white that was kept for the baby's milk.
>
> *Tuesday*. – A dead mouse found in pantry. Fish-slice taken to dig grave with. By regrettable accident fish-slice broken. Defence: 'The Cook oughtn' to keep dead mice in pantries.' (1980: 61)

Their hostility to the cook appears to originate with her complaint that they have smeared 'beastly yellow mud' on both sides of their nursery carpet (in fact the magic carpet of the title), but the chapter offers interesting hints that the animus is not solely that of the children: it begins with a somewhat glutinously lyrical account of the wonders of Sunday as a day of family relaxation, when there are flowers at the table, and the food is the sort that does 'its best to make you happy' and mother puts her feet up on the sofa and father ('who had been working hard all week') settles down to read to the family. It is at this point, with the children in 'a happy heap on the hearthrug', that the cook gives a 'surly solid knock' on the drawing-room door, opens it 'an angry inch' and requests to speak to her mistress:

> Mother looked at father with a desperate expression. Then she put her pretty sparkly Sunday shoes down from the sofa, and stood up in them and sighed.
>   'As good fish in the sea', said father, cheerfully, and it was not till much later that the children understood what he meant.' (58)

This passage works hard to develop the reader's sympathies for the hard-working, devoted parents for whom the cook's threat of resignation is just one more of life's burdens, giving subliminal justification for the aggression with which the children launch their attacks on the cook. But unlike Crompton, Nesbit is more actively attuned to the hypocrisy of class. The children later come to feel for the reality of the cook's life when they inadvertently transport her to a desert island on their magic carpet. There she is adopted as queen by the 'copper-coloured' savage inhabitants, and insists on being left there, as, even without an ability to communicate with her new – possibly cannibal – subjects, it is far preferable to her life of service: '"No more kitchens and attics for me, thank you"' (76).

The hostility towards servants that reveals itself in middlebrow novels and in children's texts is a notable feature also in the diaries of Virginia Woolf, in which she details her decade-long attempt to rid herself of her maid, in a catalogue of cowardice, hard-heartedness and sheer embarrassment on Woolf's part and what seems to have been mulish resentment and acts of petty provocation on Nelly's (a relationship brilliantly dissected in Alison Light's 2008 *Mrs Woolf and the Servants*). She repeatedly gears herself up to 'deliver sentence of death', and then backs down. Her descriptions of her mixed feelings of contempt, pity and frustration sum up the vexed mistress–maid relationship:

> This is written to while away one of those stupendous moments – one of those painful, ridiculous, agitating moments which make one half sick & yet I don't know – I'm excited too; & feel free & then sordid; & unsettled; & so on – I've told Nelly to go; after a series of scenes which I won't bore myself to describe. And in the midst of the usual anger, I looked into her little shifting greedy eyes, & saw nothing but malice & spite there, & felt that that had come to be the reality now; she doesn't care for me, or for anything; has been eaten up by her poor timid servant's fears & cares & respectabilities. (1980: 240)

Woolf is fully aware of the inadequacies of her representation of Nelly: indeed, it is the felt need to take Nelly's perspective into account that she finds so oppressive, increasingly fantasising about a house without servants, in which she is free to fend for herself domestically. The replacement of the old solid-fuel range in her Sussex kitchen with a modern oil stove in 1929 produced wistful plans of being 'able to come down here with a chop in a bag & live on my own'. She goes over in her imagination the dishes she will cook – 'the rich stews, the sauces. The adventurous strange dishes with dashes of wine in them' (257). Woolf, interestingly, recognizes that her relationship with Nelly is a rich potential source of fictional material, remarking that 'If I were reading this diary, if it were a book that came my way, I think I should seize with greed on the portrait of Nelly, & make a story – perhaps make the whole story revolve round that – it would amuse me. Her character – our efforts to be rid of her – our reconciliations' (274), but she never actually transforms the experience into fiction. The problem of the servant's point of view, as Light has so tellingly demonstrated, is one that Woolf is unable to solve: 'the figure of the servant and of the working woman haunts Woolf's experiments in literary modernism and sets a limit to what she can achieve' (2008: xviii).

Glimpses of the servant's point of view in the literature of the first half of the twentieth century often come as a shock, necessitating, as they do, a reversal of the dominant narrative which sees the middle-class housewife as the victim and the servant as powerfully capricious. One attempt to bridge that yawning chasm of understanding between the two classes of women inhabiting the bourgeois home comes in Lettice Cooper's *The New House* (1936), which encompasses one day in the lives of an upper-middle-class family as they leave their large, inconvenient old house and move to a smaller one. Rhoda, the daughter, quails in the face of servants, painfully aware of their otherness, and of the alien world of the kitchen: 'She always felt shy when she penetrated to that downstairs world. The life lived so near them and so far apart from them was a dark continent, full of unexplored mystery' (1987: 100). Attempting to bridge the divide, she goes down to the kitchen to say goodbye to the cook:

> As Rhoda came into the kitchen, the ease of cook's body changed to stiffness, and a mask fell over her face. She stopped crying. She did not dislike Rhoda – at that moment she was sorry to part from her – but Rhoda was on the other side. As soon as she came into the room Annie Hargreaves became cook. Rhoda knew it, and minded more than Annie Hargreaves. Here was a woman only a few years older than herself, living in the same house with her, full, no doubt, of hopes and fears and sorrows and wishes, and as far apart from her as a foreigner who did not speak English. It seemed absurd. (101)

The passage switches back and forth between the perspectives of the two women, yet, as with Woolf, there is an apparent hesitancy about the full subjectivity of the servant, the 'no doubt' raising precisely a doubt about the degree to which Annie does share the same sort of feelings as Rhoda. But two pages later we return to Annie and what Woolf would call her poor timid servant's fears and cares:

> She would have a bit of a rest now, but it couldn't be more than a week or two, because her people were all miners. They couldn't do without what she sent them. [...] Forty next month and in service since I was fourteen. Please may I slip out to post a letter? Would you like the chicken hashed or done in a fricassay? [...] You get sick of other people's houses. (103–4)

The novel's final view of this character is of Annie Hargreaves rather than Cook, returned in imagination to a moment of childhood bliss, running home from school, anticipating bread and jam in the kitchen. Cooper, unlike Woolf, is able to allow her servant characters full and independent inner lives. Annie is contrasted to the younger servant, Ivy, who will be coming with the family to their new house, and who is excited by the prospect of having the kitchen to herself and being able to order her work without Cook's supervision. Exuberant, shameless Ivy, with her steady young man and their plans for a tandem, and her devoted love of the household cats, is a modern creature. With her as sole servant in the new house there will be, Rhoda realizes, 'no unexplored dark continent' (102):

> Ivy was nineteen, and belonged to a generation for whom this mysterious place hardly existed. Her complete unconsciousness of it was defeating Mrs Powell and would defeat her still more as time went on, and, while deploring the old respectful servants she would find Ivy's affairs interesting. Ivy was good at telling them, racy, sturdy, sardonic, a peasant living in a town, the lineal descendant of the free-spoken, free-spirited girl of English folk-songs.

Ivy, 'bounc[ing] into the drawing-room to show them her new Marks & Spencer jumper', is kin to 'the Georgian cook' Woolf saw as exemplifying the change in human character that she dates, with provocative precision to 'in or about December, 1910': unlike the Victorian cook, a 'leviathan in the lower depths', 'formidable, silent, obscure, inscrutable', the modern cook is 'a creature of sunshine and fresh air; in and out of the drawing-room, now to borrow the *Daily Herald*, now to ask advice about a hat' (Woolf 1966: 320). Ivy, unlike Annie, does not have a life-time of service in front of her: marriage and children and her own home await, but she is content to delay this future for the moment. To Rhoda, the unmarried daughter, trapped by duty in her mother's home, Ivy's life looks something like freedom also: she sees her as 'a soldier of fortune [...] adapt[ing] herself to life as she found it' (223), and imagines, naively, that her own life would have been better if she had been forced, like Ivy, to make her own living from the age of fourteen. The kitchen in the new house is still ostensibly in the possession of the servant – Ivy has made it her own in a few short hours, with 'a gay tradesman's calendar' (292), and a chipped porcelain cat and cracked china jug she has rescued from the rubbish-heap – but the day ends with Rhoda and her sister Delia contentedly cooking themselves a late supper of scrambled eggs and toast:

> Delia was beating eggs vigorously with a fork. The golden froth rose in the white bowl. Rhoda pulled out the tray from under the griller, and looked at her toast. The pale wedges of bread were crisping, and turning a golden brown; the kitchen smelt of toast. It was the old smell of schoolroom tea, when she and Maurice and Delia jostled one another in front of the fire, toasting their bread on knives, and scorching their cheeks and noses to produce irregular pieces of toast burnt on one side, and grey with ash where they had fallen into the grate. (310)

The idea of edging aside the servant and getting to enjoy the pleasures of cooking and its processes and sights and smells has considerable potency in the interwar years. As Rhoda's sense memory of nursery-cooking suggests, it is understood more as play than as work, located somewhere between artistic practice and childhood 'messes' – a middle-class re-annexation of the kitchen which will be further explored in the next chapter.

The desire to cook is the key motivation behind the project Monica Dickens (great-granddaughter of Charles) details in her 1939 *One Pair of Hands*, in which she offers one of the most notable interwar explorations of the servant's perspective. After being 'finished' in Paris, and subsequently studying acting and cooking, she worked as a cook and housemaid for some months in order – though the narrative somewhat elides this – to write a book about her experiences. The result entertainingly exposes the realities of life below stairs, detailing the petty snobberies of mistresses and deceits of maids, graphically depicting the descent into stupidity that results from total exhaustion, and demonstrating that even the kindest of employers tended to think of their servants as alternately automatons and 'screamingly funny' music-hall turns. Much of the narrative tension derives from the reader's awareness that Dickens is not 'really' a servant: the first chapter sets up her class position very clearly, notably by way of her own inability to cook at home, due to the territorial feelings of the family's own cook:

> I once crept down there when I thought she was asleep in her room to try out an omelette. Noiselessly I removed a frying-pan from its hook and the eggs from their

cupboard. It was the pop of the gas that woke her, I think, for I was just breaking the first egg when a pair of slippered feet shuffled round the door and a shriek of horror caused me to break the egg on the floor. This disaster, together with the fact that I was using her one very special beloved and delicately nurtured frying-pan, upset cook so much that she locked herself in the larder with all the food and we had to make our Sunday dinner off bananas. (1952: 9)

It is ostensibly in order to advance her culinary skills that Dickens embarks on her servantly adventures. Cooking is presented as both chore and skill in the text, with Dickens often reaching the limits of her expertise, but depicting the processes with a degree of narrative detail that assumes readerly engagement and interest. The account of the first dinner she prepares takes us from her employer's planning of the menu, her own feverish reading of cookery books, and the various dodges she employs to manage the unfamiliar tasks: she tires of scraping the pith off oranges for the fruit salad and so 'push[es] the rest, all stringy, to the bottom of the dish' (11); she cuts her thumb when opening a tin of lobster and then produces lobster cocktails – 'a sticky mess with some tomato, thinned down with a little of my life-blood'. When burning paper spoils a Hollandaise sauce for a later dinner, she 'suddenly [has] a brainwave and turn[s] the sauce into Béarnaise by adding some chopped herbs and gherkins which effectively mingled with the black specks and camouflaged them' (60). Cooking in Dickens's text is caught between two meanings – it remains a weapon in a covert class war, with the servant deceiving her employer, covering up her mistakes and pilfering from the larder, but it is also beginning to be reimagined as a creative, cultural act: Monica messes up the sauce and deceitfully covers it up, but she knows enough about classic French cooking to do so in an artistic and effective manner. When exhausted by her life of service she takes a break to join her family on a motoring tour of Alsace-Lorraine, where she is re-inspired by the food she encounters: 'after visiting the kitchens of almost every inn and hotel, I was fired with an enthusiasm to try out some of the marvellous things we had tasted over there' (71).

The fact that she is not really in need of the money she earns is made very clear at the end of the narrative, when she takes the funds that have accumulated in the bank and 'in [her] desire to live in a way as far as possible removed from what [she] had been through [...] went out and spent the whole lot in a very short time on the adornment of [her] person' (178). She employs her acting skills to create characters appropriate to the roles she will perform: when being interviewed for a job as cook-general, she contemplates a costume of 'two slashing shades of green and Woolworth's ear-rings' but decides instead on 'the pretence of tragic gentility – plain, but clean and honest' (16–17); when approaching a job as waitress at a cocktail party, she decides 'that, to make a change and to pander to the finicky sound of Mrs Elkington's voice, I would be a very superior parlour-maid, deadly refined, and expecting to be addressed by my surname' (129). Travelling to the country for a job as a maid in a large house, she method-acts her role on the train:

At Paddington I settled myself diffidently into the corner of the carriage and read a twopenny Home Blitherings, my face innocent of make-up, shining like a young moon and my unrouged lips moving with absorbed delight while I followed the lines with my finger. (91)

The readerly pleasure that such moments produce is one very much predicated on the intense and complex class-consciousness of the 1930s. A key element of the humour, as in many middlebrow novels of the period, is a sort of pincer movement of snobbery: the upwardly mobile lower- or middle-middle class has its small pretentions skewered from above and below simultaneously. It is her most socially pretentious employers who are depicted in the harshest terms: their pettiness, the uncleanliness of their toiletries, their bedroom habits and sticky socks revealed to our fascinated disgust. These 'below-stairs' revelations gain their piquancy from our knowledge of the horror her employers would experience if they knew who they really had working in their kitchen, with tension ratchetted up by a number of moments of near-revelation, as when an ex-boyfriend is a guest at the country-house servant's ball, and when a couple she knows attend her employer's dinner party. Yet Dickens also reveals a more subtle understanding that the entire edifice of service is an elaborate masquerade. She is by no means the only one acting a part: the criminally minded butler at the large country house is 'the perfect stage butler' on 'the farther side of the green baize door', a 'good actor', who 'even had a special voice which he used when he was being a seneschal', but in the servants' hall 'relating a juicy piece of scandal [...] pop-eyed with eager appreciation' speaking in the accents of 'the lowest of the low' (94). The hired waitresses who serve the first dinner she cooks 'behav[e] like people acting in a play':

> They would sweep into the kitchen as if coming off the stage into the wings, with trays held high and a tense expression of hauteur still on their faces; relax for a moment in the frenzy of getting the new dishes loaded, and glide off again with faces prepared to make their next entrance. The cook and I were left like stage hands among the debris, as if having seen a glimpse of another world, we almost listened for the applause of the unseen audience. (13)

If service is essentially performative, so too are the lives of the employers from the perspective of the kitchen: 'when "in service" one has a rather cold-blooded tendency to regard the emotions and hazards of one's employer's lives with a certain detachment – almost as if they were people in a play, and the kitchen was the back row of the pit' (155). The relationships between the two classes of dwellers in the home are understood as essentially alienating. Although Dickens is not a 'real' servant, she experiences the arbitrary unfairness and the mind-numbing exhaustion that remain a servant's lot even in a period when they can apparently pick and choose their jobs. When an employer's boyfriend grabs and kisses her in the kitchen, she is sacked the next day. An early scene offers a reverse perspective of the dinner party in David Copperfield's lodgings with the young gal spying from the doorway: here Monica listens outside the door to the dinner-table conversations of her unlikeable fashion-designer employer and his aunt 'in order to make sure of entering in the middle of a conversation about [her], so that [she] could have the pleasure of hearing them break off suddenly as [she] went in' (52–3). The bad French with which her employer attempts to speak about her in her presence is transcribed in mocking phonetic form, and like the young gal breaking plates in her eavesdropping, Monica drops the lid of a tureen when hearing herself described as 'a rotten servant [...] and a bit of a slut' (53). The book ends with an account of Dickens delivering a speech on 'the Servant Problem' at a Household Fair at Olympia to audience of middle-class women. Her listeners are for the most part unimpressed by her account of the travails of a servant's life and instead reiterate the discourse of the put-upon employer. Her ideas about the professionalization of domestic service, with formal training and fair wages, fall on deaf ears and the last words are given to two audience members, one of whom thought the talk not worth sixpence, and the other who had fallen asleep. Domestic service, it is clear, is a doomed institution.

Coda: Imagined servants

One curious literary response to the Servant Problem was the creation of fantasy servants. This trope is most noticeable in the work of P. G. Wodehouse: the near supernatural perfection of Jeeves's service, with his anticipation of every need of his master; or Aunt Dahlia's chef Anatole, the perfection of whose cooking drives the plot in several novels (he repeatedly threatens to quit in *Right Ho Jeeves* (1922) and in *The Code of the Woosters* (1938) Sir Watkyn Bassett's persistent attempts to 'steal' him leads Bertie to offer to go to prison in an attempt to forestall the theft). The gentry-class characters in E. F. Benson's *Mapp and Lucia* series of novels are in thrall to their perfect servants, whose comically grand names – Foljambe, Grosvenor – speak to their perfection of behaviour. It is notable that these fantasy servants are considerably more 'correct' than their employers: their knowledge of the proper social forms absolves their fashionably insouciant employers from having to observe every rule.[12] The trope of the fantasy servant becomes so familiar that it is ironized by a number of writers: in Agatha Christie's *A Pocket Full of Rye* (1953) housekeeper Mary Dove performs service with a knowing perfection, able to run the entire household effortlessly and step with ease into the roles of any of the lower servants. Mary-Poppins-like, she flits quickly between posts, leaving her erstwhile employers bereft: doubly bereft, in fact, as it turns out that she is professionally connected with a team of burglars who ransack the houses using the information she provides. The truly superior servant, the text cynically assumes, has to be a con. The one apparently superior servant who falls the way of the Provincial Lady is also less impressive than he initially seems: a 'male house-parlour*man*' called 'impossibl[y]' Howard Fitzsimmons (Delafield 1991: 51–2). Flummoxed by his upper-crust name, the PL meets the 'whole situation' by 'never calling the house-parlourman anything at all except "you" and speaking of him to Robert as "Howard Fitzsimmons", in inverted commas as though intending to be funny' (52). The implied mystery of the servant's origins is never solved, and is compounded by his tendency to reply to orders with "'Right-oh!'" (typically upper-class slang, as suggested by the title of Wodehouse's 1922 novel). It is 'to the relief of everyone' that Howard Fitzsimmons gives notice shortly afterwards.

It becomes increasingly clear that the ideal for many middle-class women would be service without the servants. And this is what the new domestic technology of washing machine and floor polishers and vacuum cleaners promised. Yet it is curious how often the servant reappears in the advertising campaigns for the technology that was beginning to replace her. From Min bathroom cleaner, with its picture of a smiling uniformed servant and the slogan 'Min helps you in the house' to the extraordinary Atmos – 'the mechanical housemaid', a large metal box which claimed to be 'a clothes washer, rinser, wringer, dryer – and a vacuum cleaner', there is a very strong sense that the housewife is unable to let go of the *idea* of a servant, even as she waves good bye to the reality. By the end of the Second World War it had become largely accepted that domestic service was a thing of the past: the census of 1951 showed a halving of the number of female indoor servants compared to twenty years earlier. In the decades that followed, as 'proper' servants disappeared from popular memory, so a new type of imagined historical servant made their appearance, in television dramas like *Upstairs Downstairs* (1971–5, 2010–12) and *Downton Abbey* (2010–12), in films like *Gosford Park* (2001) and *The Remains of the Day* (1993), all of which made prominent the two lives lived in the same house: the many tensions between the culture of the kitchen and that of the drawing-room. The recently emerged genre of neo-Victorian literature very often takes the gender and sexual politics of service as one of its main themes. In both Sarah Waters's *Fingersmith* (2002) and Jane Harris's *The Observations* (2006) the plots centre on the mutual suspicions of mistress and maid and on the erotic charge associated with figure of the servant. In seeking to uncover the subtexts of service, however, none of these texts really reveal anything that was not already present in Victorian or early twentieth-century depictions. The tension, the mutual hostility and the distrust are already present in the works of Gaskell and Beeton, Cooper and Woolf; the covert eroticization in those of Collins and 'Walter'.[13] As Light notes, the figure of the 'uppish' servant reappears throughout history, always a site of tension and resentment because 'being taken care of by a person who is seen as subordinate, an outsider or an inferior, is never without its anxieties and fears' (2008: 4). Of course, even in the nineteenth century, it is not just servants who prepare food. The following chapter explores a range of other culinary roles operating within texts, in relation to the gendering of authors, protagonists and readers.

CHAPTER 4
GENDER: COOKS, CHEFS, BON VIVEURS AND DOMESTIC GODDESSES

Gender is a key component in many forms of food writing: both the gender positions adopted by the writer and the gender roles assigned to the implied reader. But despite the apparent self-evidence of this gendering process, these roles are not straightforward. This chapter will consider the various gendered identities constructed by food texts from the early nineteenth century to the present by way of topics including the role of chef, gourmet, bachelor, mother and culinary refusenik, the address of cookbooks to male and female readers, and the gendering of eating in both fictional and non-fictional texts. These gender roles are essentially performative, with no necessary connection to biological sex: male writers adopt the role of the mother, women the role of the gourmet or chef.[1] Each is considered in terms of its specific historical context and trajectory: some gendered food-identities (the chef, the gourmet) appearing in remarkably consistent form across the period and beyond, and others (the bachelor, the culinary-refusenik) being the product of particular historical circumstances.

Masculinity I: The chef

In his 1846 cookbook *The Gastronomic Regenerator*, Alexis Soyer, chef of the Reform Club and media celebrity, announced his intention to produce 'an entire change from the system of any other publication on the art of cookery' (Langley 1987: 14–15). He introduces his book with an account of having chanced, on the library shelves of 'a splendid baronial hall', upon 'the nineteenth edition of a voluminous work' on the subject of cookery, rubbing shoulders with the works of Milton and Locke and Shakespeare. The horror he feels at such an unwarranted juxtaposition – exacerbated by his opening the volume and discovering a recipe for oxtail soup – has led him to burn the papers he had collected towards his own cookbook. But 'at the request of several persons of distinction; who have visited the Reform Club, – particularly the ladies, to whom I have always made it a rule to never refuse anything in my power' he has changed his mind:

> It is only within the last ten months that I in reality commenced afresh this work; in which lapse of time I had to furnish 25,000 dinners for the gentlemen of the Reform Club, and 38 dinner parties of importance, comprising about 70,000

dishes, and to provide daily for 60 servants of the establishment, independent of about 15,000 visitors who have seen the kitchen department in that lapse of time.

Having relieved himself of this lament he launches into the book proper, with a list of 'How Everything Should Be in Cooking'. The discourse Soyer establishes here is absolutely typical of the chef-cook-book. The stress on the extreme, impossible business of the professional kitchen, the idea that a public waits, open-mouthed, for the revelations to drop from the spoon of the master, the transparent false modesty, the lordly, often arbitrary rule-giving. We find the same discursive tropes operating sixty years later in the major work of Auguste Escoffier, the greatest food personality of the later Victorian and Edwardian era. Escoffier begins his 1907 *Guide to Modern Cookery* with a potted history of the significant shifts in food culture in the previous two decades, centred particularly around the revolution in public dining effected by the rise of the restaurant, makes very clear his own primary role in these developments, explains that he wrote the book 'only with the view of meeting the many and persistent demands for such a record', and complains of the desperately exhausting life of the chef:

> What feats of ingenuity have we not been forced to perform, at times, in order to meet our customers' wishes? Those only who have had charge of a large, modern kitchen can tell the tale. Personally, I have ceased counting the nights spent in the attempt to discover new combinations, when, completely broken with the fatigues of a heavy day, my body ought to have been at rest. (1907: vii)

Just like Soyer, he dedicates the book to 'the ladies' 'whose kind appreciation has been conducive to the writing of this work'. This ultra-polite courtesy is one of the devices which the nineteenth-century chef deploys to assert his gentlemanly status. The chef of the period is a hybrid figure in class terms – a worker, a professional, an habitué of the fashionable world – and chefs use the cookbook as a means of advancing and solidifying both their fame and their respectability.

The form, content, voice and address of the domestic cookbook change dramatically across the nineteenth and twentieth centuries but, remarkably, the professional food discourse of the chef remains virtually unchanged across the entire period.[2] We find the arbitrary lordly rule-giving, for example, in Nico Ladenis's 1987 *My Gastronomy*: 'I would like to lay down unequivocally certain principles. To achieve simplicity in food and constant perfection, there should be no marriage between two meats, or between a meat and shellfish or a shellfish and fruit' (1987: 55). In the opening address of his 1990 *White Heat*, Marco Pierre White, Soyer-like, assumes a drooling public anxiously awaiting his every word:

> You're buying *White Heat* because you want to cook well? Because you want to cook Michelin stars? Forget it. Save your money. Go and buy a saucepan.
> You want ideas, inspiration, a bit of Marco? Then maybe you'll get something out of this book. (1990: 8)

The back-stage drama of the professional kitchen is glamourized by the moody black-and-white full-page photographs which occupy a solid chunk of this book, with punk-chic chain-smoking chefs wielding lethal-looking knives and cleavers. They are part of a distinctly masculine cadre, hardened and bonded by the boot-camp of the professional kitchen: 'The boys in my team know that if they want to get to the top they've got to take the shit. Harvey's is the hardest kitchen in Britain: it's the SAS of kitchens' (12). The macho hard world of the professional kitchen with its heat and its speed and its swearing is not, however, an invention of the late twentieth-century cult of the chef, nor is the lordly self-importance of their Victorian counterparts. We find identical tropes in the description of a chef in John Earle's 1628 *Micro-cosmographie*:

> The kitchen is his hell and he the very devil in it … he will domineer and rule the roast, in spite of his master, and curses is the very dialect of his calling … His cunning is not small in architecture, for he builds strange fabrics in paste, towers and castles, and like Darius his palace, in one banquet demolished. (Dover Wilson 1911: 226)

Bad-tempered, foul-mouthed, arrogant, authoritarian, but marvellously skilled: this is the mould in which chefs have cast themselves ever since. The social status of the chef and the public's interest in the profession may have gone up and down the social register, but this construction has remained remarkably consistent. And it is without doubt a heavily gendered representation. In fact, it seems clear that the chef acquires this veneer of ultra-masculinity precisely to protect himself from the feminine associations otherwise carried by food preparation.

Properly, 'chef' is a title – an honorific designating only the person in charge of the professional kitchen, but in recent decades this name, and more broadly the role it denotes, has come to be adopted by virtually all male food writers, most of whom have little to no experience in professional kitchens. In this context 'chef' is a title that appears to be claimable by anyone who cooks and is male. It is an identity slippage facilitated, I suggest, by television. With the explosion of food programmes as entertainment in the 1990s, the term started to be applied more and more loosely, coming to stand in for 'male TV cook' and then by extension, 'male food writer' (women do, of course, claim the title of chef, but almost invariably only after extensive experience in a professional kitchen). In this narrative role the 'chef' very rarely addresses his peers. The chef book is not a training manual: professional chefs learn largely in the kitchen, in a centuries-old tradition of apprenticeship. These books are marketed rather on their offer to translate the secrets and methods of the professional kitchen to the domestic one; their promise is to afford the domestic cook the skills and panache of their mentor. So in *At Home with the Roux Brothers* (1988), Albert and Michel Roux announce that 'in writing this book […] we have set out to bring our style of cooking within the reach of the cook working at home, without the equipment or the numerous staff that we are used to in our restaurant kitchens'; all they require of the grateful reader is that 'you should follow our instructions precisely' (1988: 7). Raymond Blanc, observing in his 1988 *Recipes from*

Le Manoir aux Quat' Saisons that readers often skip the introductory and explanatory chapters, exclaims 'Please do not do this!' because 'it is important to understand how and why each step is done, so that you gain a feel and complete understanding of my kind of cooking; then even a tomato will become a subject for artful discussion at a dinner party and your shopping will become a different experience' (1988: 11). But the promise is a chimera: the recipes in chef books are notorious for not working. Adapted from quantities to serve a restaurant to the 4–6 servings required in the average home, many of the economies of scale are lost. Restaurant food relies on the use of a panoply of sauces and reductions and pastes and pastries which a domestic cook would have to assemble from scratch. Restaurants have industrial equipment and fierce flames and biddable commis chefs to do the chopping and plongeurs to do the washing up. The actual function of these books is to provide a record of a moment of achieved success: capturing a restaurant and a chef at the height of their game, or on their way up, celebrating and consolidating their fame, whipping up an appetite for their cooking. It is entirely in the interests of the chef that their recipes should be unrepeatable – or at least unperfectable – in the domestic kitchen. So it is that the River Cafe's Chocolate Nemesis has rarely been known to work outside their kitchens, and that Raymond Blanc gives his recipes in three closely packed columns in type of so pale a grey it is barely legible: these recipes are not designed to be cooked, or at least, not successfully. This is not simply a modern phenomenon: Soyer's *Gateau Britannique á l'Amiral* (a cake confection in the form of a battle ship) and *Salade de Grouse á la Soyer* (in which quartered hard boiled eggs are to stand on their ends around the edge of the dish) were not possibilities for a domestic kitchen (Langley 1987: 23–4). Still less so was Escoffier's *Poularde Sainte Alliance*, which involves a young pullet, ortolans, foie gras, truffles, 'excellent' Madeira, and three waiters: one to dexterously remove the choicest morsels from the pullet, one to add the ortolan and juices, and a third to place the plate before the diner: a dish so elaborate and extravagant that its author meticulously records his inspiration in naming it and the date and place of its first service – 1905, the Carlton Hotel (1907: 491–2).

Repeatedly, the discourse of the chef distinguishes itself from that of the domestic cook by invoking speed, excitement, danger, rage and adrenaline. The celebration of chefly machismo reached its apotheosis in Anthony Bourdain's *Kitchen Confidential* (2000), which became an international best-seller with its combination of scurrilous anecdotes and its promise to let the customer into the secrets of the trade:

> There will be horror stories. Heavy drinking, drugs, screwing in the dry-goods area, unappetizing revelations about bad food-handling and unsavory industry-wide practices. Talking about why you probably shouldn't order fish on a Monday, why those who favour well-done get the scrapings from the bottom of the barrel, and why seafood frittata is not a wise brunch selection (5).

Bourdain's memoir, described by A. A. Gill as 'Elizabeth David written by Quentin Tarantino', is determinedly not in the tradition of the success narratives of great chefs.

He makes it clear that he is a 'journeyman' chef – not 'Superchef' but also 'not some embittered hash-slinger out to slag off my more successful peers' (4). The purpose of his narrative is not to provide a record of success but to open up the restaurant kitchen, and particularly its murkier corners, to public scrutiny. The major narrative method deployed is truth-telling: dishing the dirt about dangerous kitchen practices, about the disgusting things that food goes through before it lands on the plate, and about the contempt felt by restaurant staff for many of their customers: 'the slackjaws, the rubes, the out-of-towners, the well-done-eating, undertipping, bridge-and-tunnel pre-theatre hordes' (72). The commercial success of his book and its continuing reputation suggest a public both anxious about and fascinated by the secrets of the professional kitchen. The chapter on which most reviews of the book focused was 'From Our Kitchen to Your Table', in which Bourdain explains, in vigorously intemperate prose, the deceits, manipulations and unsafe practices perpetuated on the customer by the restaurant industry. The conditions in which mussels are kept, the fact that 'bacteria *love* hollandaise' (67), the '3-foot-long parasitic worms that riddle the … flesh' (69) of swordfish: all these are meticulously detailed. These warnings and revelations, the sense of seeing the things that restaurants don't want you to see, went a long way towards establishing the book's commercial success, though the note of caution sits oddly with the tone of macho bravado Bourdain is at pains to develop elsewhere in the memoir.

Kitchen Confidential is by no means the first memoir of its type. George Orwell's *Down and Out in Paris and London* (1933) is a clear influence on Bourdain with its focus on the dirt, danger and profound exhaustion of the restaurant kitchen and the eccentric personalities that people it. The first half of the book details Orwell's experiences in Paris in the winter of 1929. He had moved to the city in the spring of the previous year and had written two novels and a number of short stories which were repeatedly rejected by publishers. His funds ran out and his remaining money was stolen and so for ten weeks he lived hand to mouth, supporting himself working as a *plongeur* in the kitchens of hotels and restaurants. He first finds a job in the kitchen of what he calls 'The Hôtel X', 'a vast grandiose place with a classical façade, and at one side a little dark doorway like a rat-hole, which was the service entrance' (2013: 54). His description of his first sight of the kitchen echoes that of John Earle, evoking a place of devilish heat and fury:

The kitchen was like nothing I had ever seen or imagined – a stifling, low-ceilinged inferno of a cellar, red-lit from the fires, and deafening with oaths and the clanging of pots and pans. It was so hot that all the metal-work except the stove had to be covered with cloth. In the middle were the furnaces, where twelve cooks skipped to and fro, their faces dripping sweat in spite of their white caps. […] Scullions, naked to the waist, were stoking the fires and scouring huge copper saucepans with sand. Everyone seemed to be in a hurry and a rage. The head cook, a fine scarlet man with big moustachios, stood in the middle booming continuously. (56)

The service areas of the hotel are places of drunkenness, violence and apparent chaos: 'the chargings to and fro in the narrow passages, the collisions, the yells, the struggling with crates and trays and blocks of ice, the heat, the darkness, the furious festering quarrels' (64). Orwell dwells particularly on the filth of these regions in comparison with the gilded luxury of the dining-room: 'there sat the customers in all their splendour – spotless tablecloths, bowls of flowers, mirrors and gilt cornices and painted cherubim; and here, just a few feet away, we in our disgusting filth' (67). The filth is not simply dirt: it is a mixture of slime, detritus and bodily excretions – 'we slithered about in a compound of soapy water, lettuce-leaves, torn paper and trampled food' while coatless waiters 'showing their sweaty armpits' 'stick their thumbs into the cream pots' and wash their faces in the water in which clean crockery is rinsing (67). The room has 'a mixed dirty smell of food and sweat'. The theatrical transformation of the sweaty, swearing, farting waiters as they enter the dining room with graceful reverence is presented by Orwell not, as in the celebratory chef narrative, as part of the magic of the restaurant but as a revelation of the tawdry false nature of the 'luxury' offered by the grand hotels. Like Bourdain he presents side-by-side the most sordid revelations and the absolute ignorance of the customers: 'the staff lavatory was worthy of Central Asia, and there was no place to wash one's hands, except the sinks used for washing crockery. In spite of all this the Hôtel X was one of the dozen most expensive hotels in Paris, and the customers paid startling prices' (80–1). The 'truth' of the restaurant business for Soyer and Escoffier, for Marco Pierre White and even, perhaps, for Anthony Bourdain, lies in the culinary masterpieces it produces. For Orwell the truth is different: it is in the falseness of the divide between scullion and guest, between the two worlds that meet in the dining room. His waiters and cooks and plongeurs are a mixed bag of émigrés and slum kids, run-away rich boys and ex-students as well as the traditional working class. In neither Paris nor as a tramp in London does the old-Etonian Blair stand out from the other inhabitants of streets and slums: there are plenty of other educated men fallen on hard times. But his wider point is that the rich and the poor are 'differentiated by their incomes and nothing else, and the average millionaire is only the average dishwasher dressed in a new suit' (121). Much textual energy is expended on the demonstration of not just the difficulty of the lowliest kitchen jobs but the skill and intelligence they require. Where Bourdain's revelations of the sordid realities of the restaurant kitchen seem designed to demonstrate gleefully to the customer how he has been duped, Orwell's concern is rather that we should understand the realities of the lives of those who labour out of sight. He tells us of the chickens dropped on the filthy floor and then served, of the plates wiped on trousers, of the chefs spitting in the soup, not in warning, but so that the degraded, exhausted, dehumanizing realities of the denizens of the kitchens should be understood. Orwell's is also a macho world of swearing, rage, drunkenness, gambling, drugs and sex, but his backstage kitchen narrative has none of the celebratory exuberance of virtually every other account of this way of life. His narrative exists not to reform our relationship to the professional kitchen but to entirely remake it. What he himself takes from the experience – what he seems to want his reader to take from it also – is that he 'shall never again […] enjoy a meal at a smart restaurant' (216).[3]

Masculinity II: The gourmet

The chef book portrays a gulf between the kitchen and dining room – between those who cook and those who eat. Yet most chef narratives also contain crucial passages in which the protagonist details his own education in the grammar of food – the moments in which he learns how to eat with serious attention. Bourdain's memoir, for example, begins with an account of a trip to France as a child which divides in two around a primal moment of exclusion in which he and his brother are left in the car for three hours while their parents eat at Ferdinand Point's famous La Pyramid restaurant. Having hated French food with all the passionate insularity of the suburban young American, Bourdain describes this moment as transformative:

> Spite, always a great motivating force in my life, caused me to become suddenly adventurous where food was concerned. I decided then and there to outdo my foodie parents. At the same time, I could gross out my still uninitiated little brother. I'd show them who the gourmet was!
>
> Brains? Stinky, runny cheeses that smelled like dead man's feet? Horsemeat? Sweetbreads? Bring it on!! (2000: 13)

His first oyster, in particular, handed to him by a gnarled old fisherman, fresh from the sea – 'huge and irregularly shaped in his rough, clawlike fist' – is a moment 'more alive for [him] than so many of the other "firsts" which followed – first pussy, first joint, first day in high school, first published book'. More: the oyster does not just presage these initiations, it kick-starts them: 'I had had an adventure, tasted forbidden fruit, and everything that followed in my life – the food, the long and often stupid and self-destructive chase for the next thing, whether it was drugs or sex or some other new sensation – would all stem from this moment' (17). The key tropes here are travel, openness to experience, the overcoming of disgust, and the development of sophisticated tastes. The linking of gustatory to sexual experience is also significant. Such passages form part of another literature of food which is gendered masculine: the narrative of the gourmet.

The contemporary food memoir has its antecedents in the writings of gentlemen gourmet travellers in the late nineteenth and early twentieth centuries. Their accounts of travelling across Europe, eating as they go, are part travelogues, part narratives of sensual education. They speak of freedom, leisure, a refined appreciation for pleasure and experience. The grand tour of the long eighteenth century in which a gentleman rounded off his education by seeing the great cultural edifices of the European past is mutated in these texts into something more private, more inward, with cultural capital carried in encounters with food rather than art and architecture.[4] They form a key subset of the literary mode which Stephen Mennell categorizes as gastronomy: literary writing about food which combines, among other features, a nostalgic 'evocation of memorable meals' and 'a brew of history, myth and history serving as myth' (1996: 270–1). Always hybrid, such travel memoirs merge frequently with the travel guide, entwining recollection with guidance, segueing from lyrical accounts of lost meals of the past to guide-book rankings of particular restaurants and dishes. In their *Gourmet's Guide to Europe* (1903), co-authors Liet.-Col. Newnham-Davis and Algernon Bastard take the reader on a leisured culinary meander through the regions of France followed by a whistle-stop tour through the rest of the continent, including visits to Romania, Russia, and Turkey. Their reader is specifically understood to be male, and their information comes as from one gourmet to another: they have 'asked for information from all classes of gourmets – from ambassadors to the simple globe-trotter' in order to tell the gentleman reader 'what his surroundings will be, what dishes are the specialties of the house, what wine a wise man will order, and what bill he is likely to be asked to pay' (viii). The keynotes struck throughout are sophistication of tastes and attitudes; a man-of-the-world shared understanding; and a nostalgia for the grand dishes, restaurants and adventures of the past ('Alas for the Carpe à la Gelée and the Sole au vin Rouge and the Poularde Maison d'Or! I shall never, I fear, eat their like again.' (5)).[5] The opening chapter on France is full of the superiority of its cuisine and raw materials to those of Britain; but its address assumes not that it is imparting these correctly sophisticated attitudes to neophytes, but that the reader is already one of the company of Francophile gourmets, eager to mock insular English attitudes which can now safely be consigned to the past:

> Perhaps the greatest abasement of the Briton, whose ancestors called the French "Froggies" in scorn, comes when his first morning in Paris he orders for breakfast with joyful expectation a dish of the thighs of the little frogs from the vineyards. (3)

The sophisticated reader is assumed to understand French food well, and none of the terms or dishes are explained, but the further the text gets geographically and conceptually from this culinary centre, the stranger it finds the foods it presents. Pizza is memorably described as 'a kind of Yorkshire pudding eaten either with cheese or anchovies and tomatoes flavoured with thyme' (176), while the Turkish practice of eating spit-roasted lamb with the fingers is considered so exotically barbaric that one of the authors apologizes that his knowledge of the spectacle is only second-hand: 'I have to confess that I have not yet accomplished this feat for myself' (228). A knowing sexual sophistication is assumed to run alongside the culinary form: the reader is supposed to share an interest in observing the 'pretty ladies' from a window seat in Milan (161), and to be titillated by the fact that one lost restaurant was famous for 'extraordinary' supper parties at which the 'lights of the demi-monde of that day […] used to be present' (5). A man-to-man frankness is established in statements such as that establishing the 'golden rule, which may be held to apply to all over Germany' that 'it is safe to take ladies wherever officers go *in uniform*' (113). Dishes and menus, eating venues and patrons are accorded the same cultural status as works of art: experiences to be ticked off, elements of social capital:

> Any one who is making a leisurely journey from Marseilles to the roman cities of Provence and who halts by the way at Martigues, the "Venice of Provence" should

breakfast at the Hôtel Chabas; and if M. Paul Chabas is still in the land of the living, as I trust he is, and you can persuade him – telling him that he is the best cook in Provence, which he is – to make you some of the Provençal dishes [...] you will be fortunate. (73)

Such shared knowledge transforms the unknown terrain of 'abroad' into something safely decipherable in terms of the rules of the gentleman's club, offering the behavioural codes whereby the providers of exotic culinary specialties can be propitiated, and the reader can avoid the discomfort of being wrong-footed.

The haute-gourmet mode is reanimated by later texts in which the note of nostalgia becomes the absolutely dominant feature. The glories of pre-war eating and drinking are looked back on by Andre Simon's *Food* (1949) as to a lost world. Simon was the President of the Wine and Food Society, essentially Britain's lead gourmet, and the book was published as part of a 'Pleasures of Life' series. Combining extracts from literary and gastronomical texts from the Classical period onwards with his own recollections, the book is at its most energized when recounting memorable meals of the recent past. These are recalled in rapt, sumptuous detail, with venues, names of host and guests, and every aspect of the food and wine carefully mulled over. The approach is that of finely honed judgement and high seriousness, particularly in the matter of the relationship of the food to particular vintages. The language in which these judgements are rendered, however, is baroque, glorying in its own excesses and flourishes: a Lafite 1858 is 'perfectly proportioned, with the abstract perfection of an architectural drawing or a quadratic equation' (1949: 103); oysters 'had left their beds overnight to be with us today, with the morning's dew, so to speak, still fresh upon their scaly cheeks' (101). A virtually identical gourmet linguistic register is a notable feature of Evelyn Waugh's *Brideshead Revisited*, published a few years earlier in 1945, a novel in which the sensual self of the protagonist is discovered, in part, through new, better ways of eating. Waugh himself later noted with some distaste the 'kind of gluttony, for food and wine, for the splendours of the recent past, and for rhetorical and ornamental language' which characterized the tone: a feature of its wartime composition in 'a bleak period of present privation and threatening disaster – the period of soya beans and Basic English' (1980: 7). The protagonist Charles Ryder's first significant encounter with Sebastian Flyte, the romantically doomed aristocrat who is to provide his early sentimental education, is at a lunch party in Sebastian's Oxford college rooms. The invitation is issued in apology for Sebastian having drunkenly vomited into Charles's room from the front quad the night before (an incident Charles chooses to find charming rather than repellent). The centrepiece of the luncheon is a great dish of plover's eggs, bedded in a nest of moss. The first of the season, they have been sent by 'Mummy' from Brideshead, where 'they always lay early for her' (33): the eggs are an esoteric indulgence, representing Sebastian's family and land and house, his membership of a rarefied other world. Dazzled, Charles at this moment enters into 'the beginning of a new epoch in my life' (32). The gourmet indulgences which association with Sebastian make available to Charles are of a piece with the appreciation of beautiful buildings and art and the hinted-at sexual initiations. Visiting Sebastian's father and his mistress in their Venetian palazzo, they experience 'a Byronic night fishing for scampi in the shallows of the Chioggia', 'melon and prosciutto on the balcony in the cool of the morning', 'hot cheese sandwiches and champagne cocktails at Harry's bar' (98); at Sebastian's ancestral home they drink their way through the grand aged wines in the cellar, working their way through three at a time to compare the vintages, their descriptions becoming 'wilder and more exotic' as they become more drunk. Charles learns the language and the discrimination of the connoisseur and by the time he is living in Paris as an art student he is confident enough in the judgements of the gourmet to despise the vulgar tastes of millionaire Rex Mottram, with whom he dines one evening. He takes him to what Mottram describes as 'the sort of place you see native life' (165), where he orders 'soup of oseille, a sole quite simply cooked in a white-wine sauce, a caneton a la presse, a lemon souffle' and 'at the last minute, fearing that the whole thing was too simple for Rex, I added caviar aux blinis' (166). Throughout the meal he patronizes Rex (who is paying), advising him against eating onion with his caviar, observing that 'the sole was so simple and unobtrusive that Rex failed to notice it' (168), disapproving of the fact that Rex begins his personal confidences before the 'proper hour' of the cognac. The reader is invited to wince at Rex's *faux pas*, at his failure to recognize the superiority of the 'clear, pale' cognac over the 'vast and mouldy' bottle of 'treacly concoction' the waiters 'shamefacedly' provide for 'people of Rex's sort' (171). Although he has by now left behind the drunken and embarrassing Sebastian, the gourmet identity he learnt in his company has become a central part of Charles's sense of self.

An alternative mode of gourmet travel narrative emerges in the years following the First World War, which privileges notions of authenticity rather than luxury. The conflict had meant that many outside the gentlemanly classes had inadvertent experiences of travel, with the result that Europe and beyond seemed much closer and more accessible. A new, more muscular, form of travel narrative sets out to record rougher, less mannerly engagements with foreign cultures and foods. Writers seek above all for 'authentic' encounters: their travels taking them away from the beaten track and the guide-booked restaurant. A typical note is struck at the start of French critic and novelist Alin Laubreaux's 1931 *The Happy Glutton*, in which he establishes his 'authority' with his boast of 'having tasted every kind of food in every kind of climate: turtle in the wilds of Africa, raw fish in Tahiti, fried snake in India, and even boiled mutton and greens in England' (1931: 1). Where cultural capital for Newnham-Davis, Bastard and their forerunners lay in the knowledge and taste-experience of the most sophisticated and highly evolved of foreign cuisines, the acquisitive urge in these later gourmet texts is focused on the new, the authentic and the extreme. It is in this context that later in his narrative, Laubreaux devotes two pages to a luxuriantly lingering description of a goose being crammed to the point where its liver explodes. For the earlier gourmet tradition, the value of *foie gras* resided in its luxury – its expense, its richness of taste and texture; for the post-war gourmet the value is tied up in conceptions of authenticity which include an embracing of what the less sophisticated might dismiss as cruel, grotesque or disgusting and the idea of an ancient unchanging culture of peasant or artisanal production. Typically, in such gastronomic literature there is a tendency to conflate the people and their food. In D. H. Lawrence's *Sea and Sardinia* (1921), the people and the food merge synesthetically, both aesthetically consumable: the casual physical intimacies he observes between Sicilian men are described in culinary terms: they 'pour themselves one over the other like so much melted butter over parsnips'; the 'hugely fat' men he sees as typical of Naples and Catania have 'great macaroni paunches' (1921: 23). His aesthetic appreciation of the market in Cagliari conflates stall-holders and their produce, both equally spectacles: 'Peasant women, sometimes barefoot, sat in their tight little bodices and voluminous, coloured skirts behind the piles of vegetables, and never have I seen a lovelier show' (116). Authenticity is figured mainly in an unvarnished account of the horrors of travelling, the dirt and poverty of provisions in most restaurants and inns, and a building sense of the dislike and envy which most Italians feel for the British in the years immediately after the First World War. With rare exceptions, the food is distinguished more by its unpleasantness than its exoticism. The food that rises above the norm of overcooked, cold banality is characterized by the grotesquery of its form or production. He describes at length the method of catching the octopuses he calls 'ink-pots', where a female is captured, stored hung up in a cave 'the string going through a convenient hole in her end' and periodically towed behind a boat to attract the male 'polyp inamorati' which 'were the victims' (83). After some weeks of this treatment the female dies. Lawrence's account is simultaneously repulsed by the creatures, the tough and unpleasant form they take as food, and the cruelty of the process: 'And I think, even for creatures so awful-looking, this method is indescribably base, and shows how much lower than an octopus even, is lordly man.' Another grotesque food-object is met with in a cellar-like room in a filthy tavern where Lawrence's foul mood is lifted by the spectacle of an old man roasting 'an amazing object on a long, long spear' over the open fire. Lit only by the flames, the grotesque spectacle is slowly revealed: 'it was a kid opened out, made quite flat, and speared like a flat fan on a long iron stalk' (180). The description is fascinated by the distorted form of the animal: 'the whole of the skinned kid was there, the head curled in against a shoulder, the stubby ears, the teeth, the few hairs of the nostrils: and the feet curled curiously round, like an animal that puts its fore-paw over its ducked head.' The positioning of the feet elicits only a glancing sense of poignancy: it is the 'complete flat pattern' formed by the impossible distortions of this once-living body on which he lingers, transforming it into aesthetic spectacle through association: it is like the 'involuted creatures' of 'Celtic illuminations'. The experiential value of this moment is in the witnessing of the ancient, peculiar method of cooking: the portions of kid with which they are served much later – cold and stringy, the slovenly waiting staff having taken the best bits for themselves – are absolutely beside the point. It is no accident that the two most striking food passages in Lawrence's text centre on grotesque distortions of bodies: throughout there is an intense interest in bodies both animal and human as objects of speculation, disgust and desire. In general, in what I am calling the muscular gourmet tradition, the experiential and epistemological acquisitiveness extends to the sexual. Lawrence's curiosity about his fellow travellers and the locals he encounters frequently zeroes in on their sexual attributes and orientation: he is particularly fascinated by pairs of men where one might be considered 'the wife', by men dressing as women during a festival, by different codes of bodily intimacy.

Figure 4 *Frontispiece to Elizabeth David's* A Book of Mediterranean Food *(1950).*

The major post-war inheritor of the muscular gourmet tradition was Elizabeth David. Her first cookbook, *A Book of Mediterranean Food* (1950), was written in a Britain still bowed under the weight of years of rationing against which David, newly returned from a war spent in Greece and then Egypt, was actively rebelling. The generative impulse of the book, as she notes in a later essay, was nostalgia. Despite the format of the cookbook her primary aim was not to provide a guide for cooking of these recipes, most of which were absolutely antithetical to the tastes of her compatriots, even if the ingredients had been available, but simply to remember a food culture now lost to her: 'I sat down and [...] started to work out an agonized craving for the sun and a furious revolt against that terrible, cheerless, heartless [British] food by writing down descriptions of Mediterranean and Middle Eastern cooking' (1986a: 21). The book speaks directly to the interests and self-image of a male readership, offering a combination of 'fine' writing; a cultivated appreciation of art, culture, and wine; and an unabashed response to rumbustious peasant life. David is explicit about the masculine gourmet tradition in which she writes, building up her picture of the Mediterranean via accounts from Osbert Sitwell, Henry James, D. H. Lawrence, Norman Douglas, and Lawrence Durrell. The sparse recipes, which are often short and perfunctory, signal a distancing from the feminine mode of recipe book in favour of the masculine travel narrative. The detail-orientated precision of instructions for which she is famed is scarcely apparent here. The opening of the book makes clear its real preoccupations as the prose takes us on a tour first around the shores of the Mediterranean – 'From Gibraltar to the Bosphorous, down the Rhone valley, through the great seaports of Marseilles, Barcelona, and Genoa, across to Tunis and Alexandria' – and then, zooming in, around its kitchens and market stalls:

> The ever recurring elements in the food throughout these countries are the oil, the saffron, the garlic, the pungent local wines; the aromatic perfume of rosemary, wild marjoram and basil drying in the kitchens; the brilliance of the market stall piled high with pimentos, aubergines, tomatoes, olives, melons, figs and limes; the great heaps of shiny fish, silver, vermillion or tiger-striped, and those long needle fish whose bones so mysteriously turn out to be green. (1956: 9)

David deploys lists frequently: a device that contrasts the controlled rationed scarcity of food in Britain with the plenitude she ascribes to the Mediterranean. The foods she describes are significant not primarily for their exotic flavours but for their visual appeal: the bright contrasting colours, the plump, painterly shapes, their curious forms. The materialist lyricism owes much to Lawrence's very similar description of the market stalls of Cagliari, with their 'monuments of curd-white and black-purple cauliflowers', 'piles of sugar-dusty white figs and sombre-looking black figs, and bright burnt figs' and 'green and vivid-coloured world of fruit-gleams' (119). A composite aroma of pungency and perfume challenges the British palate. The appeal is to our desire to be there more than to our desire to eat that. John Minton, the 'decorator' of the first editions of the book, deftly captures its paradoxes with his frontispiece, in which a sailor and a market girl kneel in postures both relaxed and awkward over a cloth on which is spread a curious mixture of picnic, formal dinner (there is a soup tureen) and market stall (raw fish, baskets of fruit); behind them is a lively street scene, with the sea beyond, right in front of them the archway leading to the square which they appear to be totally blocking with their picnic. David's book is not exactly a cookbook: it is primarily an intense evocation of the unreachable pleasures of the Mediterranean for her rationing-weary British readers: a fantasy of a place where the sun always shines and food is plentiful and not brown. The embracing of the grotesque, pragmatic aspects of food culture in the interests of authenticity which we find in Lawrence and Laubreaux is also a notable aspect of David's text: the passage quoted above ends much less lyrically with a tour around the butcher's stalls of the region which are 'festooned with every imaginable portion of the inside of every edible animal (anyone who has lived for long in Greece will be familiar with the sound of air gruesomely whistling through sheep's lungs frying in oil)' (9–10).[6]

The gourmet narrative of cultural and sexual acquisitiveness is consciously rewritten in Monique Truong's postmodern postcolonial novel *The Book of Salt* (2004), told from the point of view of an imagined Vietnamese chef working for Gertrude Stein and Alice B. Toklas in the Paris of the inter-war years.[7] The traveller of the earlier gourmet narratives is replaced in Truong's retelling with the exile, whose precision of taste is a matter not of cultural capital but of survival: in the absence of linguistic mastery Bình must substitute tasting for talking. In this richly allusive text, themes of exile, of racial and sexual identity, and of food preparation as simultaneously service and art are densely interwoven as the narrative oscillates through Bình's memories and unspoken thoughts. Many of the characters are displaced and many are also queer – the famously lesbian and self-exiled Stein and Toklas are paralleled by others: Bình himself, whose exile from family and country is the result of his being caught in sexual congress with Blériot, a French chef; Bình's lover Marcus Lattimore, an habitué of Stein's salons and an African American 'passing' as white; and the 'man on the bridge', Nguyễn Ái Quốc, a fellow Vietnamese with whom Bình had spent an ambiguously romantic evening, and who is implied to be the future communist revolutionary leader Hồ Chí Minh. These forms of queerness and of exile do not simply substitute for each other – the fame and American status that render Toklas and Stein largely inviolate, the 'single drop' of black blood that allows Lattimore to pass as white, make their experiences very different from those of Bình, who has had to prostitute himself in the early months of his exile, and whose existence consists of brief sojourns as servant in homes which are not his and which he knows he will eventually have to leave.

The identity and discourse of the gourmet are central to the text's purposes. Unlike previous texts, the role is not singular: it is multiplied and complicated, including new world gourmets like Stein and Toklas who eat, incorporate and re-write the food of the old world, and colonial subjects establishing a precarious social hold with mastery over the foods of their colonizers. Bình is both gourmet and himself the object of gourmet curiosity for his many employers, who 'crave the fruits of exile, the bitter juices, the heavy hearts [...] yearn[ing] for a taste of the pure sea-salt sadness of the outcast whom they have brought into their homes' (Truong 2004: 19). With metafictive glee the text incorporates Toklas's own textual prescriptions on food in her *Cookbook*: her taxonomizing of various forms of gazpacho and their historical differences becomes an injunction to Bình; her reporting of another cook's differentiation between omelettes and fried eggs in terms of respect is transformed into 'a code that all French cooks know and understand' (101). But at the same time Toklas's culinary authority is significantly decentred: she cooks now only on Bình's day off, and always with a performative air, standing up, cooking meat loaf and apple pie, the food of her and Stein's diasporic nostalgia. Without conscious volition, these foods of their youth have been transformed by the experiences of exile: '[n]either of them seems to notice that Miss Toklas's "apple pie" is now filled with an applesauce-flavored custard and frosted with buttercream or that her "meat loaf" harbors the zest of an orange and is bathed in white wine'. The cultural acquisitiveness of the gourmet has changed the way that Toklas cooks and the way that they eat, but it is notably not a change for the better – the overly rich, culturally hybrid products are a mark not of culinary sophistication but of distortion.

Truong's text incorporates, among many other things, a critically sophisticated reading of the works, relationship and personae of Toklas and Stein. One of the striking features of *The Alice B Toklas Cook Book* (1954), written after Stein's death, and in large part a memorial to her, is the degree to which its voice echoes that of Stein's own *Autobiography of Alice B Toklas* (1933). In this book, which widely established her reputation after the dense experimentalism of works such as *Tender Buttons* (1914), Stein builds on the techniques she had developed in *Three Lives* (1909) of writing a life story in the third person in a language and register that conjured the speech patterns of its subject. The *Autobiography* is written in the first person rather than the third, but rather than telling Alice's own life story it is really the story of Gertrude Stein, with the playful advantage of its author needing to have no truck with the false modesty of the conventional autobiography. The striking similarity of the material and the voice in the two texts has several possible explanations: that it is an indication of Stein's success in ventriloquizing Alice; that Stein has in some sense 'stolen' Alice's words; that Alice herself in writing her own book returns to Stein's version of her; or that what both books record is a modernist performance in which life becomes text.[8] In this performative life Stein is the writer and Toklas the cook, even though as Toklas herself remarks she only really entered the kitchen full-time when the privations of the Second World War made this essential (Toklas 1961: 51). In Truong's rendering, Toklas's cooking is a performance in ways both culinary and sexual: 'GertrudeStein thinks it is unfathomably erotic that the food she is about to eat has been washed, pared, kneaded, touched, by the hands of her lover. She is overwhelmed when she finds the faint impression of Miss Toklas's fingerprints decorating the crimped edges of a pie crust' (Truong 2004: 27). Stein's desire for the mark of her lover's hand on their foods is partly an eroticization of touch and partly to do with the pleasure of Toklas performing the role of wife and of servant (there are shades of the relationship between Hannah Culwick and Arthur Munby here). Although Truong's narrative accords Toklas a gourmet's precision of taste that marks her out from Bình's previous employers, her expertise is of a different order to his own. A distinction is established between the Western gourmet, acquiring status through the culinary and sexual experience of other nations, and the impoverished immigrant, whose knowledge is a matter of necessity. As Bình retorts in an imagined conversation with 'Madame' (a conglomerate of his past employers) who begs for the 'secret' of his omelettes: 'if there is a "secret", Madame, it is this: Repetition and routine. Servitude and subservience. Beck and call' (154).

The tensions between expertise and servitude, cooking and eating, and their erotics are played out in the chapter in which Bình first cooks for, then eats with, then is seduced by Lattimore, his 'Sweet Sunday Man'. Having been hired by Lattimore to cook for a dinner on his day off, he plans a menu centred on a French dish of duck cooked with figs in port. The dish combines various forms of expertise and personal history. The method is one learnt from his elder brother, a sous chef – the ripe figs and the port are put together in an earthenware jug for twelve hours to 'get to know each other', this 'long and productive meeting' anticipating the tryst that will follow. But the dish itself belongs to France, specifically to the early months following his arrival, when he wandered the markets of Marseilles, living on the cheapest foods: figs, oranges and dates. Reduced to penury, he prostitutes himself one night, and then blows the proceeds of his shame on an epicurean meal of duck with figs and port. The meal he makes for Lattimore is thus a gift of his own gastronomic adventurings, speaking of multiple forms of experience. The description of the method is intensely sensual in its account of the interpenetration of flavours and textures: the figs 'plump with wine', the wine 'glistening with the honey flowing from the fruit', the duck constantly basted with 'spoonfuls of port which have grown heavy with drippings and concentrated sugars' (77). As he prepares the meal, Bình broods over the sexual intimacies he imagines between Lattimore and his intended guest, eating and sex merging as they tear at the unresisting flesh with their hands and suck fig seeds from each other's nails. The actual eating and sexual congress which occur when it is revealed that he himself is the guest go unwritten – the next present moment we see is Bình waking alone. His isolation speaks to his profound alienation in a country where he is able to communicate only haltingly. His head buzzing with all the conversations he is unable to have, he looks back constantly to the one moment of full linguistic connection in the evening he spent with the man on the bridge. The restaurant to which Nguyễn Ái Quốc takes him is notionally Chinese, though it lacks the clichéd decorative codes which signify 'Chinese restaurant' to the Westerner, and its chef, it emerges, is Vietnamese. They appreciate the meal with the intensity and precise knowledge of the gourmet, recognizing the morels which lend a sense of 'forest decay' to the *haricots vert*, noting the brown butter glaze, caught at the exact moment when it 'inexplicably acquires […] that taste of hazelnuts roasted over a wood-fed flame' (97). It is notable that much of this appreciation is unspoken, occurring in Bình's mind, communicated through brief words and questions. This reticence is not the same as the linguistic exclusion that usually silences him: it signifies a shared knowledge that does not need to be paraded or proven. The only issue on which he requires explanation is the question of the exact form of salt used to season the flash-fried watercress. It is *fleur de sel*, the most delicate form of sea salt, its evanescence, like 'a kiss in the mouth' (98) figuring the ambiguous and fleeting nature of their encounter.

The *fleur de sel*, which requires a gourmet's taste-precision to identify, joins the many other forms of salt sprinkled through the novel: the sweat of labouring bodies inadvertently dripped into and transforming dishes; the salt of the sea over which exiles travel; the salt of the lover's body; the tears of homesickness or betrayal; salt as the primary element that transforms the food of necessity into the culinary (as when the destitute Bình dips orange rinds into the sea). In an interview Truong draws attention also to the ancient symbolism of salt as salary, and as a sign of homosexuality through the connection to the biblical tale of Sodom. The 'Book of Salt' is the book we are reading, the manuscript of Stein's Lattimore persuades Bình to steal for him, and the 'story' of Bình which Gertrude Stein has herself stolen through literary ventriloquism. As Bình notes, these many forms of salt (as with forms of exile and queerness) are not all the same: they differ in '[t]heir stings, their smarts, their strengths' but 'the distinctions between them, are fine' (261). For all that Stein can 'steal' his story, she does not have the discriminatory ability to know 'which ones [he] has tasted on [his] tongue'.

Both the gourmet food narrative inverted and complicated by *The Book of Salt* and that of the chef draw on conventions of masculinity as assertive and active: alternately violent, macho, sexually and culturally acquisitive, and status-preoccupied. My final mode of masculine food writing deals in an absolutely antithetical set of tropes: home rather than travel, relaxation rather than rage: the narrative of the bachelor significantly complicates our understanding of the way the domestic and the culinary are gendered.

Masculinity III: The bachelor

In the later nineteenth century bachelors begin to assume unusual prominence in a wide range of literary texts: detective novels, social comedies and adventure stories all give an increasingly central role to the unmarried man. As I have suggested elsewhere, the figure of the bachelor becomes at this date a locus for a range of desires and anxieties around issues of masculinity, sexuality, matrimony and leisure (Humble 2011), but for our purposes here what is most significant is the centrality afforded to his domestic

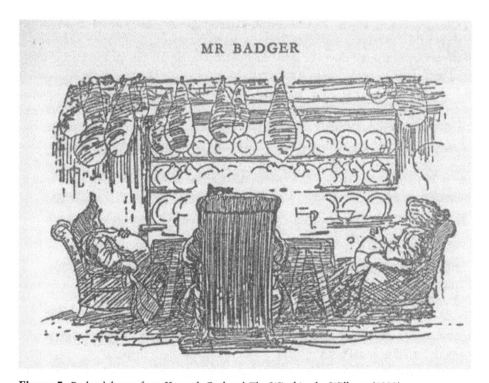

Figure 5 *Badger's house from Kenneth Graham's* The Wind in the Willows *(1908).*

arrangements. From Eugene and Mortimer in their shared flat in Dicken's *Our Mutual Friend* (1864–5), glorying in the 'domestic virtues' sure to be produced in them by their 'miniature flour-barrel, rolling pin, spice-box' and other kitchen fitments, to the Baker Street idyll of Sherlock Holmes and Dr Watson, the bachelor's domestic comforts loom large. In the comic novels of P. G. Wodehouse the figure and the domestic arrangements of the bachelor also occupy a central place. The key locations of his fantasized upper-class bachelor life – the gentleman's flat, the home-from-home that is the Drones club (a place of such luxuriant domestic comfort that its members think of each other as food stuffs: eggs, beans and crumpets), the country house weekends where the bachelor earns his bread and butter as a useful 'spare man' – these are the mainstay of his action. And it is notable how closely the domestic comfort of the bachelor is wrapped up with food and drink: with Jeeves's pick-me-ups, with the fantastic meals produced by the magnificent chef Anatole, each day punctuated by little lunches and rowdy dinners. Even in the children's and fantasy literature of the turn of the century, the focus on bachelor comfort is notable. Kenneth Graham's *The Wind in the Willows* (1908) is full of bachelor establishments: Mole's little clerkly dwelling, Rat's comfortable river-bank home and Badger's yeomanly kitchen, its rafters hanging with hams and dried herbs, onions and baskets of eggs, which 'seemed a place where heroes could fitly feast after victory, where weary harvesters could line up in scores along the table and keep their Harvest Home with mirth and song, or where two or three friends of simple tastes could sit about as they pleased and eat and smoke and talk in comfort and contentment' (1971: 67). E. H. Shepard's illustrations frequently depict interiors – fire-side scenes with two or three bachelor animals in armchairs drawn up to the blaze and with their possessions neatly arranged around them, or contentedly seated at supper tables. The kitchens are filled with every possible tool and food is quickly and easily prepared, with no women to fuss or disorder. When Mole takes Rat back to his long-deserted house he finds it embarrassingly bare and narrow, but Rat transforms it back to home for him, admiring the sleeping berths cunningly cut into the walls, finding a tin of sardines and a German sausage, mulling ale and lighting the fire. It is in this 'little home' that the book begins, as Mole spring-cleans and white-washes before leaving it for his great adventure. Tolkien's *The Hobbit* (1937) begins similarly with Bilbo's lovingly detailed hobbit hole, which means, we are told 'comfort':

> It had a perfectly round door like a porthole, painted green with a shiny yellow brass knob in the exact middle. The door opened on to a tube-shaped hall like a tunnel: a very comfortable tunnel without smoke, with panelled walls, and floors tiled and carpeted, provided with polished chairs, and lots and lots of pegs for hats and coats. (1999: 3)

The keynote in all of these homes is order: a place for everything – lots of pantries and kitchens for Bilbo and a peg for the hat and coat for every possible visitor. The fantasy of the bachelor life is like a glorified form of camping, or of life in a houseboat, with everything fitted and built in and ordered and simple. It is a life defined as one in which the home fits its owner like a well-worn tweed suit, moulding itself to his personal comforts and needs. Things are done according to personal satisfactions and logic, not arbitrary social rules. The bachelor entertains – indeed hospitality is one of the key tropes defining his role – but he does so easily, informally, without social anxiety.[9] It is a model of masculine bliss that is notably without the violence and display and fulminating of the chef: an annexing of the domestic focused mainly on control.

With the marked cultural interest in the domestic arrangement of the bachelor it is not surprising that we find cookbooks starting to appear from the late nineteenth century addressed to the domestic situation of the large numbers of men who were marrying later (or not at all) and who lived alone in apartments rather than in lodgings with a landlady.[10] Examples include Deshler Welch's *The Bachelor and the Chafing Dish* (1896), Philips A Lyman's *A Bachelor's Cupboard; Containing Crumbs Culled from the Cupboards of the Great Unwedded* (1906) and Don Wilkes's *The Bachelor Book* (1903), which is subtitled 'a goodly collection of recipes for compounding divers delectable mixtures, with toasts proper to the ceremonial drinking of the same: to which is added some chafing dish menus right seemly for the creation and appeasement of appetite: also, a chapter on the art of carving in good company, a dissertation on the philosophy of clothes in modern life, and finally some minor offences'. The knowing, cod-historical tone, the prioritizing of drinking and fellowship and appetite all work to establish the book as essentially different to those directed at female readers. The chafing dish singled out in this and in Welch's book is a table-top cooker of the sort that waiters would use in restaurants to flambé *crepes suzette*. These devices became increasingly popular for use in private homes at this date as they allowed for a flamboyant culinary performance in front of guests, while also making a virtue of the necessity of coping with fewer – or no – servants. The latter book also glories in a lengthy, elaborately punctuated sub-title: 'The Bachelor and the Chafing Dish, with a dissertation on Chums; containing some valuable recipes gathered from fascinating sources in cookery – triumphs of well-known bon vivants in clubs, yachting circles, army and navy, and the dreams of fair women – heaven bless 'em!. Again, masculine fellowship is prioritized: the term 'chums' continuing the conditions of boyhood friendships into adulthood. The world evoked is an intensely clubbish one of masculine institutions and pursuits and rituals, and it is a world in which women are doubly absent, conjured up in the echo of the drinking toast – the condition of which is that they be outside the male enclave – and creatures only of dreams, not reality. The recipes are largely confined to the first chapter with the rest of the book given over to 'The Chumship', a celebration of masculine friendship and the luxuries of life without women which consists of a series of anecdotes about the narrator's different friends and the occasions on which he has cooked for them and eaten with them. Friendship is understood by Welch, as by other authors of bachelor texts, primarily in terms of domestic comfort, offering someone to share indulgences and quiet relaxation: a pipe, a whisky, an armchair at the fireside. As with most such bachelor texts, *The Bachelor and the Chafing Dish* ends with marriage, or at least with the gloomy anticipation of it. The author persuades his beloved, Mab, to come to dinner, but she refuses to let him cook for her, considering it 'unbecoming' (Welch 1896: 55).

She instead pulls a random selection of jars from the cupboard and insists that they dine on stuffed olives, macaroons and sardines. It is a long way from the jolly sharing of culinary tips with chums: domestic enjoyment is assigned to the bachelor life, with marriage implying something much less comfortable.

The heyday of the bachelor narrative is from the 1880s to the 1920s, though texts of this sort continue to appear during the interwar years and into the 1960s, with the bachelor becoming an increasingly louche figure – James Bond or Simon Templar rather than Sherlock Holmes or Bertie Wooster. Almost all cookbooks and host books explicitly for men that appear on both sides of the Atlantic in the post-war period address themselves to the culinary needs of the single man: the idea of a married man cooking still, for the most part, appearing a contradiction in terms. Esquire's *Handbook for Hosts*, first published in 1949, assumes its readers are unmarried and that competent cookery will be a key weapon in their seduction armoury, seeing 'the culinary art as a new twist on the old "come see my etchings" routine' (1953: 11). The illustrations and the chapter titles flatter the reader's sense of himself as lover, host and chef: the first chapter is entitled 'Eat: The World's Best Chefs Wear Pants', the full-page illustration depicting a smug-looking be-toqued man putting the finishing touches to a dish while a seated woman gazes adoringly at him; other illustrations feature naked or barely clothed popsies just waiting to be lured by a good meal. The book is very much in the style of the magazine: *Esquire* was launched in 1933, aiming to be a common denominator of masculine interests. It was sued by the US Postmaster General on behalf of the government in 1946 on the charge that the magazine had used the postal service to distribute and promote 'lewd images' (*Esquire* won the lawsuit). Its themes and aesthetics focused centrally on the bachelor lifestyle. As Bill Osgerby has argued, the 'chic, gadget-laden "bachelor's lair" was a recurring icon of hedonistic, masculine consumption' in the men's magazines of the mid-twentieth century, functioning as 'a totem of forward-looking and "liberated" masculine consumerism' (2005: 99).[11] One of the keynotes of the *Handbook for Hosts* is sophistication: there is a separate chapter on caviar, a chapter on 'Continental Cooking' which includes Armenian, Russian and Turkish sections, and an extensive drink section – strap-lined 'liquor is quicker' – with a chapter on stocking the cellar. The reader is addressed as a 'gentleman' and flatteringly assumed to be au fait with the complexities of modern etiquette, needing only a 'refresher'. He is by default a bachelor, though there are rare acknowledgements that a particular reader might have a wife. What is significant is that the imagined way of life of the sophisticated bachelor has become the cultural ideal of masculinity. It is in this context that cooking is understood: as an elegant hobby rather than a necessity. The food itself is very specifically gendered masculine:

> You won't find doily tearoom fare here: no radish roses, no menus designed for their calorie content. Esky has concentrated on food of, for and by MEN. Nor will you find vitamin charts of how long to roast lamb or how to make an apple betty: we recommend that you have a standard, womanly cookbook for reference in such routine matters, for this book is concerned not with the kind of food you can get anywhere but instead with unusual dishes. Esq. suspects that you'll prove nothing

(and improve nothing) if you compete with three-meal-a-day cooks on their own territory. (1953: 11)

The food of MEN, as 'Esky' defines it, is sophisticated and worldly wise, yet also hearty and plain. It is occasion food – to be reduced to the drudgery of everyday cookery would clearly be distinctly unmanly. And it is competitive – explicitly so with women, with an overtly declared objective to reclaim the highest culinary honours from the feminine sphere – and implicitly with other men. Where the energies of earlier bachelor texts were directed towards internal pleasures and satisfactions, the focus here is outward, with all effort directed towards impressing others, whether friends, rivals, business associates, or sexual or romantic interests. The food itself is asserted to be specifically masculine – fish, because 'women don't seem to understand fish – and, we suppose, vice versa'; stew ('how to do right by a man's dish') and game ('a log cabin or an open grill is the logical place – and a man's the proper cook') (35; 43; 45). Under the latter rubric (in a chapter subtitled 'Cooking the Kill') is included bear (you eat only the paws), possum and squirrel as well as more conventional game. The resolutely hearty image built up here suggests the beer commercial that Marian, protagonist of Margaret Atwood's *The Edible Woman* (1969), tests in her capacity as a market researcher: *"Any real man, on a real man's holiday – hunting, fishing, or just plain old-fashioned relaxing – need a beer with a healthy, hearty taste, a deep-down manly flavour"*. She 'admire[s] the subtlety of "just plain old-fashioned relaxing." That was so the average beer-drinker, the slope-shouldered pot-bellied kind, would be able to feel a mystical identity with the plaid-jacketed sportsman shown in the pictures with his foot on a deer or scooping a trout into his net' (1990: 26). The novel is acutely aware of the commodified gender roles of the immediate post-war era, the products of magazines and advertising. Marian's fiancé Peter is a reader of men's magazines and manoeuvres her into sexual scenarios inspired by various periodicals: on a 'scratchy blanket in a field' after 'a hunting story in one of the outdoorsy male magazines', on a sheepskin on his bedroom floor which she imagines comes from 'one of the men's glossies, the kind with lust in pent-houses' (60). The bachelor's swinging lifestyle has become the ultimate consumable, with food, drink and women all props to build the image.

In the 1970s cook books addressing male readers begin to change. They may continue to draw from the post-war swinging bachelor lexicon of humour, sexual allusions, cartoons and a gloss of international sophistication, but they begin to acknowledge another motive for men cooking than seduction. Donald Kilbourn's *Pots and Pans: Man's Answer to Women's Lib* (1974) allows that its readers may be married and that their culinary impulses may sometimes be merely practical, the blurb offering the book as a guide 'no matter whether you wish to impress your latest girl-friend with a slap-up dinner or merely have to survive while your wife is in bed with flu'. Instead of the bombastic assertions of the age-old superiority of men over women as cooks it offers reassurance to a male reader stepping into the kitchen for the first time with advice like '[d]on't ever be discouraged' and '[d]on't be alarmed, or you will play right into THEIR hands' (1974: 3; 11). Instead of offering cooking as a means of social and sexual advancement, Kilbourn sells it as a scientific and technological activity unnecessarily complicated by arcane feminine lore: 'Cooking is basically a production job that is concerned with converting raw materials into a finished product' (1). Yet the peroration with which he follows this assertion speaks of something else – a profound gender and sexual anxiety:

> It is not cissy. Far from it. It is also fun. […]
>
> This book, then, is for men. There is, I promise you, no tarty stuff about rolling pastry and baking cakes or upside-down, inside-out, back-to-front puddings. There are no abominations along the lines of 'glazed gooseberry chicken with fried eggs and ice-cream' to titillate our already punch-drunk taste buds. (1)

Not cissy, no tarty stuff, nothing back-to-front, no abominations, no titillation: it is no accident that in the very first sentence of the book Kilbourn references his wife, his mother-in-law and his daughter, allowing not a moment of doubt to linger about his heterosexual credentials. This concern that cooking as a man will cause people to assume you are gay is not nearly so apparent in earlier cookbooks for men, though we might argue that the concerted heterosexual display of the *Handbook for Hosts* exists partly to dispel any such imputations. The explicitness of the homosexual panic in Kilbourn's text seems to me to have everything to do with its historical moment and with its relationship to the 'Women's Lib' of its subtitle. In the context of the politicization of housework by the women's movement of the 1970s, the meaning of cooking for men has changed. It is no longer primarily a hobby, an indulgence, or a display of status. It begins to look like something apparently much more threatening to secure masculine heteronormative identity: a chore.[12]

Femininity I: Culinary refusals and edible women

The post-war years in both North America and Britain witnessed the creation of a cult of domesticity centred on the figure of the housewife – or 'home-maker' in her American incarnation. Depicted in magazines and advertisements as young, modern, attractive and fulfilled, she was understood to glory in her femininity, her children, her husband and her home. The home was at the centre of this fantasy – suburban, spacious, full of labour-saving features and devices – and the kitchen was at the centre of the home. Equipped with built-in-cabinets to eradicate dirt and dust, available in a wide range of fashionable colours, with shining stainless-steel sink and wipeable surfaces, the 1950s dream-kitchen was a place where science and technology would make domestic labour a joy. The kitsch advertising images of beaming '50s housewives, resplendent in their frilly 'hostess aprons', make it difficult for us to see them today as anything other than transparent ideological manipulations, but, as Christina Hardyment notes, there were genuine material causes that led working women to turn willingly back to the home, in a reaction against the rackety impermanence of life during the war:

To understand the general enthusiasm for home-making at all levels of society, we have to bear in mind how deprived women had been of both normal home life and of any opportunity to express their own individual domestic creativity during and after the war years. (1995: 40)

On the literary evidence at least, this post-war domestic idyll had begun to sour by the early 1960s. Something historically identifiable as the woman's movement did not really emerge until the end of the decade, but it was heralded by an up-swelling of literary texts expressing profound anxieties about many aspects of women's lives. From around 1963 to 1967 a considerable number of texts were published in Britain and North America which were to later be seen as articulating many of the key principles and concerns of the women's movement: these include Doris Lessing's *The Golden Notebook* (1962), Penelope Mortimer's *The Pumpkin Eater* (1962), Margaret Drabble's *A Summer Bird-Cage* (1963), Margaret Atwood's *The Edible Woman* (written in 1965, though not published until 1969), and Sylvia Plath's *The Bell Jar* (1963) and her later poetry. The cumulative effect of texts such as these is one factor in the development of the consciousness that allowed the women's movement to come into being. Two very significant political texts have long been recognized as part of this process of pre-feminist formation: Simone de Beauvoir's *The Second Sex* (1945; translated into English in 1961) and Betty Friedan's *The Feminine Mystique* (1963). The latter, which was particularly influential in North America, focuses its argument very specifically on the post-war cult of the domestic as a factor in limiting the potential and ambitions of women. It begins with 'The Problem That Has No Name', which 'lay buried, unspoken, for many years in the minds of American women':

Each suburban wife struggled with it alone. As she made the beds, shopped for groceries, matched slipcover material, ate peanut butter sandwiches with her children, chauffeured Cub Scouts and Brownies, lay beside her husband at night, she was afraid to ask even of herself the silent question: 'Is this all?' (Friedan 1972: 13)

Friedan sees the root causes of the retreat of American women from the workplace and the enshrining of a passive model of femininity as the pervasive cultural influence of Freudianism and the bombardment effect of messages from advertising and women's magazines. Perhaps her most radical insight is a materialist one: 'Why is it never said that the really crucial function, the really important role that women serve as housewives is *to buy more things for the house?* [...] [T]he perpetuation of housewifery, the growth of the feminine mystique, makes sense (and dollars) when one realizes that women are the chief customers of American business' (181).

The literary texts of the pre-feminist moment share two features: a profound questioning of the social, ideological and sexual bounds within which contemporary women are supposed to live their lives, and a lack of answers to the questions that they raise. Like Friedan, they recognize a problem but are unable to fully name it, let alone solve it. What many of these texts also share is a sense that the domestic idyll may be a trap. The response of texts and protagonists to this suspicion is not outright rebellion but a covert resistance that most often takes the form of culinary refusals. The prototypical example of this tendency is *The Edible Woman*, a paradigmatic text for the literature of food, and a conscious reworking of Friedan's ideas in literary form. Atwood's protagonist, Marian, is a young Canadian, recently graduated from university, and working at a market research company. Her job places her at the heart of the processes of ideological manipulation that Friedan had identified as 'the sexual sell':

> Properly manipulated … American housewives can be given the sense of identity, purpose, creativity, the self-realisation, even the sexual joy they lack – by the buying of things. (Friedan 1972: 182)

Responsible for revising the 'convoluted and overly-subtle prose of the psychologists' (1990: 19) into questions that can be understood by the housewives who answer the surveys and the housewives who administer them, she is part of the 'gooey' middle layer in the ice-cream sandwich image with which she imagines the company. Blocked by gender from meaningful promotion – the 'upper crust' of executives and psychologists are collectively known as 'the men upstairs' – she is marking time until marriage, before she too turns into one of the housewives. This fate she views with passive resignation rather than anticipatory joy. She has before her the model of her friend Clara, married in college, with two small children and heavily pregnant with a third, who has been reduced to nothing but body by the experience: 'a boa-constrictor who has swallowed a watermelon' (31) or 'a strange vegetable growth, a bulbous tuber that had sent out four thin white roots and a tiny pale-yellow flower' (32). The imagery with which Marian attempts to understand her world and the traps it throws up is almost always food-related. The central trope of the novel is her gradual loss of the ability to eat, which maps her loss of an autonomous sense of self as her marriage to fiancé Peter gets closer. Everything is understood in terms of food, and food itself gets stranger and more grotesque as Marian's breakdown intensifies. From the deceptively banal opening scene, when Marian 'wash[es] down a glass of milk and a bowl of cold cereal' while listening to her flatmate, Ainsley, complain about a previous night's party spent with dentistry students obsessed with 'the insides of peoples' mouths', orality is represented as deeply problematic. Her day at Seymour Surveys begins with her roped in as 'pre-test taster' of varieties of canned rice-pudding, asked to rate them on a scale of 'Natural, Somewhat Artificial, or Definitely Unnatural' (18); her coffee break is spent watching one of her colleagues picking unwanted raisins from her toasted Danish; her afternoon writing an apology letter to a tester who has received a fly in her cereal packet. From the start food is unnatural, unwanted, vaguely unpleasant.[13] Marian's crisis as an eater begins at a dinner in a restaurant with Peter, Ainsley and Len, a friend of hers from university. Peter asserts his manhood with a loud anecdote about a hunting trip, in which he has eviscerated a freshly killed rabbit by 'just slit[ting] her down the belly and giv[ing] her a good hard shake [so] all the guts'll fall out'. Marian's mind slips away from her as she imagines the scene like a projected photographic image: the rabbit's blood and guts running down the trees, Peter and his friends with 'mouths wrenched with laughter' (69). Crucially, she 'couldn't see the rabbit'. She can't see it, of course, because she is it: she has placed herself in the role of inert violated flesh, gendered female. Her relationship with Peter has already rendered her as flesh in the men's magazine context: now she literalizes this role, shying away from meat because she identifies with it. Her active food refusals occur in the lengthy middle section of the three-part structure, where the narrative shifts into the third person to map her process of disassociation. At another dinner, she watches Peter 'operating' on a steak, dividing it into neat cubes, and compares the process to the 'diagram of the planned cow at the front of one of her cookbook', standing with placid expression, its flesh neatly inscribed into sections for the butcher's cuts. Looking at her own steak she sees it suddenly as 'part of a real cow that once moved and ate and was killed, knocked on the head as it stood in a queue like someone waiting for a streetcar' (151). Marian's refusal of meat is not really vegetarianism, nor is her gradual inability to eat at all classic anorexia: her problem is that all food becomes flesh-like, threatening animation. In a novel in which the association between women and food is so intense and problematic, it is perhaps surprising that two of its three dinner party scenes involve food cooked by men. One dinner is given by the three male graduate students into whose world Marian stumbles, Goldilocks-like, when running the survey for the beer commercial. Duncan, deceptively child-like and manipulative, lives with Trevor and Fisher, who play the roles of mother and father respectively in a bizarrely parodic family. Trevor, who is 'very proud of his cooking' (191), throws together an impromptu 'pot-luck' meal for Marian involving six or seven courses of carefully sourced and prepared food. The others eat the food without noticing (Fisher with his eyes shut while he monologues about his thesis) and only Marian pays attention to the antique family crystal, silverware and bone china and to the moment when Trevor 'appear[s] dramatically in the doorway, holding a flaming blue sword [of shishkebab] in either hand' (198). The fact that Trevor is so clearly cast as mother in the triad renders his performative cooking more a parody of femininity than a demonstration of a new masculine culinary competence. The crucial emphasis is not on his skill but on the fact that the others ignore it and take the food for granted. Throughout the novel, Marian has largely refused to cook, relying on Peter for meals out and bringing shop-bought chocolate brownies to the office party; but to accomplish her final act of domestic refusal, she bakes a cake. It is in the form of a woman: literalizing the novel's title and drawing together all of its motifs of symbolic cannibalism which render women as food. In a process that is both habitually domestic (she doesn't need a recipe) and anti-domestic (she refuses to wash the scum-laden dishes in the sink or clean the kitchen of its 'creeping skin-disease-covering of dirt' (267)), she shops for ingredients and mixes and bakes the cake and then shapes it into its woman-form. The shaping is curiously violent: rather than cut the shape from the cake, she pinches, scoops, pulls and moulds it into its new form in an echo of the social pressures that 'make' women (in de Beauvoir's phrase). She presents it to Peter as a sort of anti-engagement present, as a replacement for herself:

'You've been trying to destroy me, haven't you,' she said. 'You've been trying to assimilate me. But I've made you a substitute, something you'll like much better. This is what you really wanted all along, isn't it? I'll get you a fork,' she added somewhat prosaically. (271)

The act of making the cake is instantly understood by all of the characters to carry heavy symbolic import – Peter's response is alarm; Ainsley declares with horror that Marian is 'rejecting her own femininity' (272). But the cake-woman is more ambiguous than these reactions would suggest. There is a tension between the two meanings of eating Marian suggests to Peter – destruction and assimilation being by no means the same thing. The novel ends with Duncan, with whom she has been conducting a half-hearted affair, offering her a range of other meanings: '"Peter wasn't trying to destroy you. That's just something you made up. Actually you were trying to destroy him. [...] Maybe Peter was trying to destroy me, or maybe I was trying to destroy him, or we were both trying to destroy each other'" (280–1). In the end, he declares, none of these psychoanalytic interpretations matter, because Marian has reinserted herself into the only significant system: '"you're back to so-called reality, you're a consumer'" (281). The novel ends with Duncan eating the woman-cake 'without exclamations of pleasure, even without noticeable expression' (281). Marian succeeds only in exchanging one male consumer of her essence for another: this one child-like rather than macho, self-aware rather than oblivious, but still offering no real escape from the gender dynamic in which she is trapped.

We find a similar use of food to represent the frustrations and traps of post-war gender politics in the poetry of Sylvia Plath. Food itself is often gendered: the blackberries of 'Blackberrying' (1961) are the speaker's 'blood sisterhood', obligingly 'accommodat[ing] themselves to [her] milkbottle' (Plath 1981: 168). The mushrooms, speaking subjects of the 1959 poem of the same name, are meekly, conventionally feminine: growing overnight 'very / Whitely, discretely, / Very quietly', they are 'bland-mannered' and 'perfectly voiceless' (139). Like Atwood's Marian they acknowledge their status as food: 'we are meek, / We are edible'. But their sheer numbers pose a covert threat, a future coming to power of the powerless: their 'soft fists insist', they 'shoulder through holes' and they 'shall by morning / Inherit the earth' (140). They represent, if not a confident feminist revolt, at least the possibility of some sort of gender resistance. Mostly, however, Plath's explorations of gender politics via food and the domestic swing between cynicism and masochism. The masochism, a repeated note in her poetry, is particularly apparent in two food poems: 'Cut' (1962) and 'Glutton' (1956). The former spins out elaborate metaphors for the paradoxical pain /pleasure of a cut thumb: 'What a thrill - / My thumb instead of an onion. / The top quite gone / Except for a sort of hinge / Of skin' (235). As with many of her poems, it begins in a moment of domestic detail and then spirals out into a world of violence and pain which the exuberant rhymes and hectic rhythms seem to revel in, even as they rawly expose it. So the thumb stump is alternately a celebration ('clutching my bottle of pink fizz') and a horror: 'Kamikaze man', 'Gauze Ku Klux Klan', 'Treppaned veteran' (235–6). 'The Glutton' is the poem in which Plath most concertedly explores food as a metaphor for gender relations, with a twist on the idea of the edible woman which renders the role as sexual fantasy rather than – or as well as – social oppression. The speaker sees herself as full of 'heat such as no man could have / And yet keep kind', her sexual desire inviting a violent devouring: her 'Blood's broth / Filched by his hand' is 'Cupped quick to mouth'; her 'prime parts cram each rich meal' (40). But by the dawn at the end of the poem the metaphor of woman as edible, man as eater has been transformed: the fire of their passion burns itself out, the desiring vision is smudged with ash, their lust has devoured them both. The 'radiant limb' and the 'ardent look' could belong to either: gender difference and power differentials are erased in a moment of complete consumption. The cynicism is apparent in 'The Applicant' (1962), where the male addressee is offered various commodities by a job interviewer to fill his inadequacies, parts of women's bodies he is enjoined to 'marry': 'Here is a hand / […] willing / To bring teacups and roll away headaches / And do whatever you tell it' (221). The disembodied wifely hand is both domestic functionary, and is itself food in the form of the ambiguous 'stock' (both soup base and store product) the company makes when it obligingly dissolves with grief on the death of the husband: 'We make new stock from the salt'. The wife is an object, not a subject: an 'it', reduced to functional parts, a perk for a company man. She is interchangeable as well as divisible, easily exchanged. Plath's cut and de-membered women resemble Atwood's planned cow – their bodies divided into commodified, easily consumable parts, their subjectivity eroded. With savage humour Plath exposes an objectified post-war femininity, but sees few ways out of its pre-plotted roles. The choices she sees are to masochistically embrace one's object status, or to fantasize escape in the form of the mythic, self-destroying Lady Lazarus. She allows her edible women more anger and more agency than Atwood: the feminine mushrooms have their foot 'in the door'; the title of 'The Glutton' is carefully ambiguous – able to refer to the man who devours or the woman whose 'heat' demands to be devoured, and which ultimately consumes them both. Curiously, given the oft-repeated biographical fact that Plath introduced herself to Ted Hughes at a party by biting his face, what she does not do is reverse the symbolic polarity and have women as eaters of edible men.

The note of anger that so many have seen in Plath's poetry emerges in many of the texts of this pre-feminist moment. One of the most unlikely is a cookbook: Peg Bracken's *The 'I Hate to Cook' Book*, first published in America in 1961 and a best-seller there and in Britain. Its agenda and its tone are established from the outset:

Some women, it is said, like to cook.

This book is not for them.

This book is for those of us who hate to, who have learned, through hard experience, that some activities become no less painful through repetition: childbearing, paying taxes, cooking. This book is for those of us who want to fold our big dishwasher hands around a dry Martini instead of a wet flounder, come the end of a long day. (1978: 1)

Figure 6 *The tedium of daily cooking, from Peg Bracken's* The I Still Hate to Cook Book *(1966).*

A jokey, light, magazine style and lively comic illustrations are in tension with extreme feelings that lie just underneath the surface: the 'hate' of the title is reiterated throughout, strikingly at odds with the fun all-girls-together approach. The comparison of cooking with childbearing also adds a note of jarring seriousness. The text continually oscillates between these two moods: there is a sense of lurking darkness beneath the frothy surface foam. So the 'Good Cooks Who Like to Cook' are extravagantly praised for their bravery, energy and imagination, and their lack of fear of rotisseries but 'we've little to say to them, really, except, "Invite us over often, please." And stay away from our husbands' (9). The solutions suggested for those who hate to cook include lying, cheating, and conning other women into doing it for you: when planning a Potluck supper one must 'Beware of the entrée', as it is 'usually the most trouble as well as the most expensive'. Instead of volunteering oneself, one must volunteer somebody else:

'Ethel, would you make that marvellous goulash of yours?' you can say. The other ladies will probably join in – it would be rude not to, especially if they've ever tasted Ethel's goulash – and while Ethel is modestly dusting her manicure on her lapels, you can murmur something about bringing a couple of your delectable LEFT BANK FRENCH LOAVES. (62–4)

(The French loaves involve butter, bread and that wonder-convenience food of the 1960s, a packet of onion-soup mix). The solution never imagined by the text is that one's husband might take over some of the cooking. This possibility is fairly remote even for Shirley Conran's actively feminist *Superwoman*, published fourteen years later: in her chapter on 'How to be a Working Wife and Mother' she suggests that 'a husband who doesn't mind the occasional snack meal in a crisis – or even cooks it – is worth his weight in platinum' (Conran was married at the time to restaurateur Terrance) (1975: 153). Bracken's text advocates various forms of partial culinary refusal to women trapped by the 'Happy Housewife' myth, but like other texts of this moment is stymied by an inability to imagine larger solutions. A significant factor in the creation of this imaginative aporia is the absolute linking of food preparation with the role of mother. Bracken's book assumes that cooking for the family is one of the most inexorable parts of the lives of her readers, and one of the areas in which it is hardest to cheat. Clara is the most fully trapped of all Atwood's women characters, by the incontrovertible physical presence of her eating, defecating, demanding infants, who seem little more than their alimentary processes. Some of Plath's most striking poems are those that contemplate the absolute physical and psychological transformations wrought on women by the birth of their children – 'Morning Song' (1961), for instance, with the miraculous otherness of the child, its newness effacing the mother, reducing her to only obedient, servicing body 'cow-heavy and floral' (1981: 157). Motherhood, so fundamentally, primally, connected to nurture and nourishment, is my final category of gendered food-role.

Femininity II: The mother

The 1950s American ideal of the happy homemaker is just one of the influential constructions of the mother to appear in the literature of food. The mother as icon, as bodily source of sustenance is, of course, an absolutely primal figure, one appearing in art and mythology from the most ancient stages of human culture. In more recent cultural constructions of the mother much tends to be made of the tension between the ideal mother and the human frailties and culpabilities of actual mothers.[14] A work which presents the iconic construction of the nurturing mother figure in exemplary form is the short story 'All At One Point' from Italo Calvino's *Cosmicomics* (1965). In this ludic collection of tales about the early life of the universe, the unreliable narrator Qfwfq weaves yarns about key moments of origin – his life as an early reptile (with an uncle who was still a fish); the time when the moon and earth were so close together that you could jump between them; the birth of the sun; the creation of the elements; the extinction of the dinosaurs (Qfwfq excepted) and so on. In 'All At One Point' he describes himself and his cast of friends and relations all packed into the single primal point before the expansion of the universe:

> Naturally we were all there, old Qfwfq said, – where else could we have been? Nobody knew then that there could be space. Or time either: what use did we have for time, packed in there like sardines?
>
> I say 'packed like sardines', using a literary image: in reality there wasn't even space to pack us into. Each point of each of us coincided with every point of each of the others in a single point, which was where we all were. (1984: 43)

It is a petty world, full of irritants – the annoying Mr Pber^t Pber^d; the Z'zu family of immigrants who try to hang their washing across the point; the gossiping cleaning woman (who had nothing to do all day since 'inside one point not even a grain of dust can enter') (44). The one bright light in their world is the motherly Mrs Ph(i)Nk$_0$, whose generosity of spirit takes on such an iconic form that she is all that they can remember when they meet each other in later life 'at the bus stop, in a movie house, at an international dentist's convention' (44). It is Mrs Ph(i)Nk$_0$'s nurturing love that changes everything: her cry of '"Oh, if I only had some room to make some noodles for you boys!"' (46) initiates both space and time:

> We all thought of the space that her round arms would occupy, moving back and forwards with the rolling pin over the dough, her bosom leaning over the great mound of flour and eggs which cluttered the wide board [...]; we thought of the space that the flour would occupy, and the wheat for the flour, and the fields to raise the wheat, and the mountains from which the water would flow to irrigate the fields [...]; of the space it would take for the Sun to arrive with its rays, to ripen the wheat. (46)

The space opened up in their thoughts opens up in reality as they imagine its possibilities: 'at the same time that Mrs Ph(i)Nk$_0$ was uttering those words: "... ah, what noodles, boys!" the point that contained her and all of us was expanding in a halo of distance in light-years and light-centuries and billions of light-millennia' (47). It is this impulse of maternal love and culinary nurture that expands the universe, the process depicted in a single, extraordinary 365-word sentence. It is also in this moment that Mrs Ph(i)Nk$_0$ herself is dissipated: 'scattered through the continents of the planets, kneading with floury, oil-shiny, generous arms, and she lost at that very moment, and we, mourning her loss' (47). The nurturing mother is both absolutely physical – round and voluptuous, her body itself virtually food – and absolutely mythic, the origin of everything, never fully attainable. The resultant paradoxes reverberate throughout the literature of food.

Memorists in particular grapple with these contradictory, irreconcilable mothers. In *Tender at the Bone: Growing Up at the Table* (1998), the first of her series of autobiographies-through-food, the former *New York Times* restaurant critic Ruth Reichl begins her narrative with her mother, who she christens 'The Queen of Mold'. 'Taste-blind and unafraid of rot', Reichl's mother blithely serves up 'Everything Stew' (with two-week-old turkey and random fridge left-overs including half an apple pie), and poisons most of the guests at her son's engagement party with ancient unrefrigerated crab and chicken (1998: 4). Reichl credits her early interest in food to a need to save visitors from the worst excesses of her mother's cooking. Struggling throughout her childhood and adolescence with her mother's manic depression, Reichl finds herself alternative maternal figures whose nurture she describes explicitly in terms of food: the first is Alice, the maid of her adopted grandmother, whose physical presence embodies culinary comfort: 'she smelled like starch, lemons, and, if she was baking, cinnamon as well'. The next is Mrs Peavey, a grand patrician widow who disappeared on week-long drunken benders. The love she received from both women is rendered textually in terms of the recipes they taught her: 'Alice's Apple Dumplings with Hard Sauce', 'Wiener Schnitzel' from Mrs Peavey. In particular, it is the tips and techniques – the secrets of the kitchen – that speak love to Reichl. So, Mrs Peavey's demonstration of the way to pound the veal, lifting a big iron skillet 'high above her head and [bringing] it crashing down on the meat' (47) becomes a permanent fixture in Reichl's memory: 'every time I make wiener schnitzel Mrs Peavey is by my side, reminding me to pound the veal until it's thin' (36) and Alice, long retired home to her native Barbados, is present at Aunt Birdie's 100th birthday party in the form of the fried oysters which Reichl makes according to her recipe. Nigel Slater also begins his 2003 memoir-through-food, *Toast*, with his mother:

> My mother is scraping a piece of burned toast out of the kitchen window, a crease of annoyance across her forehead. This is not an occasional occurrence, a once-in-a-while hiccup in a busy mother's day. My mother burns the toast as surely as the sun rises each morning. In fact, I doubt if she has ever made a round of toast in her life that failed to fill the kitchen with plumes of throat-catching smoke. I am nine now and have never seen butter without black bits in it.
>
> It is impossible not to love someone who makes toast for you. People's feelings, even major ones such as when they make you wear short trousers to school, fall into insignificance as your teeth break through the rough, toasted crust and sink your teeth into the doughy cushion of white bread underneath. (2003: 1)

Slater's book is split between two consciousnesses – that of the child, resentful and contemptuous of his mother's culinary failings, and that of the adult looking back, aware of the more primal emotions conjured by food. It is in the tensions between these consciousnesses – carried here in the gap between paragraphs – that much of emotional work of the text takes place. So, in 'Christmas Cake' the text moves from culinary ineptitude: 'Mum was never much of a cook' (1), through pleasure:

'"Shh, listen to the cake mixture", she would say, and the two of us would listen to the slow plop of the dollops of fruit and butter and sugar falling into the paper-lined tin. The kitchen would be warmer than usual and my mother would have that "I've-just-baked-a-cake glow"' (3), to failure: the cake 'always sank in the middle. The embarrassing hollow, sometimes as deep as your fist, having to be filled in with marzipan' (3). The lyrical idealized pleasures of cake baking are continually interwoven with the stark actuality of Nigel's mother's dislike of the process: 'Cooks know to butter and line the cake tins before they start the creaming and beating. My mother would remember just before she put the final spoonful of brandy into the cake mixture, then take half an hour to find them. They always turned up in a drawer, rusty and full of fluff' (3). Two cooking mothers, two meanings, alternate in Slater's text: the actual incompetent, awkward, sometimes resentful woman, and the mythically-loaded Ur-mother, whose baking of a cake makes that cake mean love. The smell of the cake baking conjures this archetypal Mother: 'Warm sweet fruit, a cake in the oven, woodsmoke, warm ironing, hot retriever curled up by the Aga, mince pies, Mum's 4711. Every child's Christmas memories should smell like that. Mine did' (4), but the idyll is marred by the smell of ammonia wafting from his incontinent Aunt Fanny. The real interrupts the ideal: awkwardly, bathetically, comically. The young Nigel's impatient desire for a properly cooking mother is cruelly answered. His own mother dies when he is nine and his father soon presents him with a new mother in the form of Joan, their erstwhile cleaning lady. Joan is an excellent cook, her 'lemon meringue pie was one of the most glorious things I had ever put in my mouth: warm, painfully sharp lemon filling, the most airy pastry imaginable (she used cold lard in place of some of the butter) and a billowing hat of thick, teeth-judderingly sweet meringue' (154–5) but she sets herself up in competition with Nigel, who has to hunt through the kitchen bins to work out the ingredients of the pie. When he begins cooking lessons at school, she changes her baking day to coincide:

> Wednesday now became Joan's baking day. Each week I would proudly come home from school with a flask of vegetable soup, a sunken fruit cake, a box of eclairs (hideously squashed by Roger Mountford's satchel) or, on one occasion, an apple meringue pie whose filling had run out over the bottom of the tin, to find the house full of warm ironing, a freshly brushed dog and enough cakes, tarts and pies to feed the entire village. (184)

Joan is an anti-mother: the culinary nurture turned into a weapon. Slater makes it clear that his adolescent self, at least, blamed her for the death of his father, fed to death with luscious three-course meals every day.

The doubling of the maternal role in Slater's narrative is one that gains its cultural resonance from fairy tale. Another maternal doubling troubles the work of many women writers: the tension between *having* a mother – with all the attendant frustrations and resentments – and *being* one yourself. Nora Ephron's roman à clef, *Heartburn* (1983) sees this doubled motherhood very specifically in terms of food. The novel is a thinly disguised version of the breakup of journalist and screenwriter Ephron's marriage to Carl Bernstein, the Washington political commentator who was responsible for exposing the Watergate scandal. Bernstein's affair with Margaret Jay (then wife of the British ambassador to Washington Peter Jay, later Labour peer Baronness Jay) is depicted in very unflattering terms, with a transparency that made the novel an overnight bestseller. Ephron's alter-ego in her re-telling is Rachel Samstadt, who, unlike her real-world counterpart, is a food writer. Food plays a significant role in the text, with recipes interpolated into the prose and an index to allow the reader to locate them for kitchen purposes later (an aspect of the novel further discussed in Chapter 7). Food is intimately entwined with emotions from the title onwards. Rachel's style of food writing and television performance is personal and narrative in form: she tells stories about her family and her Jewish culinary traditions and 'work[s] the recipes in peripherally' (Ephron 1996: 17). The narrative function of her profession has everything to do with revenge. Rachel's revenge on her husband is to make his cheating public by throwing a pie at him. She is nervously aware of the slapstick implications of this action, and balances its satisfactions against the social faux pas it represents. In the event, the throwing of the pie is unimpressive as an act of revenge – but that is its point. It is of a piece with Rachel's unthreatening, nurturing, maternal profession and her vulnerability at eight months pregnant, all of which present her to the reader as intensely sympathetic and detract attention from the real act of revenge, which is Ephron's writing and publishing of the book and the public shaming it accomplished. All nurture in the novel stems from Rachel herself: with a toddler son as well as the soon-to-be-born infant she personifies motherhood. The curious unreality of her actual experiences as a mother (which seem not to prevent her jetting back and forth from Washington to New York carrying her son like a handbag) does not detract from her ownership of the maternal, which is consolidated by the fact that her own mother is defined primarily by her absolute failure as a nurturing presence:

> Even in the old day my mother was a wash-out at hard-core mothering; what she was good at were clever remarks that made you feel immensely sophisticated and adult and, if you thought about it at all, foolish for having wanted anything so mundane as some actual nurturing. Had I been able to talk to her at this moment of crisis, she would probably have said something fabulously brittle like "Take notes". (29)

A hard-bitten '40s-era Hollywood talent agent, her mother represents the feminism of the pre-war years, of independent career women defining themselves through their occupations rather than their homes and families. Rachel herself is a member of the '70s feminist-generation, and yet feminism is curiously displaced in the text, either assigned to her mother's past or rendered already-over through her comedic conclusion that 'the major concrete achievement of the women's movement in the 1970s was the Dutch treat' (81). The consciousness-raising group ('an evening a week talking over cheese to seven other women whose marriages were equally unhappy' (81)) is replaced with group therapy meetings; Rachel's successful career rendered anodyne through its home-based rituals (she spends weeks working out how to make a four-minute boiled egg in three minutes) and the folksy, familial content of her writing. With feminism and its culinary refusals rendered safely past, Rachel's cooking embraces the traditional and comforting: pies, pot roast, bread pudding and mashed potato. The latter is described in some detail in an essay on potatoes and love extracted from Rachel's own writing, in which the stages of a relationship are traced in terms of the type of potatoes one cooks: at first show-off dishes in front of the beloved; rosti or Potatoes Anna; later the potatoes moulder as the relationship sours; then comes '*the end*':

> Nothing like mashed potatoes when you're feeling blue. Nothing like getting into bed with a bowl of hot mashed potatoes already loaded with butter, and methodically adding a thin cold slice of butter to every forkful. The problem with mashed potatoes, though, is that they require almost as much hard work as crisp potatoes [...]. Of course, you can always get someone else to make the mashed potatoes or you, but let's face it: the reason you're blue is that there isn't anyone to make them for you. (126)

With Rachel the text's only source of nurture she is reduced to mothering herself. In this respect *Heartburn* anticipates a curious trend which reaches its apotheosis in the cookbooks and wider food culture of the end of the twentieth century: an intense desire for food to be comforting. This food-as-comfort narrative was to be found particularly in the glossy, TV-led cookbooks which addressed themselves to a younger generation which was marrying much later, for whom it was assumed that women would have independent careers, and for whom work took up more and more time and energy. These were the people who were to mother themselves with soft, stodgy food and – particularly – with cake. As I discuss elsewhere, baking is one of the main contexts in which the narrative role of the mother is adopted in contemporary cookbooks, with the intended recipients of these acts of ersatz mothering and culinary comforting not our children, but ourselves (Humble 2010a: 109–14). These food narratives are torn between an ideal version of mothering – just the right amount of nurture and comfort, at just the right time – and the messy, intractable reality. As Liz Lochhead's poem 'Nobody's Mother' so memorably puts it – its multiple negatives entwining us in our confused, irresolvable love and guilt and resentment: 'Nobody's mother can't not never do nothing right' (1984: 110). Mothering is so potent, so crucial, so deeply embedded in the idea of food as comfort, that our real mothers will never be up to the job – we are much better off playing mother for ourselves.

The performatively gendered texts explored in this chapter in the context of various historical moments and trajectories could equally be described generically, in terms of their formal hybridity, with many existing in the spaces between, variously, cookbook, travel book, restaurant guide, memoir, novel, political text and hagiography. The formal questions raised by food narratives form the second section of the book, with case studies exploring the experimental food texts of the modernist moment, the role of food fantasies in children's literature, and the recipe as formal mode within and beyond the cookbook.

CHAPTER 5
MODERNIST FOOD / MODERN FOOD:
LITERARY AND CULINARY EXPERIMENTS IN
THE EARLY TWENTIETH CENTURY

Modernism is a literature of disruption, contraction, reordering. The Victorian realist model is broken apart, turned inside out, its forms radically curtailed and recombined. The self and its needs, its chaotic and disordered impulses, memories and passing thoughts, are made central; for modernism, the high-realist project of representing a society in the round is both impossible and undesirable: there is challenge enough to be found in the individual. History is sidelined, the nineteenth century's faith in progress replaced by an aesthetic and philosophical focus on the new. In literary terms this leads to an emphasis on experimentation, on formalism, and on difficulty (and hence exclusivity). It is a body of writing that focusses self-consciously inward, on its own devices and its own role in creating a literature of the modern moment. It is my contention that many of these qualities can be found also in the food culture and the cookbooks and food journalism of the early decades of the twentieth century and that as a result it makes sense to begin to broaden our conception of modernism to include the notion of modernist food.[1] This chapter considers three apparently distinct understandings of the term 'modernist food': the representation of food in works of modernist literature, the modernist elements in early twentieth-century food writing, and the new food culture of the modernist moment. The discussion will begin an examination of food in modernist literary texts via a consideration of two specific types of food to which such texts accord disproportionate attention, will then move into a consideration of the modernist qualities of interwar cookbooks, and will conclude with an analysis of some of the key tropes that operate in both cookbooks and works of modernist literature and which build what I will argue is a distinctively modernist food culture.

Modernist literature is full of food. There are, of course, those iconic images and moments – Prufrock's peach, D. H. Lawrence's figs, Mrs Ramsay's Boeuf en Daube – but food plays a considerably more central and more significant role in the form and aesthetics of modernism than these celebrated isolated examples might suggest. This is particularly true of female modernists such as Virginia Woolf, Katherine Mansfield and Dorothy Richardson, in whose texts the planning, cooking, eating and social meaning of food have central significance, but it is the case also with T. S. Eliot, James Joyce, and D. H. Lawrence, for whom food is variously (in no particular order) an index of modernity, an irreducible image, a despised facet of popular culture, an incarnation of sexual pleasure, a form of religious iconography and a sign of ethnic and national identity. Just as with the literature of the nineteenth century, food remains a multivalent literary symbol, but where earlier its significance was primarily social, in modernist texts its significance is markedly individual and often experimental. Many modernist texts overflow with food – to trace all of the culinary, gustatory and alimentary references in even one of the major works of modernism is beyond the scope of this chapter. Instead, in order to facilitate comparisons, the discussion will be organized around two primal foods which appear with more than usual frequency across the range of texts critically designated as modernist: fruit and meat.

Modernist food I: Fruit

Fruit holds a curiously iconic status in much modernist literature; or rather, fruits hold such a status, because one of the most striking elements of the modernist use of these food stuffs is that it is almost without exception the individual fruit, rather than fruit rendered as indeterminate mass through cooking on which writers focus. The intense aesthetic interest in the *whole* fruit, I would suggest, is an element borrowed from the visual arts, and in particular from the work of Cezanne, Picasso and Matisse, whose many still lives with fruits focus on rendering them primarily as geometrical objects – reduced to shapes and planes – and as exercises in vivid complementary colouration. Fruit in the various experiments of post-impressionism, cubism and fauvism is valued for its everydayness – the vast majority of their many hundreds of works of *nature morte* feature apples, pears or oranges: the most quotidian of fruits, of a piece with the domestic pitchers, jars and bottles which flank them. But what they see in this everydayness is something transformative: 'I will astonish Paris with an apple,' Cezanne declared, while Matisse's oranges 'became signs of joy, discs of pure colour' (Wilson 2002a). Perhaps the modernist writer who comes closest to the cubist visual aesthetic is Gertrude Stein, who was closely associated with the birth of several key modern art movements and a patron to both Matisse and Picasso. Her 1914 *Tender Buttons* is a series of prose poems in the form of associative, repetitive lists. The work is in three parts – 'Objects', 'Food' and 'Rooms' – in which the quotidian is both de- and re-familiarized. Fruit appears as cranberries, apples, rhubarb and oranges (four times) in poems which deliberately refuse all symbolism and all pre-existing association: so rhubarb 'is susan not susan not seat in bunch toys not wild and laughable not in little places not in neglect and vegetable not in fold coal age not please' (Stein 2003: 30).[2] Not all modernist literary fruit is so formally irreducible: fruits function variously as symbol and image, emblem of pleasure and disgust, sign of the everyday and the exotic, but these textual fruits tend to share certain features that make an influence from modern visual art movements plausible: they are raw, not cooked; whole, not cut. The primary sense through which they are apprehended is the visual: they are objects for contemplation, sites of beauty, significant for their formal composition, their colours and shapes rather than (with the striking exceptions of Lawrence and Joyce) for their scents and tastes and juices.

Another explanation of the ubiquity of fruit as modernist food icon lies in the new emphasis given to fruit and vegetables in the culinary culture of the early twentieth century. These foods attain a textual prominence in the new stylish post-war cookbooks, appearing early in the books and with far more space devoted to them. In Mrs C. F. Leyel's The *Gentle Art of Cookery* (1925) the vegetable chapter is the first, with additional chapters on chestnuts, almonds and mushrooms and a chapter specifically on fruit; *Lady Sysonby's Cook Book* (1935) prefaces its vegetable chapter with the firm injunction to 'get as many vegetables as possible', while Mrs Philip Martineau's *Cantaloupe to Cabbage* (1929) is entirely devoted to the topic. Nutritional advice from the medical establishment emphasized the benefits of these plant foods and also of raw foods, while the intense fashionableness of all things American led to many recipes for 'composed salads' of vegetables, fruits and nuts. The taste for fruit and vegetables is understood as specifically modern: food writers frequently compare the new understanding of these foods with the iniquities of the recent past: Martineau, in her 1927 *Caviar to Candy*, describes the recipe book she was given by her mother on marriage in which 'there is not a single vegetable dish nor salad … and not much fruit' (1933: 3). The practice of eating fruit as a part of a meal rather than in the forbidding form of the nineteenth-century dessert course (where any who desired to eat more food after the preceding procession of courses likely quailed before the whole uncut pineapple or the arcane skills required to peel a banana with a knife and fork) is introduced in early twentieth-century food writing as an exotic custom recently borrowed from France. Martineau notes that 'at an ordinary French lunch the sweet is often absent, and one is given cheese and fresh fruit – and not a bad substitute either!' (145) and Leyel introduces her fruit chapter with a lengthy, lyrical account of the fruit-eating habits of the French, Italians and Spaniards before making the following recommendation:

> Fresh fruit should be eaten every day, and a good way to ensure it being always on the table is to use it as a table decoration. The fruits of our temperate climates – grapes, oranges, apples, peaches, apricots, plums – are very beautiful. In the winter, when flowers are expensive, a silver dish of oranges and lemons is as charming to look upon as flowers; and there are lovely Venetian glass bowls with covers to be bought in London now, and these, filled with fruit which, seen through the glass, look mysterious and fascinating, make exquisite table decorations. (1935: 273–4)

The gloss of aesthetic sophistication possessed by the innovation of the fruit bowl in this account is to be found in many similar descriptions in contemporary literary texts. In Rosamond Lehmann's *Dusty Answer* (1927) the fascinating Jennifer, who enthrals the protagonist Judith throughout her three years at Cambridge, is emblematized by a copper bowl she fills with oranges, its glowing form a repeated element in the descriptions of her glamorously dishevelled college room. Bertha, in Katherine Mansfield's 'Bliss' (1921), feels a similar aesthetic pleasure in 'a blue dish, very lovely, with a strange sheen on it as if it had been dipped in milk' and asks her maid not to turn on the light as she fills the dish and a glass bowl with fruit for her dinner party:

There were tangerines and apples stained with strawberry pink. Some yellow pears, smooth as silk, some white grapes covered with a silver bloom and a big cluster of purple ones. These last she had bought to tone in with the new dining-room carpet. Yes, that did sound rather far-fetched and absurd, but it was really why she had bought them. She had thought in the shop: 'I must have some purple ones to bring the carpet up to the table. And it had seemed sense at the time.

When she had finished with them and had made two pyramids of these bright round shapes, she stood away from the table to get the effect – and it was really most curious. For the dark table seemed to melt into the dusky light and the glass dish and the blue bowl seemed to float in the air. This, of course, in her present mood, was so incredibly beautiful … She began to laugh. (1981: 92–3)

The colours, the shapes, the arrangement, and the making strange of the everyday through the ethereal effects of light and darkness are common factors of all these descriptions. The 'mysterious and fascinating' aspect of the fruit bowl is of much greater significance than the imperative to eat the fruit. These are objects imaginatively transformed to image – Bertha's dishes that appear to float recall the paradoxical perspectives of Cezanne's still lives, in which objects and surfaces co-exist in impossible juxtaposition. These fruit-objects are understood by their observers and arrangers as primarily aesthetic entities – versions of Cezanne's apples or Matisse's oranges. And it is crucial to note that these acts of observation are not neutral. It is Judith who sees Jennifer's fruit bowl as a mesmeric emblem of her charm, not the text: in her bedazzlement Judith misses the fact that Jennifer wants more from her than friendship. When she abruptly leaves Cambridge to embark on a full-blown lesbian love affair with an older woman, Jennifer leaves behind her the copper bowl:

'Darling, I've left you my copper bowl. You always said it had nice lights in it. If I go to Italy I'll send you a crate of oranges for it. It looks best with oranges. It's the nicest thing I've ever had, so of course it's for you. Take it and don't forget me.' She lay back looking white and tired.

'Jennifer –' Judith clutched her hand and was speechless. After a while she added: 'I shall feel I haven't quite lost you. Your lovely bowl. It's always seemed such a part of you.'

'It's all of me,' whispered Jennifer. 'I leave it to you.' (1986: 178–9)

It is finally the bowl empty of fruit that emblematizes Jennifer: the promised oranges never arrive. The blissful aesthetic contemplation of the fruit holds but an illusory promise, its symbolism empty. The same is true of the aesthetic rapture felt by Mansfield's Bertha. Her impulsive desire to match the carpet to the grapes is understood to be ridiculous even by Bertha herself, and certainly by the text. Her sensory joy is not a purely aesthetic response to the beauty of the fruit, but conjured up by the prospect of seeing her new 'find' Pearl Fulton that evening. Enraptured by her own feelings for Pearl and by the sensation of diffused sensory bliss which overwhelms her, Bertha fails to realize that an entirely different story is being played out between her guest and her husband. She has had a further moment of aesthetic rapture looking out of the drawing-room window: 'At the far end, against the wall, there was a tall, slender pear tree in fullest, richest bloom' (1981: 96). Quite explicitly seeing herself as this tree she dresses in white with green shoes and stockings. She casts ambiguous, silver-clad Pearl Fulton as the moon in her internal symbolic drama and showing her the tree in the moonlight she feels a moment of absolute understanding pass between them. But later she sees her husband and Pearl arranging an assignation. The story ends in a moment of suspended animation as Bertha, uncertain of everything, gazes again at the pear tree 'as lovely as ever and as full of flower and as still' (105). The reader's judgement is as suspended as Bertha's own: was Miss Fulton attracted to Bertha; is Bertha really in love with her? Did she witness the start of an affair or one that was already in progress? As Claire Tomalin notes of Mansfield, 'the particular stamp of her fiction is the isolation in which each character dwells ... there is no history in these stories, and no exploration of motive. The most brilliant of them are post-impressionist ... grotesquely peopled and alight with colour and movement' (1988: 6–7). Both Bertha and Judith are subjects of textual irony – their desire to aestheticize their experience causing them to miss the more direct desires and manipulations of those around them – but this irony is not stable: it is also the case that the scopophilic pleasure they feel in the fruit and its arrangement spills over into the texts, inflecting the tone of each with a mesmerized sense of the beauty and strangeness of the everyday.

The same sense of intense appreciation of quotidian beauty is attributed by Virginia Woolf to Mrs Ramsay as she contemplates the bowl of fruit arranged by her daughter, Rose:

No, she said, she did not want a pear. Indeed she had been keeping guard over the dish of fruit (without realising it) jealously, hoping that nobody would touch it. Her eyes had been going in and out among the curves and shadows of the fruit, among the rich purples of the lowland grapes, then over the horny ridge of the shell, putting a yellow against a purple, a curved shape against a round shape, without knowing why she did it, or why, every time she did it, she felt more and more serene; until, oh, what a pity that they should do it – a hand reached out, took a pear, and spoilt the whole thing. In sympathy she looked at Rose sitting between Jasper and Prue. How odd that one's child should do that! (1992a: 146–7)

The arrangement of fruit is beautiful precisely in its evanescence – and poignant for just that reason. Evanescence is the dominant note of almost all Mrs Ramsay's insights and feelings in *To the Lighthouse* (1927) – in contrast to both the active grasping after artistic achievement of painter Lily Briscoe, a guest at the Ramsays' summer houseparty, or the solid, tenacious, effortful tracing of lines of reasoning of the former's philosopher husband. The beauty of the fruit is a transitory ephemeral state – a matter of angles of view, actively created by the observing eye. As such it is one of the many metaphors Woolf develops as emblems of her attempt to find a form in which to represent, impressionistically, the passing of time and the intense separateness of the individual consciousness.[3] In *Mrs Dalloway* (1925) images of fruits and vegetables work mainly as signs of these separate subjectivities. The novel opens as Clarissa Dalloway sets off from her London home to buy flowers for her dinner party that evening. The sensation of plunging out into the bright morning air takes her back to the home of her youth and an exchange with a man she might have married, about vegetables:

> Peter Walsh. He would be back from India one of these days, June or July, she forgot which, for his letters were awfully dull; it was his sayings one remembered; his eyes, his pocket-knife, his smile, his grumpiness and, when millions of things had utterly vanished – how strange it was! – a few sayings like this about cabbages. (Woolf 1996: 5)

While the eighteen-year-old Clarissa stared meditatively at the flowers and the birds Peter Walsh had remarked on her 'musing among the vegetables' remarking that he 'prefer[s] men to cauliflowers' (5). His conversion of flowers into solid, rotund Victorian vegetables renders Clarissa's abstraction ridiculous: it is such moments of intrusion, his insistence that 'he always saw through Clarissa' (67) that lead her to marry the dull, politically ambitious Richard instead. Rather than the aesthetic merging of the fruit in *To the Lighthouse*, fruit and vegetables in this novel are discrete objects, jarring in their objective particularity. Peter Walsh, dining alone in his Bloomsbury hotel, impresses the family at the next table with the moderate yet firm manner in which he says 'Bartlett pears' to the waiter (176). Septimus Warren Smith, suffering from shell-shock and trying to hold himself back from madness, looks fearfully around his sitting room, willing the objects in it to remain still and real and unexciting: 'And so, gathering courage, he looked at the side-board; the plate of bananas; the engraving of Queen Victoria and the Prince Consort; at the mantlepiece, with the jar of roses. None of these things moved. All were still, all were real' (156). But it is the bananas that obtrude, become insistently present, as he descends into madness: 'He started up in terror. What did he see? The plate of bananas on the sideboard. Nobody was there. [...] That was it: to be alone for ever. [...] He was alone with the sideboard and the bananas' (159–60). A few minutes later, as doctors force their way into the room to take him to hospital, he commits suicide, throwing himself from the window onto the basement railings beneath.

Fruit is not a static symbol in Woolf's architecturally structured novels, but rather an objective correlative for the dominant themes and aesthetic concerns. If it figures merging and ephemerality in *To the Lighthouse* and the stark separations of subjective experiences in *Mrs Dalloway*, in *Jacob's Room* (1922), whose central concern is the imminent loss of a generation of young men in the war, it mirrors the themes of unfulfilled promise and waste. So when Jacob and Timmy Durrant, aged twenty, with the world before them and fired by youthful certainties, moor their boat beneath a willow tree to lounge and eat cherries, the textual focus is not on the cherries that are eaten but on the portions that are discarded: 'as Durrant ate cherries he dropped the stunted yellow cherries through the green wedge of leaves, their stalks twinkling as they wriggled in and out, and sometimes one half-bitten cherry would go down red into the green' (Woolf 1999: 45). The life-in-death implications of the discarded cherries are underlined by the description of the grass on the bank above them – juicy and thick, not like 'the thin green water of the graveyard grass about to overflow the tombstones'. Later, arguing into the night with friends in a college room, Jacob eats dates out of a long box, preparing something profound to say when he has finished arranging the stones (56). The child's game of counting fruit stones to determine one's future profession springs to mind – a future we already realize Jacob will not possess as his fate has been prefigured from the opening lines of the novel when we are told his surname – Flanders. The missing future haunts also in the scene when Timmy's sister Clara – the girl Jacob would probably have married – cuts bunches of grapes for him from their vine, covering them gently with leaves as they 'lay curled warm in the basket' like the infants they might have had (82) while other children run wildly past the greenhouse hurling onions at each other like grenades.

The temporal movement of fruit from potentiality to waste is the major trope also of H. D.'s 'Orchard' (1916), in which the speaker seeks to arrest the processes of ripening, crying out to the god of the orchard to 'Spare us the beauty / Of fruit-trees', offering up to him fruits which in the moment of being listed tip from ripe to over-ripe: from 'fallen hazel-nuts, / Stripped late of their green sheaths' and 'Grapes, red-purple, / Their berries / Dripping with wine' to 'Pomegranates already broken, / And shrunken figs' (Dolittle 1916: 30). If it is the fecundity of the orchard that alarms H. D.'s speaker, in D. H. Lawrence's 'Ballad of Another Ophelia' (which appeared in the *Some Imagist Poets* anthology of 1915) ripeness is arrested: 'Nothing now will ripen the bright green apples, / Full of disappointment and of rain' (1915: 67–8). The poem, spoken in the mad voice of a woman betrayed or abandoned by her lover, represents the potential of new life – the green apples, the yellow chicks, her own love – wiped out by rain, a rat, a rapist. The apples figure vulnerability, femininity – potential cut short; but the 'wicked sun' winks at the end of the poem, apparently conniving at the destruction. In his fruit sequence of the 1923 *Birds, Beasts and Flowers* Lawrence has left the precise, concrete, undecorative images of Imagism behind. These poems are discursive, rambling, often approaching prose except for the insistent patterning of their symbolism and the lyrical energy of their language. Lawrence was one of the first British experimenters in the free verse form, which he defended in an essay, 'Poetry of the Present' (1919) as 'the seething poetry of the incarnate Now' (1936: 218–22). The sequence begins with two poems, 'Pomegranate' and 'Peach', which seem to argue directly with Lawrence's detractors, asserting his right to see the fissure in the whole fruit – the crack as well as the globe, the inside as well as the smooth, round whole: 'Do you mean to tell me there should be no fissure? / No glittering, compact drops of dawn? / Do you mean it is wrong, the gold-filmed skin, integument, shown ruptured?' ('Pomegranate'; Lawrence 1923: 12). His fruits are not hermetically sealed objects like the aesthetic abstractions of Cezanne and Matisse: they are things of cracks and openings, of richly realized inner textures and juices. 'Why the groove?', he asks of the peach, 'Why the lovely, bivalve roundnesses? / Why the ripple down the sphere? / Why the suggestion of incision? / Why was not my peach round and finished like a billiard ball? / It would have been if man had made it' (13). Lawrence's fruit-meditations force the reader into simultaneous awareness of three different fruits, all insistently, nakedly present: firstly the fruit itself as real-world object: not a generic peach but this particular peach, with this particular shape; secondly the fruit as part of a symbolic grammar of the sexual body; thirdly the fruit-as-poem. This latter is not in the Imagist sense of the poem as unified object, but as a discursive process. In meditating on fruits the poems map their own process of creation, tapping into the 'creative quick' (1936: 219). So the meditation in 'Pomegranate' on the aesthetic rightness of the cracked-open pomegranate over the closed smooth one becomes an assertion of the 'rightness' of the poem cracked open, showing its workings and its glinting heart. Unlike the arrested apples of 'Ballad of Another Ophelia', these later fruits are always in process, growing from flower to fruit, ripening and then rotting. The latter is the keynote of 'Medlars and Sorb-Apples': fruit traditionally eaten after they have begun to rot, or been 'bletted'; it is the rot with which the poem begins: 'I love you, rotten, / Delicious rottenness. / I love to suck you out from your skins / So brown and soft and coming suave, / So morbid, as the Italians say' (1923: 15). Medlars were known in ancient English tradition as 'openarse fruit' as a result of their open calyx, a vulgarism of which Lawrence was undoubtedly aware, and which feeds into his description of the fruit flesh as 'Autumnal excrementa' (15).[4] No symbolism is allowed to linger unliteralized: the dark autumnal rot of the fruit leads him to the chthonic – the realm of the underworld gods and in psychological terms the subconscious earthy impulses – 'What is it that reminds us of white gods?', he asks of the rotting autumnal fruits – 'Gods nude as blanched nut-kernels. / Strangely, half-sinisterly flesh-fragrant / As if with sweat, / And drenched with mystery'. The soft, morbidly parting fibres of the fruit in the mouth take him to the story of Orpheus, the journey into the underworld and the separation of lovers by death. One of the most striking features of Lawrence's fruit poems is that they are intimately concerned with the process of eating the fruit. Unlike the beautiful fruit bowls of Mansfield and Woolf, at their most fully realized when undisturbed, his fruit is sweet and dripping, marked with the traces of teeth. He sucks the medlars from their skins, has already eaten the peach of whose 'rolling, dropping heavy globule' only the stone remains. His best-known fruit poem 'Figs' begins with a discussion of how to eat the fruit:

> THE proper way to eat a fig, in society,
> Is to split it in four, holding it by the stump,
> And open it, so that it is a glittering, rosy, moist, honied,
> heavy-petalled four-petalled flower.
> Then you throw away the skin
> Which is just like a four-sepalled calyx,
> After you have taken off the blossom with your lips.
> But the vulgar way
> Is just to put your mouth to the crack, and take out the
> flesh in one bite. (1923: 18)

The intensely sexual implications of this account are baldly literalized in the next lines of the poem, as he tells us that the Italians 'vulgarly say, it stands for the female part; the fig-fruit: / The fissure, the yoni, / The wonderful moist conductivity towards the centre' (18). The inward physical form of the fig blossom and its fruit, 'Involved, / Inturned, / The flowering all inward and womb-fibrilled' (18–19), is emphasized, and this inward fruit-sex transmutes seamlessly into the assertion that 'the female should always be secret'. The ripe, 'bursten' end-of-season fig gaudily displaying its secrets to the world is a prostitute: just as the ripe fig dies, 'that's how women die too' (20). 'Our women' affirming their secret sexuality 'through moist, scarlet lips', forget that 'ripe figs won't keep': a line of thought leading to the apocalyptic anti-feminism of the poem's ending: 'What then, when women the world over have all bursten into affirmation? / And bursten figs won't keep?'

Although Lawrence's intense focus on the sucked and bitten fruit is singular among modernists, it has something in common with accounts of fruit in the novels of James Joyce, another writer strongly interested in the physical. In the 'Calypso' section of *Ulysses* (1922), a novel in which a deep litter of food references works to establish the life and culture of the city and its connections to a wider world, Leopold Bloom muses on fruit. As he walks home from the butchers he reads on the newspaper in which his meat is wrapped an advertisement for investment opportunities in the Middle East: 'You pay eighty marks and they plant a dunam of land for you with olives, oranges, almonds or citrons' (Joyce 1986: 49). This initiates a wandering meditation on the fruit and its associations:

> Silverpowdered olivetrees. Quiet long days: pruning, ripening. Olives are packed in jars, eh? I have a few left from Andrews. Molly spitting them out. Knows the taste of them now. Oranges in tissue paper packed in crates. Citrons too. [...] Nice to hold, cool waxen fruit, hold in the hand, lift it to the nostrils and smell the perfume. Like that, heavy, sweet, wild perfume. Always the same, year after year. They fetched high prices too, Moisel told me. Arbutus place: Pleasants street: pleasant old times. Must be without a flaw, he said. Coming all that way: Spain, Gibraltar, Mediterranean, the Levant. Crates lined up on the quayside at Jaffa, chap ticking them off in a book, navvies handling them barefoot in soiled dungarees. (49)

These fruits are economic entities: to be planted, traded and exported. They connect the Jewish Bloom to an ethnic homeland, an otherwise linked to the Dublin of his present by the journey the oranges, citrons and olives would take to reach him. But like Lawrence's fruit they are also sense-objects whose imagined texture and scent evoke a network of memories. Bloom takes intense and unproblematic pleasure in food, though it is notable that the only memory of eating in the passage is of Molly's spitting out of the olives: the citrus fruits remain intact, perhaps in order that they can complete their imagined journey.

Unlike Bloom, Stephen Dedalus is profoundly conflicted about food and its pleasures and processes. In a very long sequence in chapter V of *A Portrait of the Artist as a Young Man* (1916), he observes his university friend Cranly masticating figs, watching with an attention that speaks to his deep anxiety and irritation. Cranly is first seen in the chapter sheltering from the rain in the arcade of the library 'leaning against a pillar [...] picking his teeth with a sharpened match' (Joyce 2000: 233–4). The next day we see him dislodge 'a figseed from his teeth on the point of his rude toothpick and gaze [...] at it intently' (249). The fig seeds extracted from Cranly's teeth become metaphors for words and images as Stephen struggles to find a way to think about the girl he loves, comparing her inadequately to memories of sexually available women:

> That was not the way to think of her. It was not even the way in which he thought of her. Could his mind not trust itself? Old phrases, sweet only with a disinterred sweetness like the figseeds Cranly rooted out of his gleaming teeth. (253)

Cranly himself uses his fig eating as more direct metaphor. When, 'slowly and noisily' chewing, he is accosted by a 'squat student', Glynn, he first answers him 'with loud movements of his jaw' and then 'hold[s] out what remain[s] of the halfchewed fig and jerk[s] it towards the squat student's mouth in sign that he should eat it' (254–5). The joking contempt of the gesture, the substitution of chewing for words, echoes Stephen's earlier anxiety about the gross physicality of ingestion. When Stephen draws Cranly away from the group to discuss his own religious doubts, he demands that the latter cease eating: 'you cannot discuss this question with your mouth full of chewed fig' (260). In his diary later Stephen tries to reincorporate Cranly and his figs into his own narrative, casting him as John the Baptist (and so himself as Christ):

> Hence Cranly's despair of soul: the child of exhausted loins [...] The exhausted loins are those of Elisabeth and Zachary. Then he is the precursor. Item: he eats chiefly belly bacon and dried figs. Read locusts and wild honey. (270)

The horrified attention with which Stephen views Cranly's fig chewing is focussed exclusively on the action of his teeth. This is not a Lawrentian evocation of the flavours and textures of the fruit: we do not imagine ourselves into Cranly's experience of chewing the figs but into Stephen's repelled hyper-awareness of the rotating jaws and the noise of mastication. Cranly's act of eating is not neatly finished – it is drawn out to the point of the observer's screaming irritation as he continues to suck debris from the crevices of his teeth and to root around for stuck seeds.

In T. S. Eliot's poetry fruit is represented through a set of associations very similar to those deployed by Joyce: self-denial, internationalism, and religion. In the course of his career, as his work becomes increasingly focussed on issues of faith, fruit-images become entwined into an elaborate religious iconography. 'The Love Song of J. Alfred Prufrock' (1919), one of Eliot's best early poems, deploys food as part of a poetics of the petty. Prufrock bemoans his walk-on status 'I am not Prince, Hamlet, nor was meant to be; / Am an attendant lord, one that will do / To swell a progress, start a scene or two' (1974: 17). Worrying about his insignificance, his growing baldness, he wanders between London social gatherings, frustrated by his own lack of heroism, his inability to assert himself, to speak. The modern world he inhabits cannot rise to the poetic sublime – the yellow fog is imaged as a cat rubbing itself against a window; the evening sky 'like a patient etherised upon a table'. It is only as his thoughts rise to their culminating crescendo of self-loathing that the taunting possibility of something more – of richer imaginings – is held out before him, only to be snatched away in the same moment:

> I grow old … I grow old …
> I shall wear the bottoms of my trousers rolled.
> Shall I part my hair behind? Do I dare to eat a peach?
> I shall wear white flannel trousers, and walk upon the beach.
> I have heard the mermaids singing, each to each.
> I do not think that they will sing to me. (17)

The peach and the mermaids form part of the same realm of life-affirming imaginings, tantalizingly within reach (he has heard the mermaids, he *could* eat the peach) but ultimately unavailable to him. Out of all modernist fruit references this phrase resonates precisely because of the smallness of its aspirations: to eat a peach is such a tiny ambition; his implied failure to do so such a refusal of life. Bathos is the dominant note: the inadequacy of the single peach as symbol of all that is missing in the obligation-bound repetitions of his 'days and ways' (15); and yet the juicy, perfumed promise of the peach haunts unrealized, present but not present, like the mermaids' song. In *The Wasteland* (1922) 'Under the brown fog of a winter noon / Mr Eugenides, the Smyrna merchant / Unshaven, with a pocket full of currants / C.i.f. london: documents at sight, / Asked me in demotic French / to luncheon at the Cannon Street Hotel, / Followed by a weekend at the Metropole' (1974: 71). In the poem's tightly woven net of metaphors, Mr Eugenides connects to Phlebas the Phoenician of Part IV 'Death by Water'. The currants punningly connect to the 'currents' under the sea picking the bones of Phelbas who has now forgotten 'the profit and loss'. The fruits in Mr Eugenides's pocket have been variously read as the item he is trading ('c.i.f. London' meaning 'cost insurance and freight to London' as Eliot's own notes tell us) and as a code for same-sex desire.[5] In either case they are the product of Smyrna, on the border of Greece and Turkey and a place, in the English imagination marked by ethnic heterogeneity and confusion.[6] His invitation of the unnamed narrator to a dirty weekend in Brighton aligns with all those other manifestations of a 'throbbing, waiting' sterile sexuality in the poem (Lil's abortions; the encounter of the typist and the 'young man carbuncular'). The dried currants in his pocket figure the dried-up sexual potency of the Fisher King, symbolic centrepiece of the poem, whose impotence has blighted the wasteland. In Eliot's increasingly austere later poetry fruit imagery is more and more dried up, purged of its juices. *Ash-Wednesday* (1930), written after his conversion to Anglicanism, traces a lenten process of renunciation of the body in favour of the spirit, in which fruit figures only as an empty gourd, or as a 'withered apple-seed' spat from a mouth. By the time of *Four Quartets* (1935–42) fruit is a discard, a metaphor for a collective past of failure and despair, with 'time the destroyer' which is also 'time the preserver' imaged as 'Like the river with its cargo of dead negroes, cows and chicken coops, / The bitter apple and the bite in the apple' (1974: 209). The horror of the unexplained dead negroes – slaves, farmers washed away with their livestock? – attaches itself to the apple: its bitterness more than a casual reason for its discarding but a symbol of the futility of human desires and pleasures. The missing bite is as important as the bitterness – the gap (that which we do not know) as crucial as the whole. For late Eliot indeterminacy is all we ultimately have. By the end of the poem there is no more actual fruit, only, in its bleak evocation of old age, 'the bitter tastelessness of shadow fruit / As body and soul begin to fall asunder' (218).

Stephen Dedalus's anxiety about (fruit) eating and Eliot's poetics of renunciation have in common a religious code that sees the pleasures of the flesh as antithetical to the transcendence of the spirit. The paradox of this renunciation is that both Dedalus's Catholicism and Eliot's High-Anglicanism have at their centre an act of eating the flesh of their god. A profound anxiety about flesh-eating and its implications is, I will argue, the other key element in modernist literary representations of food.

Modernist food II: Murder in the kitchen

'Before any story of cooking begins, crime is inevitable' (51), declares Alice B Toklas in the third chapter of *The Alice B Toklas Cookbook* (1954), before going on to describe her first lessons in the art and crime of killing for food. Combining her own leisure reading of cookbooks with Gertrude Stein's favoured hard-boiled crime fiction, she tells the story of her 'assassination of Mr Carp' in a pastiche of Dashiell Hammett, then segues directly into a recipe for 'Carp Stuffed with Chestnuts'. Her focus is on the physical sensations of killing and its aftermath; even more so when she graduates to tougher crimes and learns how to 'murder by smothering'. Her victims on this occasion are 'six white pigeons':

> I carefully found the spot on the poor innocent Dove's throat where I was to press and pressed. The realization had never come to me before that one saw with one's fingertips as well as one's eyes. It was a most unpleasant experience, though as I laid out one by one the sweet young corpses there was no denying that one could become accustomed to murdering. (Toklas 1961: 55)

The double lens that simultaneously sees meat (and fish) as murder, and cynically acknowledges the ease with which it is possible to become accustomed to it, is paradigmatic in modernist accounts of meat eating. Unlike earlier literature which takes the pragmatic view of meat eating of those with at least a memory of a culture of home meat production, the modernist generation is primarily urban, no longer directly in touch with the life-and-death realities of meat. The result is a series of literary responses which equate meat with horror, death, even cannibalism, and which deploy it as a metaphor for the violence of modern life. The transitional moment into this modernist aesthetic of meat, we might argue, occurs in *Jude the Obscure* (1895) – the last gasp of Hardy's realist vision – when Jude is forced by Arabella to kill the pig, and the ruthless pragmatism of Arabella's approach ('Pigs must be killed', and slowly so their meat is white; 'Poor folks must live') clashes head-on with Jude's horror at a violence and cruelty which confirms his nihilistic anticipation of the modern age (2002: 59). For Virginia Woolf, the association of animal-murder with the modern is made in the scene near the end of part III of *To the Lighthouse* when some of her characters finally do reach the lighthouse. Cam, James and Mr Ramsay are rowed out to the island by Macalister and his boy, who fish as they go. The fishing connects to the story of the Fisherman and his Wife and the magic wish-granting Flounder, which Mrs Ramsay had read to the young James ten years before. While fishing, 'Macalister's boy took one of the fish and cut a square out of its side to bait his hook with. The mutilated body (it was alive still) was thrown back into the sea' (1992a: 243). It might be a passing incident, except that these two sentences form Chapter 6 in its entirety; more, they are placed in square brackets, which is exactly how the deaths of Mrs Ramsay and Prue are interpolated into the narrative in the Time Passes section – absolute truths whose random intrusion into the quotidian fabric of life makes them the more impossible to bear. The casual cruelty and the waste of life are aggravated rather than diminished by the mathematical exactitude – the straight-sided modernity – of the shape cut from the fish. The image of the fish and violence is directly associated by Woolf with her own father: on 14 May 1925 while composing the novel she notes in her diary that 'the centre is father's character, sitting in a boat reciting We perished each alone, while he crushes a dying mackerel' (1980: 18–19). The transposition of the cruelty to the unthinking boy (while Mr Ramsay elsewhere retains the self-indulgent declamation of Cowper) renders the latter less unsympathetic, but also works to make the cruelty that of an indifferent universe. After an intervening chapter concerning the characters left on land we return to the boat and to Cam Ramsay thinking 'They don't feel a thing there' – a seemingly abstract thought until we connect it back to the fish. It is a self-comfort, of course, that begs an answer in the negative: the darkness of modernity for Woolf as for Hardy is that we know that others do suffer and that we continue regardless of that knowledge.

Just this is the existential horror that illuminates Samuel Beckett's 'Dante and the Lobster', the first story in his first published work, the 1934 *More Pricks Than Kicks* collection. This loose conglomeration of narratives (short stories and fragments from a novel, *A Dream of Fair to Middling Women*, for which he had been unable to find a publisher) follows the life of Belacqua Shuah from student days to his accidental death. In the opening story Belacqua (whose name is taken from a character in Dante so renowned for his laziness that he has given up the prospect of reaching heaven) first studies Dante, then makes his lunch, goes to a pub, buys a lobster, has an Italian lesson and finally goes to his aunt's house where she is to cook the lobster for their dinner. But this bald description misses all of the fantastic grotesquery of Belacqua's life and his relationship to objects. A good third of the story is taken up with his thoughts about bread, his meticulous efforts to ensure that the toast for his lunch is burnt to a satisfying crisp, and his frustration with the fact that the piece of Gorgonzola reserved for him at the grocers is not rotten enough for his taste. Here, as in Beckett's later works, the feelings his characters have about mundane objects verge on the autistic; he feels about the bread as he might about a person – a mixture of tenderness and violence: 'He laid his cheek against the soft of the bread, it was spongy and warm, alive. But he would very soon take that plush feel off it, by God but he would very quickly take that fat white look off its face' (1934: np). Objects are safer to feel for than the living, so it is with utter horror that at the end of the story Belacqua realizes that the lobster he has been carting around in his shopping bag all afternoon is still alive:

> "Christ!" he said "it's alive."
> His aunt looked at the lobster. It moved again. It made a faint nervous act of life on the oilcloth. They stood above it, looking down on it, exposed cruciform on the oilcloth. It shuddered again. Belacqua felt he would be sick.

Connected to the savage mysteries of divine sacrifice ('Christ ... cruciform') the lobster's fate is presented as inexorable, pre-ordained: '"lobsters are always boiled alive"', his aunt declares, '"They must be."' In a moment of horrified identification Belacqua imagines the lobster's journey to this moment:

> In the depths of the sea it had crept into the cruel pot. For hours, in the midst of its enemies, it had breathed secretly. It had survived the Frenchwoman's cat and his witless clutch. Now it was going alive into scalding water. It had to. Take into the air my quiet breath.

His brief apprehension of the horror of this death is backed away from the moment it is conceived – the line from Keats's 'Ode to a Nightingale' is an invocation to 'Easeful Death', shortly followed in the poem by 'To cease upon the midnight with no pain'. In attempting to romanticize the lobster's death, Belacqua refuses to know its full darkness. But this is not an escape allowed to the reader:

> Well, thought Belacqua, it's a quick death, God help us all.
> It is not.

Our interpretation of this startling ending, with the absolute judgement of the disembodied narrator/God, depends largely on the line from Dante which Belacqua has earlier presented to his Italian teacher as an intriguing pun, and which she leaves untranslated: '*qui vive la pietà quando è ben morta*'. The pun rests on the dual meaning of *pietà*: both 'pity' and 'piety', so literally translates as 'here lives piety / pity when it is quite dead'; Stephen Connor's rendering of the phrase – 'there can only be piety where pity is dead' – captures the doubleness and the bleakness that Belacqua / Beckett presumably intends: a bitterly harsh judgement, which sees suffering as divinely ordained and pity as an indulgence.[7] God will not help us all and death will not be quick. The lobster is Christ-like but its death redeems nothing.

For T. S. Eliot also the act of killing for food connects directly and intimately with the central mystery of the Christian faith. In 'Gerontion' (1920) he conjures an image of

Christ as simultaneously predator and prey: 'In the juvescence of the year / Came Christ the tiger / In depraved May, dogwood and chestnut, flowering judas, / To be eaten, to be divided, to be drunk / Among whispers' (1974: 39). Christ, here, is a destroyer as much as a sacrifice: an animal who is never food turned into a secret, depraved blood sacrament. It is a darkly disturbing image, at one with the twisted negations of the poem which mark a transition from the wistful sense of failure of 'Prufrock' (a number of critics have seen the aged central figure of 'Gerontion' as Prufrock grown old) to the utter loss of faith of *The Waste Land* (Eliot intended to use 'Gerontion' as a prelude to *The Waste Land* until strongly dissuaded by Pound). Two decades later in 'East Coker' (1940), the second of the *Four Quartets*, Eliot again literalizes the image of the Eucharist:

> The dripping blood our only drink,
> The bloody flesh our only food:
> In spite of which we like to think
> That we are sound, substantial flesh and blood –
> Again, in spite of that, we call this Friday good (1974: 202)

By now an Anglican convert, Eliot approaches the mystery of Christ's sacrifice and the rite of Communion though their palpable absurdity. The essential cannibalism at the heart of Christianity is returned to view – dripping blood and bloody flesh rather than a dry wafer. The verse plays off a series of paradoxes: the cannibalized flesh and blood are our *only* food: interdicted yet required; not food but the only food. We like to think ourselves sound and substantial – that is, morally and physically healthy, but also unitary, whole – but we are made of the same substances that we eat in the Christ. Like Christ the tiger in 'Gerontion' we are potentially both eater and eaten. We call this Friday good in spite of the horror of the execution of our god, in spite of the cannibalistic excesses of our faith – in fact, because of these things. In these images Eliot works to return the atavistic to a creed long dried to bloodlessness. The same associations and mysteries are a source of profound distress for Joyce's Stephen Dedalus. Listening to a lengthy sermon as a school boy he is overwhelmed with doctrinal questions:

> Why was the sacrament of the Eucharist instituted under the two species of bread and wine if Jesus Christ be present body and blood, soul and divinity, in the bread alone and in the wine alone? Does a tiny particle of the consecrated bread contain all the body and blood of Jesus Christ or a part only of the body and blood? (Joyce 2000: 114)

Stephen's application of material questions to the mystery of the Eucharist does not straightforwardly destroy his faith. In fact, it is precisely the material element of this idea of eating one's god that most disturbs him: the literalism of the Roman Catholic belief that the host is not symbolically but actually the body and blood of Christ. Later, in conversation with Cranly, this paradox is expressed more directly:

> - And is that why you will not communicate, Cranly asked, because you are not
> sure of that too, because you feel that the host too may be the body and blood of
> the son of God and not a wafer of bread? And because you fear that it may be?
> - Yes, Stephen said quietly. I feel that and I also fear it. (264)

Stephen's crisis is one of faith rather than doubt: he fears the implications of his belief.
His anxiety about this act of religious cannibalism transfers to all foods: the young man
who spent his prize money on 'groceries and delicacies and dried fruits' and squares of
Vienna chocolate (104) mortifies his sense of taste by 'practis[ing] strict habits at table,
observin[ing] to the letter all the fasts of the church and [seeking] by distraction to divert
his mind from the savours of different foods' (163). In *Ulysses*, Stephen's fears of eating
are contrasted with the exuberant gustatory habits of Leopold Bloom, who is famously
introduced in the fourth chapter of the book with a description of his tastes in meat:

> Mr Leopold Bloom ate with relish the inner organs of beasts and fowls. He liked
> thick giblet soup, nutty gizzards, a stuffed roasted heart, liverslices fried with
> crustcrumbs, fried hencods' roes. Most of all he liked grilled mutton kidneys
> which gave to his palate a fine tang of faintly scented urine. (1986: 45)

Much like Belacqua's preparation of his lunch, the entire chapter is given over to an
account of Bloom's shopping for, preparing and eating a kidney for his breakfast. Joyce's
representation of his taste in offal insists on the bodily realities of the animals whose
flesh he is consuming. The physicalities shared by humanity and these creatures are
emphasized in the scene in the butcher's shop where Bloom queues, hoping to get the
last kidney on the dish, noticing the ham-like thighs of the servant girl in front of him:
'sound meat there: like a stallfed heifer' (48) and the sausage-like fingers of the butcher.
The kidney itself is associated with Bloom's own body through the movement of his
hand through pockets, brushing against different glands: 'his hand accepted the moist
tender gland and slid it into a sidepocket' (49). The cannibalistic implications of his
offal-eating hold no fear for Bloom. The description of the final eating of the kidney
(which he has just saved from burning) contains none of the elements of the grotesque
that we might expect from the foregoing account; instead, it is an act of connoisseurship:
'he put a forkful into his mouth, chewing with discernment the toothsome pliant meat.
Done to a turn' (53).

It is the atavistic rather than the sacramental aspects of killing to eat that preoccupy
both D. H. Lawrence and Katherine Mansfield. In 'Fish', Lawrence's main theme is the
profoundly alien nature of the fish's being, its absolute separateness even from other
fish: 'Even snakes lie together. / But, oh, fish, that rock in water, / You lie only with
the waters; / One touch' (1923: 93). The poem consists of a series of failed attempts to
know fish, to think its way into their separateness, their evolutionary previousness: 'Born
before God was love, / Or life knew loving. / Beautifully beforehand with it all' (96). The
experience of having killed a fish is given in the imperfect – a past act uncompleted,
as if its horrors continue to reverberate: 'I have waited with a long rod / And suddenly

pulled a gold-and-greenish, lucent fish from below' (98). The moment of the fish's death is extended, occupying stanzas, momentary sensations stretching out: 'And the gold-and-green pure lacquer-mucus comes off in my hand, / And the red-gold mirror-eye stares and dies, / And the water-suave contour dims'. It is in the extended moments of the fish's death that the speaker reaches his epiphany: 'He was born in front of my sunrise, / Before my day. / He outstarts me. / And I, a many-fingered horror of daylight to him, / Have made him die' (98–9). The God of the fish 'stands outside my God'; 'I am not the measure of creation': it is precisely in its profound otherness that the fish challenges the supremacy of humanity. And yet even after this moment the speaker returns to the fish as food, noting its 'white meat' and the 'thirst' for it of 'Cats, and the Neopolitans'. The paradox of creatures as both subject and food-object is exposed but not resolved: still the speaker proclaims 'I don't know fishes'.

The original sin of killing for food is (as will be discussed more fully in Chapter 6) a perennial preoccupation in the literature of childhood. In 'Prelude', one of a series of stories in which Katherine Mansfield recalls the New Zealand of her youth, the primal scene is the killing of a duck. A group of young cousins accompany the handyman, Pat, who has invited them to see '"how the kings of Ireland chop off the head of a duck"' (1981: 44). Greeting the prospect disbelievingly, they follow him to a pool where 'the big white ducks had made themselves at home ... preening their dazzling breasts' (45). A story-book scene is rendered more idyllic by Pat's fanciful interpretation: '"There is the little Irish navy ... and look at the old admiral there with the green neck and the grand little flag-staff on his tail."' The children are fascinated by the ducks and Pip 'nearly sob[s] with delight' when he is given one to hold while the other is 'finish[ed]' by Pat with his little tomahawk (45–6). The scene is remarkable for the mix of emotions the children evince and for the startling lack of sentimentality:

> When the children saw the blood they were frightened no longer. They crowded round him and began to scream. Even Isabel leaped about crying: 'The blood! The blood!' Pip forgot all about his duck. He simply threw it away from him and shouted, 'I saw it. I saw it,' and jumped round the wood block. (46)

The screams are of excitement rather than fear, and their response to the sight of the duck's body walking around without its head is laughter and wonder: '"It's like a little engine. It's like a funny little railway engine"'. Then it becomes clear that the smaller children did not until this moment understand the permanence of death: Kezia rushes at Pat screaming '"Put the head back"' and Rags tries to keep the head alive by giving it water to drink (47). The older children, already inducted into the ultimate secret, become angry and the group breaks up. Later, the duck is served:

> The white duck did not look as if it had ever had a head when Alice placed it in front of Stanley Burnell that night. It lay, in beautifully basted resignation, on a blue dish – its legs tied together with a piece of string and a wreath of balls of stuffing round it.

> It was hard to say which of the two, Alice or the duck, looked the better basted; they were both such a rich colour and they both had the same air of gloss and strain. But Alice was fiery red and the duck a Spanish mahogany. (50)

The duck's new status as object does not entirely rule out its previous role as subject: it lies in resignation. The comparison of the duck to Alice, the servant, complicates the issue of subjectivity, as it is Alice's perspective we have just been privy to in the scene that occurs in between the two appearances of the duck. Her internal monologue and her resentments against 'Miss Beryl' who 'talked to [her] in a special voice as though she wasn't quite all there' (49) raise questions about who exactly counts as a subject and who an object. The sentimentality that was missing in the scene of the killing of the duck returns in the response of Stanley Burnell to the meat as he carves it: 'It was a superb bird. It wasn't meat at all, but a kind of very superior jelly. "My father would say," said Burnell, "this must have been one of those birds whose mother played to it in infancy upon the German flute"' (50). This whimsical anthropomorphizing at the very moment he slices into the creature's flesh signals that hardening of the sensibilities in adults which is so often one of Mansfield's themes: the extraordinary primitive responses of the children are represented as an honesty which they are soon to lose.

Modern / Modernist cookbooks

Just as writers of modernist fiction recognize the potential of food to 'make it new' (in Ezra Pound's slogan), so too do the authors of a number of radically experimental food texts which take their lead from literary and artistic modernism. These books take the form of the cookbook and reuse it for purposes as disparate as memoir or political tract. The most striking such text is Filippo Tommaso Marinetti's *The Futurist Cookbook* (1932). Challenging the bourgeois domestic food culture of nineteenth-century Italy, Marinetti proposed instead a cuisine of speed, minimalism and modernity. The book is part serious cookbook, part artistic experiment, part political manifesto and almost wholly a joke. Written during the second stage of the Futurist movement, when many of the original members, with the exception of Marinetti himself, had departed, *la cucina futurista* is an attempt to redefine the movement and to garner press and public attention.[8] Its structure is a collage of different elements: myth-making with anecdotes about the futurist leaders ('the dinner that stopped a suicide') and accounts of 'the great futurist banquets'; guidance to enable readers to cook and eat as futurists themselves ('the definitive futurist dinners'); more ambitious rules for professional chefs and bartenders ('futurist formulas for restaurants and quisbeve'); and a 'little dictionary of futurist cooking' containing the Italian terms Marinetti wanted to substitute for despised foreign usages ('CASTAGNE CANDITE: replaces MARRONS GLACÉS') and new futurist coinages: 'CONRUMORE: term indicates the sound affinity of a given noise with the flavour of a given food. Example: the conrumore of rice in orange sauce and a motorcycle engine' (Marinetti 2014: 231; 232). Futurism as an artistic movement was extremely influential in its embracing of modernity, the urban and especially technology. Politically, its optimism about the modern world was combined with an opposition to tradition, antiquarianism and feminism and an embracing of patriotism, xenophobia and violence. Marinetti was an early enthusiast for fascism from 1915 onwards, but resigned from the party in 1920, accusing them of being reactionary. He re-engaged a few years later, and volunteered to fight with Mussolini's troops in 1942 at the age of sixty-five. 'We will glorify war – the world's only hygiene,' the 1909 manifesto had declared, also 'militarism, patriotism, the destructive gesture of freedom-bringers, beautiful ideas worth dying for, and scorn for women. We will destroy the museums, libraries, academies of every kind, will fight moralism, feminism, every opportunistic or utilitarian cowardice.' Many of the ideas expressed in *la cucina futurista* are fascist in nature, though others are more consonant with anarchism. Futurist food is determinedly masculinist in nature: very often raw rather than cooked, presented with a delight in violence, scatology, pornography, the disharmonious. The book seeks to overturn deeply held Italian culinary shibboleths: local traditions, mama, pasta. It is hard to do justice to the extraordinary provocations of the text, so a few examples must suffice. The 'Formulas' for restaurants are very often visual jokes in which the oddly assorted ingredients form an image: 'the results include a ski trip, A Fascist uniform, a woman's breasts, coitus, a tennis game and an unflushed lavatory bowl' (Chamerlain 2014: 251). The 'Definitive Futurist Dinners' draw on dishes served at previous futurist events and new inventions 'to evoke and provoke essential states of mind which cannot otherwise be evoked or provoked' (Marinetti 2014: 136). The first is a 'heroic winter dinner' whereby a group of soldiers 'who at three o'clock on a January afternoon will have to get into a lorry to enter the line of fire at four' can be put into an appropriate frame of mind. They are to be served with a DRUM ROLL OF COLONIAL FISH (poached mullet marinated in milk, liqueur, capers and red pepper then stuffed with date jam, bananas and pineapple): 'It will then be eaten to a continuous rolling of drums' (137). RAW MEAT TORN BY TRUMPET BLASTS consist of cubes of beef passed through by an electric current, marinated in a mixture of alcohols and served on a bed of red and black pepper and snow. 'Each mouthful is to be chewed carefully for one minute, and each mouthful is divided from the next by vehement blasts on the trumpet blown by the eater himself' (137). While a dessert of red-juiced fruits is served the room is sprayed with sweet and heavy perfumes 'the nostalgia and decadent sweetness of which will be roughly rejected by the soldiers who rush like lightening to put their gas masks on' (138). Simultaneously artistic 'happening' and serious attempt to create a culinary language and representation of warfare this is nowhere near to a recipe for a reproducible occasion, even if one had the battle-ready soldiers to hand. The choreographed responses of the participants in many of these dinners offer the reader the choice of seeing them as either scripts for artistic events or as passages from unwritten novels (the 'dynamic dinner', in which the other guests appear to murder the despised doctor mid-meal is in fact a passage from Marinetti's novel *The Steel Alcove*): any reader who set out to reproduce them would be the butt, rather than the perpetrator of the joke. Many of the dinners are extremely funny: the 'tactile dinner party', for instance, in which the guests are to dress in their choice of pyjamas, 'carefully prepared' by the host 'with the help of the Futurist painters Depero, Balla, Prampolini and Diulgheroff'; each pair of pyjamas 'is made of or covered with a different tactile material such as sponge, cork, sandpaper, felt, aluminium sheeting, bristles, steel wool, cardboard, silk, velvet, etc.' (170). Having donned their selected pyjamas in the dark each guest chooses a dining partner 'according to his tactile inspiration'. They are then led into the dining room and seated at a table with the partner of their choice, when, after a pause for surprise at the partners thus selected they are served with 'Polyrhythmic Salad', 'Magic Food' and 'Tactile Vegetable Garden'. 'Between one dish and the next', the instructions end, 'the guests must let their fingertips feast uninterruptedly on their neighbour's pyjamas' (171).

Marinetti's love of a practical joke might well be said to dilute the effectiveness of his text for polemical purposes, placing it more in the category of the great jest-provocations of contemporary avant-garde art – Duchamp's urinal, for example. Its many and florid castigations of pasta attracted the attention of the press but had no noticeable effect on Italian culinary practices. But where the text is deeply serious is in its deployment of food as a central element of an experimental aesthetics. This provocative act of taking food seriously it shares with the work of another experimental food writer: M. F. K. Fisher. The most celebrated of modern American food writers, Fisher wrote not conventional cookbooks, but curiously hybrid texts combining memoir, lyrical evocations of meals and places, food history, anecdote and philosophical meditations about the cultural place of food and eating. The recipes with which she occasionally lards her meandering discourse function more as curiosities than instructions. Her first book *Serve It Forth* (1937) establishes her method, covering in twenty-five brief chapters such diverse subjects as changing food tastes throughout a lifetime, Ancient Greek culinary customs, historical cookbooks, potatoes, secret food, the Ancient Roman vomitorium, slugs and snails, the pleasures of eating alone, the rival food cultures of Cane and Abel, food memories of the years she spent in Dijon with her first husband, food in England in the Middle Ages, the Elizabethan period, the cooks of Catherine the Great, post-revolutionary French cooking, bad food, favourite foods, and anecdotes that meld into short stories about waiters and butchers and eaters she has known. It is experimental in its collage-like structure: it is as if at least three separate books – a food history, a memoir and a *belle-lettrist* meditation on gourmandism – have been cut up and randomly interpolated. It is also stylistically experimental: at one point deploying a stream-of-consciousness meditation, at another the deft interweaving of evidence and judgement of the historian.[9] W. H. Auden declared of her writing that 'I do not know of anyone in the United States today who writes better prose' (1991: xii). One example will serve here as a summary of her approach: she begins 'Fifty Million Snails' with an assertion of her gastronomic hardiness – 'I have eaten several strange things since I was twelve, and I shall be glad to taste broiled locusts and swallow a live fish' (Fisher 1991: 34). Such assertions establish a tone of determinedly tough-minded masculinity of spirit – Fisher's work, like that of her English equivalent Elizabeth David, eschews all feminine associations in its approach, having much more in common with the masculine food-writing traditions of the gourmet-traveller than the conventional cookbook. Then in mid-thought she segues from boasting to horror: 'But unless I change very much, I shall never be able to eat a slug: 'Slugs', she asserts, with aphoristic intensity, 'are things from the edges of insanity' (34). This byway into the horror and disgust which lurk on the boundaries of our sense of the eatable takes her circuitously to the subject of snails: 'But I like snails. Most people like snails.' The slug sidestep is all the acknowledgement she allows to the vast majority of her American readers who are extremely unlikely to love snails or to see them as very different from slugs. This refusal to concede to the timidity of American eating tastes is in itself enough to mark her work as somewhat radical – and the soul-deadening lack of gusto in the food habits of her native land is a theme to which she returns repeatedly. But she is not talking about them here – she is talking about the French, who 'eat some fifty million every year'. The essay proceeds via a contemplation of the beauty of snails on bush and on plate, 'shell full of hot green butter like a magic cup', to an anecdote about the family with whom she lodged in France, the grandchildren, trained as gourmets and whipped up to a frenzy of delight about the annual snail hunt. The careful assessment of the exactly right moment to harvest the snails, the starving of them over days in the courtyard, the parboilings and scrubbing of the shells, the moment when 'the cadavers were tucked into their coffins again and Papazi and Madame Rigagnier made an extra trip to market for the parsley, the garlic, and the sweet butter' (36–7) are all meticulously recorded. The high seriousness of the whole process is used to demonstrate the workings of a culture in which the gathering and preparation and eating of food are part of a virtuous circle; the implicit comparison with America is made in the anecdote with which Fisher follows this first lyrical account of how differently these things are done in France. She had heard last month that a woman in her town was raising snails and had contracted to sell them to restaurants at a very high price. Going away for a weekend she leaves the snails in the charge of a friend of Fisher's who has read an article about snail culture in a magazine and proceeds to feed the snails with cornmeal until they burst, leaving the restaurants proposing to sue. The bucolic wisdom of the French snail hunt is replaced by the commercial enterprise, inflated costs, pretension and ignorance. Fisher ends the article with a postscript in which she quotes a letter from writer Dillwyn Parrish, her neighbour in California and soon to become her second husband. Parrish's anecdote about snails describes, in the blistering heat of summer in Provence, seeing peasants harvesting grapes: "'They were as brown as wood. Even the children looked old'":

> The incredible sun was in the middle of the sky. The workers in the vineyards stopped to rest and eat. They burned a stretch of grass at the edge of the vineyards along the road-side, and from the blackened ashes gathered in their hats the snails that had been roasted in the flames. Into cups, carried at their belts, they squeezed with their two hands the juice of half-rotted grapes. It tasted much like wine; it was not wasting the good grapes.
>
> Roasted snails! Raw wine!
>
> I noticed that they crossed themselves before eating, gratefully. (38–9)

Like Marinetti (whose work Fisher commented on with interest and some wry amusement), she constructs her text as a collage, layering letters and reported conversations with her own words. What Parrish's interpolated text adds to the preceding account is a powerful sense of the snail as part of an ancient peasant culture: these snails could not even be said to be gathered or cooked: they are roasted where they graze, an idea both admirably ingenious and disturbingly barbaric. The uncleaned snails and the rotted grape juice speak of the exhausted barely subsistence level of the grape-pickers' existence; their crossing themselves suggests a redeeming dignity and grace in their lives, making this meal cultural, even sacramental.

The experiments in food writing of Marinetti and Fisher I am denoting as modernist for (variously) their cut-up techniques, their generic disjointedness, their intense focus on the subjective experience and their aesthetic provocations. But there are also more general tendencies in the food writing of the interwar years which might be argued to be consonant with modernism. A number of cookbooks published in the years after the First World War share many of the formal qualities of modernist writing, eschewing traditional structures in favour of looseness, condensation and subjectivity. Historical practices and dishes are rejected or broken down and re-formed, while – in parallel to the intertextuality of modernist writing – culinary craft and skill is increasingly foregrounded, with the kitchen rediscovered as a creative space. The new food literature was absolutely antithetical to that of the nineteenth century: the monumental, encyclopaedic cookbooks of Acton, Beeton, Soyer and Escoffier are replaced by a hybrid genre of books which combined recipes and menus with essays, memoirs, social commentary, humour and artless chat. These were slim, elegant books, often expensively produced on handmade paper with lively, idiosyncratic illustrations. Most of their authors were fashionable society hostesses: women such as Agnes, Lady Jekyll (sister-in-law of the garden designer, Gertrude); Ruth Lowinsky (heiress to a South African diamond fortune and married to surrealist painter Thomas); and Dorothy Allhusen (cousin of the Mitford sisters).

The structural form of the nineteenth-century cookbook was based on that of a formal dinner, so that after prefatory material the first chapter was for soups, followed by fish, then meats, then vegetables, then puddings. Dinner was very much privileged, with foods for subsidiary meals such as breakfast and tea appearing towards the end. Foods specifically for luncheon were often not detailed at all: for much of the century it was regarded as a snack meal taken mainly by women and children. In the cookbooks of the 1920s and '30s all this is changed. Just as modernist fiction reorders the conventions of nineteenth-century realism, so writers such as Ruth Lowinsky and Agnes Jekyll break apart the formal conventions of the cookbook. Jekyll's *Kitchen Essays* of 1922 replaces the course-by-course arrangement with a series of loose, discursive essays on different aspects of contemporary food culture: 'Of good taste in food', 'Children's bread', 'Thoughts of Venice from home', 'Some breakfast-time suggestions', 'A little dinner before the play', 'Bachelors entertaining'. These are often remarkably specific – 'Luncheon for a motor excursion in winter', 'Food for artists and speakers', 'Their first dinner party', 'Cottage hospitality' – and taken together signal a focus on pleasure (travel, entertainment, indulgence) and on new forms of domestic life (men living alone, upper-middle-class people living in reduced circumstances, doing without servants). Dinners are casualized, reduced in form and in importance, often specifically designated as 'little'; luncheon is now a public meal, often more elegant than dinner because newer and more amenable to modern re-creation. Increased prominence is given to informal meals: to picnics, suppers and food for 'motor excursions' and train journeys. Lowinsky's *Lovely Food* of 1931 is arranged as a series of discursive menus for different social situations with brief recipes. Each is accompanied by one of a series of surrealist designs for table decorations 'invented and drawn' by Thomas Lowinsky and including such fantasies as 'two dead branches, one painted red, the other white to resemble coral, in an accumulator jar' and 'a bouquet of ostrich feathers in a trumpet shaped sheath of paper sunk into a painted cube of cardboard or wood' (1931: i). The menus are determinedly tongue-in-cheek: menu 1 is 'Chosen to create a favourable impression on a father-in-law, who comes prepared to judge you as either the laziest housekeeper in Europe, or the most extravagant, or even a subtle combination of the two' (8), while menu 2 is

> a slightly more pompous dinner for about ten people, none of whom have met before, and who are neither young nor amusing. They think they know all about food, but actually know only what they like. Therefore the cocktails and the wine, champagne if possible, are chosen for their mellowing effect. It is well to start with a cold *hors d'oeuvre*, as several of these guests may be late. (12)

The dominant mode is subjective: experiences are not generalized and shared but specific and personalized. Each social situation, each guest, each meal is so different that it requires a new set of rules and procedures. So Lowinsky offers 'A lunch for men of some importance in the City, who like rather substantial food but are tired of cuts from the joint' (49) and 'a maigre dinner – so much harder to think of than a lunch – for a cardinal, who is down in his hostess's book as very greedy, without further comment' (44) while Jekyll instructs her readers to 'turn your thoughts to a tropical week-end in July or August, when you might expect a jaded cabinet Minister or a depressed financier, a critic from the Foreign Office or an epicure from the Guards Club' (7). The voices of these books are highly subjective also: Jekyll's *distrait* and abstracted, with an air of a hostess languidly wandering in from the garden; Lowinsky's more urban and sophisticated: sharp and knowing, with some daringly louche asides, as in the menu she introduces by musing 'supposing your husband has gone to America on business, this might be the first of a series of little dinners with a chosen friend' (32).

Modern / Modernist food culture

I have suggested that a significant group of cookbooks from the 1920s onwards share stylistic features and experimental forms that make it reasonable to denote them as modernist. The final part of my case for the notion of modernist food rests on a key set of food tropes shared between these cookbooks and modernist literary texts or dominant in modernist aesthetics. Most importantly these include: an interest in international food, in demotic food, in technological food, in a re-ordering of the senses, and in a re-imagining of the kitchen.

One of the most striking aspects of the new food culture is its international focus. Although British food culture had incorporated the food of other nations for at least a thousand years, the process had been largely one of assimilation. What is new in the cookbooks of the years after the First World War is the intensity of interest in the specificity of the food of other nations and its connection to cultural identities. Food writers bed their recipes and descriptions in personal experience of other food cultures, and the tropes of travel writing become a part of the language of the cookbook. Alice Martineau begins *Caviare to Candy* (which is subtitled *Recipes for Small Households from All Parts of the World*) with a lyrical account of her food-travels:

> I have tasted the pearl-grey caviare of Roumania, and the exquisite wild strawberries of Norway, the sardines of the Cote Emeraude, the peasant dishes of the Basques, of Denmark, Greece, Spain, Italy, Paris, Normandy, Provence, California, Chile, Canada, Peru, Brazil, Cuba, Argentina. (1933: 1)

The self-styled Countess Morphy, author of the encyclopaedic *Recipes of All Nations* (1935), ranges even further afield, with individual chapters on many European countries, two on the United States, chapters on India, China and Japan; and a large section on 'Dishes from Many Lands' which includes the Balkans, Arabia, Persia, South America, Morocco, and a chapter on Africa notable for containing the first sub-Saharan recipes known to have been published by a major English language publisher.[10] Sisters-in-law Rachel and Margaret Ryan in their *Dinners for Beginners* (1934) offer at the end of their book a 'Special Recipe in tardy repentance for the lack of exotic novelties in this book' for a 'genuine East African dish' of sun-dried locusts (described in their introduction as 'a portmanteau meal, the chief ingredients having themselves devoured all other food available in the district') (1936: 292; 13). Just as literary modernism is an essentially international movement, so the food culture of this moment transcends national boundaries, with writers frequently relocated, translating their native foods for new national audiences or writing back to their homelands: so X. Marcel Boulestin offers the bourgeois and peasant foods of France for 'English Homes'; Countess Morphy, native of New Orleans, settled in Britain, dedicates a whole chapter of her book on world cooking to the Creole food of her home city; and Alice B. Toklas explains French food to British and American audiences and American food to the British. The same curiosity about the food cultures and eating habits of other nations, and the sense of food as a constitutive element of national identity feature in many works of modernist literature. In *Jacob's Room*, Sandra Wentworth Williams orders quails and goat and caramel custard in Greece while thinking about the peasants and fancying herself part of the tragedy of the country (Woolf 1999: 195–6); in *A Portrait of the Artist*, Stephen is given a recipe for *risotto alla bergamasca* by an Italian fellow student with whom he had argued about heresy and then remembers 'that his countrymen and not mine had invented … our religion' (Joyce 2000: 271). Joyce, writing back to Ireland from Europe, specifies his Dublin through its food as well as its streets: white puddings for breakfast, and Wicklow bacon in *A Portrait of the Artist*, barmbracks in the short story 'Clay' from *Dubliners* (1914). In Mansfield's 'Germans at Meat', the first story from her early collection, *In a German Pension* (1911), the Germans are characterized by their gross, guttural appetites. In a story palpitating with fear and loathing the English female narrator is mocked by her fellow German guests at a spa resort for the excesses of English food culture as they understand it, while they consume monstrous quantities of food, clean their ears out with their dinner napkins and attempt to offer intimate details of their experiences of sex, child-bearing and defecation. Their monstrosity verges at least symbolically on cannibalism, in the anecdote one woman tells of a friend who 'had four children at the same time. Her husband was so pleased he had a supper-party and had them placed on the table' (Mansfield 1981: 685). Their food is as grossly physical as their table manners: sauerkraut (though the Traveller from North Germany remarks that he has eaten so much that he can 'no longer retain it') and black bread on which they wipe their cutlery between courses. These Germans are already the enemy, their 'cold blue eyes' fixed upon her 'with an expression which suggested a thousand premeditated invasions' (684). We might contrast Mansfield's account of German food culture with that of Dorothy Richardson, whose *Pointed Roofs* (1915), the first volume of her thirteen-volume *Pilgrimage* sequence of novels, is set in the early 1890s at a German boarding school where the young English Miriam goes to teach. The first night at the school she takes refuge from shyness in the food:

Miriam safely ignored, scarcely heeding, but warmed and almost happy, basked. She munched her black bread and butter, liberally smeared with the rich savoury paste of liver sausage, and drank her sweet weak tea and knew that she was very tired, sleepy and tired. (Richardson 1967: 37)

The food is depicted as plentiful and delicious rather than strange and grotesque: the 'regular succession of rich and savoury meals' (83) at the school, the hot chocolate at a café above a 'Delikatessen': 'At the first sip, taken with lips that slid helplessly on the surprisingly thick rim of her cup Miriam renounced all the beverages she had ever known as unworthy' (89).

Richardson's novel, the first to have deployed a 'stream of consciousness' technique, raises another modern food trope: a new understanding of the kitchen. The reader is placed in the novel in the midst of Miriam's cultural bemusement, and shares her gradual understanding, as her language skills improve, of the fundamental differences between England and Germany. Chief among these is the different education supplied to girls, and the consequent different relationship to the kitchen: 'All could cook. Minna had startled her one day by exclaiming with lit face, "Ach, ich koche so *schrecklich gern!*" … Oh, I am so frightfully fond of cooking' (82). Both the cookbooks and the literary texts of this historical moment begin to envisage the kitchen as a place their readers and protagonists might start to inhabit. Only tentatively so – the kitchen is still a place of servants – but with a sense of excitement. As the numbers of servants start to thin, following the First World War (as discussed in Chapter 3), middle-class women needed to learn to cook. The cookbooks and magazines published in large numbers to help them to do so sell their fate to them as adventure, creativity, bohemianism, artistic experiment – anything but drudgery. The act of trespass on the kitchen is imagined as a radical act – a re-claiming of space. Labour is re-cast as play. In the opening lines of Quaglino's *The Complete Hostess* (1935) cooking is offered to a wider public than could afford to eat at the restaurant as an activity enjoyed by the upper classes: 'In England in the last twenty years the public has been taking more interest in food and cooking. It is not just only the Upper Four Hundred. Everybody is showing more keenness about it' (1935: 9). Mrs Leyel sells her *Gentle Art of Cookery* (1925) with the idea of transforming cooking into a sort of serious, mystical play: the ingredients' list at the end is tagged 'The Alchemist's Cupboard', she offers a chapter of 'Dishes from the Arabian Nights', and her chapter on 'Cooking for Children' foregrounds the notion of the kitchen as a playground with instructions for making an 'Ostrich Egg' from a pig's bladder and a dozen hen's eggs, and making strawberry jam turn white. The spirit of play is rendered distinctly avant-garde in Ruth Lowinsky's fantasy menu for 'a dream party of some of the most celebrated people of the day, whom one can never hope to meet, or, if met, be remembered by: Einstein, Mr. Charlie Chaplin, Freud, Virginia Woolf, Stella Benson, Mussolini, P. G. Wodehouse, Mistinguett, Lydia Lopokova and Jean Cocteau' (1931: 54–5): modern times indeed. In *Modernism and the Architecture of Private Life* (2005) Victoria Rosner begins her exemplary account of the changing role of interior space in modernist thinking with a chapter on 'Kitchen Table Modernism', exploring exactly this new sense of the kitchen as a space in which creativity could flourish. Many modernist characters appear in their kitchens. Bloom, for instance, preparing his kidney, and Belacqua, making his sandwich: in the description of the meticulous attention they bring to these tasks there is a new sense of freedom in the creative pleasures of the kitchen. For Woolf, in particular, the kitchen begins to open up new possibilities, as she cracks open the door to observe its functioning, offering the perspective of Lucy the housemaid as she prepares for Lady Brunton's luncheon while the cook worries about the salmon (1996: 181ff); watching the hands of the charlady washing up for Bonamy ('here all the scraps went swirling round the sink, scoured after by her purple, almost nailless hands') (1999: 138–9); and capturing the long years of work by Mrs McNab in maintaining the Ramsay's house (1992a: 177–92). There are significant ironies in Woolf's treatment of servants in her texts; in her life (as previously discussed), her relations with them veer dramatically between hostility and propitiation, and there is a sense of this too in the manner in which her texts attempt to represent the servants' perspective but also to see past them, as if what she really wants to see is the space of the kitchen itself, uninhabited. Her ambivalence is shared by the many cookbooks and household manuals which address the problem of the domestically unskilled middle-class woman.[11] Careful not to suggest that their readers may be permanently lacking servants, food writers couch their instructions in ambiguous terms: in *Kitchen Essays* Jekyll entitles a chapter 'In the

Cook's Absence', prefacing her recipes with nudging chat about 'busy holiday times of the year at which cooks, whose mothers so often specialise in sudden and disastrous illnesses, may leave us to face problems we have never really envisaged before' (1969: 10–11); Catherine Ives published a whole book for such occasions, tactfully titled *When the Cook Is Away*. At such moments, it is suggested, the reader (never, of course, imagined to be a servant herself) will be free to play. The frontispiece to Quaglino's *The Complete Hostess* captures the attitude perfectly: a modern woman, short skirted, wearing glasses, peers at a cookbook, wooden spoon held aloft, while on the floor beneath her kitchen table lie cutlery and cheese lost in her experiments. Standing disapprovingly behind her is a cook: a Victorian figure, long-skirted, voluminously aproned, and scowling protectively at the invasion of her kitchen. The modern woman's cooking is presented as play: she has a servant, but she has for the moment elbowed her aside. And yet the cook is a figure out of time, and whether by design or by an accident of failed perspective, she is not quite anchored to the floor: she appears to float, spectrally. Perhaps she is not really there at all.

The preoccupation with modern technological advances – with aeroplanes, speed, chrome – is another shared feature of many modernist art forms which finds its way also into many interwar cookbooks. Lady Jekyll suggests that the silver aeroplane cloth 'recently bought by so many when it glutted the market' (1969: 61) be used to make tablecloths and cutlery rolls for picnics, while Thomas Lowinsky's table decoration designs for *Lovely Food* are self-consciously modernist, deploying chromium-plated steel in the form of spirals, circle and blocks, and bizarre juxtapositions of found objects. The most pervasive interest in the creation of a technologically modernist food is to be found in Marinetti's *Futurist Cookbook*: devices are rigged up to cook electrically and in extreme situations (often in aeroplanes in flight); food experiments involve radios, telephones and gramophones; recipes include 'Car Crash', 'Losing a Wheel' and 'Hand Grenades'. As with all Marinetti's provocations these are partly jokes and partly not: the creations of 'aerofuturism' in particular are focussed on bringing a different scale to bear on the understanding of human experience. The excitement of the imagined meals in the clouds is being able to see the world spread out before you. It is a fantasy, above all, of power: in the 'aeropictorial dinner in the cockpit' the diners 'free five lobsters intact from their shells and boil them electrically in seawater'. The cruelty of this procedure is passed over unremarked until it is revisited in the ultimate fantasy of the experience: the lobsters are to be placed on a huge ceramic 'mattressed by twenty different kinds of salad' arranged in geometric squares: 'And so the diners, holding in their fists little ceramic bell-towers full of Barolo mixed with Asti Spumante, eat villages, farms and fields speeding by' (2014: 166). Eating, in Marinetti's polemical vision, becomes part of what he sees as a cleansing violence made possible by the power of the machine.

Marinetti's extremist food takes us to another modernist preoccupation: the reordering of the senses. A sort of figurative synesthesia operates in many modernist texts, in which the senses substitute for or stand in for each other.[12] In the case of modernist food narratives the exchange is particularly between taste and smell (though Marinetti also deploys touch, sight and hearing). Marinetti's meals frequently disrupt the 'bourgeois' enjoyment of the smells of cooked food by spraying perfumes at the diners as they eat: his concepts of 'conprufumo' (the olfactory affinities of the flavour of a food and a perfume) and 'disprofumo' (the complementary equivalent) are revealed as disruptive rather than harmonious in the definitional examples he gives: pulped potato and roses as affinities, raw meat and jasmine as complementaries. Flowers are not just to be experienced as scents: his famous recipe for 'Diabolical Roses' deep-fries them like artichokes, announcing them as 'ideal for newly-weds to eat at midnight in January' (222). Marinetti is not the only, or even the first, modern food writer to flirt with the eating of flowers. Mrs Leyel, who was by trade a herbalist (she was to found the Culpepper company in 1929), gave a chapter of Flower Recipes in her 1925 *Gentle Art of Cookery*. She places the idea of flowers as food in the context of Tudor and Classical culinary practices, but her recipes for a puree of dandelion, cowslip pudding, marmalade of violet and eggs cooked with marigold would not have been out of place in *The Futurist Cookbook*. M. F. K. Fisher also connects flower-eating with both the middle ages and with a startlingly modernist aesthetic which in her case approaches close to Marinetti's attitudes: 'What could be more ludicrously lovely than a tiny crackled piglet all garlanded with lilies and wild daffodils? Or a baked swan in its feathers, with roses on its proud reptilian head?' (Fisher 1991: 55). Flower-eating appears as a trope in a number of modernist literary texts: in *Jacob's Room* a young woman bets a young man at a formal dinner that he will not eat begonias with his fish (Woolf 1999: 76); in Mansfield's 'Carnation' (1924) a sophisticated girl seductively teases another on a boiling hot day in a French classroom, flirting with a carnation before pulling it slowly to pieces and eating it petal by petal (653); while in Lawrence's *Sons and Lovers* (1913) Paul Morel eats a flower while conveying to his mother that he will end his relationship with Miriam at her instigation, the action expressing a powerful, silent rage:

'On Sunday I break off', he said, smelling the pink. He put the flower in his mouth. Unthinking, he bared his teeth, closed them on the blossom slowly, and had a mouthful of petals. These he spat into the fire, kissed his mother, and went to bed. (1988: 359)

If modernist food culture is interested in these rarefied tastes and scents it is even more preoccupied with the smells, tastes and textures of the life of the streets. My final modernist food trope takes us into the territory of the ordinary and modernism's profound ambivalence about that state. Demotic food is everywhere in modernist literature. In *Mrs Dalloway* we see it in the description of the working-class Mrs Dempsey who views life animalistically as 'eating and drinking and mating' (Woolf 1996: 31); in *A Portrait of the Artist* in the tea-time in Stephen's increasingly impoverished family home, with 'small glass-jars and jampots which did service for teacups' (Joyce 2000: 176), his younger brothers and sisters sacrificed for his education; and in the watery tea and crusts of fried bread and yellow dripping 'scooped out like a boghole' he eats for breakfast (188). For T. S. Eliot the smells and sights of street food are an intrinsic part of the tapestry he is building for his 'vision of the street / as the street hardly understands' (1974: 24). The 'sawdust restaurants with oyster-shells' of 'Prufrock', 'the smell of steaks in passageways' of 'Preludes', and in *The Waste Land* 'the typist home at teatime [who] clears her breakfast, lights / Her stove, and lays out food in tins' (13; 23; 71): all of these images seek to understand the realities of the lives of ordinary people through their food, and all recoil in disgust. As many critics have noted, most notably John Carey in his *The Intellectuals and the Masses* (1992) modernist writers and thinkers are caught between a desire to represent the masses and a repulsion from them. It is a topic that will be explored in detail in the discussion of disgust in Chapter 8, but for the moment it is worth noting the elements that go to make up the modernist disgust at demotic food: the lingering smells, the public sight of eating (the 'damp cubes of pastry [that] fell into mouths opened like triangular bags' when Fanny Elmer has lunch at the Express Dairy Company in *Jacob's Room* (1999: 163)), and the detritus. This last appears in frequent scenes of un-cleared tables: the remains of the egg on Fanny's breakfast plate as she bemoans her unrequited love for Jacob (238), the lengthy description of the rooms used by mediums for their séances in 'The Good Anna', the first of Stein's *Three Lives*: the 'decorated woollen cloth, that has soaked in the grease of many dinners', the 'carpet grown dingy with the food that's fallen from the table', the 'all pervading smell' of soup 'made out of onions and fat chunks of meat' (1979: 54). The modernist celebration of bohemianism is forgotten in the profound distaste of the contemplation of how the other half eats. In this instance it might be argued that the writers of cookbooks are more radical. Not the socialites who author many of the cookbooks of the interwar years, but the authors of a curious duo of books: Naomi Jacob's *Me – In the Kitchen* of 1935 and Moira Meighn's *The Magic Ring for the Needy and Greedy* of 1936 which manage to out-bohemian most modernist literary writers. Novelist Jacob takes as her subject in her loose, discursive cookbook (which weaves her recipes in seamless undifferentiated form into the texture of her prose) her own eccentric diet, devoting a chapter to the infra-dig kipper and *épater le bourgeois* with her insistence that tea is better 'milk in first' (one of the key codes denoting those beyond the social pale). More shocking still was Meighn's curious book in praise of the single gas ring which addresses itself to 'educated women whom bitter necessity forces into doing their own housework' with none of the polite circumlocutions of virtually all other interwar cookbooks (1936: 28). Offering chapters of 'Suggestions for the Hard-Up' and 'Suggestions for the Servantless' she shares stories of her own experiences of life in a bed-sitting-room during the war with a young baby, waking in the night to fight rats and cooking for up to eight adults on picnic stoves. Most striking of all, given the pervasive disgust at detritus, is her suggestion that the servantless woman, when entertaining friends, should start the washing-up at the dinner table: 'Whilst slow-eating guests are chewing their last mouthfuls, the hostess can chat with such brilliancy that no one notices anything but her talk, while she wipes soiled silver and knives with a paper serviette, and puts them into a deep-mouthed jar' (29).

Modernist food culture is a matter of textual, culinary and gustatory experimentation, found equally in the representational and aesthetic reworkings of literary texts, in the provocations of generically hybrid food writers, and in the new food culture disseminated by the writers of fashionable and bohemian cookbooks. We find a similar interest in encroaching on the kitchen and in food as serious play in the children's literature which is the subject of the next chapter.

CHAPTER 6
FANTASIES OF FOOD IN CHILDREN'S LITERATURE

Food is obdurately, disproportionately present in children's literature. It has become a critical commonplace to argue that food functions in children's texts in much the same way that sex does in those for adults: producing bodily desires that operate on a level beyond a purely mental engagement with the world of the text, a source of imaginings and desires that take the reader from the page into his own body.[1] While fully accepting this model, my interest here is in exploring further ways in which children's texts engage with the visceral body through food, alongside the trope of desire. Looking at children's texts from the 1830s to the picture books of the contemporary moment, this chapter will examine the role of food as fantastic object, food-creation as play, and the curiously dominant fear of *being* food, arguing that food in children's literature figures anxiety, horror and fear as much as bodily desire and pleasure; and that its fantastic excesses, while inspiring salivatory anticipation, insist also on their own essentially textual, imaginary status.

Food as fantasy object

Food becomes an object of fantasy in many texts for children: unlimited food; hybrid food which transgresses polite codes of order and combination; magic, transformative food. Frequently it threatens to overflow its bounds: too much, too suggestive, speaking of anarchic, uncontainable drives and desires. An early example of this anxiety-provoking plenitude of food is to be found in Catherine Sinclair's *Holiday House* (1839), one of the first children's texts to depict children naturalistically, rather than as moral exemplars. Throughout the text the child protagonists are frequently immured in complexities of the social rituals around food, which they disrupt with anarchic good spirits. They gleefully issue unsanctioned invitations to tea to all the children of their acquaintance, and when their nursery maid refuses to allow them food they by default preside over an imaginary banquet; they create chaos on a picnic by rolling a large fruit cake down from the top of Arthur's Seat, sending all the children tumbling down after it. In a text which is almost entirely realist, one chapter stands out as different: 'Uncle David's Nonsensical Story about Giants and Fairies' involves a tale told to the children at their injunction – a moral tale 'about very bad boys', but one also involving 'giants and fairies' (Sinclair 1839: 130). Food looms large in this fantastic tale, in which a lazy boy, 'Master

No-book', wastes his lesson time dreaming of 'where he could get the nicest pies, pastry, ices and jellies' (131–2) and his leisure-time in whining for cake and plum-pudding. Out of the blue, as he sucks sugared oranges while lolling, odalisque-like, boots up on the best sofa, he is visited by two fairies, the gorgeously dressed Do-nothing and the book-toting Teach-all, who ask him to choose which of their palaces he will visit for a party. Naturally enough, he chooses the former, Castle Needless, where he enjoyed 'a constant holiday and a constant feast', dozing on embroidered cushions while 'admiring the view of trees covered with the richest burned almonds, grottoes of sugar-candy, a fountain of ginger-ale, [and] a wide sea which tasted of sugar instead of salt' (135–6). Excess soon palls, however, and he quickly reaches the point where he can scarcely move from the sofa. This makes him ideal prey for Fairy Do-nothing's neighbour, the giant Snap-'em-up, who she allows free range of her garden as his hunting preserve. The decadent fairy, who offers up her guests to be eaten simply in exchange for a fashionable social connection and invitations to dinner parties, is a determinedly modern take on the wicked witches and queens of fairy tale, with the inexplicable complexities of adult dining habits representing an excess beyond the child's simplistic sugar-coated food fantasies. Food in this story is excessive in quantity and amount but also in its multiple and conflicting significations and threats.

We find a similarly overdetermined depiction of food in Lewis Carroll's *Alice* books, in which it has power to transform, disorder and disturb. The intrusive power of food first emerges as Alice falls down the rabbit hole, her surprisingly leisurely descent allowing her time to pluck from a shelf a jar 'labelled ORANGE MARMALADE' which 'to her great disappointment' is empty (1968: 12).[2] The graphic form of the label is significant: the importance of the *form* of text has already been highlighted with Alice's earlier dissatisfaction with the book her sister is reading: '"what is the use of a book", thought Alice, "without pictures or conversation"' (11). The label's capitals intrude on the text we are reading, forcing an awareness of the marmalade jar as object, its powerful materiality underlined by the fact that Alice 'did not like to drop the jar for fear of killing somebody' (12). The food objects Alice first encounters in Wonderland – the little bottle and cake – are transformative, instantly and dramatically altering her size in a parodic re-enactment of the processes of childhood nourishment and growth. They are also crucially *textual* objects, with labels inviting their consumption. The drink from the bottle marked 'DRINK ME' is the only Wonderland foodstuff described in terms of flavour. When Alice ventures to taste the mixture, she finds it 'very nice': 'it had, in fact, a sort of mixed flavour of cherry-tart, custard, pineapple, roast turkey, toffee, and hot buttered toast' (17). A combination of sweet and savoury, fresh and caramelized flavour-notes, recalling the pleasures of celebratory meals, puddings, sweets and nursery teas, this 'mixed flavour' evokes primal food pleasures; the taste conjured up is fantastically desirable both because of its cornucopia-ed piling up of delights and because of the impossibility of effectively registering this combination of tastes in the imagination. This drink emblematizes that curiously over-determined nature of the food in children's literature: it is food made real through taste description, made fantastically desirable through its hybridity, made transgressive through

Figure 7 *The Mock Turtle from Lewis Carroll's* Alice in Wonderland *(1865).*

its heterogeneous combining of foods properly belonging to different orders of categorization, and made magical through the transformation it enacts. The obtrusive form of its label's capitalization foregrounds its status as a textual object, while the personal pronoun ('drink *me*') accords it an agency which aligns it with the many forms of living food which people the text.

Many later children's texts also employ the device of listing heterogeneous foods and flavours to offer fantasies of plenitude, indulgence, and enjoyable transgression. In the opening chapter of Kenneth Graham's *The Wind in the Willows* (1908), Mole discovers possibilities of pleasure beyond his provincial imaginings when Rat details the food he has packed for their boating picnic:

> 'There's cold chicken inside it,' replied the Rat briefly;
> 'coldtonguecoldhamcoldbeefpickledgerkinssaladfrenchrollscresssandwidgespotted
> meatgingerbeerlemonadesodawater -'
> 'O stop, stop,' cried the Mole in ecstasies: 'this is too much!' (1971: 13)[3]

The heterogeneous jumble of foods within the run-on word and within the hamper offers the delights of excess – more food than you need, though not more than you want. The relaxation of the rules of grammar echoes the relaxing of the social rules of dining: this is food that can be eaten in any order, or all at once, the constraints of the polite dinner table done away with as you lounge on the river bank. The wonders of the wizarding world are similarly heralded for Harry Potter when he encounters the sweet trolley on the train as he heads for his first term at Hogwarts: 'The woman didn't have Mars Bars. What she did have were Bertie Bott's Every-Flavour Beans, Drooble's Best Blowing Gum, Chocolate Frogs, Pumpkin Pasties, Cauldron Cakes, Liquorice Wands and a number of other strange things Harry had never seen in his life' (Rowling 1997: 76).[4] The list of sweets, odd, but sufficiently recognizable, acts as a conduit by which Harry and the reader can become acclimatized to the wonders of this new world. It is the Every-Flavour Beans which make it clear that the ordering and values of the wizarding world are fundamentally strange: '"You want to be careful with those", Ron warned Harry. "When they say every flavour, they *mean* every flavour – you know, you get all the ordinary ones like chocolate and peppermint and marmalade, but then you can get spinach and liver and tripe. George reckons he got a bogey-flavoured one once"' (78). The flavours in Ron's listing decline from ordinary to unusual to unlikeable to disgusting, affording the child reader the pleasures of repelled identification and transgressive delight. Harry's first experience of eating the beans yields a concatenation of contrasting tastes: 'Harry got toast, coconut, baked beans, strawberry, curry, grass, coffee, sardine and was even brave enough to nibble the end off a funny grey one that Ron wouldn't touch, which turned out to be pepper' (78). The disordered taxonomies of such flavour lists recall the much-cited opening of Foucault's *The Order of Things* (1966), in which he takes as an exemplar of 'the exotic charm of another system of thought' a passage from Borges quoting 'a certain Chinese encyclopaedia' in which animals are divided into impossible categorization ('(a) belonging to the Emperor, (b) embalmed, (c) sucking pigs, [...] (f) fabulous, [...] (h) included in the present classification [...] (k) drawn with a very fine camelhaired brush [...], (m) having just broken the water pitcher') in a list which confounds logic and challenges all our systems of thought (Foucault 2002: xvi). The jarring juxtapositions and combinations of flavours and their disruption of the rules of proper gustatory ordering open up a space for the fantastic within children's texts, in which other modes of being and thought are imagined through the exercise of sense memory. In Roald Dahl's *Charlie and the Chocolate Factory* (1964), the lists of rooms in the factory function in a similarly disruptive fashion: rendered in block capitals that at some points in the text occupy a whole page, these descriptions of curious culinary inventions telegraph the possibilities of new relations between children, adults and food ('EATABLE MARSHMALLOW PILLOWS', 'LICKABLE WALLPAPER FOR NURSERIES' (1995: 132)) and present science as a magical disruption of the natural ('COWS THAT GIVE CHOCOLATE MILK', 'TOFFEE-APPLE TREES FOR PLANTING OUT IN YOUR GARDEN' (133; 51)). They offer a world built of sugar – 'THE ROCK CANDY MINE – 10,000 FEET DEEP', 'FIZZY LEMONADE SWIMMING POOLS' (150–1), where indulgence has no consequences: 'CAVITY-FILLING CARAMELS – NO MORE DENTISTS' (151). The food fantasies constructed by these lists flirt with the sadistic ('EXPLODING SWEETS FOR YOUR ENEMIES', 'MINT JUJUBES FOR THE BOY NEXT DOOR – THEY'LL GIVE HIM GREEN TEETH FOR A MONTH' (151)) and the disgusting ('RAINBOW DROPS – SUCK THEM AND YOU CAN SPIT IN SIX DIFFERENT COLOURS' (151)). Other-worldly taxonomies conflate foods and non-foods: 'STOREROOM NUMBER 77 – ALL THE BEANS, CACAO BEANS, COFFEE BEANS, JELLY BEANS, AND HAS BEANS' (112) and fantastic realities are built on linguistic puns: 'SQUARE SWEETS THAT LOOK ROUND' (134). The food in the factory is transgressive, disruptive and excessive, the shouting exuberance of its typographic representation insisting always on its essentially imaginative, textual state.

It is notable how often these fantastic foods in children's texts are not exactly foods at all: Alice's mixture is a drink, Bertie Bott's Beans merely taste of the foods they evoke. Dahl takes such fantasy food to its limit in the chewing-gum meal which replaces real food with the *sensation* of eating: 'You can actually feel the food going down your throat and into your tummy! And you can taste it perfectly! And it fills you up! It satisfies you! It's terrific!' (122). Violet Beauregarde's excited account of her experiences as she chews the gum – 'It's hot and creamy and delicious! I can feel it running down my throat'; 'It's as though I'm chewing and swallowing great big spoonfuls of the most marvellous blueberry pie in the world!' (122–3) – privileges the pleasures of mastication, of the mouth-feel of food, but in reality, all that is in her mouth is a small stick of gum. *Actual* eating has been replaced by an ersatz facsimile of the experience. This is not really food, but something that pretends to be. The fantasy in children's texts is often as much about *not* having to eat (boring, nourishing foods) as it is about unlimited quantities of indulgent treats. Dahl's text is deeply punitive in its engagement with the child's desire for sweetness, seducing its child reader with visions of chocolate waterfalls and everlasting gobstoppers but promising terrible punishments for indulgence. Greed is only allowable in those who have literally been starved: the text's most sympathetic description of the pleasures of eating is not the exotic tastes to be found in Wonka's factory, but Charlie's experience of cramming a chocolate bar into his mouth when desperately hungry: 'Charlie [...] took an enormous bite. Then he took another ... and another ... and oh, the joy of being able to cram large pieces of something sweet and solid into one's mouth! The sheer blissful joy of being able to fill one's mouth with rich solid food!' (62). Because Charlie is starving, the chocolate counts as food, unlike the rest of the sweets in the text, which exist in a curious hinterland between fantasy and threat.

The bodily experiences of eating, as opposed to the more rarefied sensations of tasting, are represented surprisingly infrequently in literary texts from the mid-eighteenth century onwards. Children's literature is a key exception, often dwelling with some intensity on the sensations of biting, chewing and swallowing and not shying away from the associated phenomena of digestion. It is because in mastication food becomes mixed with our bodily fluids and starts to denature that we tend to find it disgusting. But, as will be discussed in Chapter 8, children's texts often welcome disgust, presenting it as a weapon that children can take pleasure in wielding against squeamish adults. The chocolate river in *Charlie and the Chocolate Factory* flips from delightful to disgusting at the moment when it is associated with human bodily fluids. Augustus Gloop, the fat boy (already rendered disgusting in textual and visual representation), contaminates the chocolate:

> Augustus was deaf to everything except the call of his enormous stomach. He was now lying full length on the ground with his head far out over the river, lapping up the chocolate like a dog.
>
> 'Augustus!' shouted Mrs Gloop. 'You'll be giving that nasty cold of yours to about a million people all over the country!' (97)

If the image of Augustus's body and his animalistic lapping are not repellent enough, we have the added component of disease. When Augustus falls into the river he himself becomes a contaminant, and his presence in the system causes us to see the bucolic-scientific scene very differently. He is sucked towards one of the huge glass pipes which conveys the molten chocolate from the river into the heart of the factory: 'The watchers below could see the chocolate swishing around the boy in the pipe, and they could see it building up behind him in a solid mass, pushing against the blockage' (99). Augustus's presence transforms the image of the flowing brown liquid from delightfully molten chocolate into something more like sewage or – even more disgustingly – renders the boy as a rectal blockage in the digestive system.[5] Yet in the next chapter, when the remaining children travel along the river in a boat hollowed out from a giant pink boiled sweet, the chocolate river has become delightful once more. Mr Wonka, realizing that both Charlie and his Grandpa Joe are half-starved, dips mugs into the river and offers them the chocolate to drink: 'Charlie put the mug to his lips, and as the rich warm creamy chocolate ran down his throat into his empty tummy, his whole body from head to toe began to tingle with pleasure, and a feeling of intense happiness spread over him' (109). As noted earlier, the expression of such intense, near-orgasmic bodily pleasure in the experience of eating is much more commonly found in children's than in adult literature. A similar description occurs in Diana Wynne Jones's *A Tale of Time City* (1987), in which evacuee Vivian Smith is transported from a railway station in 1939 to Time City, a place located outside of time, from which time-travelling Observers travel to all the Known Eras. Much like Harry Potter, Vivian first comes to know her mysterious new world through its food. The conversation in which the children who have mistakenly abducted her explain the nature of the city is punctuated by accounts of her experience of eating a

'Forty-Two Century butter-pie': 'She would have objected if she had not at that moment bitten into the butter-pie. Wonderful tastes filled her mouth, everything buttery and creamy she had ever tasted, with just a hint of toffee, and twenty other even better tastes she has never met before, all of it icy cold' (Wynne Jones 1987: 24). The physical delights of the eating experience stretch over several pages, culminating in the moment in which 'she bit through to the middle of the butter-pie. And it was hot. Runny, syrupy hot':

> 'It's *goluptous* when you get to the warm part, isn't it?', Sam said, watching her with keen attention. 'You want to let it trickle into the cold.'
> Vivian did so and found Sam's advice was excellent. The two parts mixed were even better than the cold part alone. It sent her rather dreamy again. (26)

Sam is characterized by a naked greed which is legitimated by his being younger than Vivian: her own gustatory pleasure, like that of Charlie and Harry, is rendered acceptable because of her previous experience of lack of food. Nonetheless, there is something intensely sensual about her encounter with the butter pie: a lingering focus on mouth sensations, her dreamy, drifting pleasure. In such intense representations of eating as source of both pleasure and disgust, children's texts accord food a transcendent power. Sam's onomatopoeic adjective is a compound which conveys both pleasure and the fantastic in one construct: the food is so intensely delicious that this new world has new words to describe its sensations. The transformative, hybrid, desirable and disgusting foods of children's fantasy foreground bodily sensations yet draw attention always to their own status as imaginative, essentially textual constructs.

Food as play

Another aspect of food which has an overdetermined presence in children's literature is cooking. In both realist and fantastic texts, scenes of food preparation occur unusually often when compared to literature for adults. From Jo's failed dinner party in *Little Women* with its unripe strawberries, curdled blancmange and rock-hard lobster to Pippi Longstocking's ginger-snap dough rolled out on the kitchen floor (Lindgren 2003: 21), scenes of food preparation are richly significatory moments in many children's texts. In the nineteenth and early twentieth centuries scenes of children – girls – cooking are a particularly iconic feature of North American children's literature. In a culture that strongly valorized notions of self-sufficiency, culinary skills were seen as a crucial element of a child's education. Cooking understood as essential skill and familial duty is seen most clearly in Laura Ingalls Wilder's *Little House* series, her thinly disguised autobiographical account of her late nineteenth-century pioneer childhood. Wilder's books are driven by remembered hunger, demonstrated most clearly by the extraordinary quantities of food described in the third book in the series, *Farmer Boy* (1933), which depicts not her own childhood but that of her husband, growing up on a prosperous farm, where the child Almanzo is invariably depicted stuffing himself from a board groaning with meat and dairy products.

The pleasure in these passages stems not so much from his memories of culinary plenitude as from her memories of hunger. It is hunger that animates the descriptions of the rare treats her parents manage to provide – the little white heart-shaped cakes, one each in their Christmas stockings, shine with more than simply powdered sugar: they speak of the indulgence and specialness of baked goods made with refined sugar and flour, of the parental love that affords these rare luxuries in the midst of penury. In every book the reader is given extended descriptions of the cooking, baking and preserving undertaken by Ma and the girls, who make cheese and pickles, bread and pies, with the children helping with the simpler tasks and learning by watching.[6] The most memorable passages, though, certainly for a child reader, are those where the children get to cook alone – particularly when they make treats: the molasses on snow candy of *Little House in the Big Woods* (1932), the popcorn in *These Happy Golden Years* (1943). The former scene is accompanied by an illustration in the text, showing the child Laura pouring the hot syrup, her tongue protruding from her mouth indicating both care and anticipatory pleasure:

> Ma was busy all day long, cooking good things for Christmas …. One morning she boiled molasses and sugar together until they made a thick syrup, and Pa brought in two pans of clean, white snow from outdoors. Laura and Mary each had a pan, and Pa and Ma showed them how to pour the dark syrup in little streams on to the snow.
>
> They made circles, and curlicues, and squiggedly things, and these hardened at once and were candy. Laura and Mary might eat one piece each, but the rest were saved for Christmas Day. (Wilder 2014: 204)

The pleasure conveyed by this description lies in our knowledge of how rarely the children have sugar, let alone sweets, but mainly in the agency they experience in creating their own treats, and particularly in the verb which renders the act of creation – 'they hardened [...] and *were* candy' – as imbued with profound power and mystery. Despite the fact that culinary skills are an important element of the education of girls, the food that is cooked by children in the American children's texts of this period falls almost invariably into the treat or luxury category, with candy, cakes, biscuits and grand dinners most commonly created. What this suggests is that these scenes of cooking do not straightforwardly fit within a lexicon of educative moments but are much closer to fantasy or to play. In Louisa M. Alcott's *An Old-Fashioned Girl* (1870), simple rural Polly is counterpointed to the sharp sophisticated girls who are the usual social companions of the wealthy Shaw family. Polly wins the heart of the Shaw son, Tom, when he trespasses on the kitchen and finds her giving lessons in cake baking. Allowed into the hallowed, all-female space and invited to beat the cake mixture, he compares himself in imagination to 'Hercules with the distaff' and finds his employment 'pleasant, if not classical' (1870: 276). Polly's skills as a baker, and the warm welcoming environment she creates in the kitchen, mark her out as precisely the wife Tom needs, but it is notable that it is the pleasures of *baking* rather than *eating* cake that is the means to his heart: an experience, significantly, that becomes both textual and mythic in his tongue-in-cheek retelling. In L. M. Montgomery's

Anne of Green Gables series (1908 onwards), the baking of cake plays a repeated and important part in establishing the life of the rural community of Avonlea and the travails of passionate, imaginative orphan Anne as she tries to fit in. In the opening chapter, a neighbour surveys the prepared tea-table in Marilla Cuthbert's house, assessing that company must be expected but because of the everyday china, crab-apple preserves and only one sort of cake 'it could not be any particular company' (1977: 10). Cakes in the novels are an essential part of social relations, carefully graded in number, complexity and luxuriousness so that everyone knows their place. Later in the first novel Anne begs to be allowed to bake a cake in honour of the new minister and his wife. She feels the pressure of the occasion deeply, as she confesses to her bosom friend Diana:

It's such a responsibility having a minister's family to tea. I never went through such an experience before ... We're to have two kinds of jelly, red and yellow, and three kinds of cookies, and fruit cake, and Marilla's famous yellow-plum preserves that she keeps especially for ministers, and pound cake and layer cake, and biscuits as aforesaid ... I just grow cold when I think of my layer cake. Oh, Diana, what if it shouldn't be good! I dreamed last night that I was chased all round by a fearful goblin with a big layer cake for a head. (145)

In her melodramatic imaginings Anne recognizes the seriousness of her baking task as an element in establishing her new family's social status, but her dream of the goblin-cake transforms the practical task into the stuff of fantasy. Anne's cake rises beautifully, 'it came out of the oven as light and feathery as golden foam' (146), but her triumph is short-lived: 'Mrs Allan took a mouthful of hers and a most peculiar expression crossed her face; not a word did she say, however, but steadily ate away at it' (147). Anne has flavoured the cake with anodyne liniment instead of vanilla, unable to smell the difference because of a cold. For Anne the mix-up is a source of deep shame, but for the child reader there is much enjoyment to be had in the spectacle of the stuffy guest forced to eat the uneatable under the weight of unbendable etiquette. The seriousness with which cake is taken in this text is in itself comic: the abiding assumption of the world of Avonlea is that a girl should, by the age of eleven, be already a skilled cake-maker and that much social cachet rests on her abilities.

The readerly appeal of the extended episode of the liniment cake is finely balanced between vicarious enjoyment of Anne's domestic prowess and a deep pleasure in her failure. Scenes of calamitous cooking are among the most enjoyable and memorable in children's texts – and they are many. The failed smart dinner in *Little Women*, mentioned earlier, comes in the chapter 'Experiments', where Marmee decides to allow the girls to make their own mistakes. Knowing even less about cooking than her elder sister Meg, who has already managed to burn the breakfast, Jo nonetheless invites guests to a grand dinner: 'There's corned beef and plenty of potatoes; and I shall get some asparagus, and a lobster, "for a relish," as Hannah says. We'll have lettuce, and make a salad. I don't know how, but the book tells. I'll have blancmange and strawberries for dessert; and coffee, too, if you want to be elegant' (Alcott 1953: 148). The resultant cooking 'experiment' is dwelt on in intense detail, with Jo making every possible mistake in purchasing, preparing and cooking this food:

> Language cannot describe the anxieties, experiences, and exertions which Jo underwent that morning; and the dinner she served up became a standing joke. [...] She boiled the asparagus for an hour, and was grieved to find the heads cooked off and the stalks harder than ever. The bread burnt black, for the salad-dressing so aggravated her that she let everything go till she had convinced herself that she could not make it fit to eat. The lobster was a scarlet mystery to her, but she hammered and poked it till it was unshelled, and its meagre proportions concealed in a grove of lettuce leaves. The potatoes had to be hurried, not to keep the asparagus waiting, and were not done at last. The blancmange was lumpy, and the strawberries not as ripe as they looked, having been skilfully 'deaconed'. (151)

The meal itself fully confirms Jo's dark forebodings, with her wealthy friend Laurie and their critical, gossiping neighbour subjected to course after course of undercooked, overcooked and burnt food. The one grace note of the strawberries and cream elicits wry faces and puckered lips from the guests because she has used "'salt instead of sugar, and the cream is sour'" (152). On the verge of crying, Jo instead sees the funny side and 'the unfortunate dinner ended gaily, with bread and butter, olives, and fun' (154). In this notoriously double text, the official 'message' – the one that Marmee, in her staging of just such an outcome, intends – is that you should not be puffed up, should not hanker after elegance or ape empty upper-class forms; and you should not run before you can walk.[7] But the textual *pleasure* is in the lingered-over failure. It is reminiscent of those scenes of other young people failing at entertaining in *David Copperfield*: the readerly enjoyment in such scenes is partly *schadenfreude*, but partly something else. The terms in which Meg had warned Jo against the whole culinary enterprise are significant: "'Don't try too many messes, Jo, for you can't make anything but gingerbread and molasses candy fit to eat'" (148). 'Messes' in the primary sense Meg means it refers to what the English of the same date would call a 'made dish' – a mixture of ingredients cooked or eaten together, but its secondary meaning takes over almost immediately, and it is here that much of the textual pleasure of such scenes lie: in the idea of making a mess, of cooking as play.

While there are fewer accounts of children *learning* to cook in British texts of the same period (a result of the much stronger social constraints against middle-class females being seen to perform domestic tasks), there are many instances in which the labour of cooking is transformed into exuberant and anarchic play for children of both sexes. Cooking happens behind the backs of parents and servants, or on occasions of allowed disrule – on camping trips, picnics, or in the context of fantastic adventures. In E. Nesbit's *The Phoenix and the Carpet* (1904), the children return unexpectedly to the house when their parents are away and servants out. They set about making their own tea in a passage which revels in the unexpected freedoms to raid the larder, combine foods haphazardly and to break the rules:

While Anthea was delighting the poor little black-beetles with the cheerful blaze, Jane had set the table for – I was going to say tea, but the meal of which I am speaking was not exactly tea. Let us call it a tea-ish meal. There was tea, certainly, for Anthea's fire blazed and crackled so kindly that it really seemed to be affectionately inviting the kettle to come and sit upon its lap. So the kettle was brought and tea made. But no milk could be found – so every one had six lumps of sugar to each cup instead. The things to eat, on the other hand, were nicer than usual. The boys looked about very carefully, and found in the pantry some cold tongue, bread, butter, cheese, and part of a cold pudding – very much nicer than cook ever made when they were at home. And in the kitchen cupboard was half a Christmassy cake, a pot of strawberry jam, and about a pound of mixed candied fruit, with soft crumbly slabs of delicious sugar in each cup of lemon, orange, or citron.

It was indeed, as Jane said, 'a banquet fit for an Arabian Knight'. (Nesbit 1980: 149)

Many of the cultural meanings that circle the concept of 'tea' in early twentieth-century Britain still prevail in this 'tea-ish meal': the making of the beverage is a feminine affair, presided over by the girls, with a motherly warmth accorded to the fire itself. An atmosphere of intense cosiness and safety is created by the ritual of tea-making. The foods so carefully hunter-gathered by the boys mark the meal as high tea rather than afternoon tea – the former, derived from rural traditions, being the main evening meal for children of most classes until after the Second World War; the latter a more formal, social, largely feminine affair. (Cake plays a part in both forms of tea, but it is only at high tea that plain savoury protein foods such as ham, tongue, kippers and eggs make an appearance.) The high-jacking of the 'Christmassy' cake – the modifier carefully steering away from the imputation that this is the *actual* cake intended for Christmas – large quantities of expensive candied fruit and entire pot of jam are presented with an air of gleeful anarchy. The reader is expected to take as much vicarious pleasure in this act of piratical liberation as in the viscerally detailed delights of the 'soft crumbly slabs of sugar' in the candied citrus peel. Still officially the appropriate meal for the time of day, the tea they construct themselves is also a thing of fantasy, both through its illegitimately obtained delights and because of the compound fantasy of Jane's literary malapropism, which renders the meal a thing of both Eastern and medievalist splendour.

In Richmal Crompton's William stories (as discussed in Chapter 3), there are many scenes of skirmishes with hostile cooks; other stories revolve around his stealing food and crashing parties, with the most memorable – at least for a child reader – perhaps being the glorious episode in which he gets to run a sweet shop for a day.[8] He also often indulges in renegade culinary exploration of his own: mixing noxious drinks with his fellow outlaws and cooking bizarre concoctions. Perhaps the strangest of these come in *William the Outlaw* (1927) in which William and his fellow outlaws, having failed in the opening story to live up to their name and survive in the woods on a diet of 'blackberries an' mushrooms' an' roots an' thing's, in 'The Terrible Magician', turn their hands to actual cooking:

They had made a fire in Ginger's backyard and cooked over it a mixture of water from the stream and blackberries and Worcester Sauce and Turkish delight and sardines (these being all the edibles they could jointly produce), had pronounced the resulting concoction to be excellent and had spent the next day in bed. (Crompton 1999b: 18)

Reminiscent of the random (though delicious) flavours in Alice's bottle and the exuberant food lists of *Charlie and the Chocolate Factory*, this concoction balances the reader half-way between disgust and delight. The Outlaws' joyous culinary adventures invariably take place out of doors, with the building of fires over which to scorch their purloined viands. Arthur Ransome's Swallows experience a similar joy in their campfire cooking, but where the activities of William and his friends are illicit, the Swallows have been given permission to fend for themselves on their temporary island home. A literary invocation of interwar codes of bracingly hands-off parenting ('BETTER DROWNED THAN DUFFERS IF NOT DUFFERS WONT DROWN' telegraphs their father from Malta in response to their request to spend the summer sailing and camping), *Swallows and Amazons* (1930) and its eleven sequels are balanced between a realist depiction of achievable adventures located in precisely realized landscapes and the elaborate shared fantasies with which the children heighten their experiences (Ransome 2001: 2). Cooking is treated as both an important practical skill and a key element in their serious play. A great deal of their planning for the expedition to the island involves the packing of cooking equipment and stores ('bread, tea, sugar, salt, biscuits, tins of corned beef, tins of sardines, a lot of eggs, each one wrapped separately for fear of smashes, and a big seed cake' (25)), and the eldest girl, Susan, who has been awarded the title 'Mate' takes with her '*Simple Cooking for Small Households*' (23). The account of the cooking of the first meal of their adventure, eaten once they have set up camp and found a secret harbour for their boat, locates it part-way between work and play. The opening of the description valorizes competence and culinary knowledge, describing Susan's orderly preparations in such detail that it could function as a recipe:

Then in the open space under the trees the fire was burning merrily. The kettle had boiled and was standing steaming on the ground. Susan was melting a big pat of butter in the frying pan. In a pudding-basin besides her she had six raw eggs. She had cracked the eggs on the edge of a mug and broken them into the basin. Their empty shells were crackling in the fire. Four mugs stood in a row on the ground. (50)

But Susan does not actually cook the eggs herself: she instructs her siblings to all gather round and scramble the eggs with their spoons at the same time as they eat them, in order to avoid washing up. This ingenious communal cooking is rendered fun because of its enjoyable transgression of the orderly separation of cooking and eating, but is transformed into *play* by the verbal frame within which Susan presents it: "'No plates to-day [...]. We all eat out of the common dish'" (50). Roger's objection that it is not a common dish but a frying pan makes clear that the phrase is a literary construction, which places the cooking within the shared game of explorers which they base on their reading of adventure stories. In the same vein, they re-name corned beef as 'pemmican' (a mixture of dried meat and fats used by polar explorers), toffee as 'molasses' and lemonade as 'Jamaica rum' (58; 124).

The practical interest in cooking Susan demonstrates becomes much more of a feature in the British children's literature of the post-war years, when servants have become largely a thing of the past. We find a dual representation of cooking as both fantastic play and deeply serious skill in a children's series which began shortly after the Second World War. In Mary Norton's *The Borrowers* (1952), the eponymous race of small people who live in the interstices of human dwellings devote much time and skill to 'borrowing' the necessities of existence, particularly food and cooking equipment, from the 'human beans'. A very effectively manipulated double-narrative perspective means that we see the Borrowers both on their own terms as intrepid adventurers and from the perspective of the unnamed human boy who comes to know them and to whom they seem as intriguingly curious as doll's house dolls come to life. We know that, as the mother, Homily, tells her daughter, Arrietty, her 'poor father risks his life every time he borrows a potato', but we are nonetheless amused by the spectacle of the Borrowers trying to manage the huge unwieldy potato – Arrietty nearly bowling her mother into the soup when she kicks it ill-temperedly into the kitchen, the half manicure-scissor blade which they wield like a scimitar to cut off the small slice which is all they need to make a pot of soup (Norton 1972: 17). The charm of the size difference, and the ingenuity of the repurposing of everyday human objects, lulls the reader repeatedly into a sense of the Borrowers as merely comic creatures. It is at these moments that Norton's text makes the clear the life-and-death knife edge on which they exist, forcing the reader to (in modern parlance) check their own privilege. As a number of critics have pointed out, the Borrowers are figures of a darker wartime experience than that of the British – refugees or fugitives, eking out an existence under the noses of those who would eradicate their race.[9] The acquiring of enough food to survive is a fundamental necessity for these few remnants of the species, who fear they may be the last Borrowers alive – so essential that Pod is forced to take his only child from the safety of their home under the kitchen into the dangerous world of the big house where she might be 'seen' by humans in order to train her in the skills of borrowing. The cooking arrangements of the particular family of Borrowers we come to know are a masterpiece of a sort of Heath-Robinson ingenuity: their stove is constructed from a cogwheel with a fire in the centre and a funnel from an oil-lamp which transfers the fumes to the flue of the humans' kitchen above: 'the fire was laid with match-sticks and fed with assorted slack and, as it burned up, the iron would become hot, and Homily would simmer soup on the spokes, in a silver thimble, and Arrietty would broil nuts' (20). The Borrowers are aware, on one level, that their existence is a sort of half-life lived in the shadows and on the crumbs of the humans, but they have convinced themselves that the power differential is the other way around: "'Human beans are *for* Borrowers – like bread's for butter'" (73), Arrietty tells the boy, explaining that the very small number of humans in proportion to Borrowers makes it clear that the latter are a resource for the former: "'Just a few, my father says, that's all we need – to keep us'" (69). The boy's account of 'railway stations and football matches and racecourses and royal processions [...] and "thousands and millions and billions and trillions of great, big, enormous people'" (75) stuns her into silenced reappraisal of her place in the world. For Arrietty the human beans are figures of Gulliver-esq monstrosity: 'the *food* they eat ... great, smoking mountains of it, huge bogs of stew and soup and stuff' (68), but the accounts of the meals of her own family, even though apparently focalized through Arrietty's own sensibilities, never forget the ersatz, borrowed nature of their existence:

> Tea was indeed ready, laid on the round table in the sitting-room with a bright fire burning in the cog-wheel. How familiar the room seemed, and homely, but, suddenly, somehow strange [...] She looked at the home-made dips set in upturned drawing-pins which Homily had placed as candle-holders among the tea things; the old teapot, a hollow oak-apple, with its quill spout and wired-on handle – burnished it was now and hard with age; there were two roast sliced chestnuts which they would eat like toast with butter and a cold boiled chestnut which Pod would cut like bread; there was a plate of hot dried currants, well plumped before the fire; there were cinnamon breadcrumbs, crispy golden, and lightly dredged with sugar, and in front of each place, oh, delight of delights, a single potted shrimp. [...] Arrietty drew up a cotton-reel and sat down slowly. (78–9)

The fireside tea-table, the cosy old teapot, the bread-and-butter, toast, cakes and shrimp place this as the idealized high tea of so many children's texts. But Arrietty, whose primary food culture this is, should surely think of the meal in terms of boiled and roast chestnuts rather than bread and toast. The sense of the meal as a copy of human meals is a product of the double focalization of the narrative, through both human and Borrower consciousnesses. This in turn is a product of the radical instability of truth in the text and its sequels, which are narrated by layers of tellers and in which even physical evidence is problematized. These narrative games place the Borrowers as creatures part-way between fantasy and prosaic reality; and their foods as both echoes of the privations and dodges of wartime, and imaginings of the diet of dolls or fairies.[10]

The issue of the degree to which Borrowers could free themselves from their parasitic dependence on human beans is one that the characters themselves debate throughout the text. The timid Homily is adamant that she will never follow the others of their kind and leave the house for a rural existence, mainly because she cannot reconcile herself to a diet of nuts and berries and mice. But at the end of the narrative, Mrs May (one of the storytellers) assures Kate that the Borrowers would have had a wealth of foods to choose from in the rural idyll she imagines them:

What did they eat? Did they eat caterpillars, do you think?

'Oh, goodness, child, of course they didn't. They would have had a wonderful life. Badger's setts are almost like villages – full of passages and chambers and storehouses. They could gather hazel-nuts and beech-nuts and chestnuts; they could gather corn – which they could store and grind into flour, just as humans do – it was all there for them: they didn't even have to plant it. They had honey. They could make elderflower tea and lime tea. They had hips and haws and blackberries and sloes and wild strawberries. The boys could fish in the stream and a minnow to them would be as big as a mackerel is to you. They had bird's eggs – any amount of them – for custards and cakes and omelettes. You see, they would know where to look for things. And they had greens and salads, of course. Think of a salad made of those tender shoots of young hawthorn – bread and cheese we used to call it – with sorrel and dandelion and a sprinkling of thyme and wild garlic. Homily was a good cook remember. It wasn't for nothing that the Clocks had lived under the kitchen.' (148–9)

This vision of rural subsistence draws on the revival of traditional practices which had sustained many during the Second World War, but it is also a lyrical fantasy of freedom from human (adult) constraints which sits alongside the desire of Crompton's Outlaws to subsist on the foods of the wild or the Swallow's vision of life as explorers. But while the food is wild-gathered, the meals Mrs May imagines are not campfire improvisations – proper bread, from ground wheat; custards and cakes; omelettes and salads with garlic: these foods represent considerable culinary skill and the last, in particular, come from a culinary lexicon that in the 1950s still speaks considerable sophistication. The paradox is that in the wild, away from houses, the Borrowers would finally be able to attain a full and independent culture of their own. Yet it is made very clear that the detailed account of this enriched diet and culture is produced through an exercise of the imagination – a form of play in which the child Kate (and through her, the reader) is invited to participate. As the later novels demonstrate, Mrs May's vision is overly optimistic – in particular, because a life in the wild offers not just the possibility of an abundance of wild food but also the very real risk of becoming food yourself.

Being food: Cannibalism and children's literature

The fear of being eaten haunts the lives of the Borrowers. Arrietty's parents attempt to control her desire to wander with tales of her older cousin Eggletina, who disappeared, assumed eaten by a cat. When they leave the relative safety of the house and venture into the countryside in *The Borrowers Afield* (1955), they are menaced by creatures including foxes, a crow, a snake, a moth, an owl, and a dog. The prospect of hunting their own food overwhelms them to the extent that they resolve to be vegetarians, until they meet the resourceful wild Borrower, Spiller, who provides them with meat of his own hunting, into whose origins they are careful not to enquire. These themes of killing for food and

181

the fear of *being* food reappear continually in children's texts. *Actual* cannibalism occurs relatively rarely in children's books: memorable examples include Pippi Longstocking's boasts about her father the Cannibal King and the moment in Diana Wynne Jones's *The Time of the Ghost* (1984), when adolescents collect a bowl of their own blood and drink it in order to summon a ghost. For the most part it is something that belongs to the Other, the savage, occurring in nineteenth-century imperialist adventure narratives like R. M. Ballantyne's *The Coral Island* (1858), where the plucky adolescent protagonists witness South Sea islanders sacrificing babies to the eel god and cutting slices of flesh from victims whose limbs have only just 'ceased to quiver' (1990: 176; 175). It is this sort of adventure that William and his friends re-enact when they play a game of 'canniballs', pretending a sardine is Ginger, tying it to a tree and eating it (adopting, of course, the role of cannibals rather than civilizing imperialists) (Crompton 1991b). But symbolic cannibalism, metaphorized cannibalism and the threat of the eating of creatures who are proxies for the child reader occur so often as to be a central trope of children's literature.

Master No-book's threatened culinary fate at the hands of giant Snap-'em-up is lingered over relishingly in *Holiday House*. The giant's magnificent dinners consist of dishes such as 'an elephant roasted whole, ostrich patties, a tiger smothered in onions, stewed lions, and whale soup', but little boys are enjoyed as a side dish, rather like whitebait – 'as fat as possible, fried in crumbs of bread, with plenty of pepper and salt' (Sinclair 1839: 136–7). The giant's preparation of his victim serves to foreground the active inhumanity of the treatment of meat animals: he hangs him from a hook, forces some large lumps of 'nasty suet' down his throat and positions him near the fire so that his liver will grow larger; the preparation identifies him as a luxury morsel – like a *foie-gras* goose his culinary value is enhanced by both the effort and the cruelty. On reflection, the giant decides to kill him in a new and ingenious way: 'as pigs were considered a much greater dainty when whipped to death [...] he meant to see where children might not be improved by it also' (139). Master No-book is ultimately saved by the good fairy Teach-all and is redeemed by a regimen of gardening, reading, and moderate and nourishing food, but his erstwhile companions are not so lucky: the larder also contains 'the dead bodies of six other boys, whom he remembered to have seen fattening in the fairy Do-nothing's garden' (138). Framed as an amusing cautionary tale, 'Uncle David's Nonsensical Story' can be dismissed as fairy tale, but the equating of children with consumable animals, the detailing of real-world horrors in the treatment of those animals, and the teasing pleasure their uncle takes in piling up the horror all contribute to a sense of profound unease.

The prospect of being eaten preoccupies many of the creatures Alice encounters in Wonderland.[11] She inadvertently terrifies the small animals she meets in her pool of tears by talking about her cat, Dinah, who is 'such a capital one for catching mice' (Carroll 1968: 26) and who will 'eat a little bird as soon as look at it' (35). The pigeon she encounters when her neck has expanded to enormous length insists that she must be 'a kind of serpent' (57) when she confesses to eating eggs. Most dramatically illustrative of this theme is the Mock Turtle, "'the thing Mock Turtle Soup is made from'" (97), as the Queen explains – a creature whose physical form in Tenniel's illustrations is a recipe, with an ox's tail and the head of a calf (which is clearly dead, resembling the illustrations in cookbooks). The Mock Turtle's final act in the text is to sing the song of his own demise, sobbing as he does so: "'Beautiful Soup, so rich and green, / Waiting in a hot tureen! [...] / Soup of the evening, beautiful Soup!'" (111), but before this, he and the Gryphon (another hybrid creature) tell Alice stories of their school days under the sea. They discuss whiting – which to Alice are a dish, but to the others, characters – and Alice attempts to recite a poem which, like all the verse she tries in Wonderland, comes out very differently than she had remembered. Her version of ''Tis the voice of the sluggard', Isaac Watts's moral verse of 1715, turns into the voice of the lobster, declaring, "'You have baked me too brown, I must sugar my hair'", with a second verse in which an Owl and a Panther share a pie:

> The Panther took pie-crust, and gravy, and meat,
> While the Owl had the dish as its share of the treat.
> When the pie was all finished, the Owl, as a boon,
> Was kindly permitted to pocket the spoon:
> While the Panther received knife and fork with a growl,
> And concluded the banquet – (110)

Alice is interrupted before she finishes the final line, but the power of the rhythm and rhyme is such that 'by eating the Owl' is the only possible conclusion: its omission requires the child reader to supply the ending and to complete the thought – an apparent textual self-censorship that highlights the thing it does not say. The theme of animate food continues in *Alice through the Looking Glass* (1872), where she is introduced to insects like the Snap-dragon-fly, whose 'body is made of plum-pudding, its wings of holly leaves, and its head [...] a raisin burning in brandy' (177) and the 'Bread-and-butterfly', whose 'wings are thin slices of bread-and-butter, its body [...] a crust, and its head [...] a lump of sugar' (178). These creatures subsist precariously on substances associated with themselves – the former on 'frumenty and mince-pie' (p. 177), the latter on 'weak tea with cream in it', which is so difficult to find that it always dies. Creatures less aware of their status as potential food are the young oysters in 'The Walrus and the Carpenter', the poem recited to Alice by Tweedledee, who are persuaded out for a walk along the beach by the nefarious protagonists. The creatures are rendered as schoolchildren and therefore as figures with whom child readers might identify – 'all eager for the treat: / Their coats were brushed their faces washed, / Their shoes were clean and neat' (190). The oysters are consumed as the Walrus and Carpenter talk, ostensibly to their victims, whom they praise with double-edged cunning: "'It was so kind of you to come! And you are very nice!'" (192). The poem piles cruelty on betrayal – the oysters are young and eager, their betrayers force them to walk far and fast before they consume them and they are of course, though the verse does not specify this, eaten alive. The themes of living food and the fear of being eaten come together in the banquet with which the story ends. Alice, as the new Queen, is required to carve the leg of mutton, but before she can do so, the Red Queen introduces them: "'Alice – Mutton; Mutton – Alice.'" As a result, she is unable to serve it because "'it isn't etiquette to cut anyone you've been introduced to'" (272). The nonsense of adult codes of manners and the nonsense that is language games merge. In an attempt to regain control, Alice insists on cutting the pudding, whose response is a robust assertion of equality: "'What impertinence!' said the Pudding. "I wonder how you'd like it, if I were to cut a slice out of *you*, you creature!'" (273). As the fantasy starts to dissolve, the food and the people change places: the guests climb into the dishes, the leg of mutton sits in the White Queen's Chair and the Queen disappears into the soup tureen. Alice takes control and destroys the fantasy world with an act which is transgressive both in its violence and in its repudiation of all manners, seizing the tablecloth and pulling, so that 'plates, dishes, guests, and candles came crashing down together in a heap on the floor' (277). The hidden term of Carroll's fantasies is death – the 'softly and suddenly vanishing away' of the Snark, the thing that, as the Gnat points out, 'always happens' (178). To be named as a 'creature' – to be interchangeable with food – takes Alice herself too close to the darkness that lurks behind the fantasy, so hastening its end.

In portal fantasies such as the Alice stories, the possibility of stepping back outside the fantasy world is always in prospect – for the text itself, if not the protagonists. The Looking-glass world can be dissolved when it gets too frightening. This is not the case in high fantasy, where the fantasy world is all that there is and where that world's logic often produces a frighteningly violent environment.[12] In J. R. R. Tolkein's *The Hobbit* (1937) the prospect of being eaten is very real, and is the first threat of the book, occurring in the second chapter. Having reluctantly agreed to join the party of dwarves in their quest, in the role of 'burglar', Bilbo stumbles upon a trio of trolls, who are bemoaning the lack of 'manflesh' in their diet, and is captured in the act of trying to pick one of their pockets. They converse with him as an individual – "'Re, 'oo are you?'", but nonetheless leap instantly to the prospect of consuming him:

'[C]an yer cook 'em?' said Tom
'Yer can try', said Bert, picking up a skewer. (Tolkein 1999: 35)

The text has fun with the expectedly rough manners of the trolls, apologizing for their habit of wiping their mouths on their sleeves and the fact that their language is not 'drawing-room fashion' (34), but in the process draws attention to the fact that they *have* sleeves and manners, however rudimentary: they are not wild creatures but people with a culture of their own. They intend to eat Bilbo not raw but cooked and spend a considerable amount of time debating the best ways in which to prepare him. William suggests that he "'wouldn't make above a mouthful, [...] not when he was skinned and boned'" (35), which Bert counters with the suggestion that they find "'more like him'" (36) and make a pie. When they also capture Bilbo's companions they tie them ('neatly') up in sacks and sit down to argue about 'whether they should roast them slowly, or mince them fine and boil them, or just sit on them one by one and squash them into jelly' (39). Bilbo, in his role as trickster, manages to extend their argument by imitating their voices in turn, keeping them disputing until the sun comes up and turns them to stone. It is notable that Bilbo's first defence against being cooked is to offer his services as cook instead: "'Please don't cook me, kind sirs! I am a good cook myself, and cook better than I cook, if you see what I mean. I'll cook beautifully for you, a perfectly beautiful breakfast for you, if only you won't have me for supper'" (36). His difficulty in separating the two senses of 'cooking' linguistically plays for humorous effect, but also speaks to the impossibility of imagining oneself being eaten. The different species of Tolkein's Middle Earth function in practice much more as races, with interbreeding possible between many of them. In this context, the prospect of being eaten by another talking, clothed, cultured being takes us beyond the idea of humans (or dwarves, or hobbits) as a prey species and into the territory of cannibalism.

The threat of being eaten is also a key element in the form of adult to child sadism we call teasing: it is a trope that appears strikingly often in those adult texts whose intense interest in the child's experiences makes them part of a literature of childhood. Early in Dickens's *Great Expectations* (1860), young protagonist Pip is subjected to prolonged needling from his adult sister's guests, who 'stick the point' of their barbs into him as if he was 'an unfortunate little bull in a Spanish arena' (1985b: 56–7). Over Christmas dinner Mr Wopsle and Mr Pumblechook expatiate at length on the subject of "'Pork'", which they consider contains "'many a moral for the young'" (57). Pip is explicitly compared to the "'plump and juicy'" pork on the table in front of them, and told that he should be grateful not to have been "'born a Squeaker'" (infant pig), or he would not have found himself in the assembled company – "'Unless in that form'", said Mr Wopsle, nodding towards the dish' (58). Expanding on the theme, Mr Pumblechook details the horrors of the imagined life of piglet-Pip, who would have been "'disposed of for so many shillings'" to Dunstable the butcher who "'would have come up to you as you lay in your straw, and he would have whipped you under his left arm, and with his right he would have tucked up his frock to get a penknife from out of his waistcoat-pocket, and he would have shed your blood and had your life'" (58). The precision with which the scene is imagined – the named, known butcher, the details of his various gestures – and the lingering, relishing pace of the culminating phrase all indicate the sadistic pleasure Mr Pumblechook has in toying with Pip's fears and the darker pleasure he takes in imagining him as meat.[13] The scene follows soon after the opening chapter in which Pip is persuaded to steal food for the convict Magwitch by the latter's dire threats of his hidden accomplice, the "'young man'" who "'has a secret way pecooliar to himself, of getting at a boy, and at his heart, and at his liver'", which organs will be "'tore out, roasted and ate'" (38). In Henry James's *What Maisie Knew* (1897), the infant Maisie, displaced by her parents' divorce and hereafter a weapon in their bitter wranglings, comes to consciousness of her own physical being in the experience of being manhandled by her father's friends:

> Some of these gentlemen made her strike matches and light their cigarettes; others, holding her on knees violently jolted, pinched the calves of her legs till she shrieked – her shriek was much admired – and reproached them with being toothpicks. The word stuck in her mind and contributed to her feeling from this time that she was deficient in something that would meet the general desire. She found out what

it was: it was a congenital tendency to the production of a substance to which Moddle, her nurse, gave a short and ugly name, a name painfully associated at dinner with the part of the joint that she didn't like. (James 1984: 21–2)

In typical Jamesian circumlocution her physical appearance is defined by an object to pick food from the teeth and negatively as a riddle the answer to which is 'fat', and which causes her to directly associate her body with food, an early lesson in her commodified role in the elaborate battle played out between her parents and their new partners.

We find these themes explored in their most naked terms in the most surprising place – in the picture books designed for young children. Picture books are one of the first places where the realities of the connections between death and eating are broached for infants, but these books also lay bare a profound cultural confusion around these issues. They are part of an enculturation that, along with nursery rhymes, songs, soft toys, nursery decoration, and so on, requires very young children to perform their first acts of imaginative identification with animals: not just any animals, but specifically those animals – ducks, hens, lambs, calves, pigs – that we farm and kill for food. The fact of the death of those animals is an open secret – something children are supposed to know and not know simultaneously, and children's picture books engage with these processes of secrecy and knowledge, identification and betrayal, pleasure and horror with an intensity that is perverse, if not outright sadistic. In requiring the child reader to identify with precisely those animals – and animate objects – that are most commonly eaten, children's texts play with the infant's primal fear that he himself is edible.

For Beatrix Potter, immersed in the pragmatic logic of a farming community, there was no need to draw a veil over the life-and-death realities of animal husbandry – the very first thing Peter Rabbit and his sisters are told in her first book, published in 1902, is not to go into Mr McGregor's garden because 'your father had an accident there: he was put in a pie by Mrs McGregor' (1984: 9). This curious, and comic, transfer of agency – the father's having an accident rather than Mrs McGregor's act of cooking (and the elision of, we assume, Mr McGregor's act of killing) – thematizes this central paradox: Mr Rabbit Senior is both person and food, someone who can have an accident and something which can be put in a pie. The issue of food is of pre-eminent importance in *The Tale of Peter Rabbit*, with its acquisition, preparation and consumption represented on virtually every page: from Mrs Rabbit's shopping at the bakers, the blackberry-gathering of Peter's 'good little' sisters, Peter's theft of Mr McGregor's lettuces and French beans and radishes to the camomile tea he is given in lieu of supper while his siblings eat bread and milk and blackberries. The other animals Peter encounters also devote much of their time to the pursuit of food, from the old mouse carrying peas and beans one at a time to her family, to the cat staring transfixed at the goldfish. The landscape of the story is Mr McGregor's garden, full of fruit and vegetables and the means of their production and protection – cucumber frames, gooseberry nets and scarecrows. The central threat of the narrative is that Peter will follow his father's fate, though this is never directly articulated: Mr McGregor chases him as a thief, rather than a potential foodstuff. The threat of becoming someone else's dinner, often in the process of searching for one's own, becomes more and more overtly the theme of the sequels. In *The Tale of Benjamin Bunny* (1904), which takes place immediately after the first story, Peter's cousin Benjamin accompanies him back to the garden to try and retrieve his coat and shoes, which Mr McGregor has used to make a scarecrow. The clothes are important – with them, Peter walks upright and fulfils a human-like role; without them he is a generic rabbit, moving 'lippity – lippity – not very fast' and looking much more like prey (16). In each subsequent story about these characters, the risk of becoming food is more overt: in this tale, Peter and Benjamin are trapped in an upturned basket by a cat, who sits on top of it for '*five hours*' until she is attacked and driven off by Benjamin's father (1984: 31); in *The Tale of the Flopsy Bunnies* (1909) the many (unnamed and unclothed) children of feckless parents Benjamin and Flopsy (one of Peter's sisters) are put in a sack by Mr McGregor, who gloats at his capture of 'one, two, three, four, five, six leetle fat rabbits!' and plans to sell them to buy himself 'baccy' (1984: 44–5); while in *The Tale of Mr Tod* (1912), Mr Brock, a badger, steals the grandchildren of his friend old Mr Bouncer (more unnamed flopsy bunnies) to put in a rabbit-pie. Benjamin and Peter track him down to one of the lairs of Mr Tod, a fox, where, through the window Benjamin spies 'preparations upon the kitchen table which made him shudder. There was an immense empty pie-dish of blue willow pattern and a large carving knife and fork, and a chopper' (1984: 58). The older rabbits wait outside all night, unable to rescue the babies, who have been shut up in the cold oven. Meanwhile a lengthy subplot ensues, when Mr Tod returns home and rigs a trap to pour water over the interloping badger. The slapstick of their battle contrasts ominously with the gruesome midden heap of bones outside the house and the long-unresolved fate of the baby rabbits. It is only when the predator-animals take their fight outside the house that the adults are able to rescue the infants.

The central aim of the animal protagonists of Potter's work is not to become food. This need is handled in a somewhat orderly psychological manner in those texts in which it is humans who wish to turn the protagonists into food, but it becomes more disturbing when the animals try to eat each other – particularly when, as in *The Tale of Mr Tod*, the attempt transgresses codes of friendship and hospitality. It is at its most radically disruptive in those texts – most notably *The Tale of Samuel Whiskers* (1908) – when there is competition over the role of eater and eaten. Naughty, adventurous Tom Kitten, hiding from his mother, is captured by the rats Anna Maria and Samuel Whiskers and put into a roly-poly pudding. Tom is rendered simultaneously as protagonist – pictured in a darkly gothic image squalling in pain and fear as the rats truss him up – and as foodstuff, as the rats discuss him only as 'the pudding', worrying that it will not be good as he is covered in chimney smuts, and arguing about the recipe, which Samuel Whiskers wants 'made properly' with breadcrumbs, and Anna Maria insists on making with 'butter and dough' (Potter 1989: 54–5). But the roles of predator and prey are not straightforwardly divided in this text: it is not just the rats who eat infants – at the beginning of the story Tom's mother notes in passing that she had caught a dozen young rats and served them for Sunday dinner. The twist of the knife in this 'dog-eat-dog' world is not so much that these creatures eat each other's young, but that they do so in the context of 'civilized' constructs such as recipes and Sunday dinner (or Mr Tod's willow-pattern dish). As

Jonathan Swift's *Modest Proposal* (1729) with its suggestion of fricassee or ragout makes clear, the worst barbarism would not be eating the babies of the poor, but exchanging recipes for the best way to serve them.[14] The recipe transforms necessity to pleasure – Potter's animals are at their most disturbingly barbaric when they act like people.[15]

Beatrix Potter's tales may start out with a benign agenda of introducing children to the life-and-death realities of the countryside and of interactions between animal species, but they get much darker and stranger when the animals become most human, raising the question of what the function might be of representing these themes in a picture book. It seems odd only if we think of children's literature as an essentially benevolent force. But as many critics, from Jacqueline Rose (1984) to Jack Zipes (2001: 147–69) have argued, there is a significantly sadistic element running through adult writing for children. We can trace this quality, which ranges from a desire to terrify to a teasing based on adult access to meanings unknown to children, from the fairy-tale oral tradition, through the dark warnings of the puritan stories which were the first written texts produced specifically

Figure 8 *Tom Kitten trussed up ready for the pie in Beatrix Potter's* The Tale of Samuel Whiskers *(1908).*

for children in Britain, to the present day. Children's texts have always played with the idea of children as victims – warning of dire fates if adult instructions are not obeyed, introducing fears in order to allay them. As a culture, some of the earliest stories we tell children involve the threat of their edibility – 'Little Red Riding Hood', with the much-lingered on prospect of the Wolf's great big teeth and the grandmother's being already in his stomach; 'Hansel and Gretel', with the temptation of the house made entirely of sweets, the details of the cage in which they are to be fattened, the stove on which they are to be cooked; 'Beauty and the Beast', when the father dispatches his daughter into the clutches of a creature he thinks will eat her; 'Jack and the Beanstalk', with the giant's memorable plan to 'grind his bones to make my bread'. These tales flow as a dark undercurrent beneath our shared cultural systems of understanding, suggesting that food is a thing it is possible to *be* as well as have, especially if you are young and tender.

Since around the 1960s there has been a tendency for children's books to situate themselves as a site of rebellion against the authority of adults and the rule of law, refusing morals and offering more open-ended, anarchic narratives. Picture books, at

Figure 9 *The Giant eating the Hen in Jon Scieszka and Lane Smith's* The Stinky Cheese Man and Other Fairly Stupid Tales *(1992).*

the same time, have become less clearly directed only at very young children, as graphic narratives and comic books have become an increasingly significant element of the reading of adults, young adults and older children. This has created an ambiguity around their audience, legitimating darker, unresolved narratives. Such books tease children with the fear of being food in ever more ingenious ways, from Maurice Sendack's creepy midnight bakers of *In the Night Kitchen* (1970), baking little naked Mickey into a cake, to the anarchic rewriting of fairy-tale happy endings in Jon Scieszka and Lane Smith's *The Stinky Cheese Man and Other Fairly Stupid Tales* (1992), which uses the visual games of the postmodern graphic novel to deconstruct classic fairy tales. Inviting the reader to view such tales with a cynical detachment, the text blurs the lines between stories, deploying self-reflexivity, typographical play, intertextuality and the incorporation of paratextual material into the main text in order to short circuit the narrative logic of the fairy tale. So the ugly duckling grows up to become an ugly duck, while the frog-prince is only a frog and tricks the princess into kissing him. The Stinky Cheese Man of the title story is so unpleasant that no one wants to eat him (the story playing with a child's sense of disgust about adult food), but he dies anyway, dissolving in the river. A governing narrative trope is the little red hen, who forces her way onto the endpapers and into other narratives, shouting annoyingly about her plan to plant the wheat and make the bread. At the end of the book she shouts so loudly that she wakes Jack's sleeping giant. His enormous face fills the penultimate page, mouth open: '"BREAD?" said the Giant. "EAT?" said the Giant' (Scieszka and Smith 1992: 48). When we turn the page there is one last image: the Giant with a half-eaten sandwich, filled with a mysterious red meat, as he picks feathers from his teeth; tiny hen's legs protrude from the corner of his mouth and a little bonnet falls unheeded to the floor. There is no textual gloss, only the legend 'The End'. The text is unusual in the lexicon of children's texts about the threat of being eaten as it deploys not the child's fear and capacity for identification but a sort of cheerful sadism which the child reader is invited to share.

One of the most radical explorations of the threat of being food can be found in the extraordinary narratives of Mini Grey. In Grey's *Biscuit Bear* (2004), the biscuit of the title, having survived his first night of existence uneaten, goes to the kitchen and bakes himself a whole circus of friends – performing the role of cook as if to refuse the role of food. Grey's multilayered, scrapbook style of illustration offers additional subtextual stories that run parallel to the written narrative – so the double-page spread immediately before the genesis of Biscuit Bear involves a series of snapshot images of Horace, the child-creator of the biscuit, engaged in anarchic play with raw pastry: putting it on his head, fighting for it with the dog and rolling it out on the toilet seat. In contrast, the new clean piece of dough that becomes Biscuit Bear involves a sparse single image of his act of creation. The pages in which Biscuit Bear himself cooks are in the style of a child's first recipe book, with images of the labelled ingredients providing a visual recipe. The scenes of the decoration (dressing) of the multiple biscuit friends, and their dazzling circus performances, are illustrated in vivid colours against dramatic backgrounds, designed to encourage the child to whom the book is read to linger in delighted absorption. All is good until the arrival of the household dog, Bongo, who 'liked biscuits (But not in a way that is necessarily good for the biscuits)': only Biscuit Bear survives the resulting massacre (Grey 2004: 21). Seeking a place where a biscuit could be safe he finds a refuge in the window display of a pastry cook where he can survive forever uneaten, belying the fact that (in a pun that only really works for a culinary-minded adult reader) 'the life of a biscuit is usually short and sweet' (28). The protagonist of Grey's much darker 2002 *Egg Drop* is not so lucky. It is an egg who wants to fly: at once a creature, a potential creature and an object, it is shown in the title pages in a sea of identical eggs, the only one with eyes. The story opens with a retrospective narrative, told, according to the accompanying image, by a hen to an assembled crowd of chicks: 'The Egg was young. [...] We tried to tell it, but of course it didn't listen' (Grey 2002: 6). It is the warning that underlies cautionary tales and motivates the horrors of fairy tales, but in this case it has failed. The Egg is portrayed as a visionary, shown with fantastic designs for flying machines, which fail because it doesn't understand aerodynamics. Eventually it climbs all the way to the top of a tall tower and jumps off. It is a moment of exhilarating triumph for the egg (and for the reader who identifies with him), aloft in the bright sky, his ovoid form cracked open to reveal a huge yolky-smile of delight at flying. But the next page's image pulls back the focus to show us the tall bleak brick tower, the darkening sky and the tiny image of the egg, dropping. The next double-page spread reveals the story to be a re-writing of Humpty Dumpty, with snapshots of the many ingenious ways they tried to put him back together again – with string, sticky tape, plasters, sewing, nails and screws, chewing gum and tomato soup – the images both comical and monstrous, as the egg's little eyes peer out of his broken, mangled form – 'nothing really worked and shells don't heal' (26) – we are told, the 'heal' placing the egg still as living being rather than object to be mended. We cut to the mother hen, weeping, as on the nest at her side one of the more patient sibling eggs is cracked open by a beak and then to the final pages and the devastating concluding statement: 'Luckily he was not wasted' (30). On a cheerful checked tablecloth, a plate of breakfast awaits, positioned so that it is in front of the reader. The egg is at the centre, fried. It is clear that as well as now being food it is also dead, but it is peacefully smiling. The transition from agency to food is particularly abrupt and painful for the identifying reader. We have been with him in his bizarre, overweening, human aspirations – and now the knife and fork are waiting for us.

Australian artist Shaun Tan takes the paradoxes of identification with food creatures in a new direction in his 2018 *Tales from the Inner City*. In Tan's previous work, dealing with issues including depression, social isolation and immigration, food and food animals are often of significant importance: in *The Red Tree* (2001) depression is rendered in the form of an enormous grey fish floating the city streets above the protagonist, its dead eye that of an old corpse on a fishmonger's slab. In his multi-award-winning wordless story *The Arrival* (2006), Tan, who is himself the son of immigrants from many cultures (his father is Chinese-Malaysian, his mother Anglo-Irish), tells a fable of immigration which takes place in a fabulous steam-punk world, but which is grounded in historical reality through the end paper renderings of passport photographs of immigrants from all periods and places. The experiences of alienation and then gradual integration are rendered through a hotchpotch of experiences in which food is central. The food in

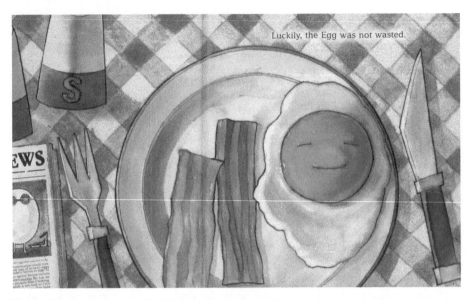

Figure 10 *The final image of Mini Grey's* Egg Drop *(2004).*

the new country is profoundly alien, with strange foodstuffs part-way between gourds and sea creatures, and curious implements, tableware, and modes of acquisition (food is prepared at table with blow-torches, it is purchased from boxes in a wall). In learning to navigate this strange new food culture, and in sharing tips and life stories with other immigrants, a new sort of home is finally found. In *Tales from the Inner City* the dead food-creatures of his earlier work are replaced by living animals, his central theme: the horrors of our relationship to other species. He deploys a fabular style of storytelling to depict a chaotic modern city on the verge of a dystopian moment. In this city, animals live alongside humans in modes both fantastic and horrific: in the frontispiece deer inhabit a high-rise building which has become, unexplained, a forest; giant snails mate on bridges; the last rhino is shot dead because it is blocking the motorway. A number of stories dwell particularly on the animal as food. One focuses on a teacher imploring his students to '"respect the sheep"', as they line up to hug its 'hot woolly body, trembling with animal life, something much bigger than any lesson' (Tan 2018: 135). The sheep is to be respected because of its immense importance to their society: its wool and meat, bones and skin '"all worth more to this city than gold"', but the horror and grief the teacher feels about its fate has everything to do with the 'gigantic livestock ship' loading outside, its stink so vile that people cancel all outdoor activities, in which the sheep will be treated with something very far from respect. Another story begins surreally: 'In the room at the back of our apartment there is a pig, sinking' (85). The double-page image following the story renders this pig, its back to us as it sits in the dark, peering towards the light from a partially opened door. Its hind quarters are invisible, so that it does appear to be disappearing through the floor but, as the child speaking subject had gone on to reveal, it is not actually sinking, it is being sliced, bit by bit, 'just like every other pig in every other family in every other city apartment'. Although assured by their father that the pig feels no pain and does not want to leave the apartment, the children are not so sure, so one moonlit night they transport him by trolley to the local park, 'screw in the trotters we made out of cardboard tubes and paint' (86–7) and release him into a field suddenly filled with all the other pigs, who squeal and grunt, 'meeting their brothers and sisters and telling each other everything they know and everything they don't' (87), creatures with families and thoughts and confusions just like the humans. The temporary nature of the idyll is conveyed by the fact that the children have to raise their hands to block out the view of buildings and wires and lights so that they can imagine a bucolic scene consisting of nothing but trees and pigs. A simultaneous mood of hope and despair is evoked in both the text and images throughout the book, with brief lights of sublimity or awakened empathy glowing in the gathering dark. In place of a contents page there is a double page of silhouettes of numbered animal species, evoking old scientific tomes; in the midst of the other animals, in no way visually distinct, is a (female) human. The numbers, we come to realize, denote the pages on which the story of each animal's fate is disclosed, with the story of the human-as-animal ending the book. In this final story, when 'our time is long past', the remains of our species delight in excavating the fossils of our culture while we 'chatter and chatter in our simian way' about all of the many unanswered questions about humanity (217). Disinterring bodies from the 'granulated plastic and brittle, faintly radioactive ash' these future forms of ourselves, only distantly curious about what they had been, wonder most about the separate loneliness of our species, isolating itself so much from all the other animals, the 'brothers and sisters in sediment, each husk and bone much the same carbonate' (219). Finally, hearing the song that is 'the vast murmur of every living thing that ever moved across the face of this planet' we bury our tools and run to join the rest, simply animals at last. Instead of the animal-as-human-avatar of earlier children's texts, Tan's eco-narrative insists on an ethically radical equality between all species, in which the eating of our fellow beings and the elaborate social mechanisms that support such consumption are understood as untenably horrific.

The food in children's texts, I have suggested, is inherently paradoxical: both viscerally imagined and insistently textual, with cooking rendered simultaneously as serious life-skill and as form of imaginative play. From fairy tales to the postmodern reinventions of the picture book, children's texts play out a drama of child-as-animal-as-food which is both evocative of a primal terror and a mark of curious, unresolved, adult to child sadism. The next chapter will examine a similar set of paradoxes in considering the denotative and connotative tensions at the heart of the recipe form.

CHAPTER 7
READING RECIPES

The subject of this chapter is the recipe, the ways it has been written and read, and its relationship to the texts in which it finds itself. The cookbook has always been a hybrid genre, offering recipes but also folding into itself, at different times and places, household manuals, travel guides, lifestyle and etiquette guides, and personal memoirs. The closer the form gets to a 'pure' collection of recipes – probably the text books of catering colleges – the less 'readable' it becomes. It would seem, then, that it is the apparently extraneous matter – the artless chat of a Nigella Lawson, the patrician lifestyle-construction of a Martha Stewart, the encyclopaedic information of an Isabella Beeton – that makes the cookbook readable as 'literature'. And yet, we can read recipes too. The form has its own voice, its own grammar – like any other textual construction, it communicates more and other meanings than those on its surface. The recipe offers possibilities of new and different lives, skills, experiences. It tempts and cajoles, challenges and reassures. When cut free from its 'natural' context in the cookbook it sets up contrapuntal resonances, creating new and curious meanings in the texts in which it finds itself, in novels and memoirs, blogs and newspaper columns. The discussion will begin with the forms of the recipe itself and the ways in which it makes and resists meanings, in itself and in the various contextual frames which incorporate it. It will trace some notable textual engagements with recipes – projects in which writers take the cookbook literally and in so doing reveal the contradictions at its heart. It will conclude with a discussion first of food memoirs, and then of the paradoxes of memory and re-creation that trouble the exchange which the recipe mediates between author and reader.

Reading the recipe

A recipe in its 'purest' form would be shorn of narrative: a bare list of ingredients, a series of instructions free of all ambiguity. In the history of its development as a communicative form, the impulse towards this sort of transparency of meaning has been one 'pull', represented in the separation of method from ingredients pioneered by Eliza Acton in her *Modern Cookery for Private Families* (1845), which replaces the earlier practice of giving ingredients and (sometimes) quantities only at the moment they appear in the description of method; instead, Acton offers what she calls 'a novel feature': a 'summary appended to the receipts, of the different ingredients which they contain, with the exact proportion of each, and the precise time required to dress the whole' (1993: 2). Subsequent food writers built on and refined Acton's innovation, with Isabella Beeton adding the crucial logical step of giving the list of ingredients before rather than after the method. The various movements of the later nineteenth and early twentieth centuries for the professionalization of domesticity continued the tendency towards the eradication of randomness in recipes and unpredictability in the results they produced in the kitchens of their readers. As Laura Shapiro notes in *Perfection Salad*, her study of women and cooking in turn-of-the-century America, the development of 'domestic science', with its emphasis on measurable nutritional outputs, led to the production of cookbooks which privileged clarity and brevity: considering Fanny Farmer's substantial and highly influential rewriting of Mrs Lincoln's *Boston Cook Book* (1884) as *The Boston Cooking-School Cook Book* of 1896, she notes that the new book 'was written to be consulted, not read, and its aim was to be authoritative, not simply companionable' (Shapiro 1986: 114). Farmer's innovations included the standardization of all measurements: the contents of measuring cups and spoons were to be levelled with a knife and the old, haphazard notions of rounded or heaped measures outlawed; her sense of specificity was such that 'she could measure out spices by the grain' (Shapiro 1986: 116). Books like Farmer's were developed in and designed to be used by the considerable number of cooking schools and domestic institutes that sprang up across the country, designed to train servantless housewives how to approach domestic work as a scientific endeavour. Reinvented as 'home economics' in the early twentieth century, it had a major influence on both sides of the Atlantic on styles of recipe writing and on readerly expectations of their precision and reproducibility. At its plainest, a 'scientific' recipe seeks to convey the specific ingredients needed and their precise quantities, the exact cooking time and temperature, and the order and particulars of culinary method in sufficient detail to be clear, but not so much as to allow for any confusion, ambiguity or distraction.[1] A typical (British) example is the recipe for 'Victoria Sponge Sandwich' in the fourteenth edition of *The Cannon Cookery Book* (1953):

VICTORIA SPONGE SANDWICH
Mark 5–20-25 minutes

3 ozs. butter.	*4 ozs. castor sugar.*
5 ozs. flour.	*Pinch of salt.*
2 eggs.	*Level teaspoonful baking powder.*

(1) Cream butter and sugar together. (2) Add beaten eggs gradually. (3) Fold in lightly, flour, sifted with baking powder and salt. (4) Put into a greased tin, 7 ¾ inches wide. (5) Place in oven on 3rd runner and bake for 30 minutes. (6) When cold, split and sandwich together with jam, or butter icing. (78)

Issued by the makers of the Cannon gas cooker to accompany the sale of a particular model ('your A125 Cooker'), the book is firmly embedded in the traditions of domestic science instruction. Its recipes admit of no ambiguities, giving precise timings and temperatures and specifying exactly which shelves of the oven to use in each case. Its methodological stages are clear and apparently succeed in the crucial avoidance of any vagueness or confusion. And yet even this plain, straightforward recipe reveals some key problems with the scientific model. Firstly, it does not acknowledge that ingredients are not all standardized: eggs, for example, come in radically different sizes, and the choice of a large or a small one will have a significant effect on the cake. Secondly, and for obvious reasons, it does not acknowledge the possibility of the temperature of individual ovens being calibrated differently. It makes little allowance for unskilled cooks, giving no explanation of 'creaming' or 'folding' or 'sifting', and failing to detail the fact that a sponge cake needs to be removed from its tin and left to cool on a rack. We are not referred to instructions for butter icing. The recipe does not explain the reasons for its specifications, so a reader who does not own a cake tin precisely 7 ¾ inches in diameter does not know whether it is possible to substitute a different size (8 inches, perhaps?) and whether this would affect cooking times, temperature or placement in the oven; nor are they told how deep the tin should be or even what shape. The specificity of *castor* sugar is not explained, so a reader with only soft brown sugar or granulated sugar may not know if a substitution is possible (the former would produce a damper, 'fudgier', possibly 'sad' cake; that latter would not fully cream into the butter, leaving a gritty texture). It is virtually impossible, of course, for a cookbook to cover every recipe in just this detail and to take into account all of the variations in ingredients, equipment, knowledge and skill of every potential reader. The food writers who do attempt such a feat end up taking their recipe writing into a very different territory, becoming inevitably discursive. So, in *Dinners for Beginners: An Economical Cooking Book for the Single-Handed* (1934), sisters-in-law Rachel and Margaret Ryan devote nearly 300 pages to twenty-eight simple seasonal menus, offering their neophyte readers instructions on every aspect of timing, order and process of operations, but also on shopping, serving, washing-up and even how to eat. They include injunctions to wash hands, to have a rest, and instructions about what direction your guests should nibble their Corn on the Cob ('along the row from one end to the other – not round and round the cob') (Ryan 1936: 171). Their instructions for 'Sunshine Cream' (a simple lemon mousse with three ingredients) run for a full two pages: the level of detail can be seen in the description of how to separate eggs:

> Take two basins. Separate the yolks of five eggs from the whites by cracking each egg against the edge of a basin and letting the white drip down into the basin while you turn the yolk from one half of the shell to the other until it is free of white. Put all the yolks in the second basin. (180)

Unlike the author(s) of *The Cannon Cookery Book*, the Ryans do explain what 'folding' means in culinary terms:

> To do this, add the whites gradually, in about five instalments, and as each bit of frothed white falls into the yellow, lift the latter over and round it with the flat side of a pastry-knife. Continue in this way, not stirring round and round, but lifting

over and over, until the white is taken right into the yellow and can no longer be seen separately. (181)

Not content with this explanation, they expand on it in a further paragraph, explaining precisely the effect, in this particular recipe, of failing to follow these instructions to the letter: 'It is very important that all the yellow and white should be completely blended, if not, the yellow will turn hard and glossy and the white will sink into a watery substance at the bottom of the glass' (182). The detail of *Dinners for Beginners* arises from the same impulse for clarity as that of the books of the domestic science movement, but its attempts to explain rather than simply direct lead it inexorably into narrative – in a path followed by some of highly admired food writers of the mid-twentieth century, including Constance Spry and Elizabeth David in Britain and Julia Child in America.

Practitioners of scientific food writing resisted the narrative impulse because of its potential for endless digression, for its tendency to pull us towards the book rather than the kitchen. But as all students of post-structuralism know, the potential for ambiguity is a product not of narrative but of language itself. No recipe can entirely control its meanings: even the most reading-resistant reveals far more than it intends. The *Canon Cookery Book*'s 'Victoria Sponge Sandwich', for example, is interesting for the tautology of its title – the 'correct' name of the cake is 'Victoria Sandwich' (it was named in the latter half of the nineteenth century in honour of the Queen), and denotes a cake which is an adjusted form of the traditional pound cake (equal weight of eggs and all other ingredients), which substitutes more baking powder for some of the eggs. The resulting cake is served as the British traditionally serve sponge cakes (which are much lighter cakes, made without fat, and raised by whisked egg whites): sandwiched with jam and sometimes cream or butter icing, the top un-iced and dusted with sugar. It is, strictly speaking, incorrect to call a Victoria Sandwich a Victoria Sponge, and the authors of the book know that, listing the recipe in a section on 'Cakes Made by the Creaming Method' and having a separate section on 'The Making of Sponge Mixtures'. They call the cake a 'sponge' because a significant number of their readers do so (a usage that almost certainly developed because of the way a Victoria Sandwich is served). In using both designators the recipe marks itself as interested in tradition and authenticity but also eager to use the terms with which the reader is familiar – there is no educative impulse: here and throughout, the book is not trying to expand its readers' culinary repertoires but give them fool-proof methods for making the dishes they already know and like. As are all recipes, it is also interesting for all the things it does *not* say and do and for what it assumes. It is not at all concerned with issues of taste, in either of its meanings. At no point in this recipe, or in any of the others in the collection, is there any discussion of flavour, of how the dishes are supposed to taste, of how to vary flavour intensity or profile for different recipients. There is no discussion of the occasions on which different dishes might be served, for what function and for what effect. The 'register' of the dishes collected is very safe: almost all the recipes are for very traditional, 'ordinary' British food. Almost all of the dishes could have been found in a recipe collection 100 years earlier – indeed, Isabella Beeton's *Household Management* of 1861 contains far more 'exotic' dishes, and Beeton does not feel the need to explain, as *The Cannon Cookery Book* does, that curry powder is 'a combination of Eastern Spices used for flavouring meat, poultry, fish, cereals and vegetables' (1953: 59). All of this suggests that the authors do not consider their readers to be people who will deploy their culinary skills in the interests of social mobility (or, at least, that they consider such purposes outside their purview). Most striking of all are the formal qualities of the recipe, which structurally and graphically shouts its concern to avoid narrative: there are full stops after each item in the listed ingredients, the stages of the method are separated by numbers, oven temperature and timings are given in bold and laid out as a subheading. Everything possible has been done to prevent a drift into continuous prose.

A distinction should be made between the digressive potential of the recipe and the text in which it is imbedded. Food, and therefore food writing, as this book has aimed to demonstrate, exerts a centripetal force capable of dragging all sorts of apparently diverse areas into its field: power, politics, sex, violence, national identity, body image, familial relations, the means of production, gender, history, the avant-garde – all these and more have, throughout its history, been considered a reasonable part of the discourse of the cookbook. For the most part, however, the more wildly digressive elements have not formed part of the recipe proper, and have instead been part of introductory material at the start of books or chapters or sections. Despite her abrupt ways with an inter-recipe adjective, Isabella Beeton, for example, allows herself almost as many chapters of encyclopaedic information on the history, geography, culture, literature, science and so on, of food as she has chapters of recipes.[2] It is in the twentieth century that food writers begin to allow themselves specific space for digression within the formally delineated structure of the recipe itself. We see this new mode at work in the chatty, sophisticated cookbooks produced in Britain immediately after the First World War: in Lady Jekyll's *Kitchen Essays* (1922), for example, the titles of recipes are interpolated into the chat: 'This *Bombe Néro* was one of the successes of the artist chef of the Cannes Casion during a recent conference', while in *Caviar to Candy* (1927), where Mrs Philip Martineau offers recipes from around the world, the discursive matter is often folded into the instructions, so a recipe for Cumberland Sauce begins 'Can anything be nicer with cold ham than a Cumberland sauce? And this, once made, will keep for many days. You take two shallots, minced as finely as possible, and put them into a saucepan with the rind of an orange cut into the finest strips' (Jekyll 1969: 147; Martineau 1933: 134) (In her essay 'The Anatomy of a Recipe' M. F. K. Fisher parodies exactly these 'slim and beautifully printed volumes which float out of London, through wars and pestilence': 'The style is always informal: one is discussing, between peers, what was a *succès fou* at last night's little stand-up supper for Imogen (Lady) Craddo, or may be so tonight after Wallie's new opening' (Fisher 1983: 21)). By the 1950s a new protocol has been tacitly agreed on: preliminary discussion can come before or after the recipe title but it is kept graphically distinct from the methodology. Many writers freely vary their practice: in *The Constance Spry Cookery Book* (1956) a recipe for Lemon Soufflé has the title followed by a note of recommendation while the consecutive recipe for Mousse au Chocolate Basque is preceded by exactly the same sort of recommendation (Spry and Hume 1961: 943). It is this model that still remains the dominant practice in most contemporary food writing, giving us a four-part structure of title, preliminary remarks, ingredients and methodology with some flexibility about the ordering of these elements. The recipe as thus established is insertable into a variety of contexts, appearing in instructional manuals, newspaper columns, magazine pages and food blogs, but also in less immediately obvious forms such as memoirs, novels and essays. The discussion will return to some of these forms shortly, but will first consider the emergence of a curious literary genre predicated on taking recipes (too) seriously.

Engaging with recipes

It is so unusual to cook one's way through all – or even the majority – of the recipes in a single cookbook that those who choose to do so are considered remarkable. Veteran food writer, restaurateur and campaigner Prue Leith 'taught herself her craft by working doggedly through Constance Spry's book section by section ("suet puddings and all") as lunch-time cook to a prosperous firm of West End solicitors', while Paul Levy, the influential food journalist, taught himself to cook as a student in similar manner: 'he bought a book by Louis Diat (of the Ritz Carlton) and worked his way through the stations of a large hotel restaurant' (Driver 1983: 161; Barr 1988: 10). In 2002 a young New York temp secretary lighted on a similar project: Julie Powell, in need of comfort as she dealt with issues about her fertility and her failure to become an actress, found her mother's copy of *Mastering the Art of French Cooking* (1961), and decided to cook her way through it. She recorded her encounters with the book's recipes in a blog – 'The Julie / Julia Project', which soon achieved considerable popularity. Her book about the experience of writing the blog was published in 2005 under the title *Julie & Julia: 365 Days, 524 Recipes, 1 Tiny Apartment Kitchen*, and a film adaptation entitled *Julie and Julia* directed by Nora Ephron, which combines episodes of Powell's experience with episodes from the life of Julia Child, appeared in 2009.[3] The titles of the various projects highlight one central element: Powell's engagement with these recipes is conceived as a relationship with their author. The fact that the source book is not solely authored by Julia Child, but also by her co-authors Louisette Berthole and Simone Beck does not in any way interrupt the intensity of her focus on Child: they are mentioned in the first post and then quietly forgotten.[4] This omission is due to the fact that Child's public profile in America rests not so much on the book as on the TV show which followed, which turned her into a household name and kick-started a food revolution. As a TV star, Child cut a very curious figure: she was six-foot tall, solidly built and clumsy. British audiences complained about 'that mad, drunken American woman', but the Americans took her to their hearts:

> At first some viewers assumed that Julia [...] was parodying the traditional cooking show. But even when they realised the show was entirely serious, viewers watched her shenanigans with enthusiasm. Mrs Child huffed, puffed, and galumphed

across the screen, her high-pitched voice cracking like an adolescent schoolboy's, and she was famous for dropping things and demonstrating cuts of meat with her own body. All of this enchanted viewers and assured them that if this seemingly average American woman could cook French food, then so could they. (Lovegren 1995: 226–7)

By the time Powell 'discovers' Child, she has ceased to be a name to conjure with in food-conscious circles – 'this book hasn't been on the must-have list for enterprising gourmands in decades' – but she responds to something in the book's project and voice: 'I have never looked to religion for comfort – belief is just not in my genes. But reading *Mastering the Art of French Cooking* – childishly simple and dauntingly complex, incantatory and comforting – I thought this was what prayer must feel like. Sustenance bound up with anticipation and want' (Powell 2009: 15). She imagines Child speaking to her throughout her project, and although she is momentarily abashed when someone brings the blog to the attention of the still-living Julia Child, who dismisses her as 'not serious', she continues to relate to 'her' Julia as variously mentor, challenger and friend. When Child dies, she notes the intensely self-centred tone adopted by commentators: 'these statements tend toward the possessive – "*I* saw Julia in this-and-such restaurant," or "*My* whatever-Julia-dish is *really great*," or "I never really *bought* Julia's opinion on this-or-that ...."' (306). She imputes this relational thinking about Child to some unique quality in her work (ultimately, she declares, it is a capacity for joy), a quality that can be apprehended *through* the prose: 'it's the best word I can think of for the heady, near violent satisfaction to be found in the text of Julia's first book. I read her instructions for making béchamel sauce, and what comes throbbing through is that here is a woman who has found her way' (305). Child's instructions for making béchamel do not, to my mind, noticeably throb with joy, though they do convey a particular pleasure in the 'Frenchness' of innovations such as adding extra butter, which 'imparts that certain French taste which seems to be present in no other type of cooking' (Beck et al. 1976: 78). Rather, I would suggest, Child's recipes read in the conglomerate drip-feed a sense of authorial personality through asides, digressions, opinions, tone of voice, even word choice. This phenomenon is not unique to Julia Child: many readers of Elizabeth David, for example, respond similarly, as Artemis Cooper noted in her biography: 'behind those crisp sentences, one can feel the pressure of her loves and hates, her enthusiasm and her passion. The reader becomes acutely aware of these emotions, although they are never mentioned' (2000: xiii). It is in part a function of the discursive quality of their prose, in part the effect of the intense focused engagement of a project like Powell's; but it is also, on some level, something that recipes inevitably do: in the act of instructing, they speak to us, and in speaking, they gain a particular voice and convey a sense of a personality operating behind that voice. The effect is at its most pronounced when we *do what they say*, when we literalize their words: which perhaps accounts for the cult of personality that built around the most influential food writers long before the phenomenon of the TV chef. In 'Recipes for Reading: Summer Pasta, Lobster à la Riseholme, and Key Lime Pie' (1989), a highly influential essay that did much to insert food writing into academic critical discourse, Susan J. Leonardi argues that the central feature of a recipe is that it represents an interchange between individuals: 'even the root of *recipe* – the Latin *recipere* – implies an exchange, a giver and a receiver' (1989: 340).[5] It is the act of sharing that she finds fundamental to the nature of the recipe in its many and various embedded contexts. Leonardi considers Irma S. Rombauer's *The Joy of Cooking* (1931), and the ways in which the quirky, relatable personality of the original is systematically undercut in the edits performed by her daughter, Marion Becker Rombauer, for the revised edition of 1963. It is notable for our purposes (although Leonardi does not emphasize it) that *both* versions of the book convey personality – but Marion's is controlled, and self-consciously distant and 'scientific': 'one cannot imagine the reviser of this book ever having made either a first cake or a cutting remark' (342). The persona of a cookbook is a product of narrative devices, but it is also constructed through *active* reading, reading between the lines and the recipes, hearing a tone of voice through the directions, building a continuous narrative through the discontinuities and hybridities of the form. When people remark (and many do) that they read cookbooks like novels, it is this process to which they are referring: the construction of a narrative personality through the reading between the lines and gaps of discontinuous text. In Powell's case, she beefs up this sense of authorial personality by interspersing her account of her own life with imagined scenes from Julia Child's biography, often focalized through the perspective of Child's husband, Paul. These scenes focus on Julia Child as unlikely ingénue – newly married, first discovering the glories of French food, bringing her closer in age and experience to Powell herself.

This equalizing device is at one with the role in which Powell casts herself – she is not so much eager acolyte as bolshie, disrespectful high school student. She evinces little interest in classic French food or its cultural context, and challenges Child at every turn. Despite her account of her long dalliance with upmarket food magazines and the works of Martha Stewart, she is not a sophisticated eater: she doesn't eat eggs, is 'nervous about the Roquefort, being generally a bit squeamish about eating mold', and quails at kidneys and other 'organ meat' ('The Julie / Julia Project', Sept 3, 2002; Powell 2009: 257). A running motif is horror at the amount of butter Child's recipes use. Her decision to cook her way through *this* book is profoundly counter-intuitive: the food is unfashionable, not to her taste and does not fit her lifestyle. But this is the point – her hapless grappling with live lobsters, aspic and ladyfingers in a tiny filthy 'loft' kitchen in the outer boroughs after a long day as a beleaguered democrat desk-slave in a republican political office makes for great copy. The blog and the projects that spin out from it are not about 'mastering' French cooking, or anything else; they are about being *mastered by* an obsession. What Child's book provides Powell is order: a syllabus, to be followed step by step. In the chaos of an urban twenty-something life, this order – the very lack of choice or decision – is in itself deeply comforting, while for her blog readers there is an intense satisfaction in the chaotic encounters with individual recipes. In some cases these encounters are slapstick scenes of failure and disgust – her attempts to remove marrow from bones without a cleaver, the disaster of trying to cook eggs poached in red wine at nearly midnight after a day of moving house, the maggots that emerge from under her unwashed sink rack – and the effect for the reader is part rueful sympathy, part schadenfreude. The blog is at its most inclusive, though, at the moments when it dramatizes the ultimate impossibility of the recipe as form – the places where linguistic ambiguity and imprecision short-circuit its ability to convey physical actions and precise material states. On the blog on 1 September 2002 she attempts crème brulee, which is 'one of those scary recipes that involved pouring hot things into cold things in thin streams while beating vigorously but not too much, where milk can curdle, butter separate, egg yolks congeal':

> Julia's descriptions usually bring me much comfort, but today she only intones obscurely. I'm meant to beat the egg yolks and sugar 'until the mixture is pale yellow and forms the ribbon'. Granted, she refers me to another page where this enigmatic phrase is expanded upon, but there she only terrifies me by saying that 'when a bit is lifted in the beater it will fall back into the bowl forming a slowly dissolving ribbon on the surface of the mixture. Do not beat beyond this point or the egg yolks may become granular'. Granular?! I heat the egg and hot cream mixture in a saucepan, stirring constantly, until the 'sauce' – sauce? I'm making a sauce? – 'thickens just enough to coat the spoon with a light, creamy layer'. I have no idea what this means. Doesn't liquid pretty much always coat a spoon? 'Do not', says Julia, 'let the custard' – now it's a custard? – 'come anywhere near the simmer'. I'm meant to be using a candy thermometer to assist in this determination, but I lost my candy thermometer in a nasty incident involving mercury-tainted fried chicken some time back, so I have to muddle through without. When the coating looks creamy-ish, I take it off the heat, beat in some vanilla, and set it aside to cool. The distinctly liquid nature of it is leading me to suspect this is not going to be crème brulee as I know it.

Powell conveys well the panic of reading-while-doing that complex cooking from a recipe often involves, as well as the confusions caused by near synonyms (the mixture-cum-sauce-cum-custard) and the metaphoric language necessarily employed to convey changes of state. Child's language is more precisely detailed than most recipe writers, but it still has the potential to confuse. Powell's project highlights the ultimate paradox of the recipe form – it communicates very easily all sorts of things that are not its primary purpose – personality, social and cultural context – but can struggle to convey the one thing that is its absolute raison d'etre: the precise actions the reader must perform in order to produce a dish.

Fictional recipes

When cookbook and recipes make brief appearances in nineteenth-century novels it is with a focus on the gap to be bridged between the manual's blithe reassurances and glib instructions and the inadequacies of the harried reader. In Wilkie Collins's *No Name* (1862), the hapless giantess Mrs Wragge, wife of the scurrilous captain who functions as protagonist Magdalen's *aide de campe* in her elaborate campaign to regain her inheritance, breaks down over the complications of the instructions in her 'old-fashioned Treatise of the Art of Cookery', marking the pages with her tears:

> 'As sure as I ever sit down to this book, the Buzzing in my head begins again. Who's to make it out? Sometimes, I think I've got it, and it all goes away from me. Sometimes, I think I haven't got it, and it all comes back in a heap. Look here! Here's what he's ordered for his breakfast tomorrow: – "Omelette with Herbs. Beat up two eggs with a little water or milk, salt, pepper, chives, and parsley. Mince small." – There! mince small! How am I to mince small, when it's all mixed up and running? "Put a piece of butter the size of your thumb in the frying pan." – Look at my thumbs and look at yours! whose size does she mean? "Boil, but not brown." – If it mustn't be brown, what colour must it be? She won't tell me, she expects me to know, and I don't. "Pour in the omelette." – there! I can do that. "Allow it to set, raise it around the edge; when done, turn it over to double it." – Oh, the number of times I turned it over and doubled it in my head, before you came in to-night! [...] Oh, the lots of omelettes all frying together in my head and all frying wrong.' (1992: 149–50)

The problems Mrs Wragge has with the recipe's instructions are two-fold: the inexactitude of its language and its difficulty in conveying physical actions. The first is particularly a matter of temporal ordering: she is told to mince – the parsley, we must assume – *after* she has been told to put it in the egg mixture. The seemingly self-evident requirement to arrange the stages of the method in the sequence in which they must be performed is one that has posed a perennial problem for food writers; the difficulty seems to be a conceptual survival from an essentially oral tradition, the instructor standing next to the instructee, offering details and refinements as they work. The recipe as written form is crucially dependent on order in time, as Eric Griffiths notes in a somewhat tongue-in-cheek article relating Delia Smith's food writing to Hegel's anti-materialist theories of aesthetics:

> The calm of Delia's work expresses itself best in her over-arching and point-instant grasp of time. She is so narrative, it is surprising she hasn't been more written about by Gerard Genette or Gillian Beer. [...] She [...] mark[s] time, like a piano teacher [...] stay[ing] with you all the way, ticking off the instructions – 'First of all ... When ... Now ... Next ... Then ... Next ... Now ... Then ... Then ... Now ...' – until we arrive together at a 'Finally'. (Griffiths 1996)

The other inaccuracy in the cookbook in *No Name* is one of rough and ready measurements. Novelist Julian Barnes, in his 2003 *The Pedant in the Kitchen*, complains of exactly this in contemporary cookbooks, his concern about cavalier measurements virtually identical to that of Mrs Wragge: 'how big is a lump, how voluminous is a "slug" or a "gout" [...]. Are we meant to write to the late Mr Olney's executors and ask how big his hands were? What if children made this jam, or circus giants?' (2004: 19–21).

The larger problem lies in the conveying in prose sufficiently precise instructions for physical movements. The omelette is a particular challenge, as it relies on a specific manual knack. It is the point at which many cookbooks founder: Julia Child attempts to solve the conundrum with eleven pages and ten diagrams, including arrows showing the directions in which your hands should be moving at particular stages; she also advises that 'a simple-minded but perfect way to master the movement is to practise outdoors with half a cupful of dried beans' – an instruction that Julie Powell has great fun following (Beck et al. 1976: 152; Powell 2009: 85). (The instructions in Mrs Wragge's book, even if followed correctly, would produce a profoundly inauthentic omelette for French tastes, cooked solidly on the outside and set in the middle.) When Magdalen has translated the instructions to Mrs Wragge's satisfaction, the latter becomes reconciled to the textual rhythms that have previously haunted her: '"And then turn the frying-pan, then turn the frying-pan, then turn the frying-pan over. It sounds like poetry, don't it?"' (Collins 1992: 150). Now that she has had the method explained to her, the book's words can be allowed an incantatory, purely textual status. In Dickens's *Our Mutual Friend* (1865), another cookbook proves equally ineffective. 'The Complete British Family Housewife' is the property of the erstwhile Bella Wilfer, now the newly married Mrs John Rokesmith, who indulges herself in happy domesticity when her husband is at work in the City. Her servantless domestic routine is depicted as inherently blissful as, wearing 'trim little wrappers and aprons', she indulges, like Doris Day's finally feminised Calamity Jane, in 'such weighing and mixing and chopping and grating, such dusting and washing and polishing, such snipping and weeding and trowelling and other small gardening, such making and mending and folding and airing': all this labour imagined by the text as essentially play, with the exception of the 'such severe study' she is forced to give to the book of household management, which 'she would sit consulting, with her elbows on the table and her temples in her hands, like some perplexed enchantress poring over the Black Art' (Dickens 1918: 796–7). Her perplexity is directly related to the *language* of the book: 'the complete British Housewife, however sound a Briton at heart, was by no means an expert Briton at expressing herself with clearness in the British tongue, and might have issued her directions to equal purpose in the Kamskatchan language'. Bella's response has much in it of the insubordination with which Julie Powell approaches Julia Child: 'in any crisis of this nature, Bella would suddenly exclaim aloud, "Oh you ridiculous old thing, what do you mean by that? You must have been drinking!"'. She finds the imperative tone of the British Housewife 'highly exasperating': 'She would say "Take a salamander", as if a general should command a private to catch a Tartar. Or, she would casually issue the order, "Throw in a handful -" of something entirely unattainable'. This imperative mode, a feature of traditional recipes so distinctive that it forms part of a general parodic trope about old cookery books ('first take your hare'), establishes a dictatorial relationship between the text's persona and the reader which Bella, at least, finds so objectionable that she 'would shut her up and knock her on the table'.

In twentieth-century fiction these self-defeating, reader-resistant recipes are replaced by a very different conception of the recipe form, which sees it as a profoundly expressive mode. At the centre of E. F. Benson's *Mapp and Lucia* (1931) is a competition over the much-prized recipe for 'Lobster à la Riseholme'. The book is the fourth of a series of six, which originally started life as two separate series: the first two books, *Queen Lucia* (1920) and *Miss Mapp* (1922), cover the lives of their respective titular protagonists as they rule over the genteel communities of Riseholme and Tilling; in *Mapp and Lucia*, the latter moves to Tilling, initiating a battle royale about status which fuels the rest of the series. Much of the elaborate game of social one-up-manship centres around food, in particular the use of invitations to luncheon, tea, dinner and parties as a means of manipulation, competition and exclusion. 'Lobster à la Riseholme' and variations on it are served a number of times: the dish represents Lucia's former home in her present one, an exoticism which the Tillingites, and particularly Elizabeth Mapp, are eager both to experience and to absorb into their own culture. The town worthies' first encounter with the dish occurs offstage, and is only mentioned retrospectively; the first time the reader hears of it is in the context not of the dish itself, but of its recipe:

> It had already produced a great deal of surmise in the minds of the housewives at Tilling, for no one could conjecture how it was made, and Lucia had been deaf to all requests for the recipe: Elizabeth had asked her twice to give it to her, but Lucia had merely changed the subject without attempt at transition: she had merely talked about something quite different. This secretiveness was considered unamiable, for the use of Tilling was to impart its culinary mysteries to friends, so that they might enjoy their favourite dishes at each other's houses. (Benson 1970: 178–9)

The idea of the secret recipe is not one that has much valency in British culture (unlike America, where there is much more of an emphasis on culinary invention and on personalized recipes): Lucia's secretiveness is unusual, and Elizabeth Mapp takes her refusal as both insult and challenge. She first attempts to 'guess' the recipe, but 'lobster *à la Riseholme à la Mapp* had been found to consist of something resembling lumps of India-rubber (so tough that the teeth positively bounced away from them on contact) swimming in a dubious pink gruel'; when that fails she tries to bride Lucia's cook – 'actually fingering a bright half-crown, [she] had asked point blank for the recipe' (179). When she tastes the dish again Elizabeth tries to 'read' its flavours: 'she took into her mouth small fragments of lobster, in the manner of a wine-taster, appraising subtle flavours. There was cheese, there were shrimps, there was cream: there were so many things that she felt like Adam giving names to the innumerable procession of different animals' (182). Finally, in the throes of obsession, she lets herself into Lucia's kitchen on Boxing Day when the servants are out celebrating, in order to find the recipe in the cook's book. At this moment, Benson's social comedy tips into a sort of high camp surrealism: just as Lucia discovers Elizabeth in the act, an enormous flood swirls into the kitchen, leaving the two of them only moments to climb into the upturned kitchen table before they are swept out to sea. Months later, they return, having spent the interim in an Italian fishing trawler on the Gallagher banks, and Elizabeth's first act, on reclaiming her home, is to draw from the pocket of her 'frayed and sea-stained jacket, a halfsheet of discoloured paper' on which are 'the mystic words "take two hen lobsters"' (264). As Susan Leonardi notes, these words – the only scrap of the recipe to which the reader is ever privy – emblematize Mapp and Lucia themselves and their rivalous scrapping (1989: 345). The novel ends with another serving of the dish, at a luncheon hosted by Elizabeth. It is a moment of wild speculation on the part of the assembled guests about how the recipe was obtained and whether the dish will succeed:

> The ghastly silence continued as the lobster was handed round. It came to Lucia first. She tasted it and found that it was exactly right. She laid down her fork and grubbed up the imperfectly buried hatchet.
>
> 'Are you sure you copied the recipe out quite correctly, Elizabeta mia?' she asked. 'You must pop into my kitchen some afternoon when you are going for your walk – never mind if I am in or not – and look at it again. And if my cook is out too, you will find the recipe in a book on the kitchen-shelf. But you know that, don't you?' (285)

The battle ends in a draw, with neither fully successful: Miss Mapp has 'won' the recipe, but only at the cost of overt social exposure; Lucia has lost control over the recipe, but demonstrated her moral superiority. As Leonardi points out, it is significant that the reader continues to be at a loss as to the precise ingredients and method that will produce Lobster à la Riseholme – it remains as an entirely fictional dish, one not translatable into material reality. Given the weight of signification it bears, any actual reproduction of the dish would be bound to disappoint. As I have argued elsewhere, Benson's novels function as a sort of parodic commentary on the themes and ideological concerns of the inter-war feminine middlebrow novel, turning up the heat on its intense class-consciousness and effortful bohemianism so that the comedy of manners boils over and is condensed into something much stranger (Humble 2001: 59–60). In particular, the novel's queer sensibility remakes gender as essentially performative, transforming the trivial elements of the domestic scene into vital symbolic objects. In rendering the recipe as both quest object and talisman it both valorizes feminine power and draws attention to the toxic effects of limiting that power to the domestic sphere: like *Villette*'s Mme Beck, who 'ought to have swayed a nation', Mapp and Lucia waste their energy and natural authority on bitterness and petty social control. In this reading, the textually unwritten remainder of the recipe might be said to speak of as-yet unwritten possibilities for women's lives beyond the circular plots of interwar domestic fiction (Brontë 1993a: 71).

Later in the twentieth century, a number of novels do lard their text with actual recipes, the texts of which work in interesting counterpoint to their prose frames: prominent examples include Nora Ephron's *Heartburn* (1983), Laura Esquivel's *Like Water for Chocolate* (1989) and John Lanchester's *The Debt to Pleasure* (1996).[6] The protagonist of *Heartburn*, as discussed in Chapter 4, is a food writer and broadcaster, whose books are 'cookbooks in an almost incidental way', with chapters about 'friends or relatives or trips or experiences', with the recipes worked in 'peripherally' (Ephron 1996: 17). The novel follows exactly this blueprint, with recipes flowing seamlessly from Rachel's artless chat about her life. There is no graphic separation of text and recipe: the only indication that a recipe is beginning is the use either of the imperative – 'Take 4 cups of washed sorrel' (35) – or the deployment of a language of gifting or exchange: 'Here's Amelia's cheesecake recipe' (49). The recipes are an integral part of the texture of the novel, telling us much about Rachel's cultural background, her historical moment, her influences. Her life is measured out in the meals she has eaten and prepared, the recipes she has written, and those she has been given. In giving the recipes to us she is creating a climate of feminine intimacy, giving us access to something fundamental about herself. The recipes take us into her emotional state, offering conduits to deeper intimacy:

> (Another thing I like to eat when I'm feeling blue is bacon hash. Cut some bacon into small pieces and start to cook it over a slow flame so that some of the fat is rendered. Then add diced cooked potatoes and cook slowly until the potatoes and bacon are completely crunchy. Eat with an egg.) (42)

The invitation to identification of the traditional novel is here amplified, but also troubled, since the implied suggestion (or sometimes, command) that we make these dishes is compounded by the presence of a recipe index on the final page of the text. It is one thing to read *through* the recipes to the nostalgia and pain they represent; it is another to actually make them ourselves. To cook bacon hash *from* this recipe represents a particular sort of textual engagement: would I be imagining myself *as* Rachel, or trying to bring her experience to life, or simply engaging in a sort of self-conscious play? There is quite a contemporary taste for recipes from literature, with a small publishing industry supplying collections of recipes from Jane Austen, from Charles Dickens, from children's books like the *Little House on the Prairie* series, but to cook from these books is not quite the same thing as to cook from a recipe in a novel, because the recipes have been extrapolated from brief textual mentions, or collected from contemporary sources rather than given by a character in the novel.[7] The act of cooking Rachel Samstadt's bacon hash is problematic because it draws attention to all the tacit mental contortions we willingly undertake in order to convince ourselves, for the length of the reading experience, that realism is *real*. In undertaking this ultimate act of readerly identification we are forced to realize that Rachel Samstadt is textual, unable to give us the validating practical experience we require of the author of a recipe because she does not exist. Precisely because the recipes are so firmly woven into the narrative, as elements of plot and characterization and back-story, they are troubling as detachable reproducible objects. This is particularly the case with the key lime pie with which Rachel ends her marriage, by throwing it in the face of her cheating husband at a dinner party. In writing the recipe for this pie she turns what might otherwise read as hysterical outburst (and does in the film version of this scene), into a planned, considered decision: '*If I throw this pie at him, he will never love me. But he doesn't love me anyway. So I can throw the pie if I want*' (175). In offering the reader the recipe for this marriage-ending pie, Ephron inserts her text into a contemporary tradition of feminist consciousness-raising. For Leonardi, the key feature of the recipes included in *Heartburn* is the way in which they literalize a feminine tradition of sharing and mutual support, they are 'an act of trust between women' (346), extended to the reader. In the context of the world of the novel this reading is absolutely convincing – Rachel entrusts her friends and her readers with the recipes that are important to her; they trust that she has rendered them completely and accurately; but who, exactly, would the kitchen-bound reader of *Heartburn* be trusting: Rachel Samstadt, a fictional character, or Nora Ephron, a film-maker who has wrapped up her act of revenge and public shaming in the unthreateningly post-feminist form of a food writer? It is the recipes and the strong tonal injunction to use them that more than anything else move this text into the territory of the postmodern, a place where both realism and the real are ludically up for grabs. Laura Esquivel's magic realist *Like Water for Chocolate* similarly operates in this territory, its subtitle – 'A Novel in Monthly Instalments with Recipes, Romances and Home Remedies' – indicating the formal play in which it will indulge. Each monthly chapter begins with a decorated title page, on the recto of which is given the month and the name of a recipe and on the verso the ingredients. The decorated linear panels containing this information are physically arranged so that they could be cut from the pages to form a collection of recipe cards: the format imitates not so much a cookbook as the food pages of a magazine. Each chapter then begins with the title 'PREPARATION:', with the first paragraph detailing the method in a diffuse, discursive mode, and the matter of the novel proper segueing from this, but separated from it by both paragraph break and tense. So, the recipe / chapter for 'Champandongo' begins thus:

> The onion is finely chopped and fried in a little oil with the meat. While it is frying, the ground cumin and a tablespoon of sugar are added.
>   As usual, Tita was crying as she chopped the onion. The tears clouded her vision so completely that before she realised it she cut her finger with the knife. (Esquivel 1993: 133)

The recipe is rendered in the present continuous form, given by an authority who is not fully identified until the final pages of the novel, when it is revealed that the source is Tita's cookbook, the only thing remaining when the family ranch is burnt down by the long-delayed passionate consumption of her love for Pedro. In this Cinderella-like narrative, Tita, the youngest daughter, is forced to remain unmarried, cooking for her demanding mother, while her sister is married to the man Tita loves. But cooking is not simply drudgery for Tita: the kitchen is her home from infancy, and for her 'the joy of living was wrapped up in the delights of food' (11); the food she cooks for her family and friends contains within it her emotions: the tears she cries into her sister's wedding cake create desperate longing in all who eat it; the quails in rose petals, cooked with a bunch of roses given to her by Pedro, drives her other sister mad with lust. Clearly the recipes that operate within the novel are not the same as the recipes we are given, though textually they are identical.[8] The cut-out-and-keep format of the 'recipe cards', like Ephron's recipe index, invites the literalization of the dishes in the kitchen of the reader, but unlike *Heartburn*'s recipes, which are perfectly workable (and often, like the recipes for Key Lime Pie and Amelia's Cheesecake, highly conventional and much-circulated forms that ultimately derive from food manufacturers), those in Esquivel's novel are not always what they seem. The quail in rose petal sauce, for instance (as Julie Powell discovers to her cost), with its twelve roses and two drops of attar of roses to six small birds, would produce an unbearably perfumed dish.[9] Others, like the recipe for making matches, are simply curiosities, and many are not practically reproducible because of the extraordinary amounts of time and trouble they involve: the making of (hot) chocolate from scratch, beginning with three types of raw, unroasted beans, for example. The food in the novel is prepared in extraordinary quantities: twenty-five trays of roasted chilies stuffed with nut paste; a wedding cake for 180 people, using 170 eggs. Ingredients have to be grown, harvested and prepared by hand: quails and turkeys killed, eggs slowly gathered as the hens lay and then preserved over months; nuts one by one roasted, shelled and the bitter inner skin removed. Food in this culture and time can fill – and use up – a whole life, and part of the point of the recipes is to speak to the gap between our world and theirs. The recipes themselves are magic realist devices – making strange the ordinary (matches, a cake) and making the magical real by giving us a set of rules which will apparently reproduce it.

While the recipes in Esquivel's and Ephron's novels speak to a female tradition of recipe sharing as community building, those in John Lanchester's *The Debt to Pleasure* come from a very different tradition. Lanchester's murderous narrator, Tarquin Winot, is a self-consciously intense gourmet, given to long meandering disquisitions which treat food as a serious art form (one which rivals the sculpture for which the elder brother of whom he is intensely jealous is famous). The food writing which structures his narrative is the menu rather than the recipe, but recipes are strewn through his narrative, and he begins with a disquisition on the form:

> One of the charms of the genre is that it places an unusually high premium on accuracy. The omission of a single word or a single instruction can inflict a humiliating fiasco on the unsuspecting home cook. Which of us has not completed a recipe to the letter, only to look down and see, lying unused by the sauté pan, a recriminatory pile of chopped onions? One early disaster of my brother's, making a doomed attempt to impress some hapless love object, was occasioned by the absence of the small word 'plucked' – he removed from the oven a roasted but full-fledged pheasant, terrible in its hot sarcophagus of feathers. (Lanchester 1996: 1)

The trap which Lanchester lays so masterfully is that for the contemporary food-obsessive, Winot is correct about many things, and it may take the reader a little while to realize that his grandiloquent statements are not to be taken at face value.[10] The role played by the recipes in the novel is primarily to force the reader into an unwanted complicity with the narrator, as they are *right* – offering precise advice and accurate, if extraordinarily digressive, contextual information. Although the menus are given in a graphically separate form, centred and in italics, the recipes flow in the main text, with no presentational division between instructional and discursive or narratorial text. The first menu, for Winter, begins with Blinis with sour cream and caviar. The 'recipe' covers five and a half pages, beginning with a disquisition on 'the many extant batter, pancake and waffle dishes', with an analysis of how the blini is taxonomically distinguished from other pancakes: 'it is thick (as opposed to thin), non-folding (as opposed to folding) and raised with yeast (as opposed to bicarbonate of soda)' (13), and so on. The fact that it is made with buckwheat leads to a discussion of Ceres, Roman god of agriculture, and thence, with no transition, to the start of the recipe:

> Blinis. Sift 4 oz. buckwheat flour, mix with ½ oz. yeast (dissolved in warm water) and ¼ pint warm milk, leave for fifteen minutes. Mix 4 oz. flour with ¼ pint milk, add 2 egg yolks, 1 tsp sugar, 1 tbs melted butter, and a pinch of salt, whisk the two blends together. Leave for an hour. Add 2 whisked egg whites. Right. Now heat a heavy cast-iron frying pan of the type known in both classical languages as a *placenta* – which is, as everybody knows, not at all the same thing as the caul or wrapping in which the foetus lives when it is inside the womb.

The forced change of subject leads to a full page of meandering, covering his own birth 'in the caul' and the luck this is supposed to confer, via Freud and *David Copperfield* to the 'intense jealousy and anger' that this can cause between siblings, to self-serving anecdotes about his brother's apparent ill treatment of him as a child. The recipe then continues: 'When smoke starts to rise out of the pan add the batter in assured dollops, bearing in mind that each little dollop is to become a blini when it grows up, and that the quantities given here are sufficient for six' (15). The accompaniments occupy the remaining three and a quarter pages. The first is dismissed (and we with it) in one sentence: 'Sour cream is completely straightforward, and if you need any advice or guidance about it then, for you, I feel only pity' (15), while caviar accords him the opportunity for a discussion that covers rarity value (via Veblen, and also Marmite), the natural history of the sturgeon, the process of salting the eggs, and the work of the master caviar taster, segueing into a discussion of artistic judgement which becomes an account of a dream. This first recipe ends, self-reflexively, with a discussion of the name 'recipe':

> With liberal additions of sour cream and caviar the above recipe – I prefer the old-fashioned spelling 'receipt', but it was pointed out to me that 'if you call it that, nobody will have a f***ing clue what you're talking about' – represents adequate quantities for six people as a start, providing several blinis each. Perhaps I have already said that. (18)

In *Heartburn* and *Like Water for Chocolate*, the recipes intrude into and are embedded in the narrative; in *The Debt to Pleasure*, the whole text is ostensibly a collection of recipes, into which the narrative intrudes, slyly and haphazardly. While technically correct, and full of useful tips and precise details, the recipes also express a distinct hostility to the reader. The description of the layering of the ingredients for Irish stew – potatoes, then onions, then meat and so on – is followed by the injunction to 'Sprinkle each layer with salt and herbs' and the triumphant rejoinder that 'You will, of course, not be able to do that if you have been following this recipe without reading it through in advance. Let that be a lesson to you' (24). As the book progresses, the dual plots (of Winot, in disguise, following a young honeymoon couple through France, as he simultaneously dictates the book into a recording device; and his gradual revelation of the grand artistic project of destruction which has occupied his entire life) occupy more and more textual space, and the menus proportionately less, though the former are still ostensibly contained in the latter. Winot increasingly refuses to give recipes, having become bored with the detail required: of lemon tart he announces 'this is something for which I am not going to be bothered to give a recipe: simply purchase the relevant pudding from someone authoritative' (46), and his suggestions for a summer menu half way through the book of 'An Aperitif, Vegetables and Saladings, A Selection of Cold Cuts' are announced as not 'recipes and menus *per se*' but 'sparks flung from the wheel' (122). From this point onwards there are no recipes, though the learned disquisitions on food and food ways continue to the very end. The food book format is exploded from within, the reader's putative trust in the giver of recipes turned against them as Winot's true – murderous – culinary purposes are slowly revealed.

Food memoirs

It is no coincidence that all three of these modern recipe-driven novels are also fictional memoirs or biographies, with recipes used to tell a life story. The food memoir suddenly took off in the last decades of the twentieth century as a defined publishing category, with prominent examples including *New York Times* restaurant critic Ruth Reichl's *Tender at the Bone: Growing Up at the Table* (1998) and sequel *Comfort Me with Apples* (2001); cookery writer Nigel Slater's *Toast: The Story of a Boy's Hunger* (2003); Patricia Volk's *Stuffed: Growing Up in a Restaurant Family* (2001); and Nora Seton's *Kitchen Congregation: A Memoir* (2000).[11] The form has become so ubiquitous that food scholars have begun developing generic terms to refer to it, with candidates including 'foodoir' and 'recipistolary' literature.[12] Of course, the memoir element had been long established in more hybrid forms of food writing (for instance, the works of M. F. K. Fisher; *The Alice B Toklas Cook Book*). The 'new' food memoir is not essentially different from its predecessors, except that it is now explicitly acknowledged that the recipes and discussion of dishes serve to express the life story, rather than the memories existing mainly to frame the recipes. The difference is an extremely subtle one – as I have noted, recipes very often contain an expressive power even when this is not foregrounded. The framing of a recipe in the memoir form raises some significant questions about both its function and its relationship to the act of remembering. I will return to the question of memory later but want first to consider the particular purposes that the recipe plays in the food memoir. I would argue that we can divide food memoirs into a number of sub-categories: those which tell 'the story of the development of my taste', those which deploy food as a means of exploring a particular racial or ethnic or national identity, and those which record encounters with the foods of other nationalities. Examples of the former – which include Reichl's and Slater's texts, as well as Anthony Bourdain's *Kitchen Confidential* – are discussed in detail elsewhere in this book. My concern here is particularly with the use of recipes to explore issues of identity.

My examples are the best-known and most highly regarded of what is a significant sub-genre of African American women's food memoirs: Edna Lewis's *The Taste of Country Cooking* (1976) and Vertamae Smart-Grosvenor's *Vibration Cooking* (1970).[13] Writing about food and self as an African American woman is an immediately political act: in declaring themselves as cooks, Rafia Zafar stated in 'The Signifying Dish', black women must 'engage with the reigning ghosts of American racism' (1999: 450). As Doris Witt has persuasively argued, the figure of the be-turbaned 'Mammy' of plantation mythology lies problematically behind the role of cook for black women. In her brilliant deconstruction of the 'Aunt Jemima' figure Witt notes the ways in which a fetishized image of 'the black female kitchen dominatrix' (2004: 61), beating biscuits, presiding over her realm, is used in the narratives of white southerners as a way of attributing power to slaves which they in reality absolutely lacked, while making white power – particularly that of white men – invisible.[14] The subordinate role of black women in white kitchens continued long after emancipation – domestic service was still by far the commonest form of employment for African American women when Lewis and Smart-Grosvenor were writing in the 1970s. Part of the success of these books lies, I would suggest, in the fact that the personal circumstances and histories of both writers offered them opportunities to sidestep those associations of service and therefore construct narratives of black-owned kitchens. Edna Lewis was born in 1916 in Freetown, Virginia, a village community founded in the years after emancipation by a group of freed slaves which included her grandfather. Her text foregrounds reminiscence, taking us season by season through the practices and events of the largely self-sufficient farming community. The growing, harvesting, preserving, preparation, sharing and consumption of food are at the heart of their lives. The food culture delineated is not an impoverished one: provisions are carefully husbanded for the non-productive periods of the year, but each season has its plenty. Recipes function in the text as both memorial and prompt to revival. They are arranged according to the dictates of the remembered rural year, with sections headed 'A Spring Breakfast When the Shad Were Running', 'Morning-After-Hog-Butchering Breakfast', 'The Night for a Boiled Virginia Ham Dinner', but they are designed to be cooked: Lewis had already had a long career as a chef when she wrote the book, and the recipes are meticulously detailed for the purposes of modern cooks and kitchens. The narrative perspective is that of the child, gradually inculcated into the skills and rituals of kitchen and fields, eagerly anticipating seasonal pleasures such as wild strawberries and home-cranked peach ice cream, observing the communal labour of harvesting, hunting and hog-killing. The voice employed most consistently throughout is also communal, that of both the children remembering and of the community following its seasonal traditions. *Vibration Cooking*, in contrast, is firmly individual and contemporary in its voice and focus: writing at the height of the Black Arts Movement, and deploying a hip, urban African American vernacular, Smart-Grosvenor uses food as a form of black consciousness-raising.[15] Both the book and the narrative persona nimbly sidestep categorization: subtitled *The Travel Notes of a Geechee Girl*, it melds travel journalism with cookbook with memoir with letters with manifesto, while Vertamae herself moves through roles and identities with virtuoso ease, appearing variously as actress, dancer, costume designer, urban bohemian, traveller and country girl. The first identity she claims, in the book's title, is that of a Geechee. The Geechee people (now more usually referred to as Gullah) are those from the Sea Islands off the coast of South Carolina and Georgia and the coastal plain area of the mainland; from the eighteenth century the area was used to grow rice and indigo in huge plantations and the relative isolation from whites allowed for the retention of large elements of African culture by the people enslaved there. The Gullah people's creole language and distinctive culture have been increasingly celebrated in recent decades, but at the time of the writing of *Vibration Cookery* the culture was less widely known, and Smart-Grosvenor's proud championing of this identity places her in the vanguard of 'a much broader movement to reinterpret and revalue the African heritage of black Americans' (Witt 2004: 174). While the farming year structures Lewis's book, Smart-Grosvenor's circles around aspects of identity, with sections including 'Home', 'Away from Home', 'Madness', and 'Love'. Name-dropping, quoting and directly addressing friends and family both famous and unknown (some perhaps imaginary), she uses recipes to illustrate anecdotes, and anecdotes to talk about food in terms of racial identity, politics, history and gender. Trickster-like (and it is worth noting that the Brer Rabbit stories are Gullah in origin), she contradicts herself, takes up positions and then abandons them, her 'riffing, razzing [and] sassy talk' rendering food and its culture immediate and urgent (Williams-Forson 2011: xviii).

For both writers, food and its preparation are available to be celebrated precisely because they can be separated from a long history of service. The women whose cooking Edna Lewis recalls are crucially cooking for their families and communities, not as servants: their labour is self-determined and joyous, with food understood as gift rather than duty:

> The women of Freetown were amazing because they participated in the work of the fields and barnyard and yet would step right out of the field work when an unexpected friend or traveller turned up. They would make a quick fire in the wood cookstove, and in a few minutes emerge from the kitchen with a pot of hot coffee, a plate of biscuits – flannel-soft, a thin slice of ham inserted in each – a bowl of home-canned peaches, and perhaps some sugar cookies. (Lewis 2017: 135)

Vertamae Smart-Grosvenor raises the spectre of service on the first page of her text in the dedication 'to my mama and my grandmothers and my sisters in appreciation of the years that they worked in miss ann's kitchen and then came home to TCB in spite of slavery and oppression and the moynihan report'. This apparently artless statement demonstrates the covert complexities of her approach with its simultaneous encapsulation of political, historical, familial and aesthetic references; the 'TCB' ('taking care of business') an echo of Aretha Franklin's version of the anthem 'Respect'. The ironically referenced Moynihan report of 1965 had investigated the larger number of births outside marriage to African American women and concluded that it was the result of a matriarchal culture spread from slavery and ghettos which had weakened the ability of black men to function as authority figures: for Smart-Grosvenor, the ability of her foremothers to run their own homes and families in the time left over from service to 'miss ann' is something to be celebrated rather than reviled. Throughout her text she focusses on food prepared with love rather than from duty: for family and friends, children and lovers. Working as a maid is the one job she refuses to contemplate, and her memories of her mother's employers demonstrate one of the many complex uses to which she puts the recipe form. Beginning with her experience of being a latchkey child, and an incident in which she sets the apartment on fire with a candle of a cupcake as she celebrates her birthday alone, she describes her intense resentment of the family for whom her mother worked, and then offers a recipe from a later employer:

Mrs Greenstein (of late my mother's former employer) now lives in Miami and during one of her visits to Philadelphia visited my mother. Hearing of the cookbook she sent this recipe via my mother to me.

SPONGECAKE
1 box Duncan Hines Yellow Cake Mix
1 3-ounce box lemon-flavor Jell-O
2/3 cup milk
2/3 cup Wesson oil
4 eggs

Combine all ingredients except eggs. Beat eggs and add to other ingredients and mix. Bake in preheated oven, 325 degrees, for 50 minutes. (2011: 34)

What is crucial here is what is *not* said: there is no comment, no recommendation, no anecdote, merely an ironic silence about this junky convenience food cake which represents whiteness. Throughout her text, Smart-Grosvenor uses recipes not simply as recommendations but as representations of relationships, with her feelings for the individuals who briefly people the book revealed through the recipes she imputes to them or connects with them. Lewis's recipes, in contrast, are communal: they belong to the community of Freetown rather than to a specific individual. In her passages of memoir she will discuss the culinary virtuosity of particular people: in the chapter on the Revival Dinner – a church picnic which was the chief event in their social calendar – she offers a detailed account of the huge labour of her mother in preparing piles of fried chicken and cakes and tarts to take to the picnic, and the groaning tables of their neighbours, each with her own specialities, but the recipes – for cooked meats, corn pudding, biscuits, sweet potato and apple pies, caramel layer cake, lemonade and iced tea – represent a consensus, assigned to no one individual. This might not seem remarkable, as the impersonal mode is one often adopted by the writers of recipes, as discussed at the start of the chapter. But it is striking in a memoir, whose very function is to indicate the personal dimensions of the writer's relationship to food. It is a device which speaks to Lewis's fundamental purpose: to speak not of her own memories specifically, but of the memories of the community whose mutual support emblematizes the possibilities for African American self-determination. Her text is more quietly political than Smart-Grosvenor's, but it is political nonetheless.

One of the ways in which food was immediately political for black people in the America of the 1970s was the issue of 'soul food'. A term which gained currency in the early 1960s, it referenced particularly the rural Southern food traditions which many African Americans had left behind during the Great Migration to northern cities.[16] Having been generally celebrated, soul food became a site of debate and contestation in the Black Power era of black nationalism towards the end of the decade; some objected to what they saw as a revival of the foods of slavery, others to its co-option by whites and a growing black middle class: '[d]iverse voices – including those of numerous African American women – began to engage in a public debate over the proprietorship, origins, ingredients, and meanings of soul food' (Witt 2004: 96). Defining soul food became increasingly problematic, with many authors of the flood of soul food cookbooks insisting that definitional indeterminacy was one of its key features. Whether the concept was understood to contain the food of the rural South more broadly, or also the foods which nourished African Americans during the Migration and in the restaurants they founded in the north, at its core were the foods which were fed to the enslaved who laboured on plantations: greens, black-eyed peas, corn and the 'less-noble parts of the pig' (Harris 2011: 73). With the rise in influence of the Nation of Islam in the late 1960s and early 1970s the eating of pork became particularly contentious: leader Elijah Muhammad enjoined his followers to reject it absolutely: 'Do not eat the swine – do not even touch it' (Harris 2011: 73).[17] Both *Vibration Cooking* and *The Taste of Country Cooking* situate themselves aslant from the concept of soul food. Lewis never uses the term, instead claiming a wide range of foods as her own. She is concerned to delineate the precise food culture of Freetown as one with its own history and internal logic: the food she describes is Southern, but in a specific rather than generic way. Southern classics like coconut layer cake, shad roe, country ham, hominy grits and divinity mix with a food heritage that is understood as specifically black, with black-eyed peas, pickled watermelon rinds, and greens stewed in meat stock. These foods are notably presented not as the products of slavery but as a prized African inheritance: 'some varieties of leafy greens we would gather and cook every day, mostly because we knew instinctively they were of nutritional value – an instinct that comes from our African heritage, I'm sure' (Lewis 2017:174); the black-eyed pea is 'truly an African bean first introduced into our area by Thomas Jefferson, via France' (174). The French influence on the food culture of her part of Virginia is frequently suggested, in the blanc mange which is a familiar pudding (made in the ancient manner with a base of pounded almonds) and in the fact that 'Every aged person in Freetown drank their coffee from a bowl' (24), suggesting a further elaboration of their inherited food culture beyond the ingredients of bare survival.

Smart-Grosvenor was at pains to assert that her book was not a soul food cookbook: arguing that 'while certain foods have been labelled "soul food" and associated with African Americans, African Americans could be associated with all foods. I would explain that my kitchen was the world' (2011: 189). She frequently engages, however, with both the concept and the foods, offering a spirited defence of both the taste and historical importance of soul food in a letter to *Time* magazine interpolated into the text: 'So you white folk [...] keep on eating Minute Rice and instant potatoes [...] and stick to your instant culture. And I will stick to the short-lived fad that brought my ancestors through four hundred years of oppression' (175). As Witt notes, throughout the book she is 'continuously embracing and distancing herself from the rubric of soul', skilfully negotiating the complex politics of African American food by continually redefining her position. A comparison of the two authors' treatment of the most primary soul foods gives a sense of their different approaches. Lewis's recipes for greens spread throughout the book, as she details the wide variety picked at different seasons and the many ways of serving them. It is notable, however, that the recipe in which she delineates the most 'soulful' mode of preparation – stewed with fatty pork as in the classic method for collard greens – appears directly below an entry on black-eyed peas. The textual proximity of these two dishes clearly speaks to the debates around soul food, particularly since, as Lewis notes, the black-eyed pea was not used as a food crop in her area of Virginia. Her recipe is not really a recipe at all, although it is titled as such – 'Purée of Green Black-Eyed Peas'; instead it recalls the brief single moment in the year when this pulse – later rendered iconic in the fetishizing rubric of soul – was actually eaten by her community:

> They were not planted in the garden but were planted by farmers as a green manure crop. Before the sowing of wheat, when in full foliage, they were chopped into the soil. A week before, everyone was welcome to gather the green pods before the crop was chopped under. Everyone responded and we enjoyed fresh black-eyed peas for a short period. (174)

Part of a trope of the serendipitous and accidental which structures many of Lewis's accounts of food (turtles that wandered onto their land after a flood made into delicious soup; animals accidently damaged by the hay mower necessarily killed and cooked), the black-eyed peas thus function as bounty in a land of carefully tended plenty rather than the bare subsistence diet of slavery. The purée of the title similarly distances them from subsistence, placing them taxonomically in the category of cuisine. Smart-Grosvenor's treatment of black-eyed peas is very different:

> COW PEAS
>
> Remove all the peas that look weird and wash and soak in cold water. Cook in some kind of boiled meat until done. Cow peas by the way, came here via the slave trade, from Africa where they grow wild. Dried cow peas are called black-eyed peas. (2011: 19)

The consciously perfunctory mode is typical of the ways in which she treats 'soul' foods in particular, a manner which works to evoke oral transmission and an African American culture of food preparation driven by both tradition and personal inspiration (qualities which come together in her grounding concept of 'vibration cooking'). Like Lewis, her impulse is to by-pass the associations of slavery and to take 'soul' foods back to their African roots. So okra is discussed in a chapter titled 'Name-Calling', in which she relates her own dislike of being 'called out of [her] name' to a determination to restore to foods their original names:

SO-CALLED OKRA
Boil your meat and then add washed and carefully trimmed so-called okra.
Do not cut the tip. Cook for 20 minutes.

If you are wondering how come I say so-called okra it is because the African name of okra is gombo. Just like so-called Negros. We are Africans. Negros only started when they got here. I am a black woman. I am tired of people calling me out of my name. Okra must be sick of that mess too. So from now on call it like it is. (74–5)

The practical elements of the recipe are once again vanishingly brief – the type of meat is not specified nor its mode of preparation; the only significant detail being that the tips of the okra should remain intact (so that its mucilaginous fluids should not leak out). Her guiding assumption is that she is speaking to a reader with a similar food-cultural background to whom the basics of African American food are already known. The most contentious of all soul foods was chitterlings, or the bowels and intestines of the pig. Celebrated as a form of soul food too soulful to be appreciated by the (white) uninitiated, they were also disavowed as a fundamental sign of the filth of the pig. As Witt argues, 'in the US social order hog bowels are overdetermined to be both fetishized and abjected – an object of cathexis and catharsis, of desire and disavowal' (86). Lewis, typically, does not mention chitterlings at all, but her lengthy, lyrical account of the annual ritual of hog killing creates a speaking silence around them: we are told that the slaughtered hog was hung up, and then cut down the centre, 'a large round tub was placed underneath for the entrails to fall into. My father would remove the liver and the bladder, which he would present to us. We would blow the bladders up with straws cut from reeds and hang them in the house to dry. By Christmas they would have turned transparent like beautiful balloons' (2017: 182). The bladder-balloons transform the excretory organ to something delicate and celebratory; no other entrails are mentioned, though one assumes that the intestinal membranes would be used for sausage skins. Owning their own land and their own pigs, the people of Freetown have no need to eat the bowels. Grosvenor-Smart's treatment of the dish complicates the arguments around it by broadening the cultural frame through which it should be viewed:

People think chitterlings is something only the southern nigras eat but let me tell you about the time I was in this fancy restaurant in Paris and the people said, "Let us order, we know this place." You know the type. They are usually found in

Chinese restaurants. [...] So these people order for me and they are just on pins and needles, dying, really dying for me to taste this enjoyable rare dish. Well thank you Jesus the food arrives and it ain't nothing but CHITTERLINGS in the form of a sausage. They call it andouilette. (2011: 93)

We might expect the recipe that follows to be for the French bowel sausage, but it is for chitterlings, from a chef friend who used to cook at a soul food restaurant. Unlike her own recipes, it is detailed and focussed, broken down into fifteen numbered instructions, with tips to avoid the pungent smells which are a feature of the cooking experience. The strategic move here is typical of the ways in which Smart-Grosvenor approaches African American food traditions – situating them in a broad international context to afford them the status of serious cuisine before circling back to the dishes themselves as the most authentic versions *for her*. A key example comes in a section of reminiscence about one of her grandmothers, which ends with a food memory – 'Mostly I remember the hoe cakes she made'. The next paragraph apparently opens a different subject, about her travels: 'In Paris I used to eat what they called crepes – a thin pancake. They are very good but I don't make them. In Paris on the Rue Grégoire des Tours there is a place that serves nothing but crepes and jelly – honey – anything you can name'. The shift into the genre of travel reminiscence, with its typical specificity – street name and all – does not yield an accompanying specificity of recipe: she does not make crepes – 'I prefer the hoe cake of bread like Grandmama Sula used to make'. She then launches into the recipe proper:

GRANDMAMA SULA'S HOE CAKE
2 handfuls sifted corn meal
pinch salt
pinch soda and melted bacon grease
(if you eat swine – peanut oil if you don't)
About 1 cup sweet milk

Mix all together and wait a few minutes to see if more water is needed – then pour the whole mixture into a hot greased heavy black cast-iron skillet. Put it on your plate. Pour some thick syrup and sop it up and it's out of sight. Hoe cakes are also good with pot likker. Hoe cake got its name from the hoe. Slaves would cook batter on the flat edge of the hoe in the fields for the noonday meal. You don't have to cook it on the metal part of the hoe cause we ain't slaves no mo'. (16–17)

Once again, the method is minimal, with more focus on the act of eating than of making. This is in keeping with the attitudes she expresses at the beginning of the book – that cooking is (or should be) simple and instinctual: 'White folks act like they invented food and like there is some weird mystique surrounding it – something that only Julia and Jim can get to. There is no mystique. Food is food. Everybody eats!' (xxxvii). To give elaborate instructions would put her on a par with mysticizing Julia [Child] and Jim

[Beard?]: instead, she emphasizes heritage and pleasure. It is the last sentence of the recipe that really epitomizes the radicalism of her approach: the clarity of the address to a specifically black audience, and the triumphant assertion of travails undergone, and freedom attained, all transgressively addressed not in the discursive matter, but within the recipe itself.

Smart-Grosvenor's book announces itself as 'Travel Notes' in its subtitle and demonstrates a clear formal influence from *The Alice B Toklas Cookbook*, with its similar accounts of food at home and abroad, and recollections of a bohemian existence in Paris.[18] Unlike Toklas, however, it is not part of her purpose to offer a guide to authentic French foods for her American readers: instead, the foods she encounters in her travels are transformed, re-made by her sensibilities. So an omelette, named after her Paris home on the rue des Ursulines, is a solidly cooked cake of onions, peppers and ham much closer to the Spanish than French tradition, and in her recipe for Salade Niçoise she adds two cups of cold cooked rice, commenting that it 'is a French name but just like with anything else when soul folks get it they take it out into another thing' (60). The concept of authenticity, so often ritually evoked by the writers of food-travel narratives, serves another purpose in her work. Instead of insisting on the correct replication of the foreign dish, she holds it up for comparison with the foods of her own heritage, and finds it lacking. So, the 'recipe' for Fish Head Stew begins with the excellence of her mother's version – 'My mother used to get the heads from the fish market on Ridge Avenue for five cents a pound. She would stew them down with onions and bell pepper. Served over grits, head stew is an epicurean delight' (38) – before recounting the similar stews encountered on her travels: the 'terrible' fish stew in Iceland, the inadequate bouillabaisse in Paris and *zuppa di pesce* in Rome. Although she acknowledges her failure at cooking bouillabaisse, the real failure is not hers, but the stews which 'didn't make it'. Her mother's head stew is superior, she concludes, because there '[a]in't nothing like the real thing'. Concepts of culinary authenticity are raised only in order to be trumped by the more 'authentic' authenticity of the black experience represented by her mother's virtuosity with the cheapest of ingredients. Smart-Grosvenor's responses to her travels are entirely without the cultural cringe which typifies the responses of white American – and British – authors to the cuisine and culture of other nations. The food of other nations is there to be incorporated into the culinary culture of African Americans. This is nowhere more the case than when she considers the foods of other black nations. In a curious early chapter called 'First Cousins and the Numbers', she details the travel experiences of a number of relatives: there is 'Queen Esther', who 'is married to a maharishi or mahara or anyhow she married a rich Indian' (42) and who sends Vertamae the information that black-eyed peas are prehistoric; and cousin Markana who won money gambling and 'took off to the West Indies to live' (42). The recipes in the chapter – for Rastafari meat patties, Souse from the Virgin Islands, Curried Goat, Fried Plantains and so on – come ostensibly from Markana (as well as from a West Indian neighbor), but Markana's voice is suspiciously like Vertamae's in the one interpolated letter, which lists types of yams and finishes with the consciously Steinian 'a yam is a yam is a yam' (43). Witt suggests that Smart-Grosvenor employs the device of fictional travelling friends and relatives in compensation for her own geographical fixity in her years of single motherhood; or it may be that she ventriloquises the voices of her associates much in the way that Gertrude Stein does Alice B. Toklas, in order to more fully own their experiences. Whatever the case, her project is one of incorporation: incorporating the voices of other black women and the foods of black nations in order to effect a reintegration of the culinary culture of the African diaspora. This is demonstrated most fully in the epistolary chapter with which the book ends: in a series of letters to and from her travelling friend Stella (again sounding very much like Vertamae), who visits Bolivia, Brazil, France, Italy, Egypt and finally Africa. Her arrival in 'black Africa' is triumphantly heralded: 'Child, after 350 years, I am home. Africa, the motherland' (175). There is no specificity about which countries she visits: Africa itself is the end of the journey: the symbolic homecoming for all the descendants of all of the stolen people across the continent; but the recipes she gives, the last in the book, are carefully accorded their regional identities: 'Lumumba Gombo, from Kinshasa', 'Boeuf aux Gombos, from Cameroons', and 'Northern Labajabaja', which is noted as 'an adaptation of a Sengalese dish' (176–7). Here in Africa, the originating home of so many of the foods at the heart of her diasporic model of soul food, she will at last have truck with notions of culinary authenticity.

Memory and the paradoxes of the recipe

The tricksiness of Smart-Grosvenor's construction of self in her recipistolary memoir is extreme but by no means unique. In fact, I would argue that the inclusion of recipes in a memoir (whether a whole text or a fragment within a cookbook or travelogue) almost inevitably creates distortions in the representation of self. By example, we might consider Elisabeth Luard's 1996 *Family Life: Birth, Death and the Whole Damn Thing*, one of the first of the millennial publishing boom in food memoirs. Luard, a British cookery writer, told the story of her marriage in swinging London to Nicholas Luard (co-founder, with Peter Cook, of the Establishment Club and one of the proprietors of satirical magazine *Private Eye*), her difficult pregnancies, including a still-born baby, her years bringing up her four children in an Andalusian cork forest, and the death of her eldest daughter from AIDS. Prominent in the narrative is the food she cooked for her young children, her experience of cooking and eating the same foods as her peasant neighbours in Spain, the foods they ate in a year's sojourn in France. Each chapter ends with a collection of recipes, graphically separated from the narrative, framed with ruled lines and accompanied by small illustrations. The discursive sentences that begin the recipes are not continuations of the memoir proper, but the recommendations and asides of the conventional modern cookbook. Yet there is still something disturbingly intimate in the offering of the recipes for these very personal dishes: in sharing with us the improvised campfire meal made on one of their annual trips south across Europe, or the favourite birthday cake of the daughter we know will die (and whose own account of her illness is interpolated into the narrative). Just as we might feel self-conscious about cooking the key lime pie with which Rachel Samstadt pelts her cheating husband, a cooking of one of Luard's family recipes feels uneasily intrusive. Primarily, I would suggest, this unease is a product of the fact that the recipe framed in the memoir already belongs to someone else. So, the recipe for 'Starvation-Diet: Rice-Bowl' belongs to the 'family mythology' of her month-long disciplinary lesson of giving her picky children a third-world diet. The act of giving this recipe functions more as an ironic comment on the very activity of recipe-giving than as a transferrable set of instructions, despite the fact that, removed from its framing narrative, it is a highly detailed and effective account of how to cook rice. If Luard's recipes belong to someone else, they also belong to some*where* else – another time and place, the moment of their first cooking and eating. The central motivating device of the memoir as a literary form is an act of remembering. Unlike an autobiography, which reshapes memory into coherent, seamless narrative, a memoir repeatedly foregrounds memory as a process, and is constructed as a series of moments of remembering, linking past and present either explicitly or through a formal structuring device. In the case of Luard, the recipe itself plays this function, bringing the past memory into the textual present through a transformation of a culinary experience into a reproducible set of instructions. While some of the recipes may have existed as written recipes in the past – those given by friends, for example – many are for improvised, oft-repeated dishes which are re-created as recipe in a process which is part remembering and part invention.

Food and memory are intrinsically linked, as indicated by the most famous of all food texts, Marcel Proust's *Remembrance of Things Past*, its enormous narrative spinning out from a moment of memory triggered by the taste of cake crumbs in a spoonful of herb tea. In the meandering, hybrid, discursive cookbooks which are the antithesis of the domestic science school with which this chapter began, memory is frequently evoked. Yet memory, the foundational process for the food memoir, is often faulty, incomplete, manipulable. Its failures and fractures become, surprisingly often, the central focus of discursive food narratives. M. F. K. Fisher's meandering disquisitions on the foods and hungers of her past (discussed in Chapter 5) often come up against the inadequacies and lacunae of the memory. Her intensely hybrid work moves in and out of the world of memoir, recalling the foods of her childhood (variously horrific and imbued with the glow of loving nostalgia), her travels around America and Mexico and across Europe, the food she offered to friends and family and lovers, the changing of her tastes as she ages. Like Toklas, she lived in France during the 1930s, accompanying her first husband, Al Fisher, who had a post at the University of Dijon. In *The Gastronomical Me* (1943), she compared her experiences of cooking in France and in her native California:

> There in Dijon, the cauliflowers were small and very succulent, grown in that ancient soil. I separated the flowerlets and dropped them in boiling water for just a few minutes. Then I drained them and put them in a wide shallow casserole, and covered them with heavy cream and a thick sprinkling of freshly grated Gruyère, the nice rubbery kind that didn't come from Switzerland at all, but from the Jura. It was called *râpé* in the market, and was grated while you watched, in a soft cloudy pile, onto your piece of paper.

I put some fresh pepper over the top, and in a way I can't remember now the little tin oven heated the whole thing and melted the cheese and browned it. As soon as that had happened we ate it.

The cream and cheese had come together into a perfect sauce, and the little flowers were tender and fresh. We cleaned our plates with bits of crisp bread crust and drank the wine, and Al and Lawrence planned to write books about Aristotle and Robinson Jeffers and probably themselves, and I planned a few things, too.

And as I say, once back in California, after so many of those casseroles, I found I could never make one. The vegetable was watery, and there was no cream thick enough or unpasteurized and fresh. The cheese was dry and oily, not soft and light. I had to make a sauce with flour in it. I could concoct a good dish, still … but it was never so *innocent*, so simple … and then where was the crisp bread, where the honest wine? And where were our young uncomplicated hungers, too? (Fisher 1991: 441)

The perfect cauliflower cheese is lost both geographically and to the past. She can never go back – this France is gone with the war, but even if she could, the people who made and enjoyed this dish are no more. Fisher mourns throughout her extensive oeuvre not just for the foods of her past but for the gusto with which she was able to eat them. The appetites, tastes and digestive powers of youth are lost treasures; she writes elegiac accounts of eating mounds of mashed potatoes with catsup (ketchup), of potato crisps, of macadamia nuts, made poetic by their constant awareness that she would not, or could not, or should not eat such foods in her later years. The cauliflower cheese is poetic not because she sees it as anything other than a prosaic everyday dish, but because it is irrecoverable. It is notable that she cannot remember the culinary alchemy whereby the oven melted and browned the cheese and combined it with the cream into a sauce. The dish is bathed with the spirit of magic precisely because it cannot be had again. Fisher's prose resurrects it, gives it new life, but simultaneously consigns it to the past. Despite the fact that she gives us all the details necessary to forensically reconstruct the dish – the name and origin of the cheese, the information that the cream is unpasturized, the place to source the cauliflowers – the passage insists that this is wasted effort: the dish cannot exist again.

This insistence on the situational uniqueness of a particular dish is also a striking characteristic of the work of Elizabeth David. Above all, David's commitment as a food writer is to getting it *right* – her recipes are designed to take the English reader as close as possible to the original dish. However, this impulse pulls against another increasingly strong factor in her work – the recording of her life as an eater. Her stories about travels in search of a particular dish or local variant, or anecdotes about perfect meals stumbled upon serendipitously always resolve in a tension between the original dish in its generative setting and the sort of facsimile that can be produced elsewhere, with different ingredients and equipment. Despite the fact of her enormous reputation as a culinary instructor her work repeatedly mourns food that is now lost:

JAMBON À LA CORSOISE

HAM WITH TOMATO AND GARLIC SAUCE

This is a dish I remember from my first visit to Corsica, which now seems a very long time ago. In the little town of Piana of the red rocks, I took a room in the house of a very humble family. There were a large number of children in their teens. Their mother was a great big brawny woman with a robust sense of humour. Amid a tremendous clatter we would all sit down to meals at one big table. Madame's cooking was of the same nature as her own: rough, generous, full of character and colour. There were great dishes of ham and tomatoes, eggs and olives, plenty of salads and oil, huge hunks of bread and great bowls of bursting ripe figs. In all the years since then I have never quite forgotten the very special savour of that food. The ham dish was made with thick slices of the Corsican version of *prosciutto*, or raw ham, fried and served on top of a tomato sauce freshly cooked in oil and well spiced with garlic, pepper and herbs. Nowadays I sometimes make it with gammon rashers, but cooked in a baking tin, just covered in water, in the oven, then drained and just barely browned in olive oil. Served on a big round earthenware dish, surrounded by the tomato sauce, flavoured with plenty of dried basil as well as garlic, and with some croutons of bread fried in oil, this makes a splendid quickly cooked dish for lunch or supper. (David 1986b: 234)

Unlike Fisher, David claims that this dish can be reproduced, and makes vague gestures towards giving us a recipe – but how limp those gestures are: gammon rashers rather than prosciutto, the prosaic details of the baking tin, the water, the dried basil. This is not a recipe she really believes in. David, above all, is scrupulously in control of her prose – that slip into 'bright' women's magazine jargon – 'a splendid quickly cooked dish for lunch or supper' reveals her deep insincerity: this is not the same dish: she knows it, and she really wants us to know it too. The recipe book was in some ways a rather uncomfortable form for Elizabeth David. Her first book, *Mediterranean Food* (1950), was published and attained fame precisely because of the irreproducibility of its recipes: the oft-repeated legend goes that the publisher's reader at John Lehmann recommended it for its audacity in including a recipe for a whole roast sheep at a time when the country was still immured in rationing. That first book (as noted in Chapter 4) was essentially a travelogue-cum-memoir, mourning for the lost tastes and sensations of the Mediterranean, where she had spent a rather salubrious war: 'Even to write words like apricot, olives, butter, rice and lemons, oil and almonds, produced assuagement' (David 1986a: 21). Although her mid-career books – *French Provincial Cooking* and *Italian Food* – are rich with recipes, a sense of loss still pervades them. In a fascinating series of prefaces in successive editions of her *French Provincial Cooking* (in 1960, 1977, 1983), she gradually withdraws hope: the little inns, the fantastically competent chefs tucked away in motorway service stations – all going, going, gone. The France she evokes is lost to us – strikingly, just as it becomes possible for the mass

British public to retrace her steps. The recipes function only as bleak compensation – we can no longer find such food in France, but we can make a bare approximation of it in our own kitchens.[19]

The paradoxes of memory as both recommendation of and impediment to a recipe continue to be a feature of modern cookbooks. This is Nigella Lawson, for example, explaining the inclusion of dried mushrooms in a recipe for fish pie:

> Fish pie is not particularly labour-intensive to cook, but it's hard to get right: if the flour / butter / milk balance is off, the sauce bubbling beneath the blanket of nutmeggy mashed potato can be too runny or too solid. [...] I added porcini because I'd been given some by my Austrian Aunt Frieda, who was coming for lunch. Perhaps it would be more correct to say Great Aunt; the title is honorific but she's the generation, was the companion, of my grandmother. She was the matron at my mother and aunts' boarding school and my grandmother, not I think extraordinarily maternal, was so dreading the school holidays that she asked Matron to stay during them. Over forty years later, she's still here, an important fixture in all our lives. I wanted to use the mushrooms because she'd given them to me. But I thought they'd add a creaturely muskiness, a depth of tone, to the milkily-sweet fish-scented sauce. They did.
>
> This is how I made it. You can change the fish as you want. (1998: 266–7)

This anecdote accomplishes many things: it creates a sense of readerly empathy by revealing personal details: though it is notable that Nigella, like Elizabeth David, is accomplished at only appearing to reveal, measuring out the intimacy with a careful hand, concealing as much as she shows. It is a nice example of her cunning manipulation of class, which she plays rather like Hugh Grant's filmic characters, in a bumblingly apologetic way that reads as effortlessly *haute bourgeois*. It evokes maternity, family, continuity – though in a rather twisted way. It insists on the power of food to comfort and console. It functions as explanation, as recommendation: why *this* fish pie, rather than all other versions of this well-known recipe, is the best one. It creates a reassuring sense of cookery as serendipity – the idea that the best dishes arise from accidental circumstances, a chance concatenation of events, rather than through rigorous effort or lengthy training or great skill – so reassuring us that such inventions are within our reach. But her little narrative also reveals the great paradox at the heart of recipe writing – the myth of reproducibility. This is the idea on which its existence as a form is predicated – that we can read about dishes and then receive the instructions to make them ourselves. And yet there is always also a nagging awareness of the extent to which this idea is a myth. We cannot make Nigella's special fish pie. We will not have the right dried mushrooms, specially delivered from Austria by her faux Great Aunt, and even if we do have them we will have different fish and different scales and different ovens and are different people with different senses of taste. Even Nigella cannot reproduce this one Ur-fish pie, as the past tense ('this is how I made it') and the faintly nostalgic tone of her account suggest.

Repeatedly we find accounts of food bathed in a melancholic glow: food that is lost. These texts are more memorials than memoirs. What all these recipes and reminiscences say to the reader cuts to the paradox at the heart of the cookbook. They say: you can't have this. You can't have this because I already had it. This food is unrepeatable. The cauliflower cheese made in California cannot be the same as that in Dijon. Food is a one-off, a fugitive moment, best appreciated as memory. We cannot catch it and keep it; and at their heart, all cookbooks know this, even as they try to freeze the dish in photographic form, to arrest the process of its destruction in consumption. Food is always in process: growing, being prepared, being chewed, digested and defecated. The only place it is ever fixed whole in time is in memory. In reality, its flavours and substance dissolve in our mouths and are gone.

For many novels and memoirs the power of the recipe lies in its promise to bring the fleeting, ephemeral sensations of the past into the present; in its establishment of identity, of intimacy between speaking subject and reader – yet an awareness of the problematics of those promises lurk close to the surface. In its very form, the recipe dramatizes the tensions between food as text and food as bodily experience, between the food we read and the food we eat. The final chapter of this book will consider another fundamental paradox of food writing: the many curious and contradictory purposes for which it evokes and deploys disgust.

CHAPTER 8
DOWN THE ALIMENTARY CANAL: FOOD, DIGESTION AND DISGUST

Throughout this book we have encountered moments where literary responses to food take us into the realm of disgust: Orwell's account, in *The Road to Wigan Pier*, of the Brooker's boarding-house-cum-tripe, shop, where the dank hole containing the ageing, slimy, disturbingly textured tripe is partly blocked by the sofa on which the permanently ailing Mrs Brooker lies day and night, wiping her mouth on her blankets and on the slimy wads of newspaper with which she litters the surrounding floor (Chapter 1); the sights and sounds of the gobbling mouths of Thackeray's 'A Dinner in the City' (Chapter 2); the modernist disgust about the eating of the masses: in public, visibly chewing, leaving behind them smells and detritus (Chapter 5); the snot-flavoured Every-Flavour Beans of *Harry Potter*; Augustus Gloop lapping from the chocolate river, disregarding his 'nasty cold' in *Charlie and the Chocolate Factory* (Chapter 6); and the accounts, from Orwell to Bourdain, of restaurant kitchens as places of sweat, dirt and rot, where spit in your soup is the least that you risk (Chapter 4). These food-disgusts fall into several distinct categories: a revulsion from certain food textures, the association of consumables with disease-causing pathogens, an anxiety about dirt and mess produced by or in connection with food, and a revulsion from the alimentary process itself, and its stages of chewing, swallowing, digesting and defecating. The textual attitudes to these moments of disgust range widely: for many modernists disgust marks the precise, viscerally felt limit of their sympathetic engagement with the poor, while for Orwell it is a matter of moral importance that we should both confront disgustingness and look beyond it for its root socio-economic causes; for many children's authors disgust marks another limit, that between adult probity and rectitude and a realm where children can take pleasure in the sticky, scatological, transgressive energy of the disgusting.

Disgust theory

Disgust as a topic has attracted a great deal of academic interest over recent decades precisely because of its multiple and ambiguously overlapping functions and triggers. Among its curious features is the fact that it is the only primal emotion which we seem to have to learn to some extent: infants are not disgusted by the same things as adults, as anyone who has parented a curious toddler will know, and part of their process of socialization involves caregivers removing worms, mud, food from the floor, and faeces from eager hands and even mouths with an 'urgh – dirty' and accompanying disgust-face, with its characteristic pinched nostrils and gaping mouth.[1] The response might have to be learnt, but the retching 'gape face' which expresses disgust seems to be innate, as it is found across all cultures and manifested by people born blind.[2] The function of disgust as an evolutionary mechanism has been much debated among biologists, geneticists and psychologists, with two primary arguments being that it works as a barrier against contact with potential pathogens and parasites, or as a protection against the ingestion of potentially toxic substances in the form of food. Proponents of the former model tend to emphasize the features of disgust that seem unique to humans (notably its 'decidedly cognitive, symbolic, and conceptual character'), with some arguing that the emotion arises specifically in response to the uniquely human knowledge of our own mortality and the need to ward off the existential terror produced by this fact.[3] Those who emphasize the food-avoidance theory, in contrast, find similar processes of taste aversion in other mammalian species and an approximation of the gape face in other primates, and relate the mechanism of food-rejection to what experimental psychologist Paul Rozin has called 'the omnivore's dilemma' (1976): the question of how a creature which can eat almost anything selects the foods which are most nutritious and least harmful. In this model food aversion is a learned response which causes the body to violently reject through nausea and vomiting foods which it has previously associated with illness. It is a mechanism which can easily throw up false positives, so foods which were consumed close to the time of a gastric episode but were not themselves the cause will nevertheless lead the subject to develop a profound aversion to them. In *Yuck!*, his survey of *The Nature and Moral Significance of Disgust*, Daniel Kelly interweaves philosophy, psychology and evolutionary biology to offer what he calls 'the entanglement theory', which sees the mechanisms of food aversion and pathogen protection as separate evolutionary inheritances which became entangled in the human species at an early stage of our development. This model, he argues, provides the best explanation for the curious interchangeability of disgust responses: '[t]he reaction to potential carriers of parasitic infection came to involve nausea and gaping of the mouth. Alternatively Garcia aversions [false positives of food aversion, named after the lead author of the first study to systematically investigate the mechanism in rats] and misgivings about certain sorts of cuisine can turn the offending food not just inedible but offensive and contaminating' (2011: 53).

The complex interchangeability of the mechanisms contributes also, in his model, to the potentiality of the co-option of disgust for seemingly unrelated moral and psychological purposes, including 'dining practices or issues of sexual norms' (119) and 'more insidious roles in the psychology of ethnic boundaries and group membership' (124).[4] So (in my examples) putting your knife in your mouth or consuming horse-meat may well serve to mark you as 'out-group' (in anthropological parlance), eliciting disgust in others and resulting in some degree of social shunning; conversely, your own expressed disgust at the prospect of eating snails or raw fish may function as the mechanism of exclusion from another sort of social group. Arguing with those who see moral disgust as essentially metaphoric rather than literal, Kelly points to experimental evidence that finds the same facial expressions and overlapping neurological responses to both universal physical disgust triggers (vomit, for example) and 'sociomoral' issues (130–1). The human disgust mechanism, he argues, has both a 'hair-trigger' sensitivity 'that is easily activated by a relatively wide array of cues' (132) and a rigidity of response, so that whatever the trigger the 'disgust system produces a characteristic inferential signature that involves a sense of oral incorporation, a sense of offensiveness, and sensitivity to contamination' (133). The result, crucially, is that 'anything that triggers the disgust response will have disgustingness projected onto it and will be thought about and treated *as if* it were mildly revolting, offensive, and contaminating' (133). The social and political implications of this model of disgust are clear: once a sense of disgust is elicited in response to a particular individual or ethnic group or social class rational responses become considerably more difficult. Kelly concludes his study with a consideration of the 'normative ethics' that can be derived from the emotion and its objects. He counters the arguments of those who advocate treating moral disgust as an arbiter of the boundaries of the natural and the unnatural, a source of 'deep wisdom' about what should be our moral limits, arguing instead for a strong scepticism about what we might think disgust 'communicates' to us about ethical issues.[5] It is exactly this issue, incidentally, that Orwell grapples with in the second half of *The Road to Wigan Pier*. Elaborating on his controversial assertion that the real block to socialism is that the middle and upper classes are brought up to believe that the working classes smell, he gives a demonstrative account of his own viscerally disgusted anticipation when travelling in the third-class carriage of a train at the age of thirteen, of the moment when he might be required to put his mouth to the bottle of beer being passed around the carriage of 'shepherds and pig-men' (equating disgust very specifically with issues of ingestion and the urge to protect bodily boundaries) (1989a: 122). Despite his sense of such disgust as forming an 'impassible barrier' between the classes, he asserts the moral imperative of resisting it, claiming that he has managed to cure himself of this 'fundamental' 'physical repulsion' by spending time living among tramps, sharing their beds and drinking tea from the same vessel (119). He retains the distaste about shared drinking containers, but he imputes this disgust not to the class of those other soiling mouths, but to their gender: 'I still don't like drinking out of a cup or a bottle after another person – another man, I mean: with women I don't mind – but at least the question of class does not enter' (122). The disgust at the mouths of other men is here re-understood as a matter of sexual orientation, his revulsion from the contact mediated by the bottle at one with the repulsion from 'sodomites' and 'nancies' he expresses throughout this and other texts.[6] Rather than having trained himself away from disgust, he has relocated it to a group he considers it much less ethically problematic to despise – a confirmation of Kelly's case of the suspect ideological purposes for which disgust can be deployed.

Before the recent 'turn' to the cognitive sciences, those interested in disgust in the humanities engaged primarily with three theoretical models: those of Mary Douglas, Julia Kristeva and Mikhail Bakhtin. In her 1966 *Purity and Danger: An Analysis of Concepts of Pollution and Taboo*, structural anthropologist Douglas examined the language and the rituals associated with dirt and cleanliness in many societies and religions. Starting with the grounding claim that dirt – the disgusting – is 'matter out of place', she developed a theory which emphasized the principle of exclusion in the establishing of cultural meaning systems. Things defined as dirty or unclean, and the use of pollution beliefs, are deployed primarily, she argues, as boundary markers, delineating between that which is of the tribe and that which is outside it. In her model, it is the things which do not fit into the classificatory systems that order particular social domains that are polluting (and, by extension, though she does not say so, disgusting). It is the anomalous, the ambiguous that disturbs. In *An Anatomy of Disgust*, social historian William Miller incorporates some of Douglas's insights into his own classificatory model of the disgusting, though notes the limitations of her method: '[t]he risk to this kind of structuralism is that it ends in reduction and tautology': we 'can only pretend to get at the structure through the very thing we need the structure to explain' (1997: 44). He notes that Douglas's model works best in situations when the rules are already 'spelled out and an object of official cultural knowledge', as in food-prohibitions. Douglas's recognition of the often metaphoric, symbolic nature of ideas of the unclean strongly influenced psychoanalytic theorist Julia Kristeva's model of the abject, which she developed in *Powers of Horror: An Essay on Abjection* (1982). The abject, as Kristeva defines it, is that which the individual must reject in order to delimit the boundary of his subjectivity. The abject is 'a threat that seems to emanate from an exorbitant outside or inside, ejected beyond the scope of the possible, the tolerable, the thinkable. It lies there, quite close, but it cannot be assimilated' (1982: 1). In a passage headlined 'The Improper / Unclean' she defines the physical and psychic manifestations of disgust as the process whereby the self (particularly the super-ego) establishes its separation from that which is other.[7] Her prime exemplar of the abject is the corpse, 'that thing that no longer matches and therefore no longer signifies anything' (3), but the category also includes bodily wastes – pus, faeces – and food:

> Food loathing is perhaps the most elementary and most archaic form of abjection. When the eyes see or the lips touch that skin on the surface of milk – harmless, thin as a sheet of cigarette paper, pitiful as a nail paring – I experience a gagging sensation and, still farther down, spasms in the stomach, the belly; and all the organs shrivel up the body, provoke tears and bile, increase heartbeat, cause forehead and hands to perspire. (3)

She sees an infant's first categorically disgusted rejection of food as initiating a specific psycho-sexual stage of development, located between the inchoate early infancy in which there is no separation felt between self and mother or even self and world, and the 'mirror stage' which, following Jacques Lacan, she defines as the moment that the infant self identifies with its own image and is able to build a model of its place in a larger imaginary order representing the world beyond the self. The stage between, the moment of abjection, Kristeva sees as 'a precondition of narcissism' (i.e. the mirror stage): before the self can recognize itself, it struggles to separate itself from the mother. The rejection of the 'milk cream' through nausea, sobs and vomiting 'separates me from the mother and father who proffer it' (3). The abject marks, or sometimes constitutes, the border between 'I' and 'not I'; it is that which must be excluded in order for the symbolic realm of language, law and gender difference to function.[8] When it reappears in the symbolic – in literature, for example – it figures a profound ambivalence because it represents the return of the very thing that has had to be excluded in the process of self-definition. So, for Kristeva, literary accounts of food as, or in association with, the abject represent particularly the knowledge of the absolute material fact of death:

> [A]s in true theater, without makeup or masks, refuse and corpses show me what I permanently thrust aside in order to live. These body fluids, this defilement, this shit are what life withstands, hardly and with difficulty, on the part of death. There, I am at the border of my condition as a living being. (3)

Rather like pathogen-theory biologists, Kristeva sees disgust as a matter of the protection of the horrifyingly porous body envelope which has ultimately to do with our species' unique knowledge of our own mortality, though from her psychoanalytic perspective the 'self' seeking to protect itself is a psychic construction rather than a material body.[9]

The Kristevan abject, with its interweaving of disgust, horror and the uncanny, is a profoundly negative state, marking a site of psychic distress at the boundary of the self. The work of Mikhail Bakhtin, in contrast, casts the disgusting as a source of transgressive energy and radical possibility. Bakhtin's ideas about the grotesque body and the carnivalesque, outlined in *Rabelais and His World* (1965), have been particularly influential in the field of literary studies.

Broadly, he argues that the inversion of official values in the pre-modern carnival represents an anticipation of a utopian, anarchic, anti-hierarchical world: 'During carnival time life is subject only to its laws, that is, the laws of freedom' (Bakhtin 1984: 7). He reads the grotesque bodies of the giants in Rabelais's *Gargantua and Pantagruel* (1532–65) as similarly celebratory, arguing against the dominant critical readings of Rabelais's work as satirical, and coining the term 'grotesque realism' to describe it:

> Grotesque realism imagines the human body as multiple, bulging, over- or under-sized, protuberant and incomplete. The openings and orifices of this carnival body are emphasized, not its closure and finish. It is an image of impure corporeal bulk with its orifices (mouth, flared nostrils, anus) yawning wide and its lower regions (belly, legs, buttocks and genitals) given priority over its upper regions (head, 'spirit', reason). (Stallybrash and White 1986: 9)

The scatology and sexual grotesquery of the work he reads as manifestations of a deeply positive model of the body and its relationship to the world. The grotesque body is the antithesis of the 'closed', unitary classical body: it is open to the world, constantly taking in and emitting substances. Eating and drinking and their various digestive consequences are at the heart of this model: the 'open unfinished nature' of the grotesque body and its interaction with the world 'are most fully and concretely revealed in the act of eating' where the body 'transgresses [...] its own limits: it swallows, devours, rends the world apart, is enriched and grows at the world's expense':

> The encounter of man with the world, which takes place inside the open, biting, rending, chewing mouth, is one of the most ancient, and most important objects of human thought and imagery. Here man tastes the world, introduces it into his body, makes it part of himself. [...] Man's encounter with the world in the act of eating is joyful, triumphant; he triumphs over the world, devours it without being devoured himself. (Bakhtin 1984: 281)

Recent work has raised powerful objections both to the positivity of Bakhtin's reading of Rabelais and most particularly to the sentimentality of his portrait of the medieval carnival. As a number of critics and historians have pointed out, the social function of carnival in the medieval and early modern period is as safety valve, a period of allowed disrule and 'fooling' which reconfirms rather than challenges the authority of the state: 'Carnival, after all, is a licensed affair in every sense, a permissible rupture of hegemony, a contained popular blow-off as disturbing and relatively ineffectual as a revolutionary work of art. As Shakespeare's Olivia remarks, there is no slander in an allowed fool' (Eagleton 2009: 148). William Miller is particularly acerbic at the expense of Bakhtin and those inspired by him:

> For the Jews murdered during carnival, the women raped, the animals set on fire and tormented it would have been small solace that late-twentieth-century scholars would find cause for admiring such 'authentic rites', 'sites of resistance', or 'counter-hegemonic practices'. (1997: 184)

Yet whatever the historical inaccuracy of Bakhtin's model of carnivalesque, this idea and the associated concept of the radical power of the grotesque body continue to have significant valency within literary studies. Often they are deployed in tension with Kristeva's abject as the positive and negative poles of the fundamental ambivalence of disgust.[10] The reason for the continued power of these concepts, despite the existence of more finely nuanced models of disgust derived from the social and cognitive sciences, lies perhaps in their extremism: the clear ambivalence of disgust as both visceral response and moral agent is acknowledged, but transformed through the complexities of their systemic approaches into deterministic absolutes: for Kristeva all disgust speaks ultimately to the unrepresentable fact of our fate as mortal flesh; for Bakhtin the play of the disgusting, representing both growth and decay, life and death, resolves always in the ability of popular festivity to outlast the hierarchies of official power; of the body to incorporate and overcome the world. What we find when we turn to literary representations of the disgusting in association with food is that very often *both* of these elements are in play: the horror of the restaurant kitchen evoked in Anthony Bourdain's account flirts always with a macho bravado that gleefully embraces the disgusting as a means to *épater* the bourgeoisie who are his customers and readers; the close focus on the decaying mouth of the 'very lean old Bellows-Mender' in Thackeray's account of the turtle dinner repels, but this repulsion is complicated by the sympathetic acknowledgement of the limitations of earthly pleasure and by the exuberant delight the text takes in detailing the noisy greed of the gobbling eaters. In tracing the lineaments of disgust and the disgusting in some emblematic literary food texts what follows will not deploy schematically any of the models outlined above; rather, it will consider the complex textual play of disgust as it moves between the various conceptual positions that these theories represent.[11] The texts considered belong to four literary categories – modernism, memoir, feminist fiction and children's literature – which deploy disgust in distinctive ways to advance a particular poetics and readerly response. The first category is represented by Joyce's *Ulysses* and Beckett's *Molloy*; the second by Nigel Slater's *Toast*; the third by Margaret Atwood's *The Edible Woman* and Angela Carter's *Nights at the Circus*; the fourth by the works of Roald Dahl and later children's writers.

Modernist disgust

The 'Laestrygonians' episode of James Joyce's *Ulysses* (1922) is rich in representations of food-disgust. In Joyce's schema for the novel, each of the eighteen episodes, based on the stages of Odysseus's journey in the Homeric epic, is assigned a colour, symbol, literary technique and bodily organ or process.[12] This episode, in which Leopold Bloom looks for somewhere to eat lunch, maps onto Odysseus's encounter with a race of giant cannibals; it is associated with the oesophagus and its assigned literary technique is 'peristaltic'. The notion of peristalsis as a literary process is Joyce's own coinage; the physical process described by this name is the primary action of the oesophagus: a series of muscular contractions which produce a wave which propels a chewed bolus of food from the mouth to the stomach. The wave of the oesophageal contractions pushes the wad of chewed and denatured food before it, as Bloom is pushed forward through the Dublin streets by his insistent hunger; while the stop-start of the contractions represents the nature of his journey, as his search for an eating place is derailed by the sights and sounds of the city and the thoughts and memories they throw up, by the seagulls he stops to feed, and the old acquaintance he pauses to chat with.[13] In this epic of the body, the thoughts of the protagonists and the language in which they are depicted reveal the dominant bodily processes which hold them in sway.[14] Where the metaphors in the previous episode, identified with the Aeolian winds, circle around scents and breezes, they shift, as Bloom's hunger grows, to food. Tired clichés come to life, revivified by their precise application: 'eat you out of house and home' (124), 'the fat of the land' (124), 'proof of the pudding' (125), 'no accounting for tastes' (126), 'drop him like a hot potato' (134). He sees everything through a miasma of food: passing acquaintances, he thinks of meals he has shared with them and foods he associates with them; thinking of the pyramids leads him to the diet of the slaves whose labour constructed them: '[b]uilt on bread and onions' (135). As he grows hungrier and more frustrated the food-language becomes more fanciful: he spies the brother of Irish nationalist leader Charles Stewart

Parnell, whose 'woebegone walk' suggests that he has 'Eaten a bad egg. Poached eyes on ghost' (135); the diet of vegetarians is rendered as '[o]nly weggebobbles and fruit' (136).[15] Yet when he enters the Burton restaurant his insistent hunger is suddenly overwhelmed by intense nausea:

> Stink gripped his trembling breath: pungent meatjuice, slop of greens. See the animals feed.
>
> Men, men, men.
>
> Perched on high stools at the bar, hats shoved back, at the tables calling for more bread no charge, swilling, wolfing gobfuls of sloppy food, their eyes bulging, wiping wetted moustaches. A pallid suetfaced young man polished his tumbler knife fork and spoon with his napkin. New set of microbes. A man with an infant's saucestained napkin tucked around him shovelled gurgling soup down his gullet. A man spitting back on his plate: halfmasticated gristle: no teeth to chewchewchew it. Chump chop from the grill. Bolting to get it over. Sad booser's eyes. Bitten off more than he can chew. Am I like that? See ourselves as others see us. Hungry man is an angry man. Working tooth and jaw. Don't! O! A bone! (138–9)

The hurriedly dining men represent the cannibals of the *Odyssey*, their frantic gulping at 'meatjuices' the equivalent of the blood drinking of the Laestrygonians. It is a scene of horror, with Bloom suddenly plunged from his anticipatory food-thoughts into a maelstrom of disgust: the smells, the sounds, the sights all viscerally repellant. The passage focuses in horrified fascination particularly on the orality of the eaters: their gobfuls and gullets and frantically chewing jaws. The verbs luxuriate in the disgustingness of observed mastication: 'swilling', 'wolfing', 'shovelled', 'gurgling', 'chewchewchew'. In part the eating men are disgusting in their infantilization: swaddled in napkins, spilling their food, spitting out the gristle. They are creatures of a pre-civilized life-stage, and yet they are triply emphasized men, complete with moustaches and long life histories. Against his will, Bloom is drawn into an engagement with what he sees, comparing himself with the man with the 'sad booser's eyes' who has also 'bitten off more than he can chew', warning him, if only in imagination, about the bone he is about to bite down on. As the passage continues the disgust is drawn out, lingered on, one sense at a time: first the smells of the restaurant which cause Bloom's gorge to rise: '[s]paton sawdust, sweetish warmish cigarettesmoke, reek of plug, spilt beer, men's beery piss, the stale of ferment' (139), then the sights – 'look on this picture then on that' – of 'old chap picking his tootles' and 'fellow ramming a knifeful of cabbage down as if his life depended on it', and finally the sound of someone talking with his mouth full 'I munched hum un thu Unchster Bunk un Munchday'. It is this last individual that pushes Bloom beyond his limits:

> Mr Bloom raised two fingers doubtfully to his lips. His eyes said.
>
> - Not here. Don't see him.
>
> Out. I hate dirty eaters. (139)

As he is overwhelmed the senses merge synesthetically – the repellant sound connected to the sight which Bloom tries to block out and to his own oral sensations (specifically, we assume, an anxiety about vomiting). All merge together into the concept of 'dirty eat[ing]', a conglomerate food-disgust that propels him out of the restaurant, the food and the acts of eating within merging as he leaves into a peristaltic stop-start of word-boluses convulsively swallowed: 'Gulp. Grub. Gulp. Gobstuff' (139). The horror in this scene is absolutely abject – from the microbial anxieties to the existential nausea which forces Bloom out of the door in total refusal of the multiple horrors within. Yet orality, the alimentary and the other territories of the disgusting do not consistently provoke abjection for Bloom or for the novel itself. As we saw in Chapter 5, his breakfast kidney's 'fine tang of faintly scented urine' (45) is a key part of the pleasure it affords him. The alternative lunch he purchases in Davy Byrne's pub – a gorgonzola sandwich laced with mustard – is pleasurable not because it represents the antithesis of the disgusting meat dinners being gobbled by the men in the restaurant, but because its disgustingness is tempered and balanced by other qualities:

> Mr Bloom ate his strips of sandwich, fresh clean bread, with relish of disgust pungent mustard, the feety savour of green cheese. Sips of his wine soothed his palate. Not logwood that. Tastes fuller this weather with the chill off. (142)

The disgust adds piquancy as the mustard does: the bodily odours of the cheese balanced by the freshness of the bread, the flavours tempered by the roundedness of the Burgundy. This second attempt at lunch makes clear that the really disgusting element in the restaurant was the insistent pressure of the bodily processes of others: the disgusting consciously embraced rather than forcefully imposed can enhance pleasure.[16] This is particularly emphasized as Bloom's lunchtime meditation leads him to remember a long-ago moment in his relationship with his wife Molly (who is that day cuckolding him as Bloom wanders the Dublin streets trying to repress this knowledge). The wine '[t]ouched his sense moistened remembered', conjuring a memory of a sexual encounter during a picnic:

> O wonder! Coolsoft with ointments her hand touched me, caressed: her eyes upon me did not turn away. Ravished over her I lay, full lips open, kissed her mouth. Yum. Softly she gave me in my mouth the seedcake warm and chewed. Mawkish pulp her mouth had mumbled sweetsour of her spittle. Joy: I ate it: joy. Young life, her lips that gave me pouting. Soft, warm, sticky, gumjelly lips. (144)

In the throes of ecstasy from Molly's manual attentions, Bloom experiences what would otherwise be repellant – well-chewed food from another's mouth – as the epitome of joy; sexual intimacy enhanced by its transgression of the psychic as well as physical limits of another's body. Molly's sticky 'gumjelly' lips, coated with the sweet residues from the food she has been eating, could so easily figure disgust, but become alluring through the absolute intimacy that contact with them represents. The paradox of disgust as relish is here played out in an erotic context. Bloom's meandering thoughts on the trope of food and disgust then travel from orality to anality, following the path of the alimentary canal. His appreciation of the smooth curve of the pub's wooden bar leads him to the curves of the sculptures of naked goddesses in the museum, and then to the foods of the gods, imagining nectar as like 'drinking electricity' (144), and comparing the 'golden', 'ambrosial' dishes of the gods with the quotidian food of mortals, which takes him to the alimentary processes which hold humanity in thrall: 'And we stuffing food in one hole and out behind: food, chyle, blood, dung, earth, food: have to feed it like stoking an engine' (144–5). The processes of alimentation are notably rendered here as a cycle: faeces as dung which forms earth which grows food: this is not a Kristevan abject in which bodily processes point ultimately to death; but nor yet is it a Bakhtinian celebration of the grotesque body's triumph over the world, but rather a recognition of the body's place in a cycle of necessity, with life rather than death the thing that threatens to disgust. William Miller offers the best explanation of this mode of disgust, hoting, in a chapter called 'Thick, Greasy Life', that '[w]hat disgusts, startlingly, is the capacity for life, and not just because life implies its correlative death and decay: for it is decay that seems to engender life' (1997: 40).[17] As he leaves the pub and makes his way to the library, he searches his teeth for debris of the meal 'his tongue brushing his teeth smooth' and passes a vomiting dog, 'a ravenous terrier [who] choked up a sick knuckly cud on the cobble stones and lapped it with new zest' (147). The primal disgust evoked by this image belongs mostly to the reader: Bloom meditates on rather than recoils from the sight: 'Surfeit. Returned with thanks having fully digested the contents. First sweet then savoury.' All digestive processes have been considered, culminating with that which disturbs most because it reverses the 'properly' unidirectional nature of the alimentary canal.

Samuel Beckett traverses the territory of the disgusting in a similar way to Joyce (it may be remembered that the sandwich Belacqua prepares for his lunch in *Dante and the Lobster* also consists of gorgonzola and mustard, in what is almost certainly a conscious echo of Bloom's lunch).[18] In *Molloy*, as discussed in Chapter 1, food is deeply problematic: the meal proffered by the social worker is 'filth' that Molloy is unable to bring himself to eat: he consumes only enough to keep himself marginally alive. He is much more interested in the end of the alimentary process than the beginning, with the anus figuring as the fundamental locus of his understanding of birth, sexuality and death. Near the start of the book, he turns from recalling his much-loved bicycle to the less restful subject of his mother:

> What a rest to speak of bicycles and horns. Unfortunately it is not of them I have
> to speak, but of her who brought me into the world, through the hole in her arse if
> my memory is correct. First taste of the shit. (2003: 16)

The shit tasted during this aberrant imaginary birth process is both actual and metaphorical; at one with the filth that is food in general to him, and the abject horror of the world he inhabits. Sexual intercourse as well as birth he imagines as a matter for the anus: knowing little about female anatomy, he is surprised, at the start of his only sexual relationship – with 'a woman who might have been my mother, and even I think my grandmother, if chance had not willed otherwise' (56) – to find that 'the hole between her legs' is 'not the bunghole [he] had always imagined, but a slit'. He believes it is into this orifice that his partner inserts his 'so-called virile member, not without difficulty', but is not sure, and wonders later if 'perhaps she put me after all in her rectum', concluding that it is 'a matter of complete indifference' to him, but wondering if it can be 'true love' (as his partner has informed him it is) 'in the rectum' (57). Molloy's bemused disinterest ('A mug's game in my opinion and tiring on top of that' (56)) and absolute ignorance (he later wonders if his partner could have been a man, but concludes that he or she must have held her testicles out of the way if so) establish a tone which teeters on the knife-edge between comedy and tragedy, as do the descriptions of their encounters, with her 'bent over the couch, because of her rheumatism' (57). The episode is more horrifically poignant than disgusting, but is explicitly connected to both disgust and food by the nature of their meeting:

> We met in a rubbish dump, unlike any other and yet they are all alike, rubbish dumps […] Anyway it was she who started it, in the rubbish dump, when she laid her hand upon my fly. More precisely, I was bent double over a heap of muck, in the hope of finding something to disgust me for ever with eating, when she, undertaking me from behind, thrust her stick betweens my legs and began to tickle my privates. (57)

Molloy's abjection is both sexual – he is assaulted from behind with a phallic-like object – and a matter of the rubbish dump setting, but his relationship to neither element contains the horror and the threat to self of the Kristevan abject: his response to the sexual approach is passive but accepting; his encounter with rubbish one actively sought. Disgust, and food-disgust specifically, is something he is deliberately courting in order to weaken the tenacious grip his body has on life. Material existence, for most of Beckett's characters, is a state to be got over as quickly as possible, so a disgust that prevented eating would be a welcome friend. The implications of anality for the novel as a whole are explicitly returned to towards the end of Molloy's narrative, as he shifts from an audit of the parts of his body and their relative states of collapse at the moment he is recalling, to a disquisition on the anus and its cultural status, which in self-evident pun he declares 'fundamental':

> I apologise for having reverted to this lewd orifice, 'tis my muse will have it so. Perhaps it is less to be thought of as the eyesore here called by its name than as the symbol of those passed over in silence, a distinction due perhaps to its centrality and its air of being a link between me and the other excrement. We underestimate this little hole, it seems to me, we call it the arse-hole and affect to despise it. But is it not rather the true portal of our being and the celebrated mouth no more than the kitchen-door. Nothing goes in, or so little, that is not rejected on the spot, or

very nearly. Almost everything revolts it that comes from without and what comes from within does not seem to receive a very warm welcome either. (79–80)

Reversing the usual entrance / exit, upper / lower, positive / negative polarities of the two openings of the alimentary canal, he reads the anus as the 'true' door of being and the mouth as the lesser, menial back door precisely because of what they do and don't let in. The anus imagined here is not the gaping, open orifice of the Bahktianian grotesque body, but a tightly clenched 'little' hole, remarkable for its resistance to ingress (though he wavers over this in the light of his previous experiences) and its reluctant opening even for egress. The mouth, in contrast, is too open, too accepting of all comers: seen as the kitchen door it is figured as a lowly opening, without discrimination. Earlier, Molloy had proposed bringing an end to language by 'fill[ing] in the holes of words till all is blank and flat and the whole ghastly business looks like what it is, senseless, speechless, issueless misery' (13); he fantasizes also a closed body, one in which the processes finally shut down. In this context the wide-open voracious mouth is considerably more disturbing than the shut-tight, discriminating anus.[19]

Disgust memoirs

Both Beckett and Joyce play in the territory of bodily and food-disgust, at times working to elicit strong visceral responses of repulsion from the reader while at others taking us into the realm of the disgusting but producing only pity or laughter or an alienated lack of affect. For neither writer is it a matter of a straightforward oscillation between a Kristevan abject and a Bahktinian celebration: disgust and its purposes are more various and subtle than this opposition would suggest. For many of the writers who deploy disgust, it functions not as the rearing psychic bulwark of abjection nor as the absolute licence of carnivalesque, but as a field of play in which the emotional responses of protagonist, reader and text shift continually between revulsion, amusement, nausea, and that curious sense of achievement that comes from overcoming one's disgust mechanisms. This is certainly true of Nigel Slater, whose memoir *Toast* (2003) returns to disgust more often than any other mode of response, resolutely lingering on the moments that sepia-coloured memory would rather forget. His first engagement with a cookbook is the copy of Marguerite Patten's *All Colour Cookbook* which is kept in the hidden cupboard at the back of his parent's bookcase, along with Philip Roth's *Portnoy's Complaint*; his excited flicking between the two leaves them both 'slightly stained' (2003: 12); the family's first, dramatic encounter with spaghetti bolognese in 1960s Wolverhampton is accompanied by Aunt Fanny's terrified pants-wetting and the horrified realization that the Parmesan cheese 'smells like sick' (20). The disgust that often accompanies food in Slater's narrative does not invariably result in a cancelling out of pleasure; the two frequently exist side-by-side, observed, but separate: so the weekly treat of blackcurrant pie fresh from the bakery is enjoyed regardless of the proximity of his hungover brother's noxious leavings: 'There, where the edge of the sofa had been, is a pile of my brother's warm vomit. But pie is pie and I tuck in regardless' (40). At times disgust alienates the child Nigel: so the fact that his father 'always had something disgusting in his mouth, a Setler, a glug of kaolin and morphine, his pipe' (48) leads his son to 'flinch on the rare occasion he kissed me, even though I wanted him to'; at others Nigel waits in thrilled anticipation for something disgusting to happen: he longs for the permanent dewdrop of snot to fall from Aunt Fanny's 'hooked beak' of a nose into the jug of Nestlé's tinned cream passed around at Sunday lunch, just to see how the adults respond. Disgustingness as carnivalesque celebration is not only deployed in situations where Nigel himself is not disgusted: the violent nausea with which he responds to milk leads to one of the most dramatic textual explorations of this mode of affect. Having moved to a new class where the teacher makes everyone drink their milk, he solves the problem by 'offering my small bottle of milk to any girl who would show me her knickers' (62); when a couple of girls 'failed to keep their side of the bargain' he turns to boys, who are happy to show him their 'dicks' in exchange for the milk. This element serves to establish early on and casually the bisexuality which Slater wants the reader to take for granted. It also makes for significant comic payoff at the end of the scene. The inevitable consequences when the teacher finally confronts Nigel and forces him to drink the milk are lingered over in the text: his pretence at drinking, the slow realization of inevitability, the warmth of the milk which 'had been standing in its crate in the sun for a good hour' and the horror of the first taste: 'a great bubble of warm creamy milk hit my tongue, then filled my mouth. It was like vomiting backwards' (63). The scene of the actual vomiting is long and detailed, rendered in virtual slow-motion:

> The vomit came so quickly I didn't have time to move the milk bottle. The straw shot out across the floor, the bottle fell with a clatter and I closed my eyes. Partly to block out the horror of it all and partly because I always close my eyes when I throw up. The puke splattered down my green school pullover and on to the floor, it splashed the bottom half of the bookcase with its Conan Doyles and Kiplings, Sylvia Mountsey's satchel and a marrow on the harvest festival display. At least it missed my bare legs. When I opened my eyes there was milk over the floor, running over the radiator and Mrs Walker's desk. There was thin, milky-yellow vomit over my shoes [...]. (63–4)

The comedy and the disgust are very intricately entwined: the precision with which the path of the vomit is mapped, and the incongruous details such as the marrow are comedic, but the vomit is dwelt on to an extent that is likely to cause the reader's gorge to rise. Notable, though, is the fact that his fellow children respond differently: bending to pick up the bottle as he is forced to return to his seat, still vomit-soaked, he spies 'a flash of three pairs of green knickers and Peter Marshall's dick, fully erect and waving back and forth like a child's flag' (64). For them the scene has been pure carnivalesque: they are much more concerned with the absolute challenge to the authority of the teacher than with Nigel's abjection. Later scenes of nausea-inducing foods are rendered as absolute abjection, however: there is nothing carnivalesque about the painful recollections of the way in which, each weekend, his recently widowed father tries to force his young son to eat eggs:

> My mother had never forced me to eat anything in her life. He cut the egg in small pieces, now as hard as toffee. He held me by the shoulder. He told me to open my mouth or he would hit me. He shook almost as much as I did. The sulphurous smell of the egg made me gag. I shuddered and shook my head from side to side. As the egg on the fork got near to my closed lips I threw my head fast from left to right. The fork went flying. The egg hit first the table and then the floor. I was crying. Snot hit my top lip. I felt something coming up into my mouth from my stomach. Something burning and vile. I pushed my chair back and ran upstairs to the bathroom, my face smeared with tears and egg and snot and vomit. (103)

The disgust evoked by this passage is as much moral as physical: egg is not a universally disgusting substance like vomit, so our disgust is secondhand. We understand that the hardened texture of the egg and its smell evoke intense nausea in Nigel, but what specifically produces our own reactions is the emotional tension built by the rapid succession of very short sentences, his father's aggressive desperation and his own absolute physical revulsion. The scene is very similar to the rejection of milk-skin described by Kristeva, with her spasms in the stomach and belly provoking tears and bile and perspiration. Slater's 'tears and egg and snot and vomit' place the offending egg with offensive bodily emissions, so that, in terms of the two primal forms of disgust outlined by Daniel Kelly, the mechanism of food aversion becomes conflated with that of pathogen protection, and the egg itself becomes a polluting substance. The fact that his father becomes preoccupied with Nigel eating eggs soon after his mother's death is by no means coincidental: his mother has protected him for years from the parental insistence that eggs were a crucial component of manliness: 'It was quite obvious that to turn a nine-year-old nancy boy (his phrase) into a strapping son to be proud of you simply added an egg' (103). The egg, 'the ovum' (104), psychic symbol of motherhood, emblematizes the responsibility for child nurture that now falls to his father's lot.

As Nigel enters adolescence, food and disgust are more and more bound up with sexuality. The opaque parental rules around the way in which different forms of chocolate bar can be eaten are interpreted by Nigel as encoding attitudes about sexual orientation: 'we'd all sit round watching Tony Curtis and Roger Moore, our tongues ferreting around inside our Walnut Whips. Quite why I was encouraged to practise this particular form of culinary cunnilingus, yet was barred from sucking a Mars bar, was something my father chose not to expand upon' (168). The Walnut Whips feature again in Nigel's illicit nightly dog walks to the lay-by employed by couples for car-sex. Crouching in the bushes he observes the goings-on with fascination; he is undeterred even when a used condom lands on his back. The resultant 'thick, shining line of semen' on the back of his school blazer is more disturbing to him for the possibility of discovery it represents than because it is disgusting. It is only when he returns to the lay-by on a healthy country walk with his father that the scene reveals itself to him as sordid:

In the cold light of day there are no twinkling stars and distant lights, no naked bottoms, no spread legs, no muffled cries. Just hundreds of used condoms, little piles of dog shit and dozens upon dozens of Walnut Whip wrappers. (176)

The sexual and culinary leavings are rendered disgusting by the harsh light of day, but particularly by their juxtaposition to the dogs' excrement. Later incidents of virtually performative disgust in which food is associated with either semen or excrement are features of Nigel's early forays into professional kitchens: at a country hotel where he lasts a week, the repellant cooks crumble tired apple pies into the filling for fresh ones, and instruct Nigel to wash the batter off old fillets of fish and then re-batter them. Both disappear for lengthy sojourns during meal service, announcing that they have 'the squits'. The state of the staff toilets is the final coda, with its stamped on cockroaches, eye-watering stench of stale pee, and horrifically untouched bar of soap 'as dry and cracked as the batter on my rebattered fish' (221). The back-stage revelations of the horrors of the professional kitchen are very much of the order of those of Orwell's *Down and Out in Paris and London* and particularly reminiscent of Anthony Bourdain's *Kitchen Confidential*, which was published three years before *Toast*, and the commercial success of which perhaps encouraged the inclusion of these particular episodes in Slater's memoir. The disgust evoked by the revelations of the cheating with old food and wilful lack of hygiene in the latter is more moral than visceral; these are not personal explorations of Slater's own relationship to food and the memories it evokes. Similarly, the sexual highjinks of the young cooks and waiting staff at the more upmarket hotel where he works later – involving a used condom in a seafood salad (the dishes all come back to the kitchen empty, every squid-ring consumed), and a chef masturbating into 'a slice of soft, rose-pink roast beef' (239) – raise only the same level of emotional affect as a viewing of *American Pie*. While not precisely ludic – or carnivalesque – these final moments of disgust offer a comic coda to the sadness of Nigel's orphanhood, a last gasp of ribald adolescence before he moves into the temporal space of adulthood and beyond the text's remit.

Disgust and the woman's novel

While the shifting polarities of food-disgust map a life history to adulthood for Slater, and function as tools of existential exploration in the modernist poetics of Beckett and Joyce, in the women's novels of the later twentieth-century disgust is a feminist issue. In Margaret Atwood's *The Edible Woman* (1969), as discussed in Chapter 6, protagonist Marian's fear of the looming inevitability of marriage and suburban domesticity manifests itself in an increasing inability to eat and an alienation from the female body – both her own and those of others. At the all-female office party, Marian is vaguely repelled by the table loaded with the food prepared by the women: 'all that abundance, all those meringues and icings and glazes, those coagulations of fats and sweets, that proliferation of rich glossy food' (1990: 165). More repellant still are the bodies of the mature women:

'the roll of fat pushed up across Mrs Gundridge's back by the top of her corset, the ham-like bulge of thigh [...] the way her jowls jellied when she chewed, her sweater a woolly teacosy over those rounded shoulders' (167). Female bodies and food become increasingly interchangeable. Women's bodies are threatening to her particularly in their permeability, their openness to the outside world:

> What peculiar creatures they were; and the continual flux between the outside and the inside, taking things in, giving them out, chewing, words, potato-chips, burps, grease, hair, babies, milk, excrement, cookies, vomit, coffee, tomato-juice, blood, sweat, liquor, tears, and garbage [...]. (167)

The list of substances and objects that make their way in and out of the porous envelope of the female body might suggest a connection to the Bahktinian grotesque body, but this is not a celebratory grotesque: these are not bodies triumphing over the material world, but passively subject to it. It has more in common with the abjection which equates egg to tears, snot and vomit in Slater's account of his father's forced feeding, but what is missing is any sense of resistance to the bodily processes of taking in and giving out. Women, for Marian, are the victims of their own bodies, of the lack of clear boundaries between self and other produced both by biology and the mechanisms of socialization. Men's bodies, by contrast, she sees as 'solid, clear', offering a point of resistance to the 'liquid amorphous other', the 'thick sargasso-sea of femininity' (167). A particular disgust attaches itself to the processes of gestation, as the ultimate sign of the permeability of the female body. Her friend Clara's body is seen as monstrous in its invasion by another being: 'a swollen mass of flesh with a tiny pinhead, a shape that had made her think of a queen-ant, bulging with the burden of an entire society, a semi-person – or sometimes, she thought, several people, a cluster of hidden personalities she didn't know at all' (115). Maternity is not exactly *un*natural, but it is natural in an alien way, reducing the female body to something less than mammalian: an insect life-form, or, elsewhere, a bulbous vegetable – 'the gigantic pumpkin-like growth that was enveloping her body' (114). Marian's attempts to comfort Clara in very late pregnancy turn into bizarre imaginings of monstrous births, as she makes 'cheerful but notably uncheering remarks intended to lighten the atmosphere, such as "Maybe it's got three heads", and "Maybe it isn't a baby at all but a kind of parasitic growth, like galls on trees, or elephantiasis of the navel, or a huge bunion [...]."' (114). The threat to the body's physical and psychic envelope of which maternity is the prime exemplar offers a clue as to how we might read Marian's progressive inability to eat: not so much an anorexic fear of adulthood, but a resistance to the bodily openness which she sees as specifically and peculiarly feminine. The connection of gestation to culinary disgust is made explicit not by Marian but in the regression to infantile neurosis of Len, old college friend of Marian's and inadvertent father to her roommate Ainsley's baby. Roué Len is horrified to discover that Ainsley intentionally got pregnant, having 'trapped' him by pretending to be an innocent young girl and not 'college educated'. His horror at impending fatherhood is not centred on issues of responsibility (she wants nothing from him), but a visceral abhorence at the very concept of pregnancy: "'Now I'm going to be all mentally tangled up in Birth. Fecundity. Gestation. Don't you realise what that will do to me? It's obscene, that horrible oozy [...]'" (159). He experiences this psychic distress at the generation of life in terms of violent disgust as well as horror: Ainsley's reminder that 'you were all curled up inside somebody's womb for nine months just like everybody else' produces the classic symptoms of disgust – a 'cringe' face, a warding-off of physical contact and a fear of contamination: "'Don't remind me. I really can't stand it, you'll make me sick. Don't come near me! [...] You're unclean!'" (160). This phobia has its origins in a classic moment of childhood trauma – one which is notably produced by food:

> Marian decided he was becoming hysterical. He sat down on the arm of the chesterfield and covered his face with his hands. 'She made me do it', he muttered. 'My own mother. We were having eggs for breakfast and I opened mine and there was a little chicken inside it, it wasn't born yet, I didn't want to touch it but she didn't see, she didn't see what was really there, she said Don't be silly, it looks like an ordinary egg to me, but it wasn't, it wasn't and she made me eat it. And I know, I know there was a little beak and little claws and everything [...].' He shuddered violently. 'Horrible. Horrible, I can't stand it,' he moaned, and his shoulders began to heave convulsively. (160)

The egg horrifies Len because he sees it as a womb: it is not the fact of eating chicken that figures absolute disgust, but the fact of eating *unborn* chicken. The safe, homely breakfast food has been transformed into a site of monstrous fecundity, of life where it should not be. It seems to be not so much the death of the chick which horrifies, but its near-complete development, with beak and claws. Len's horror is of gestation as a transitional, in-between state; it is 'oozy', neither solid nor liquid, capable of horrifying, slow, contaminating movement: a state akin to Miller's 'thick, greasy life'. One of the issues with Atwood's novel is the question of how we are to read ingestion: as a process of destruction or incorporation? For Len, it seems clear that it is the contaminating act of ingesting the half-formed chick, rather than his role in its destruction, that is the dominant element in his horrified disgust. Marian herself 'catches' Len's food phobia, with eggs becoming the next food she finds herself unable to eat: 'when she opened her soft-boiled egg and saw the yolk looking up at her with its one significant and accusing yellow eye, she found her mouth closing together like a frightened sea-anemone. It's living; it's alive, the muscles in her throat said, and tightened' (161). Throughout, it is the sense of life in relation to food that repels her – from the self-evidently once-living meat which she first refuses, and the carrot which she fears is still alive as she prepares to slice it, to the cake which 'felt spongy and cellular against her tongue, like the bursting of thousands of tiny lungs' (207). Throughout the novel, this aberrant life is intimately connected with femininity, with fecundity, and with the central image of the edible woman.

It is the adult female body, its openness and its ability to create life, from which Marian recoils in disgusted refusal; the thing which she resists becoming. This idea of bodily femaleness as well as cultural femininity as forms of oppression is a function of the text's historical moment, poised on the cusp of the feminist movement whose fictions would seek to reimagine femininity and to celebrate the female body in an unfettered state and as a source of power. Angela Carter's *Nights at the Circus* (1984), for example, actively embraces the (sometimes grotesque) physicality of the female body in the interests of feminist empowerment. The body of Fevvers, the figure at the heart of the novel, is both central mystery and incontrovertible physical fact. A woman with wings, she is a creature of the *fin de siècle*: brought up in a brothel, star of music hall and circus, courted by artists and monarchs throughout Europe. Our meeting with Fevvers in the lengthy opening part of the novel is mediated through the eyes of Jack Walser, a young American reporter attempting to interview her after a show, with the aim of answering the central question posed by the slogan on her own advertising posters: 'is she fact or is she fiction?' (1985: 7). Freeing herself from the glamorous trappings of the stage in her dressing room she is a viscerally physical presence, ripping off her false eyelashes, and slapping her hefty 'marbly thigh' (7) with gusto. The crowded, fetid dressing room is an extension of her body: the smell a 'hot, solid composite of perfume, sweat, greasepaint and raw, leaking gas' (8) compounded with 'a powerful note of stale feet' (9) and a 'marine aroma' that may stem from 'the Cockney Venus' (8) herself. Just as the smell takes on a virtually physical presence – 'ma[king] you feel you breathed the air [...] in lumps' (8) – so her clothes function as bodily detritus, her 'elaborately intimate garments' strewn around the room, 'wormy with ribbons, carious with lace, redolent of use' (9). These manifestations of Fevver's body are actively grotesque, the whole section a knowing reworking of Jonathan Swift's 'The Lady's Dressing Room' (1732) in which the discarded clothes, dirty brushes, medicinal creams, make-up, washpot and commode reveal to the intruding man the horrific bodily realities which lie beneath the burnished public appearance of the 'haughty' 'goddess', culminating in the devastating realization that 'Celia, Celia, Celia shits!'. In Carter's echo of Swift's excremental scene, Fevvers is fully in control of the emanations of bodily grotesquery, and the male response is much more ambivalent. The dressing room's detritus is understood as an aesthetic creation: it is 'a mistresspiece of exquisitely feminine squalor' whose function, like Fevver's tricksy speech, is 'to intimidate a young man' (9). She is consciously disgusting, transgressing bodily proprieties as an assertion of power: drawing attention to her farting, and eating with conspicuous gluttony. The food consumed throughout the lengthy interview is used by Fevvers as a tool in the construction of her ambivalent persona: a magnum of champagne chilling in ice which 'must have come from the fishmonger's for a shiny scale or two stayed trapped within' (8), and which she opens with her teeth, serves as emblem for the rich *fin de siècle* atmosphere of the demi-monde: the sordid and the glamorous in potent stew. She consumes a quintessentially East End meal of 'hot meat pies with a glutinous ladleful of eel gravy on each; a Fujiyama of mashed potatoes; a swamp of dried peas cooked up again and served swimming in greenish liquor' (22) with ostentatious grotesquery:

her mouth was too full for a riposte as she tucked into this earthiest, coarsest cabbies' fare with gargantuan enthusiasm. She gorged, she stuffed herself, she spilled gravy on herself, she sucked up peas from the knife; she had a gullet to match her size and table manners of the Elizabethan variety. (22)

The Rabelaisian reference implied by 'gargantuan' is clearly deliberate, as is the engagement with Bakhtin's reading of Rabelais's grotesque: Fevvers's eating, as with her other forms of bodily self-presentation, is a self-conscious political act which claims the grotesque potential of the female body in the interests of self-empowerment and resistance to patriarchal gender norms. The grotesque body is not the final truth, however: the robust Cockney self revealed under the greasepaint and spangles is not presented by either text or Fevvers herself as her authentic identity, but as another performance. The apparent stripped-down honesty of her dressing-room self, with its smells and appetites and unrestrained abundant flesh, is rendered unstable by the magic or manipulation which freezes time in the room for the course of the interview and by the unanswered questions about her physical self: the huge bulge of her back under her dressing-gown which is either a deformity or a wonder; the question of whether she lacks a navel, as her story of being hatched from an egg would require; the anatomical problem of her possessing both wings and arms. Even the issue of whether or not she is a virgin forms part of her mystery. Crucial for Carter's feminist dynamics is that it is Fevvers who controls both her body and its multiple revelations and withholdings. Her self-presentation and bodily autonomy are a crucial element in the text's ludic atmosphere of wonder. In the context of a patriarchal world which wants to own, imprison and use women's bodies (in brothels and palaces, circuses and torture chambers), she is an image of hope: flying above it not in fey delicacy, but with an intensely corporeal presence, and landing with heaviness and well-fed weight, securely on her own feet. Fevvers is deliberately, consciously disgusting, evoking the power of the grotesque body in the interests of feminist self-assertion. Despite her miraculous otherness, in her insistent, large materiality, the product of her active appetite – her 'face broad and oval as a meat dish', her body which close up 'looked more like a dray mare than an angel' (12) – she asserts the right of women to take up space in the world. It is notable that Walser, as the reader's avatar, is not actively disgusted by her, despite her efforts, but is instead intrigued and aroused.

Disgust and children's literature

Much like Carter's deployment of the disgusting in the interests of rebellion, many children's texts transgress social prescriptions about disgustingness in order to draw a line between the realms of adulthood and childhood. Food and the things it does to bodies feature prominently in these disgust-rebellions. Roald Dahl is the high priest of this ludic disgust, his books – and particularly their striking popularity with child readers – opening a door to a new genre of disgust-literature, particularly for the very young.

Food-disgust is played with in most of Dahl's children's texts: the anticipation of vomit as Bruce Bogtrotter is forced to consume the giant chocolate cake in *Matilda* (1988); the 'disgusting paste' of goose livers Farmer Bunce stuffs into doughnuts in *The Fantastic Mr Fox* (1970); and the fanciful horrors of the diet outlined in the Centipede's song in *James and the Giant Peach* (1961), with 'jellied gnats', 'earwigs cooked in slime', 'minced doodlebugs and curried slugs' and 'tasty tentacles of octopi' (2016a: 65–6). Notable in these evocations of the disgusting is how often it is the sophisticated tastes of adulthood – goose-liver paté, octopus – that are singled out for the horrified contemplation of the child reader. The use of disgust to draw a firm line between the realms of adults and children – and thus establish a sense of conspiratorial connection between reader and text – works in both directions: adult food tastes (as with the disgusting things Slater's father puts in his mouth) are represented as repulsively incomprehensible to children, just as the ludic joy of the slimy, the messy and the borderline food object wilfully transgresses the rules with which adults seek to constrain children. In many of Dahl's texts disgust-evocation is just one among many such polarizing devices, but in two texts – *The Twits* (1980) and *The BFG* (1982) – it takes centre stage. The entire plot of *The BFG* revolves around issues of food: the Big Friendly Giant differs from his fellow giants in his refusal to hunt and consume 'human beans', thus reducing his diet to a single item – the revolting snozzcumber:

> 'Here is the repulsant snozzcumber!' cried the BFG, waving it about. 'I squoggle it! I mispise it! I dispunge it! But because I is refusing to gobble up human beans like the other giants, I must spend my life guzzling up icky-poo snozzcumbers instead. If I don't, I will be nothing but skin and groans.' (2016b: 42)

A great deal of textual attention is devoted to the many ways in which this vegetable is disgusting: for the BFG it is 'disgusterous', 'sickable', 'rotsome' and 'maggotwise' (43), its repulsiveness expressible not in terms of its intrinsic qualities but in its comparability with the absolute acme of the disgusting: vomit, decay and infestation. The child Sophie declares that it tastes 'of frogskins [...] and rotten fish' (43), which the BFG tops with 'cloakcoaches and slime-wranglers' (44), making its flavour a compound of the slimy, the rotting and the disease-carrying, neatly tapping in to a full set of disgust-producing triggers. The 'snozz' of the name also suggests the slime and contamination of 'snot' (the word spoken with a stuffed-up nose), while for the child reader specifically, the full comedic horror of this food stuff is that it is in the form of that most despised object: a vegetable. The textural horror of the vegetable is lingered on when Sophie is forced to climb into its 'wet and slimy' (50) interior, displacing seeds each as big as a melon, in order to hide from one of the human-eating giants. The diet of these more conventional giants is much discussed, with a whole system of taste and discrimination applied by them to their food-stuffs: both 'human Chile beans' and 'Esquimos' are 'cold eats' good for hot weather (53); 'English school-chiddlers [...] has a nice inky-booky flavour' (54), people of Wellington have a 'booty flavour', those of Panama a 'hatty taste' (26). The puns and associations render the giant's diet more amusing than horrifying, with something humorous in their habit of swallowing children by the handful, like sweets, or selecting particularly tasty looking humans from city streets, 'like choosing from a menu' (69). It is notable that while this diet is depicted as terrible, it is not represented in terms of disgust. The BFG rebukes Bloodbottler for his eating habits by declaring 'you is disgusting' (54), but this is a matter of morals rather than affect: the giant's diet is represented as a cuisine, while the BFG's daily grappling with the disgust of his bare subsistence diet is the price he pays for his superior moral position.

While the snozzcumber works to elicit disgust in the child reader, other elements of the disgusting are deployed as fantastic rebellions against the behavioural prescriptions of adults. The delightful fizzy frobscottle which the giants drink instead of water offers the BFG some compensation for the horrors of his diet. While the flavours of other consumables are described with nonsense words or puns, the taste of this drink is afforded a focussed analysis with shades of oenology: 'it tasted of vanilla and cream, with just the faintest trace of raspberries on the edge of the flavour' (60). The precision and delicacy of the flavour description are in tension with the other effect of frobscottle: because its bubbles run down rather than up, unlike human 'pop' it causes the drinker to release its gas through farting rather than burping. For the BFG – and, the text assumes, the child reader – this is the central delight of the drink. The extended conversation in which Sophie and the BFG discuss what he calls 'whizzpopping' and its place in giant culture – '"Whizzpopping is a sign of happiness. It is music in our ears"' (59) – offers the child reader the delight of 'rudeness' and transgression, and a space to contemplate the arbitrary nature of the social prescriptions against certain bodily functions. The fart as sign of the other alimentary consequence of eating is played with in the chapter near the end of the book when the BFG is entertained to breakfast at the palace by the Queen. Seated on a chest of drawers balanced on a grand piano, he is served tray after tray of eggs, sausages, bacon and fried potatoes, after which he feels the need of some frobscottle. In its absence, he declares his ability to '"go whizzpopping perfectly well without it if I is trying hard enough"' (163). The 'sly little smile' which accompanies this declaration indicates his conscious transgression of behavioural norms, inviting the complicity of the child reader. Farting in the palace might seem the epitome of carnivalesque transgression against authority, except that the Queen is made party to the joke, comparing the BFG's violent explosion to bagpipes, and unable to stop herself from smiling. This is in keeping with the transgressions elsewhere in Dahl's work, which, however radical they seem at first glance, almost invariably turn out to operate in the service of an old-fogeyish little-Englander mentality: we might think, for example, of the distaste for the nouveau-riche Salts and for the horrors of modernity as represented by television and chewing gum in *Charlie and the Chocolate Factory* (1964), of its astonishing racism; of the startling misogyny of *The Witches* (1983) ('if only there were a way of telling for sure whether a woman was a witch or not, then we could round them all up and put them in the meat-grinder' (2016e: 5)); and most particularly of the continual preoccupation throughout his oeuvre with the socially unacceptable body. Dahl's works are perhaps best understood as part of a tradition of radically conservative disgust-literature that has its origins in the work of Jonathan Swift. Like Swift, Dahl returns constantly to a horror of the body, which is rendered disgusting because of its aberrant size and shape, its dirtiness and the revelation of its grotesque functions. Distortions of size allow for a microscopic focus on bodily grotesquery: just as Gulliver is monstrous to the Lilliputians, and in his turn a repelled witness to the monstrosities of the Brodignagians, so the ugliness of the giants of *The BFG* is magnified by their scale in relation to Sophie. But it is not just the giants whose bodies are grotesque: adults in Dahl's fiction are frequently represented in similarly repelled terms. Aunt Spiker and Aunt Sponge in *James and the Giant Peach* are 'ghastly hags', their ugliness of spirit matched by a physical ugliness that is rendered in terms of a disgust which is notably inflected through food and orality:

> Aunt Sponge was enormously fat and very short. She had small piggy eyes, a sunken mouth, and one of those flabby white faces that looked exactly as though it had been boiled. She was like a great white soggy overboiled cabbage. Aunt Spiker, on the other hand, was lean and tall and bony [...] She had a screeching voice and long wet narrow lips, and whenever she got angry or excited, little flecks of spit would come shooting out of her mouth as she talked. (2016a: 5–6)

The unpleasant parents in *Matilda* are physically distasteful: Mrs Wormwood 'had one of those unfortunate bulging figures where the flesh appeared to be strapped in all around the body to prevent it from falling out' (2016f: 21) while her husband 'is a small ratty-looking man whose front teeth stuck out underneath a thin ratty moustache' (17) The 'nasty and mean' farmers in *The Fantastic Mr Fox* (1970) are characterized by their diet and their physical forms, which are intimately and specifically related: Boggis is 'enormously fat' because he eats 'three boiled chickens smothered with dumplings every day for breakfast, lunch and supper'; Bean lives on a diet of strong cider and is 'as thin as a pencil' (2016c: 1; 2; 4). Most disgusting of all are the bodies which are lingered over with horrified fascination in *The Twits* (1980). Unlike most of Dahl's children's stories, it is not focalized through the perspective of a child protagonist: the disgustingness of Mr Twit is universalized. The text begins not with the introduction of specific characters, but with a chapter devoted to the phenomenon of men with beards, and the narrator's anxiety about how, and if, they wash their faces; it is only in the next chapter that Mr Twit is introduced, as the realization of all of the nagging anxieties about the cleanliness of men with facial hair. His hair is intrinsically repellant because of its texture – 'in spikes that stuck out straight like the bristles of a nailbrush' – and its placement – it 'even sprouted in revolting clumps out of his nostrils and earholes', and rendered more so because he 'hadn't washed it for years' (2016d: 2–3). But its fundamental disgustingness – developed at length, in its own chapter, with detailed visual aids – is in its association with food and eating. Once again, the disgust is universalized: all hairy faces, we are told, are problematic in relation to eating: 'things *cling* to hairs, especially food. Things like gravy go right in among the hairs and stay there' (3). The smooth faces of the narrator and the child reader are the normative state: 'you and I can wipe our smooth faces with a flannel and we quickly look more or less all right again'; the hair-sprouting face of the adult, and particularly ageing, male (Mr Twit is 60), is pathologized. *All* beard-wearing men, in this account, are potentially disgusting, very likely to leave morsels of ice-cream or chocolate sauce on the hairs around their mouths. Mr Twit is simply the epitome of that disgust. His repulsiveness is a concatenation of several distinct forms of disgust. His sprouting, bristle-like hairs are multiply repellant because of where they sprout (hair in the ears and nose being both comically aberrant and unpleasant) and their texture, which renders them individually distinct rather than a mass (we are told that Mr Twit's facial hair 'didn't grow smooth and matted as it does on most hairy-faced men' (3)): as Miller points out, scalp hair is much less disgusting than hair elsewhere, because it can be understood as a unitary mass rather than as individual sproutings (1997: 55). But their disgustingness is squared by the fact that these hairs contain permanent remnants of his meals: 'there were always hundreds of bits of old breakfasts and lunches and suppers sticking to the hairs around his face' (4). The text zooms in ever closer on these repellant morsels of food waste, forcing our attention on them even as it acknowledges our resistance: 'if you looked closely (not that you'd ever want to) [...]. If you looked closer still (hold your noses, ladies and gentlemen), if you peered deep into the moustachy bristles sticking out over his upper lip' (4–5). An illustration of Mr Twit eating is followed by a close-up circular image (as in a microscope slide), showing his mouth, with its few brown scraggly teeth, and nostril, complete with sprouting hairs, and sundry food-scraps embedded in the hair, labels helpfully identifying the fragments. These morsels function doubly as 'matter out of place': as food waste they are intrinsically contaminating, distinct from their mis-placement in the beard. The foods themselves – the 'disgusting things Mr Twit liked to eat' – are chosen precisely because of their likelihood to be found repellant by a child reader: 'dried-up scrambled eggs', 'spinach', 'minced chicken livers', 'maggoty green cheese', tinned sardines (4–5). Any reader who had survived these drawn-out revelations with equanimity is likely to be confounded by the revelation that '[b]ecause of all this, Mr Twit never went really hungry. By sticking out his tongue and curling it sideways to explore the hairy jungle around his mouth, he was always able to find a tasty morsel here and there to nibble on' (5). Mr Twit's contravention of virtually every social law of hygiene, health and propriety in relation to food and the body renders him so foul that the tricks played upon him by his wife and sundry other mistreated creatures throughout the rest of the text, and even his eventual death, are received as welcome catharsis. The revelations of his physical foulness come in the text before the descriptions of his meanness and cruelty, because they are primary: his disgustingness elicits an 'ethical' response before we know anything of his behaviour. Unlike Orwell, Dahl does not resist the ways in which the disgust response can be co-opted for moral judgements: rather, his texts work actively to produce precisely this conjunction. Mrs Twit, we are told, is fearfully ugly: not because she was born that way, but because her 'ugly thoughts' (7) have shaped her countenance. Our distaste for her appearance, then, is rendered appropriately ethical, and we are free to enjoy her textual comeuppance alongside her repellant husband. As in Dahl's other texts, disgust is presented as a game: a 'naughty' behaviour encouraged by an indulgent uncle behind the backs of the other adults. The wormy spaghetti Mrs Twit serves her husband falls into this category – the child reader can squirm in delighted disgust at the prospect of Mr Twit chewing his way through the wriggling bowl. But the more fundamental disgust elicited for fat, ugly, hairy, uncontrolled bodies is not really a game: it taps into a child's disbelief that their own compact, biddable flesh will one day morph into an adult form in order to express a profoundly conservative body horror.

The Swiftian element of Dahl's disgust is not one shared by most of the children's writers who follow his invitation to the disgust-playground. We find something much closer to a Bahktinian celebration of the bodily grotesque in texts such as Raymond Briggs's 1977 graphic novel *Fungus the Bogeyman*, with its exuberant imaginings of the inverted world of the Bogeys, with their liking of damp, slimy environments and rotting food, and incomprehension of the repellent ways of the human 'Drycleaners'. Illustrated in a dingy, greyed palette throughout, the brightest things are the Bogeys themselves, their virulent green skin shining through the murk. Copious footnotes and encyclopaedia entries make their world clear, developing the child reader's instinctive gleeful disgust into a more nuanced understanding of the internal logic of their different social practices. Disgust in Briggs's text is importantly reciprocal: we find disgusting their assiduous cultivation of boils, consumption of mould and encouragement of snails in their mattresses; but they are equally disgusted by the heat and dryness and unnatural cleanness of the human world. Disgust is not the categorical limit of sympathy as in many adult texts, but the starting point for the investigation of the same in the other.

A significant number of children's texts published around the millennium deploy not just the disgusting, but the specifically scatological, as the marker of a divide between the sensibilities of adults and children, but, unlike Dahl, use disgust with a redemptive rather than a punitive impulse. *The Giggler Treatment* (2000), the first children's novel of celebrated Irish novelist Roddy Doyle, revolves around the question – drawn out over the whole length of the text – of whether Mister Mack, biscuit-factory tester and father of Robbie, Jimmy and baby Kayla, will or won't step in an enormous pile of dog poo on his morning walk to the station. The poo is the product of the next-door dog, Rover, but has been placed in Mister Mack's path by the Gigglers, small, furry creatures who, from the beginning of human history, have punished adults who mistreat children by dint of 'the Giggler Treatment': 'poo on the shoe' (2000: 22). The fantastic elements, the childish disgust-humour and the representation of adults as cruel might seem to echo Dahl, but there are crucial differences: Mister Mack, it turns out, is not actually cruel to his children. The scene of anger the Gigglers overhear is his momentary rage elicited by his sons breaking a window for the eighth time, and responding to his rebuke with cheek. He soon regrets his initial impulse to send them to bed with no supper, though by this time the Gigglers have left to plan his punishment. Unlike Dahl, Doyle makes the child reader privy both to the perspective of the children and to that of the adult: Mister Mack's bad day at work (which included a vulture stealing his lunchtime sandwich) and the fact that he had cut his finger replacing the glass in the window in question only five minutes earlier are presented as significantly mitigating circumstances. When his children meet the Gigglers and learn their plan they and Rover make it their mission to prevent their father's foot making contact with the poo: the text becomes a race against time in defence of the adult. The child reader is still invited to delight in the finely elaborated toilet humour: the Gigglers, particularly the youngest, who is coming to poo-work for the first time, are avatars for the reader, gleefully anticipating the outcome of their nefarious plans; Mister Mack's children narrate their own chapter 'JIMMIE AND ROBBIE GIVE THEIR SIDE OF THE STORY', in which they are torn between approval of the Giggler Treatment because 'it's fair and it's funny' ('funnier even than doing rudies in the bath') (83–4) and a sense that their own father doesn't really deserve it, despite his many crimes against childhood: 'even though he wouldn't let me pick my nose, even though there was a brilliant bit of snot up there and I wanted to flick it at Grandad because he was asleep and his mouth was open' (84–5). Fairness and fun are the joint moral systems which dominate the story, to the extent that we are offered two denouements: one where the 'left leg of [Mister Mack's] brand-new trousers was up to its knee in Rover's—' (96) and one where he is saved in the nick of time. The foot-in-poo ending is curtailed by Rover himself, who insists that, regardless of whether this is the funnier outcome, he, as the producer of the poo, should have a say in its use. Rover's argument with the narrator is one of many meta-textual games which stop and start the narrative flow, including character interventions, false narratives, and a running gag about the names, numbers and status of chapters. These elements establish storytelling as a co-operative endeavour between reader and writer, and moral issues of guilt and punishment as matters of societal negotiation rather than arbitrary imposition. Just as narrative form is open to ludic exploration in Doyle's text, so too is the very nature of disgust. The status of dog excrement as unequivocal signifier of disgust is interrogated and problematized – at first by an insistence on the very everydayness of the substance, and then by a consideration of the dog's experience in producing it: 'Poor Rover has to stand out on the street, usually late at night, in the rain and snow, thunder and lightening, in the glare of passing car lights, and go to the toilet while his owner stares straight at him' (42). In fact, Rover reveals, dogs are perfectly able to use human toilets, and do so when their owners have gone to bed: '[a]ll dogs do this and they never, ever get caught' (45). He further reveals that dog poo is a commodity – the Gigglers pay for it at a rate of twenty-pence a go, and Rover stores his wages in the hollow interior of the bones he buries in the garden. Rover's poo is thus simultaneously sign of both difference and sameness: his public, street-level emissions are a mark of his abject position as pet; his toilet-using abilities and wages showing a secret membership of the systems from which humans derive their dignity and self-respect. Dog poo plays a central role also in Andy Stanton's 2006 *You're a Bad Man, Mr Gum*, the first of a series featuring antagonist Mr Gum, who is clearly a close relative of Dahl's Mr Twit. A wilfully unpleasant, fulsomely bearded old man with a positive taste for the disgusting, Mr Gum 'was a complete horror who hated children, animals, fun and corn on the cob. What he liked was snoozing in bed all day, being lonely and scowling at things. He slept and scowled and picked his nose and ate it' (2006: 2). Like the Twits, he plots nefarious schemes against children and animals, in this novel poisoning Jake the dog, a local mascot much beloved by the people and animals of the eccentric town of Lamonic Bibber. So loved is Jake – 'a furry wobbler and friendly as toast' (15) – that 'a rumour began that if Jake the dog visited your garden it meant you were in for some good luck, and if he left a "little gift" on the lawn you were in for double good luck and maybe even a telegram from the Queen' (17). Jake's leavings are categorized as 'only natural', and the only person who has any problem with them is the monstrously disgusting Mr Gum, who finds them so horrific that the text, when focalized from his perspective, cannot name them: 'There was something lying under the oak tree that Mr Gum did not even want to think about' (23). Since Jake's excrement is as natural as the grass, flowers and other animals, the vengeance that Mr Gum enacts is seen as entirely unreasonable, a function of his 'hat[red] of all the joy the world was having' (108). But the visual dimension of the text tells another story: above the first description of Jake's 'little gifts' is a detailed drawing of a large spiral of excrement, complete with pinched-off summit and encircled by buzzing flies. The importance of this image is highlighted by the fact that repeats of it, interspersed with bottles of rat poison, decorate the book's endpapers. The image revels in the intractably disgusting nature of the poo, and asks the reader to join in the sense of pleasure in Mr Gum's beautiful garden being thus despoiled. Disgustingness – which at first seems the province only of Mr Gum – is more widely dispersed by this and other peritextual elements, particularly the printed 'grime' which subtly decorates the corners of many of the pages, just where dirty fingers may have held them. It is not Mr Gum's fingers which we imagine besmearing our copy of the book, but our own, or those of other readers, so that dirt then becomes a marker for our material engagement with the physical text.

Like Dahl's, both Doyle's and Stanton's disgust narratives pay particular attention to food. Two food shops in Lamonic Bibber represent the rival poles of pleasure and horror: Mrs Lovely's sweet shop and the horrific butcher's shop run by Billy William the Third. It is from the latter that Mr Gum obtains the rotten cows hearts with which he will poison Jake: the hearts are already rotten when he buys them, as Billy William, as consciously disgusting as Mr Gum, has left the parcel sitting out in the sun for over a week because 'I like watching the flies go mad over it' (39). It is at Mrs Lovely's Wonderful Land of Sweets that Mr Gum reluctantly purchases lemonade powder to disguise the taste of the poisoned rotten hearts, a place so antithetical to his negativity that it disgusts him:

> The powdery smell of sherbet lemons mingled with the odours of strawberry bombs and liquorice whips. Mr Gum felt sick. He felt as if he was being attacked by the forces of good. When he was a boy he had loved eating sweets, but that was before he turned into a bad man. Yet now he seemed to hear the voice of the boy he had once been, calling to him down the years. (74–5)

As for Dahl, sweets represent a world of lost childhood delights, though it is one still available to the innocent-hearted adults such as Friday O'Leary, side-kick of the hero, Polly, with his surreal refrain 'THE TRUTH IS A LEMON MERINGUE!' (138). Mister Mack's role as biscuit-tester serves a similar purpose: his job a child's fantasy of an occupation. The success or failure of his day depends on the biscuits he will be testing (the factory conveniently making 365 varieties). As with the children's texts discussed in Chapter 6, food stuffs attain the roles of characters in the novel: biscuits have personalities as far as Mr Mack is concerned: his favourites, fig rolls, he considers 'intelligent' because they are 'delicious without needing any help from chocolate' (Doyle 2000: 9). The profoundly boring nature of his least favourite, cream crackers, is demonstrated by their being given a voice in the text – first in Mister Mack's dreams and then in their own chapter – where they intone blindingly obvious facts in a monotone ('If you put your feet in water, they get wet. Isn't that interesting' (33)). In both texts, foods are a device of imaginative power, but it is striking that in neither do the excremental and the gustatory connect. It is not *these* foods that produced the poo, and we don't see the foods that the dogs eat. Dog poo is both more abject than that of humans – in its public production and lingering presence, its smell, the likelihood of its contaminating transference to the shoe – but also less worryingly, embarrassingly connected to us. Those children's books which fully embrace the entirety of the human alimentary process do so most often with the aim of amusing toddlers: large numbers of books with 'poo' in the title have been produced for very young children in the last couple of decades, some of which market themselves on their ability to facilitate toilet training, but all of which rely on the young child's sense that talking about poo is screamingly funny.[20] A striking exception in terms of the sophistication of its address is *Vesuvius Poovius* (2003), a large-format picture book intended for six- to eleven-year-olds, written by Kes Gray and illustrated by Chris Mould. Set in Ancient Rome it tells the story of a city overcome with 'the whiff of the unmentionable' until saved by Vesuvius Poovius's timely invention of the toilet. The early pages detail not just a city overrun with excrement, but a social system in which the very concept is so shameful that elaborate verbal circumlocutions have to be employed, by order of the emperor. In order not to embarrass his wife, citizens must, on pain of being chopped in bits and fed to the emperor's dogs, employ 'delightful words' such as 'marzipan or strawberries or jewels' to describe their excrement (2003: 4). This poses problems for Vesuvius Poovius, who needs to be able to sell the emperor on his new invention and the sewage system it necessitates. His solution is to invite the emperor and his wife to a private party, at which he stuffs them so full of delicacies that they need to defecate, at which point he directs them to his shiny new (double) toilets. The disgust-play of the narrative alternates between the humour of poo being everywhere and yet unmentionable, and the repellant nature of 'Ancient Roman' food, which includes 'prune cocktail, sheep's eye dumplings, eel jelly, frog burgers, beetle pizza, snail squash, crow soup and lots, lots more!' (16). The illustrations depict a table heaving with repulsive dishes: a huge pudding is studded with eyeballs, frog's legs emerge from burger buns, while live slugs, snails and insects crawl all over. The hugely fat Emperor and his wife, their wobbly pink flesh barely covered by their togas, cram their mouths with these disgusting morsels, the Emperor spearing a whole, disgruntled-looking eel while his wife sucks at multiple sugared snails. Vesuvius, notably, claims, with a shudder, not to be hungry: both his food (dis)tastes and his anticipation of modern technology placing him on our side of the disgust-dynamic. The moment when his guests realize the imminence of their bodily functions is stretched out over several double pages, with the reader gleefully anticipating the bodily and social discomfort as their stomachs gurgle and their faces turn green, until they are forced to declare their need in specific language rendered in huge and desperate block capitals: "A POO! Vesuvius!" screamed the Emperor. "WE

NEED TO DO A POO!!!'" (24). The toilets which, the text tells us, are made of gleaming marble, in the illustrations resemble highly generic 1970s low-cisterned models, in the avocado green distinctive of the bathroom fittings of this period. Their everyday familiarity (to the parent if not the child reader), incongruous next to the marble pillars, arches and urns that comprise the rest of the interior fittings of the house, renders their function safely anodyne. The emperor and his wife are so thrilled with them that they order their installation throughout the city, and remain in Vesuvius's house, stuffing themselves with honeyed hedgehogs and squid ink tea in order that they can 'have another go' on the wonderous contraptions. The abjectly disgusting can be safely flushed away (the fact that the sewage system has not yet been built is glossed over), while the enjoyably grotesque elements of the Roman diet remain to entertain us.

Figure 11 *Roman food in Kes Gray and Chris Mould,* Vesuvius Poovius *(2003).*

The stark memorableness of the moments of textual disgust discussed in this chapter might obscure the fact that they are comparative rarities: the texts which take us into the territory of the disgusting in association with food are unusual. The bodily experience of eating – of chewing and swallowing – is represented surprisingly rarely in most accounts of food, as opposed to the more rarefied sensation of tasting, which is to be found everywhere. When food-disgust is predominantly present in a text it is because that text has an agenda: the savage satire of the Swiftian tradition, the determined breaking and remaking of literary convention of the modernists, the transgressive play of certain children's writers, the political energy of Orwell (or Mayhew or Engels), feminist transgressions against the acceptably feminine, the confessional energy of Slater (or Bourdain). Disgust always has an agenda, though these agendas are not always the same.

CONCLUSION: GO TO WORK ON AN EGG

What is true of disgust is also true of literary food in general: it very often has an agenda, but its agendas are not always the same. Food, as I said at the outset, is a thing of power within many texts: power to emblematize and power to disrupt. To draw together the threads of my argument, I will return to the food with which I started: the egg. In culinary terms the egg is strange – even miraculous. It can be and do so many things. It can raise a cake, swelling out a dense mixture of flour, sugar and fat many times its weight with little bubbles – spaces frozen into fixity by the oven's heat; separated, its yolk can thicken a custard, a mayonnaise, its unctuousness binding with the liquidity of oil, of milk to produce smooth, sheeny perfection. The whites can rise to enormous billows, so firm the bowl can be turned upside down and they miraculously cling. But these culinary promises are tainted always with the threat of failure: the egg is tricky, demanding. The cake can sink, its middle soggy – the technical term for which is 'sad'. The mayonnaise and custard can curdle, separating into islands of fat in a disappointed liquid. The meringue or soufflé falls, the promised spectacle diminished to a flat pancake. Symbolically, the egg has been many things for many cultures: alpha and omega: the beginning and the end; the spring time; the earth; the universe; the central paradox of nature (what comes first … ?). The egg emblematizes food and our curious attitudes to it in that it is both absolutely ordinary and always somehow strange.

Because eggs are both ubiquitous in cooking and multivalent in meaning, we can trace the argument of the book by following the fragments of their discarded shells. In nineteenth-century narratives of hunger, the egg figures simple, homely nourishment. The harmonious meal at the start of *Mary Barton*, when the Bartons entertain their friends to a high tea of fried eggs and ham, positions the egg as at the heart of a culinary culture, rather than the subsistence level diet figured by the potato. Adolescent Mary's competence as both shopper and cook makes clear that there is a working-class food culture from which the characters are increasingly alienated throughout the rest of the novel. One of the few wholesome meals David Copperfield eats in the years after the destruction of his infantile idyll is a 'nice little' loaf of brown bread and egg boiled for him by an old woman just before his first night at school (1985a: 125–6). Her home is poor, and he has had to purchase the egg and little loaf for himself, but the meal stands for comfort and simple nourishment, at odds with the random chaotic diet of his later street-life. The manner of cooking an egg changes its associative meanings. A soft-boiled egg speaks of childhood, of tea-time or breakfast with a row of toast soldiers lined up to dip into the yolk; it is simple condensed protein – unequivocally good for you. The soft-boiled egg is the egg that 'reads' as closest to the natural state. It is bucolic, rural, innocent. It is also specifically British, depending on the technology of the egg-cup (something not traditionally used by other nations). The 'pale fried egg' which is part of Orwell's breakfast in the Brooker's lodging house has nothing of comfort about it, its paleness signalling its age and the sickly, poorly fed state of the hen which laid it; its colour at one with the monochrome horror of the tripe. Sally Bowles's prairie oyster, with its raw egg whisked up with brandy and Worchester sauce stands for the hectic chaos of the lives of the bohemians of 1930s Berlin: barely sufficient nourishment binding spice and intoxication. The stolen egg M. F. K. Fisher's Sue warms in the teapot and breaks randomly over the largest dish of food similarly marks the limit of what is needed to survive with bodily and mental processes intact.

Since the egg so clearly speaks of bucolic comfort and basic sustenance, it is unsurprising that it does not appear in its elaborate, showy menus of the Victorian dinner party. Egg dishes, for the most part, were a matter for breakfast or luncheon. This designation begins to change in the late 1880s, when French haute cuisine became established as the *dernier cri* of fashionable dining. Eggs formed a major part of this new culinary repertoire – Escoffier's 1907 *Guide to Modern Cookery* contained 60 separate recipes for soufflés and 150 more for other egg dishes. (It is entirely fitting that he was sacked from his job at the Savoy in 1897 for fiddling the egg account.) The souffle, in particular, speaks luxury. Its value is in its tricksiness and ephemerality, the threat that it will fall, or fail to rise. Their success relies on physical technique and on timing, hence their role at the centre of the new, showy, restaurant culture of the fin de siècle, where they dramatize chefly skill and waiterly aplomb. The technical power of whisked egg whites to give height and to spell the luxury that is technical virtuosity harnessed to one's pleasures is figured also in the mentally illuminating effects of the meal Virginia Woolf enjoys in the men's college at 'Oxbridge': the 'confection which rose all sugar from the waves', surely having the sculpted glossy curves of meringue somewhere in its make-up (1992b: 13). Eggs are connected to kitchen labour, also, in the politics of service, forming a sign both of the everyday banality of the domestic, and of the first incursions of the middle class woman (back) into her own kitchen. The former sense of the quotidian impositions of daily routine is figured in texts of the interwar years, surprisingly, in the trope of eggs for cakes: the Provincial Lady's fantasy of herself as culinary expert after the war is interrupted by a servant with a message from the cook wanting permission to order 'half-a-dozen of eggs for the cakes'; while beleaguered Mrs Brown, about to be left with no servants at all, adds too many eggs at once to her cake mixture, causing it to 'curdle' (Delafield 1991: 473; Crompton 1956: 145–6). But eggs also represent the pleasures of the physical actions of cooking in interwar literature: the late-night supper of scrambled eggs on toast sisters Delia and Rhoda cook for themselves in the kitchen on the new house at the end of the day of moving, their access to the kitchen emblematic of new independence and new futures, the quiet lyrical delight of the 'golden froth rising in the white bowl' (Cooper 1987: 310). A similar incursion on the territory of the kitchen is that of Monica Dickens, when she creeps downstairs in the middle of the night to make omelettes, horrifying the family cook: a scene which she deploys as reason for her decision to train as a professional cook herself, as the only way to get her hands on the omelette pan. The technical skill required to make an omelette elevates it above many other egg preparations, a fact recognized by the cook employed by Gertrude Stein and Alice B Toklas during their early years living in Paris. Toklas tells the story of how the cook, who disliked Matisse, changed her planned dish from omelettes to fried eggs on learning he was staying to dinner – 'it takes the same amount of butter and same number of eggs, but it shows less respect, and he will understand' (Toklas 1961).

Eggs appear in numerous guises and with strikingly various tropic power in the context of gender. In the haute gourmet tradition they figure exoticism: the plovers' eggs of the first luncheon Charles attends in Sebastian Flyte's college rooms, representing rarity value and his world of landed privilege (they come from Brideshead; they lay early for 'Mummy'). In the bachelor confines of the Drones club, eggs (along with beans and crumpets) are a marker of identity, part of the chummy code whereby the members – refusing to grow up, embracing the silly as a defence against the horrors of the modern – name each other with generic slang designators which speak of childhood simplicities. The egg figures both the pleasures and the distractions of domesticity in the context of the culinary refusals of the women's texts of the 1960s and '70s: Ephron's Rachel Samstadt spends weeks trying to find a method for making a four-minute egg in three minutes: a literal wasting of time while her marriage crumbles unnoticed. The egg also stands for the loving labours of motherhood, in the great mound of eggs and flour kneaded by the universe-expanding Mrs Ph(i)Nk$_0$ in Calvino's 'All At One Point'.

Eggs appear in modernist texts either as sign of the banality of the demotic (the smeared remnants on Fanny's breakfast plate in *Jacob's Room*); as jest provocations (Agnes Jekyll's 'Ostrich Egg' constructed from a pig's bladder and twelve hens' eggs); or as a making profoundly strange of the ordinary, as in the many elliptical references in Stein's *Tender Buttons*, where eggs are 'Kind height, kind in the right stomach with a little sudden mill' and 'Cut up alone the paved way which is harm' (2003: 23–4).[1] Eggs figure often in those children's texts which engage with cooking as an index of learned competence: there are many eggs used in the cakes which emblematize the culinary skill of girls in the American children's fiction of the turn of the nineteenth century. The scrambling of eggs in the 'common dish' of *Swallows and Amazons* captures a dual state of cooking as skill but also as play. The wild bird eggs imagined for the newly rural Borrowers by Mrs May represent both the bucolic and a modern culinary sophistication – the latter figured particularly in the idea that they will make omelettes and salads with wild garlic. The passage is unworried by the implications of eating the eggs of wild birds – unlike *Wonderland*, where Alice is accused by the pigeon of being a sort of serpent when she confesses to eating eggs. The fears of being eaten which figure so strikingly often in children's texts are most graphically demonstrated in Mini Grey's *Egg Drop*, where we emphasize with the ambitions and the pain of the egg-protagonist until the horrific final moment when we are required to eat his dead and smiling fried corpse. Eggs loom large in the discussion of recipes partly because they are such a ubiquitous element of cuisine and partly because their manipulation involves technical skills which take the recipe writer to the limits of what is conveyable: the lengthy, laborious instructions for separating eggs in *Dinners for Beginners*; Julie Powell's problems identifying 'the ribbon' when beating eggs with sugar to Julia Child's instructions; the many complexities involved in the writing and reading of instructions for making omelettes for *No Name's* Mrs Wragge and for Julia Child herself.

Finally, the egg is a potent index of disgust. The scene of young Nigel being force fed eggs by his newly widowed father (who believes that 'to make a man you just add an egg') evokes both moral and visceral disgust at the absolute abjection of 'tears and egg and snot and vomit' (2003: 103). For *The Edible Woman's* Len, the egg is a thing of absolute horror, a site of monstrous, oozy fecund life.

Like all food the egg hovers awkwardly between object and process, pleasure and disgust, banality and intense, fascinating strangeness. To read the scenes of the egg – to read the literature of food in general – opens up for us a profound sense of its many and various purposes, its disturbing plenitude. It is hard to stop reading, and writing, about food.

NOTES

Introduction

1 'In the spirit of "what's eating us?," food and eating continually branch into areas that may at first seem unconnected, yet in their rhizomatic logic are deeply entwined' (Probyn 2000: 7–8).

2 Tigner and Carruth's *Literature and Food Studies* (2018) offers a series of historical case studies focussing on issues of social justice and injustice and on the intersection of critical food studies perspectives with those of literary scholarship. Shahani's edited collection of essays, *Food and Literature* (2018) contains contributions on a broad range of approaches to food and literature. Another recent work, Gilbert's *The Culinary Imagination: From Myth to Modernity* (2014) surveys a very broad historical field, producing fascinating readings but in a necessarily much looser, more associative structure. Until very recently, book-length studies on food and literature have tended to focus on single genres, or periods, or both: there are important studies of food in relation to, for example, the eighteenth-century novel (Moss 2009), romantic-period texts (Morton 2004), the mid-twentieth-century women's novel (Sceats 2000), children's literature (Daniels 2006; Keeling and Pollard 2009), nineteenth-century British fiction (Cozzi 2011; Lee 2016; Scholl 2016), race and colonialism in American literature (Carruth 2013; Tompkins 2012; Vester 2015), and post-colonial writing (Parama 2010).

3 Shahani (2018: 8) examines the anxiety in food studies about this sense that food is trivial.

4 De Certeau (1984).

5 The 'ordinary' as de Certeau defines it is not the same as the commodified forms of mass culture; rather, it consists of those everyday practices – reading, cooking, walking – which are performed as if by rote, and which for de Certeau and his co-authors offer (partial) sites of resistance to the institutions and systems of power (1998: 3).

Chapter 1

1 Examples of the former include Houston (1994) and Cozzi (2011). Studies of voluntary hunger and self-starvation focus on an alternative canon of hunger narratives which begins in accounts of the lives of medieval saints, reaches its modernist apotheosis in Franz Kafka's stark fable of 'A Hunger Artist' (1922) and ends in anorexia narratives; these hungers are mostly outside the purview of this study, but have been extensively considered elsewhere – most strikingly in Ellman (1993); see also Silver (2002).

2 See Scholl's work on the early nineteenth century (2016) and work on the literature of the Irish famine, particularly Fegan (2002).

3 'Modern historians have rightly pointed out that the term "hungry 40s" is a retrospective invention, coined in the early 20th century by supporters of free trade' (Gurney 2009: 101).

4 See Kinealy (1994: 32); Ó Gráda (2006: 9); Woodham-Smith (1991: 69).

Notes

5   For more on hunger in *Mary Barton*, see Scholl (2017).

6   Fegan (2002); see also Kelleher (1997).

7   See also Bourke (1993).

8   A note in her collected works indicates that the poem was first published in an article by her husband, William Wilde, on 'The Food of the Irish', published in the *Dublin University Magazine* in 1854.

9   Cowen gives examples of Jewish soup kitchens and La Soup, the first Huguenot soup kitchen, which opened in Brick Lane in 1797.

10   'Souperism' has become a key element in later literary and folkloric representations of the Famine. Modern historians have tended to conclude that it was not as widespread as contemporary suspicion suggested, but have found evidence of a number of cases. See Whelan (1995).

11   The book uses the same device as his earlier *Modern Housewife* (1849), which addresses itself to a middle-class female readership through the use of two female personae who discuss household affairs.

12   A fourth volume was published in 1861.

13   Saloop was a cheaper substitute for tea or coffee made from orchid roots or sassafras roots and leaves, popular in the eighteenth century when the price of the former put them out of reach of all but the wealthy; its popularity as an item for public consumption declined when it began to be touted as a treatment for venereal disease. See Chase (1994: 45–6).

14   For a discussion of the pineapple as object of fascination, see Boyce and Fitzpatrick (2017: 1–3).

15   This is by no means the case in Europe: one of the most striking literary studies of hunger is Knut Hamsun's *Sult* (1890), usually translated as *Hunger*. This proto-modernist text follows the mental and physical meanderings of its protagonist, a would-be writer, around the city of Kristiania (Oslo), as he starves to the point of near death. It goes further as a representation of the physical and mental effects of starvation than previous texts, focusing on the stomach's inability to retain food after a certain stage of starvation and the feverish mental state produced when 'drunk with starvation' (1991: 62). The narrator catalogues the particular physical pains produced by his hunger spells – the gnawing pain in his chest he can alleviate by walking doubled, the pain in his back and shoulders that nothing can expel. We follow him through the steps of his degradation: the pride that prevents him from asking for help; that causes him to give away money to beggars whenever he acquires any; his attempt to keep himself alive on the bits of meat clinging to a raw bone he told a butcher he wanted for his dog. Hamsun's text is remarkable for deploying none of the distancing devices that other writers use to hold hunger at arm's length.

16   See Warnes (2004) for a discussion of hunger in Wright.

17   For a fuller discussion of British wartime food culture, see Humble (2005: 81–111).

18   Sylvia Townsend Warner's 1926 *Lolly Willowes* involves a contemporary woman who turns to witch-craft.

19   Shahani (2018: 7) cites the memory 'cookbooks' compiled by Czech women in concentration camps (De Silva 1996): 'they create new vocabularies of hunger and new forms of expression to endure, even defy it.'

20   See Carruth (2013: 82) and Moody (2012: 266): 'If Ireland provided Beckett with a cultural and political tradition of hunger, it was France that allowed him to become intimately acquainted with the everyday realities of malnutrition.'

21   See note 15 for discussion of Hamsun.

Chapter 2

1   Boyce (2006: 1–3) makes a similar point about the conventional invisibility of the Victorian fictional dinner.

2   For further detail on the historical form of the dinner in the nineteenth century, see Symonds (2010) and Attar (1992).

3   In Barthes's account, the reality effect produced by realist texts depends of a significant proportion of 'stuff' that is uninterpretable in order to, as Freedgood puts it, 'maintain a convincing equilibrium between the realistic and the allegorical. [...] A complicated exchange between narrative agency and the anomie of the real must take place for realist fiction to feel real and at the same time for it to mean something that reality by itself cannot'. (2006: 147).

4   Gigante reads Jos as a satirical portrait of George IV (2005: 173–6).

5   For an interesting discussion of appetite in the novel, see Lee (2016: 47–62).

6   Lindner reads the novel's intense materialism as dramatizing commodity fetishism (2002: 564–81).

7   For further discussion of dinners in *David Copperfield*, see Cozzi (2011).

8   'The points of formal dinner knives in the West became rounded during the seventeenth century, apparently beginning in France. We have learnt to use forks instead of knives for introducing food into our mouths, partly in order to spare our companions the faintest suggestion of the consequences which could result from that knife-point approaching our faces' (Visser 1992: 98).

9   Wilson (2002b: 66). See also Wilson (2012: passim).

10 See Humble (2010b: 226).

11 Gillian Beer also finds this absence significant: 'food has little presence in *Middlemarch* save as a source of unease. [...] Appetite is almost entirely absent' (2006: 30–1).

12 Lee mounts a similar argument about the 'simultaneous attraction to and repulsion from food and eating in conceptualizations of fiction as an art form' in the work of both Henry James and George Eliot (2016: 108).

13 See also Mennell (1996: 157–63).

14 The image of white circles on a patterned background is strongly reminiscent of the aesthetic style of Virginia's sister, Vanessa Bell.

Chapter 3

1   Because the servant–employer relationship is so culturally specific, the discussion will focus largely on the British situation. There is much fascinating work on service in America, encompassing the history and legacy of slavery: see Witt (2004), Harris (2011), Zafar (1999), Tompkins (2012) and Warnes (2004).

2   Beeton, instructing that the housemaid should be required to clean every room and every piece of furniture thoroughly every day, notes that 'In the country, a room would not require sweeping thoroughly like this more than twice a week' (1989: 991).

3   The involvement of the mistress of the house in cooking and preserving had been a given from the Elizabethan period to the end of the Georgian: as Burnett notes 'in earlier times,

and throughout the eighteenth century, [the female employer] had worked with and personally supervised her domestic staff, at least in all but noble households; servants were assistants, who helped the housewife to bake and brew, wash and mend linen, cook and clean' (1974: 165).

4   On the basis of the numbers of servants and of middle-class families in the 1871 census, Flanders concludes that 'most families had at best one servant, and [...] far more women were helping their single servants do the family cooking – or doing it entirely on their own – than our perception today would allow for' (2004: 94). See also Branca (1974: 179–91).

5   According to Beeton, a good kitchen should be 'sufficiently remote from the principal apartments of the house, that the members, visitors, or guests of the family, may not perceive the odour incident to cooking, or hear the noise of culinary operations' (25).

6   Bloaters are a form of kipper, cured with the guts in.

7   For a fuller account of the growth of this distrust, see Robbins (1986: 108–12).

8   See also McCuskey (2000: 359–75).

9   See Reynolds and Humble (1993: 140–7).

10 'Walter', *My Secret Life,* vol II, p. 218. See also Marcus (1969).

11 For example, an account of an interview with a maid-of-all-work includes her as an 'amateur' prostitute, when all she admits to is a 'young man', a 'sweetheart' who is 'in the harmy, not a hoffisser, but a soldier' and with whom she goes out on Sunday afternoons (Mayhew 1968: IV, 258).

12 See Humble (2001) for more on such imagined servants.

13 Robbins makes a similar point, noting the essential continuities in the depictions of servants across the history of the English novel: 'From the beginning, the functional, secondary, second-hand presence of servants in the novel is extraneous, absurd, modernist' (1986: 49).

Chapter 4

1   The gendering of food has been a dominant element in academic discussions in the fields of psychology, sociology and gender studies over recent decades. See, for example, Silva (2000), Hollows (2003), Probyn (2000).

2   The shifting historical form of the British cookbook is the focus of my *Culinary Pleasures* (2005).

3   It is notable that it was female chefs who pioneered the open kitchen, a performative space open to the restaurant, allowing no place for the violence and horror of the masculine chef tradition.

4   On the Grand Tour and its afterlife, see Colletta (2015), Buzard (2002) and Fussell (1987).

5   Symons (2004: 295) argues that Newnham-Davis constructs the 'sovereign consumer': he 'became a modern *aribeter elegantiae*, promoting, on the one hand, great chefs and their practices and, on the other, informed consumers'. See also Broomfield (2012).

6   Floyd (2003: 127–43) also considers David in relation to the gourmet / gastronomic tradition, though her focus is more on notions of national identity.

7   *The Book of Salt* has generated considerable critical interest: see Tigner and Carruth (2018), Cruz (2013), Xu (2008).

8 For more on these paradoxes of writerly identity and ventriloquism in Stein and Toklas see Gilmore (1992), Gilbert and Gubar (1989), Linzie (2006).

9 Though Bilbo's panic at having to feed thirteen uninvited dwarves might be taken as an exception.

10 See Snyder (1999).

11 See also Hollows (2002) and Inness (2001).

12 Neuhaus (2003: 216–18) in her study of American cookbooks places this fear of homosexuality somewhat earlier, seeing it as a function of Cold War paranoias whipped up in the McCarthy era.

13 I differ here from Sceats, who sees Marian's relationship with food as unproblematic until the moment Peter proposes (2000: 95).

14 See Chodorow (1999), Rich (1995), Thurer (1994).

Chapter 5

1 The term 'modernist food' is increasingly applied to a school of experimental food also known as molecular gastronomy, influenced by the technological experiments of Hervé This, Ferran Adrià and Heston Blumenthal, but I am using it here to refer to a modernist culinary moment running alongside those in literature and the arts in the first half of the twentieth century. For a comparison of the two forms of modernist food, see Carruth (2018: 220–36).

2 For more on Stein's experiments in severing the word from the object, see Schwenger (2001: 103–6). For the 'still-life poetics' of Stein and other modernist poets, see Delville (2008).

3 Tromanhauser (2011), following the logic of Adams's *The Sexual Politics of Meat* (1989), reads the fruit as a feminine 'vegetarian dish' working in opposition to the daube, which she sees as part of a 'sacrificial structure' confirming masculine authority.

4 Grigson (1983: 235).

5 Perloff (1981: 12); Israel (2006: 128).

6 See Roessel (2002), who notes that inhabitants of Smyrna were thought to be the last surviving descendants of the Ancient Greeks.

7 Connor (1982). For a full discussion of the phrase and its implications, see Slote (2010).

8 The Futurist movement had been effectively launched by the publication of Marinetti's first Futurist manifesto in 1909; manifestos appeared annually until 1916, with many of the original members leaving the movement around 1917. Marinetti rebranded the movement as a Second Futurism, with a focus particularly on aeroplanes and radio. For further discussion of the food-agenda of Futurism, see Delville (2008: 100–9) and Novero (2010).

9 Carruth (2013: 50–77) also considers Fisher in relation to modernist aesthetics.

10 Very little is known about her: a native of New Orleans, she was born Marcelle Azra Forbes, or possibly Hincks, and seems to have assumed the name and title when she moved to England as a young woman, having spent some time travelling in Italy.

11 See 'The Invention of the Housewife' in Humble (2005).

12 For a fuller discussion of this feature of modernist aesthetics, which figures notably, for example, in the work of Huysmans, Rimbaud, Faulkner and Forster, see Tajiri (2001) and Thacker (2004).

Notes

Chapter 6

1   Nodelman (1996: 196) argues that 'the sensuous delight of these descriptions of food reveals that in children's fiction, eating seems to occupy the place that sex does in adult fiction'. See also Katz (1980: 192) and Daniels (2006: 81–2).

2   Texts which usefully consider food in Carroll's work include Vallone (2002), Nicolson (1987), Boyce and Fitzpatrick (2017: 231–5), and Lee (2014).

3   Katz (1980) discusses food in Graham's text, as does Hunt (1996), Sullivan (2005), Hemmings (2007) and Nikolajeva (2000), who reads meals as part of a system of ritualized temporal markers that integrate the child into the community.

4   See Harris (2012) for food in the Harry Potter series.

5   For more on the excremental elements in this text, see Bosmajian (1985) and Gooderman (1994).

6   Keeling and Pollard (2018: 209) make the point that Ma's sense of civilization rests on the existence of a stove and a table in each of her temporary homes.

7   Blackford (2009) employs a Kristevan reading of Jo's cooking, seeing its violence as rage directed at the maternal body; see also Pelletier (2009). For more on Alcott in relation to concepts of virtuous eating, see Tigner and Carruth (2018), chapter 3.

8   'William's New Year's Day', *Just William* (1922).

9   See Wilson (2005: 522) and Rustin (2001).

10 For food restrictions during the Second World War and afterwards, see Driver (1983: 16–57) and Humble (2005: 81–136).

11 'Carroll gives us a world in which everything and everyone is potentially on the menu' (Lee 2014: 490).

12 Critics of fantasy are generally agreed on a division between high fantasy, which takes place in a completely fictional fantasy world with its own logic, and low fantasy, which involves 'nonrational happenings that are without causality or rationality because they occur in the rational world where such things are not supposed to occur' (Stableford 2009: 256). They are divided about how to categorize 'portal fantasies' such as the *Alice* books and the *Chronicles of Narnia*, which move between a rational and a fantastic world.

13 See also Houston (1994: 18, 164).

14 Jonathan Swift, *A Modest Proposal for Preventing the Children of Poor People in Ireland, from Being a Burden to Their Parents or Country; and for Making Them Beneficial to the Publick* (1729).

15 See also Pollard and Keeling (2002: 117–30).

Chapter 7

1   For further discussion of the domestic science movement in the British context, see Humble (2005: 59–61).

2   Beeton unashamedly lifted many her recipes from Acton's work of sixteen years earlier. In editing them she deliberately removed all digressive elements: all opinion, niceties of taste, serving suggestions and discussions of flavour. See Humble (2000: xiv–xv) and (2005: 10–13).

3   The 2007 paperback edition of the book was retitled *Julie & Julia: My Year of Cooking Dangerously*. The blog is no longer functional but can be accessed on The Wayback Machine at https://web.archive.org/web/20021013043154/ and http://blogs.salon.com/0001399/2002/08/25.html.

4   The three had founded a cooking school, *L'Ecole des Trois Gourmandes*, together in Paris in 1951, and the book draws on their extensive experience of teaching.

5   Leonardi's paper yielded such a crop of letters that the journal devoted a section in a later edition to printing a small selection: some were horrified at an august publication descending to trivia, others took issues with her readings, and a surprising number wanted to offer their own recipes.

6   Sceats (2003: 169–86) also discusses exactly these three novels – the central texts of the genre we might call 'recipe-novels' – at some length, but thinking about them primarily in terms of power and gender comes to rather different conclusions to mine. See also Gopnik (2006).

7   These 'delicious supplements' to children's texts are analysed by Slothower and Susina (2009).

8   A similar paradox to that which structures Jorge Luis Borges's initiatory post-modern parable 'Pierre Menard, Author of the Quixote'.

9   Powell attempts, in her pre-Julia Child days, to woo her boyfriend with a version of the dish, using 'roses from a bin at the 7-Eleven and papaya instead of pitaya', with inedible results (2009: 216).

10 Sceats makes a similar point, noting the ways that Winot's 'culinary elitism' plays to the reader's desire to be acknowledged as 'part of the club' (2003: 177).

11 Not all of this new crop of food memoirs incorporated recipes – Slater's *Toast* has only one: an ironic anti-recipe, which lists the horrifically chemical ingredients of the ubiquitous convenience-food favourite of the seventies' childhood: Butterscotch Angel Delight.

12 'Foodoir' is a coinage of Gilbert (2014); Doris Witt (2004) suggests the term 'recipistolary' to embrace memoirs, travel writings and novels which centre on the recipe. For other important critical engagement with the recipe, see Tigner and Carruth (2018), who focus on chocolate in their case study of early recipe transmission, and Coghlan (2018).

13 Smart-Grosvenor has been brilliantly discussed in Witt (2004), and Gilbert (2014): my approach differs in my particular interest in her use of the recipe form.

14 Egerton (1993: 16) elucidates this 'difficult to eradicate' stereotype of the black female cook: 'They were "turbanned mammies" and "voodoo magicians" and "tyrants" who ruled the back rooms with simpleminded power; they could work culinary miracles day in and day out, but couldn't for the life of them tell anyone how they did it. Their most impressive dishes were described as "accidental" rather than planned. Their speech, humourously conveyed in demeaning dialect in many an old cookbook, came across as illiterate folk knowledge and not to be taken seriously.'

15 The Black Arts Movement was the aesthetic and cultural 'wing' of Black Power, focused on the establishment of distinctively black cultural institutions and aesthetic traditions and practices.

16 Between 1916 and the 1970s six million African Americans migrated from Southern rural areas to cities in the Midwest, Northeast and West.

17 In his two volumes *How to Eat to Live* (1967 and 1972). For a detailed account of African American food politics in the civil rights era, see Wallach (2014).

Notes

18 She both confirmed and denied this influence at different times; see Witt (2004: 156).

19 Floyd (2003: 142) reads David's deployment of memory similarly, arguing with some irony that 'David's Mediterranean is only ever an Other space in the sense of being the focus of memories of happier times. The Europe of the present, by contrast, is merely an arena in which she works tirelessly and with little success to taste the last traces of an authenticity already utterly lost to Britain.'

Chapter 8

1 Theorists are in some disagreement about whether disgust is an emotion or a drive.

2 See Kelly (2011: 16; 64); Ekman (2003: 205–21); Oaten et al. (2009: 303–21).

3 Kelly (2011: 43); see also Rozin et al. (2008).

4 '[D]isgust is capable of exhibiting great diversity and variation, and [...] an important part of the explanation for this lies in the flexibility of its acquisition system. Such flexibility also makes for an emotion easily activated by new types of cues and thus well suited to be co-opted to perform new roles' (Kelly 2011: 118).

5 One of the major proponents of the 'deep wisdom' argument is Kass (1997), who uses disgust as a moral arbiter in his arguments against human cloning and stem cell research. See Kelly (2011: 138–9; 147).

6 For example, in the opening chapter of *Keep the Aspidistra Flying* (1936).

7 She is clear that the abject is not an object in the post-Freudian terms established by Jacques Lacan – it is 'not my correlative, which, providing me with someone or something else as support, would allow me to be more or less detached and autonomous', nor is it 'an otherness ceaselessly fleeing in a systematic quest of desire': rather, it is made up of those things that the psyche jettisons and radically excludes: that which 'draws me toward the place where meaning collapses' (1982: 2).

8 The symbolic is the fourth stage in the Lacanian psychoanalytic model of infant psycho-sexual development, in which the subject, through the acquisition of language, enters into the symbolic order, the social world of intersubjective relations, knowledge of ideological conventions and acceptance of the law.

9 Trotter offers a useful challenge to the problematic universalism of Kristeva's model in his extraordinary *Cooking with Mud*: 'Although I shall draw on Kristeva's work, and on Douglas's, I believe that they are both too quick to generalize. After all, the in-between, the ambiguous, and the composite account between them for a very large proportion of human experience; if these disturbances were consistently to provoke abjection, we should all feel abject all the time. By the same token, there surely are other events, such as a lack of cleanliness or health, which nauseate us without unsettling any symbolic universes' (2000: 159n).

10 Critical approaches that play Kristeva and Bakhtin against each other include Rushdy (1991) and Anspaugh (1994).

11 Trotter follows a similar approach, noting that 'I shall only draw upon commentaries on the aetiology of disgust as and when they help to explain why a writer or a painter should have chosen to invite a particular response' (2000: 161).

12 The schema was produced by Joyce in 1921 to explain the underlying structure of the work to his friend Stuart Gilbert. With Joyce's agreement, Gilbert published it in his *James Joyce's 'Ulysses': A Study* (1930).

13 What this might mean as literary practice has intrigued critics: e.g. Vike (2010) and *James Joyce Quarterly* (2009): special issue on Joyce and Science.

14 Joyce was explicit about this process: 'Among other things my book is the epic of the human body. [...] In my book the body lives in and moves through space and is the home of a full human personality. The words I write are adapted to express first one of its functions then another' (Budgen 1972: 21).

15 The 'ghost', as well as being a pun on 'toast' and a reference to Parnell's unhealthy pallor, also suggests that he appears to Bloom as a ghostly revenant of his illustrious sibling (Charles Stewart Parnell died in 1891; *Ulysses* is set in 1904).

16 'When it comes to cuisine [...] the disgusting and the delicious do not always function as opposites. A good deal of recondite and sophisticated eating actually seems to be built upon (or even to be a variation of) that which disgusts, endangers, or repels' (Korsmeyer 2011: 62).

17 'Our bodies and our souls', he later suggests, in riposte to the suggestions of the Rozin school that disgust is driven by a deep need to avoid knowledge of our animal origins, 'are the prime generators of the disgusting. What the animals remind us of, the ones that disgust us – insects, slugs, worms, rats, bats, newts, centipedes – is life, oozy, slimy, viscous, teeming, messy, uncanny life. We needn't have recourse to the animals for that reminder; all we need is a mirror' (Miller 1997: 50).

18 Beckett, early in his career, worked as Joyce's secretary in Paris, and Joyce is one of the most significant influences on his early work.

19 Miller makes a similar case for the greater potential for disgustingness of the mouth over the anus: 'The mouth routinely risks contamination simply by carrying out its role as entry point. Its job is to admit things and make the final judgment about their swallowability. The anus is not at risk from so many sources' (99). For more on disgust in Beckett's trilogy, see Gigante (2004: 183–201).

20 For example, *Liam Goes Poo in the Toilet: A Story about Trouble with Toilet Training* (Whelan-Banks 2008) and *Everybody Poos* (Gomi 2004). A play on the tension between poo as object – smelly, silly and amusingly disgusting to the three-year-old; and poo as process – difficult, stressful and bound up with adult rules about when and where – is explored in *The Story of the Little Mole Who Knew It Was None of His Business* (Holzwarth and Erlbruch 2007), in which a furiously dignified little mole marches through the pages trying to work out who is responsible for the large poo which balances on his head throughout.

Conclusion

1 After writing this meditation on eggs I discovered Maria Christou's *Eating Otherwise: The Philosophy of Food in Twentieth-Century Literature* (Cambridge University Press, 2017), which frames its brilliant discussion of avant-garde reformulation of food and ontology via the treatment of eggs in the work of Beckett, Bataille, Marinetti and Atwood.

BIBLIOGRAPHY

Note: Primary texts are shown in bold.

Acton, Eliza (1993) *Modern Cookery for Private Families* (Lewes: Southover Press).
Adams, Aubrey (2013) 'Racial Indigestion: Eating Bodies in the 19th Century', *Food, Culture and Society* 16 (4): 694–6.
Adams, Carol (1989) *The Sexual Politics of Meat* (Chicago: University of Chicago Press).
Adams, Samuel and Sarah (1989) *The Complete Servant* (Lewes: Southover Press).
Addyman, Mary, Laura Wood and Christopher Yiannitsaros, eds. (2017) *Food, Drink, and the Written Word in Britain, 1820–1945* (London: Routledge).
Albala, Ken, ed. (2014) *The Food History Reader: Primary Sources* (London: Bloomsbury Academic).
Alcott, Louisa M. (1870) *An Old-Fashioned Girl* (London: n.p.).
Alcott, Louisa M. (1953) *Little Women* (Harmondsworth: Penguin).
Andrews, Geoff (2008) *The Slow Food Story: Politics and Pleasure* (London: Pluto Press).
Angelella, Lisa (2011) 'The Meat of the Movement: Food and Feminism in Woolf', *Woolf Studies Annual* 17: 173–95.
Anspaugh, Kelly (1994) 'Powers of Ordure: James Joyce and the Excremental Vision(s)', *Mosaic* 27 (1): 73–100.
Appadurai, Arjun, ed. (1986) *The Social Life of Things* (Cambridge: Cambridge University Press).
Armstrong, Nancy (1987) *Desire and Domestic Fiction* (Oxford: Oxford University Press).
Armstrong, Nancy (2005) *How Novels Think: The Limits of Individualism 1719–1900* (New York: Columbia University Press).
Ashley, Bob, Joanne Hollows, Steve Jones and Ben Taylor (2004) *Food and Cultural Studies* (London: Routledge).
Attar, Dena (1987) *A Bibliography of Household Books Published in Britain 1800–1914* (London: Prospect Books).
Attar, Dena (1992) 'Keeping Up Appearances: The Genteel Art of Dining in Middle-Class Victorian Britain', in *The Appetite and the Eye: Visual Aspects of Food and Its Presentation within Their Historic Context*, ed. C. Anne Wilson (Edinburgh: Edinburgh University Press).
Atwood, Margaret (1990) *The Edible Woman* (London: Virago).
Auden, W. H. (1991) 'Introduction', in *The Art of Eating*, ed. M. F. K. Fisher (London: Macmillan).
Bakhtin, Mikhail (1984) *Rabelais and His World*, trans. Hélène Iswolsky (Bloomington: Indiana University Press).
Ballantyne, R. M. (1990) *The Coral Island* (Oxford: Oxford University Press).
Barnes, Julian (2004) *The Pedant in the Kitchen* (London: Atlantic Books).
Barr, Ann (1988) Introduction to Paul Levy, *Out to Lunch* (Penguin: Harmondsworth).
Barthes, Roland (1989) *The Rustle of Language* (Berkeley: University of California Press).
Beck, Simone, Louisette Bertholle and Julia Child (1976) *Mastering the Art of French Cooking* (Harmondsworth: Penguin).
Beckett, Samuel (1934) 'Dante and the Lobster', *More Pricks than Kicks*, http://www. evergreenreview.com/dante-and-the-lobster-samuel-beckett.
Beckett, Samuel (2003) *Molloy*, in *Trilogy* (London: Calder Publications).
Beer, Gillian (2006) 'What's Not in Middlemarch', in *Middlemarch in the Twenty-First Century*, ed. Karen Chase (Oxford: Oxford University Press).

Beeton, Isabella (1989) *Beeton's Book of Household Management* (London: Chancellor Press).
Beeton, Isabella (2000) *Book of Household Management*, ed. Nicola Humble (Oxford: Oxford World's Classics).
Belasco, Warren (2008) *Food: The Key Concepts* (London: Bloomsbury).
Benedict, Barbara (2009) 'The Trouble with Things: Objects and the Commodification of Sociability', in *A Companion to Jane Austen*, ed. Claudia L. Johnson and Clara Tuite (Chichester: Wiley-Blackwell).
Bennett, Jon (1987) *The Hunger Machine* (London: Polity Press).
Benson, E. F. (1970) *Mapp and Lucia* (Harmondsworth: Penguin).
Blackford, Holly (2009) 'Recipe for Reciprocity and Repression: The Politics of Cooking and Consumption in Girls' Coming-of Age Literature', in *Critical Approaches to Food in Children's Literature*, ed. Scott Pollard and Kara Keeling (London: Routledge).
Blackwell, Mark, ed. (2007) *The Secret Life of Things: Animals, Objects and It-Narratives in Eighteenth-Century England* (Lewisburg: Bucknell University Press).
Blanc, Raymond (1988) *Recipes from Le Manoir Aux Quat' Saisons* (London: Guild Publishing).
Blodgett, Harriet (1997) 'Food for Thought in Virginia Woolf's Novels', *Woolf Studies Annual* 3: 45–60.
Bordo, Susan (1993) *Unbearable Weight: Feminism, in Western Culture, and the Body* (Berkeley: University of California Press).
Bosmajian, Hamida (1985) '*Charlie and the Chocolate Factory* and Other Excremental Visions', *The Lion and the Unicorn* 9: 36–49.
Boulestin, Marcel (1923) *Simple French Cooking for English Homes* (London: William Heinemann).
Bourdain, Anthony (2000) *Kitchen Confidential: Adventures in the Culinary Underbelly* (London: Bloomsbury).
Bourke, Austin (1993) *The Visitation of God? The Potato and the Great Irish Famine* (Dublin: The Lilliput Press).
Boyce, Charlotte (2006) 'Tell Me What You Eat': Representations of Food in Nineteenth-Century Culture', PhD dissertation, University of Cardiff.
Boyce, Charlotte (2012) 'Representing the "Hungry Forties" in Image and Verse: The Politics of Hunger in Early-Victorian Illustrated Periodicals', *Victorian Literature and Culture* 40 (2): 421–49.
Boyce, Charlotte and Joan Fitzpatrick (2017) *A History of Food in Literature from the Fourteenth Century to the Present* (London: Routledge).
Bowen, Elizabeth (1962) *The Heat of the Day* (Harmondsworth: Penguin).
Bracken, Peg (1978) *The 'I Hate to Cook' Book* (London: Corgi).
Braddon, Mary Elizabeth (1991) *Lady Audley's Secret* (Oxford: Oxford University Press).
Braddon, Mary Elizabeth (1996) *Aurora Floyd* (Oxford: Oxford University Press).
Branca, Patricia (1974) 'Image and Reality: The Myth of the Idle Victorian Woman', in *Clio's Consciousness Raised*, ed. Mary Hartmann and Lois Banner (New York: Harper Torchbooks).
Brontë, Charlotte (1974) *Shirley* (Harmondsworth: Penguin).
Brontë, Charlotte (1987) *Jane Eyre* (Harmondsworth: Penguin).
Brontë, Charlotte (1993a) *Villette* (London: Everyman).
Brontë, Emily (1993b) *Wuthering Heights* (London: Everyman).
Broomfield, Andrea (2012) 'The Soldier of the Fork: How Nathanial Newnham-David Democratized Dining', *Gastronomica: The Journal of Food and Culture* 12 (4): 46–54.
Brown, Bill (2001) 'Thing Theory', *Critical Inquiry* 28 (1): 1–22.
Budgen, Frank (1972) *James Joyce and the Making of 'Ulysses'* (Oxford: Oxford University Press).
Burnett, John, ed. (1974) *Useful Toil: Autobiographies of Working People from the 1820s to the 1920s* (London: Allen Lane).

Bibliography

Buzard, James (2002) 'The Grand Tour and After (1660–1840)', in *The Cambridge Companion to Travel Writing* (Cambridge: Cambridge University Press).

Calvino, Italo (1984) *Cosmicomics*, trans. William Weaver (London: Abacus).

Cannon Cookery Book, The **(1953) (London: Cannon).**

Carey, John (1992) *The Intellectuals and the Masses* (London: Faber).

Carlyle, Thomas (1899) *Past and Present* (London: Chapman and Hall).

Carlyle, Thomas (1971) *Chartism*, in *Selected Writings* (Harmondsworth: Penguin).

Carlyle, Thomas (1971b) *Past and Present*, in *Selected Writings* (Harmondsworth: Penguin).

Carroll, Lewis (1968) *Alice's Adventures in Wonderland and through the Looking-Glass* (London: Macmillan).

Carruth, Allison (2013) *Global Appetites: American Power and the Literature of Food* (Cambridge: Cambridge University Press).

Carruth, Alison (2018) 'Avant-Garde Food Writing, Modernist Cuisine', in *Food and Literature*, ed. Gitanjali G. Shahani (Cambridge: Cambridge University Press).

Carter, Angela (1985) *Nights at the Circus* (London: Pan).

Chamerlain, Lesley (2014) 'Afterword', in *The Futurist Cookbook* (Harmondsworth: Penguin).

Chase, Holly (1994) 'Suspect Salep', *Look and Feel: Studies in Texture, Appearance and Incidental Characteristics of Food*, Proceedings of the Oxford Symposium on Food and Cookery 1993 (Totnes: Prospect Books).

Chase, Karen and Michael Levenson (2000) *The Spectacle of Intimacy: A Public Life for the Victorian Family* (Princeton: Princeton University Press).

Chodorow, Nancy (1999) *The Reproduction of Mothering: Psychoanalysis and the Sociology of Gender* (Los Angeles: University of California Press).

Christie, Agatha (2002) *A Pocket Full of Rye* (London: HarperCollins).

Christou, Maria (2017) *Eating Otherwise: The Philosophy of Food in Twentieth Century Literature* (Cambridge: Cambridge University Press).

Cline, Sally (1990) *Just Desserts* (London: Deutsch).

Coghlan, J. Michelle (2018) 'The Art of the Recipe: American Food Writing Avant la Lettre', in *Food and Literature*, ed. Gitanjali G. Shahani (Cambridge: Cambridge University Press).

Cohen, William (2009) *Embodied: Victorian Literature and the Senses* (Minneapolis: University of Minnesota Press).

Colletta, Lisa, ed. (2015) *The Legacy of the Grand Tour: New Essays on Travel, Literature, and Culture* (London: Fairleigh Dickinson University Press).

Collingham, Lizzie (2012) *The Taste of War: World War Two and the Battle for Food* (Harmondsworth: Penguin).

Collins, Wilkie (1985) *The Woman in White* (Harmondsworth: Penguin).

Collins, Wilkie (1992) *No Name* (Oxford: Oxford University Press).

Connor, Stephen (1982) 'Samuel Beckett's Animals', *Journal of Beckett Studies* 8: 29–42.

Conran, Shirley (1975) *Superwoman* (London: Sidgwick & Jackson).

Cooper, Artemis (2000) *Writing at the Kitchen Table* (Harmondsworth: Penguin).

Cooper, Lettice (1987) *The New House* (London: Virago).

Counihan, Carole (1999) *The Anthropology of Food and the Body: Gender, Meaning and Power* (London: Routledge).

Counihan, Carole and Penny van Esterik, eds. (2008) *Food and Culture: A Reader* (London: Routledge).

Coveney, John (2000) *Food, Morals and Meaning: The Pleasure and Anxiety of Eating* (New York: Routledge).

Cowen, Ruth (2006) *Relish: The Extraordinary Life of Alexis Soyer: Victorian Celebrity Chef* (London: Weidenfeld & Nicholson).

Cozzi, Annette (2011) *The Discourses of Food in Nineteenth Century British Fiction* (London: Palgrave).

Crompton, Richmal (1954) *William the Pirate* (London: George Newnes Limited).

Crompton, Richmal (1956) *William and the Tramp* (London: George Newnes Limited).

Crompton, Richmal (1988) *William Carries On* (London: Macmillan).

Crompton, Richmal (1991a) *Just William* (London: Macmillan).

Crompton, Richmal (1991b) *William in Trouble* (London: Macmillan).

Crompton, Richmal (1995) *More William* (London: Macmillan).

Crompton, Richmal (1999a) *William Does His Bit* (London: Macmillan).

Crompton, Richmal (1999b) *William the Outlaw* (London: Macmillan).

Crouzet, François (2013) *The Victorian Economy* (London: Routledge).

Cruz, Denise (2013) '"Love Is Not a Bowl of Quinces": Food, Desire, and the Queer Asian Body in Monique Truong's *The Book of Salt*', *Eating Asian America: A Food Studies Reader*, ed. Robert Ji-Song and Martin G. Manalansan Ku (New York: New York University Press, 2013), 354–70.

Dahl, Roald (1995) *Charlie and the Chocolate Factory* (Harmondsworth: Penguin).

Dahl, Roald (2016a) *James and the Giant Peach* (Harmondsworth: Penguin).

Dahl, Roald (2016b) *The BFG* (Harmondsworth: Penguin).

Dahl, Roald (2016c) *The Fantastic Mr Fox* (Harmondsworth: Penguin).

Dahl, Roald (2016d) *The Twits* (Harmondsworth: Penguin).

Dahl, Roald (2016e) *The Witches* (Harmondsworth: Penguin).

Dahl, Roald (2016f) *Matilda* (Harmondsworth: Penguin).

Dalley, Lana (2008) 'The Economics of "A Bit O' Victual," or Malthus and Mothers in *Adam Bede*', *Victorian Literature and Culture* 36 (2): 549–67.

Daniels, Carolyn (2006) *Voracious Children: Who Eats Whom in Children's Literature* (London: Routledge).

David, Elizabeth (1956) *A Book of Mediterranean Food* (Harmondsworth: Penguin).

David, Elizabeth (1986a) 'John Wesley's Eye', in *An Omelette and a Glass of Wine* (Harmondsworth: Penguin).

David, Elizabeth (1986b) *French Provincial Cooking* (Harmondsworth: Penguin).

Davidson, Alan, ed. (1999) *The Oxford Companion to Food* (Oxford: Oxford University Press).

De Certeau, Michel (1984) *The Practice of Everyday Life*, vol I, trans. Steven Rendall (Berkeley: University of California Press).

De Certeau, Michel, Luce Giard and Pierre Mayol (1998) *The Practice of Everyday Life*, vol II: *Cooking and Eating*, trans. Timothy J. Tomasik (Minnesota: University of Minnesota Press).

De Silva, Cara, ed. (1996) *In Memory's Kitchen* (Northvale, NJ: Jason Aronson).

Delafield, E. M. (1991) *The Diary of a Provincial Lady* (London: Virago).

Delville, Michel (2008) *Food, Poetry and the Aesthetics of Consumption: Eating the Avant-Garde* (London: Routledge).

Dickens, Charles (1918) *Our Mutual Friend* (London: Chapman & Hall).

Dickens, Charles (1978) *Nicholas Nickelby* (Harmondsworth: Penguin).

Dickens, Charles (1985a) *David Copperfield* (Harmondsworth: Penguin).

Dickens, Charles (1985b) *Great Expectations* (Harmondsworth: Penguin).

Dickens, Monica (1952) *One Pair of Hands* (London: Michael Joseph).

Dolittle, Hilda (H. D.) (1916) 'Orchard', in *Sea Garden* (London: Constable and Company).

Döring, Tobias, Markus Heide and Susanne Mühleisen, eds. (2003) *Eating Culture: The Poetics and Politics of Food* (Heidelberg: Universitätsverlag Winter).

Douglas, Mary (1991) *Purity and Danger: An Analysis of the Concepts of Pollution and Taboo* (London: Routledge).

Dover Wilson, John (1911) *Life in Shakespeare's England* (Cambridge: Cambridge University Press).

Doyle, Roddy (2000) *The Giggler Treatment* (London: Scholastic).

Bibliography

Driver, Christopher (1983) *The British at Table, 1940–1980* (London: Chatto & Windus).

Drummond, J. C. and Anne Wilbraham (1991) *The Englishman's Food* (London: Pimlico).

Eagleton, Terry (1995) *Heathcliff and the Great Hunger: Studies in Irish Culture* (London: Verso).

Eagleton, Terry (2009) *Walter Benjamin: Or, towards a Revolutionary Criticism* (London: Verso).

Egerton, John (1993) *Southern Food: At Home, on the Road, in History* (Chapel Hill: University of North Carolina Press).

Ekman, Paul (2003) 'Darwin, Deceit, and Facial Recognition', *Annals of the New York Academy of Sciences* 1000: 205–21.

Eliot, George (1913) *Felix Holt, the Radical* (Oxford: Oxford University Press).

Eliot, George (1977) *Adam Bede* (London: Dent).

Eliot, George (1985) *Middlemarch* (Harmondsworth: Penguin).

Eliot, George (1986) *Daniel Deronda* (Harmondsworth: Penguin).

Eliot, T. S. (1974) *Collected Poems 1909–1962* (London: Faber & Faber).

Ellis, John (1993) *The World War II Databook: The Essential Facts and Figures for All the Combatants* (London: Aurum Press).

Ellis, Sarah Stickney (1843) *The Wives of England: Their Relative Duties, Domestic Influence, and Social Obligations* (London: Fisher, Son, & Co.).

Ellman, Maud (1993) *The Hunger Artists: Starving, Writing and Imprisonment* (Cambridge, MA: Harvard University Press).

Engels, Friedrich (1844) *The Condition of the Working Class in England* (Oxford: Oxford University Press).

Ephron, Nora (1996) *Heartburn* (London: Virago).

Escoffier, A. (1907) *A Guide to Modern Cookery* (London: William Heinemann).

Escoffier, Georges Auguste (1957) *A Guide to Modern Cookery* (London: Hutchinson).

Esquival, Laura (1993) *Like Water for Chocolate*, trans. Carol Christensen (London: Black Swan).

Esquire (1953) *Handbook for Hosts* (New York: Grosset & Dunlap).

Fegan, Melissa (2002) *Literature and the Irish Famine 1845–1919* (Oxford: Clarendon Press).

Fernandez, Jean (2009) *Victorian Servants, Class, and the Politics of Literacy* (London: Routledge).

Fisher, M. F. K. (1983) *With Bold Knife and Fork* (London: Chatto and Windus).

Fisher, M. F. K. (1991) *The Art of Eating* (London: Macmillan).

Fitzpatrick, Joan (2013) 'Food and Literature: An Overview', in *Routledge International Handbook of Food Studies*, ed. Ken Albala (London: Routledge).

Flanders, Judith (2004) *The Victorian House* (London: HarperCollins).

Floyd, Janet (2003) 'Simple, Honest Food: Elizabeth David and the Construction of Nation in Cookery Writing', in *The Recipe Reader: Narratives-Contexts-Traditions*, ed. Janet Flood and Laurel Foster (Burlington, VT: Ashgate).

Foucault, Michel (2002) *The Order of Things* (London: Routledge).

Frank, Robert H. and Ben S. Bernanke (2007) *Principles of Macroeconomics* (Boston: McGraw-Hill/Irwin).

Fraser, Evan D. and Andrew Rimas (2010) *Empires of Food: Feast, Famine and the Rise and Fall of Civilizations* (London: Arrow).

Freedgood, Elaine (2006) *The Ideas in Things: Fugitive Meaning in the Victorian Novel* (Chicago: University of Chicago Press).

Friedan, Betty (1972) *The Feminine Mystique* (Harmondsworth: Penguin, 1972).

Fussell, Paul, ed. (1987) 'The Eighteenth Century and the Grand Tour', in *The Norton Book of Travel* (London: W. W. Norton).

Gaskell, Elizabeth (1848) *Mary Barton* (Harmondsworth: Penguin).

Gaskell, Elizabeth (1986a) *Cranford* (Harmondsworth: Penguin).

Gaskell, Elizabeth (1986b) *North and South* (Harmondsworth: Penguin).

Gigante, Denise (2004) 'The Endgame of Taste: Keats, Sartre, Beckett', in *Cultures of Taste/ Theories of Appetite: Eating Romanticism*, ed. Timothy Morton (London: Palgrave Macmillan, 2004).

Gigante, Denise (2005) *Taste: A Literary History* (New Haven: Yale University Press).

Gilbert, Pamela K. (2003) 'Ingestion, Contagion, Seduction: Victorian Metaphors of Reading', in *Scenes of the Apple: Food and the Female Body in Nineteenth- and Twentieth-Century Women's Writing*, ed. Tamar Heller and Patricia Moran (Albany: State of New York Press).

Gilbert, Sandra (2014) *The Culinary Imagination: From Myth to Modernity* (New York and London: W. W. Norton).

Gilbert, Sandra and Susan Gubar (1989) *No Man's Land: The Place of the Woman Writer in the Twentieth Century Volume 2: Sexchanges* (New Haven: Yale University Press).

Gilmore, Leigh (1992) 'A Signature of Lesbian Autobiography: Gertrice/Altrude', in *Autobiography and Questions of Gender*, ed. Shirley Neuman (London: Cass).

Gooderman, David (1994) 'Deep Calling unto Deep: Pre-Oedipal Structures in Children's Texts', *Children's Literature in Education* 25 (2): 113–23.

Gomi, Taro (2004) *Everybody Poos* (London: Frances Lincoln).

Graham, Kenneth (1971) *The Wind in the Willows* (London: Methuen).

Gregg, Melissa and Gregory J. Seigworth, eds. (2010) *The Affect Theory Reader* (London: Duke University Press).

Grey, Mini (2002) *Egg Drop* (London: Jonathan Cape).

Grey, Mini (2004) *Biscuit Bear* (London: Jonathan Cape).

Griffiths, Eric (1996) 'Hegel's Winter Collection: Defending Delia; Fairy-Tale Cookery and the Art You Cannot Eat', *Times Literary Supplement*, 8 March.

Griffiths, Sian and Jennifer Wallace, eds. (1988) *Consuming Passions* (London: Mandolin).

Griggs, Barbara (1986) *The Food Factor* (London: Viking).

Grigson, Jane (1983) *The Fruit Book* (Harmondsworth: Penguin).

Gopnik, Adam (2006) 'Cooked Books: Real Foods from Fictional Recipes', *The New Yorker* 9 April: 80–5.

Grossmith, George and Weedon Grossmith (1892) *The Diary of a Nobody* (London: Simpkin, Marshall, Hamilton, Kent & Company).

Gurney, Peter J. (2009) '"Rejoicing in Potatoes": The Politics of Consumption in England during the "Hungry Forties"', *Past & Present* 203 (1): 99–136.

Gymnich, Marion and Norbert Lennartz, eds. (2010) *The Pleasures and Horrors of Eating* (Bonn: Bonn University Press).

Haber, Barbara (2002) *From Hardtack to Home Fries: An Uncommon History of American Cooks & Meals* (New York: Putman).

Hamsun, Knut (1991) *Hunger*, trans. Sverre Lyngstad (London: Cannongate).

Hardy, Thomas (2002) *Jude the Obscure* (Oxford: Oxford University Press).

Hardyment, Christina (1995) *Slice of Life: The British Way of Eating since 1945* (London: BBC Books).

Harris, Jessica B. (2011) *High on the Hog: A Culinary Journey from Africa to America* (New York: Bloomsbury).

Harris, S. (2012) 'Glorious Food? The Literary and Culinary Heritage of the Harry Potter Series', in *J.K. Rowling: Harry Potter*, ed. C. J. Hallett and P. J. Huey (Basingstoke: Palgrave Macmillan).

Hayes-Conroy, Alison and Jessica Hayes-Conroy (2008) 'Taking Back Taste: Feminism, Food and Visceral Politics', *Gender, Place and Culture* 15 (5): 461–73.

Haywood, Ian (1995) *The Literature of Struggle: An Anthology of Chartist Fiction* (London: Scolar Press).

Hemmings, Robert (2007) 'A Taste of Nostalgia: Children's Books from the Golden Age – Carroll, Grahame, and Milne', *Children's Literature* 35 (2007): 54–79.

Hollows, J. (2002) 'The Bachelor Dinner: Masculinity, Class and Cooking in *Playboy*, 1953–61', *Continuum: Journal of Media and Cultural Studies* 16 (2): 143–55.

Hollows, J. (2003) 'Feeling like a Domestic Goddess: Post-Feminism and Cooking', *European Journal of Cultural Studies* 6 (2): 179–202.

Holzwarth, Werner and Wolf Erlbruch (2007) *The Story of the Little Mole Who Knew It Was None of His Business* (London: Pavilion).

Houston, Gail T. (1994) *Consuming Fictions: Gender, Class, and Hunger in Dickens's Novels* (Carbondale, IL: Southern Illinois University Press).

Humble, Nicola (2000) *Introduction to Isabella Beeton*, in *Household Management* (Oxford: Oxford University Press, 2000), vii–xxx.

Humble, Nicola (2001) *The Feminine Middlebrow Novel 1920s to 1950s* (Oxford: Oxford University Press).

Humble, Nicola (2005) *Culinary Pleasures: Cookbooks and the Transformation of British Food* (London: Faber).

Humble, Nicola (2010a) *Cake: A Global History* (London: Reaktion Press).

Humble, Nicola (2010b) 'Domestic Arts', in *The Cambridge Companion to Victorian Culture*, ed. F. O. Gorman (Cambridge: Cambridge University Press, 2010), 219–35.

Humble, Nicola (2011) 'From Holmes to the Drones: Fantasies of Men without Women', in *The Masculine Middlebrow 1880–1950: What Mr Miniver Read*, ed. Kate Macdonald (London: Palgrave Macmillan).

Hunt, Peter (1996) '"Coldtonguecoldhamcoldbeefpickledgherkinsaladfrenchrollscresssandwid gespotted-meatgingerbeerlemonadesodawater …": Fantastic Foods in the Books of Kenneth Grahame, Jerome K. Jerome, H. E. Bates and Other Bakers of the Fantasy England', *Journal of the Fantastic in the Arts* (1996): 5–22.

Hyman, Gwen (2009) *Making a Man: Gentlemanly Appetites in the Nineteenth-Century British Novel* (Athens, OH: Ohio University Press).

Inness, Sherrie (2001) 'Bachelor Bait: Men's Cookbooks and the Male Cooking Mystique', in *Dinner Roles: American Women and Culinary Cuisine*, ed. Sherrie Inness (Iowa City: University of Iowa Press).

Isherwood, Christopher (1940) *Goodbye to Berlin* (London: The Hogarth Press).

Israel, Nico (2006) 'Geography', in *A Companion to Modernist Literature and Culture*, ed. David Bradshaw and Kevin J. H. Dettmer (Oxford: Blackwell).

Ives, Catherine (1951) *When the Cook Is Away* (London: Gerald Duckworth & Co).

James, Henry (1947) *The Portrait of a Lady* (Oxford: Oxford University Press).

James, Henry (1963) *The Siege of London*, in *The Complete Tales of Henry James*, vol V (London: Rupert Hart-Davis).

James, Henry (1981) *Roderick Hudson* (Harmondsworth: Penguin).

James, Henry (1984) *What Maisie Knew* (Harmondsworth: Penguin).

Joyce, James (1986) *Ulysses* (London: The Bodley Head).

Joyce, James (2000) *A Portrait of the Artist as a Young Man* (Harmondsworth: Penguin).
James Joyce Quarterly (2009) 46: (3–4).

Jekyll, Lady Agnes (1969) *Kitchen Essays* (London: Collins).

Kapetonios Meir, Natalie (2006) '"Household Forms and Ceremonies": Narrating Routines in Elizabeth Gaskell's *Cranford*', *Studies in the Novel* 38 (1): 1–14.

Kapetonios Meir, Natalie (2008) '"What Would You Like for Dinner?": Dining and Narration in *David Copperfield*', *Dickens Studies Annual* 39: 127–47.

Kass, Leon (1997) 'The Wisdom of Repugnance', *New Republic* 216 (22): 17–26.

Katz, Wendy (1980) 'Some Uses of Food in Children's Literature', *Children's Literature in Education* 11 (4): 192–9.

Keeling, Kara and Scott Pollard, eds. (2009) *Critical Approaches to Food in Children's Literature* (London: Routledge).

Keeling, Kara and Scott Pollard (2018) 'Utilizing Food Studies with Children's Literature and Its Scholarship', *Food and Literature*, ed. Gitanjali G. Shahani (Cambridge: Cambridge University Press).

Kelleher, Margaret (1997) *The Feminization of Famine: Expressions of the Inexpressible?* (Cork: Cork University Press, 1997).

Kelly, Daniel (2011) *Yuck!: The Nature and Moral Significance of Disgust* (London: MIT Press).

Kiell, Norman (1995) *Food and Drink in Literature: A Selectively Annotated Bibliography* (Lanham, MD: Scarecrow Press).

Kilbourn, Donald (1974) *Pots and Pants: Man's Answer to Women's Lib* (London: William Luscombe).

Kinealy, Christine (1994) *This Great Calamity: The Irish Famine 1845–52* (Dublin: Gill & Macmillan).

Korsmeyer, Carolyn (1999) *Making Sense of Taste: Food and Philosophy* (Ithaca, NY: Cornell University Press).

Korsmeyer, Carolyn (2011) *Savouring Disgust: The Foul and the Fair in Aesthetics* (Oxford: Oxford University Press).

Kristeva, Julia (1982) *Powers of Horror: An Essay in Abjection*, trans. Leon S. Roudiez (New York: Columbia University Press).

Ladenis, Nico (1987) *My Gastronomy* (London: Ebury Press).

Lanchester, John (1996) *The Debt to Pleasure* (London: Picador).

Langley, Andrew, ed. (1987) *The Selected Soyer* (Bath: Absolute Press).

Laubreaux, Alin (1931) *The Happy Glutton: How to Eat and How to Cook*, trans. Naomi Walford (London: Ivor Nicholson and Watson).

Lawrence, D. H. (1915) 'Ballad of Another Ophelia', in *Some Imagist Poets: An Anthology*, ed. H. D. (Hilda Doolittle) and Richard Aldington (Boston: Houghton Mifflin).

Lawrence, D. H. (1921) *Sea and Sardinia* (New York: Thomas Seltzer).

Lawrence, D. H. (1923) *Birds, Beasts and Flowers* (London: Martin Secker).

Lawrence, D. H. (1936) 'Poetry of the Present', in *Phoenix: The Posthumous Papers of D. H. Lawrence*, ed. Edward D. McDonald (New York: Viking).

Lawrence, D. H. (1988) *Sons and Lovers* (Harmondsworth: Penguin).

Lawson, Nigella (1998) *How to Eat* (London: Chatto and Windus).

Lee, Michael Parrish (2014) 'Eating Things: Food, Animals, and Other Life Forms in Lewis Carroll's Alice Books', *Nineteenth-Century Literature* 68 (4): 484–512.

Lee, Michael Parrish (2016) *The Food Plot in the Nineteenth-Century British Novel* (London: Palgrave).

Lehmann, Rosamond (1986) *Dusty Answer* (Harmondsworth: Penguin).

Leonardi, Susan J. (1989) 'Recipes for Reading: Summer Pasta, Lobster à la Riseholme, and Key Lime Pie', *PMLA* 104 (3): 340–7.

Levi, Primo (1988) *If This Is a Man* (Harmondsworth: Penguin).

Levy, Paul (1988) *Out to Lunch* (Harmondsworth: Penguin).

Lewis, Edna (2017) *The Taste of Country Cooking* (New York: Alfred A. Knopf).

Leyel, C. F. (1935) *The Gentle Art of Cookery* (London: Chatto and Windus).

Liena, Marianne and Brigitte Nerlich (2004) *The Politics of Food* (Oxford: Berg).

Light, Alison (2008) *Mrs Woolf and the Servants* (Harmondsworth: Penguin).

Lindgren, Astrid (2003) *The Best of Pippi Longstocking* (Oxford: Oxford University Press, 2003).

Lindner, Christoph (2002) 'Thackeray's Gourmand: Carnivals of Consumption in *Vanity Fair*', *Modern Philology* 99 (4): 564–81.

Linzie, Anna (2006) *The True Story of Alice B. Toklas: A Study of Three Autobiographies* (Iowa City: Iowa University Press).

Bibliography

Litvak, Joseph (1997) *Strange Gourmets: Sophistication, Theory and the Novel* (Durham: Duke University Press).

Lochhead, Liz (1984) *Dreaming Frankenstein & Collected Poems* (Edinburgh: Polygon Books).

Lockie, Stewart (2002) 'The Invisible Mouth: Moblizing 'the Consumer' in Food Production-Consumption Networks', *Sociologia Ruralis* 42 (2): 278–94.

Logan, Thad (2001) *The Victorian Parlour* (Cambridge: Cambridge University Press).

Lovegren, Sheila (1995) *Fashionable Food: Seven Decades of Food Fads* (New York: Macmillan).

Lowinsky, Ruth (1931) *Lovely Food: A Cookery Notebook* (London: The Nonesuch Press).

Lupton, Deborah (1996) *Food, the Body and the Self* (London: Sage).

McCuskey, Brian (2000) 'The Kitchen Police: Servant Surveillance and Middle-Class Transgression', *Victorian Literature and Culture* 28 (2): 359–75.

McFeeley, M. Drake (2001) *Can She Bake a Cherry Pie? American Women and the Kitchen in the Twentieth Century* (Amherst: University of Massachusetts Press).

Mansfield, Katherine (1981) *The Collected Stories of Katherine Mansfield* (Harmondsworth: Penguin).

Marcus, Stephen (1969) *The Other Victorians* (London: Corgi).

Marinetti, Fillipo Tommaso (2014) *The Futurist Cookbook*, trans. Lesley Chamberlain (Harmondsworth: Penguin).

Martineau, Mrs Philip (Alice) (1933) *Caviar to Candy: Recipes for Small Households from All Parts of the World* (London: R. Cobden-Sanderson).

Mayhew, Henry (1968) *London Labour and the London Poor*, vols I–IV (London: Dover Publications).

Meighn, Mora (1936) *The Magic Ring for the Needy and Greedy* (London: Oxford University Press).

Mennell, Stephen (1996) *All Manners of Food; Eating and Taste in England and France from the Middle Ages to the Present* (Urbana: University of Illinois Press).

Mennell, Stephen, Anne Murcott and Annette H. van Otterloo, eds. (1992) *The Sociology of Food: Eating, Diet and Culture* (New York: Sage).

Michie, Helena (1987) *The Flesh Made Word: Female Figures and Women's Bodies* (Oxford: Oxford University Press).

Miller, Daniel, ed. (1995) *Acknowledging Consumption* (London: Routledge).

Miller, Daniel (2001) *Consumption: Critical Concepts in the Social Sciences*, vol I, *Theory and Issues in the Study of Consumption* (London: Routledge).

Miller, William (1997) *The Anatomy of Disgust* (Cambridge, MA: Harvard University Press).

Mitford, Nancy (1986) *The Pursuit of Love*, in *The Nancy Mitford Omnibus* (Harmondsworth: Penguin).

Moe, Bryan W. (2014) 'The Rhetoric of Food: Discourse, Materiality, and Power', *Food, Culture and Society* 17 (2): 343–5.

Montanari, Massimo (1990) *The Culture of Food*, trans. Carl Ipsen (Oxford: Blackwells).

Montgomery, E. L. (1977) *Anne of Green Gables* (Harmondsworth: Penguin).

Moody, Alys (2012) 'The Non-Lieu of Hunger: Post-War Beckett and the Genealogies of Starvation', in *Early Modern Beckett; Beckett Between*, ed. Angela Moorjani et al. (Amsterdam: Rodopi).

Morash, Christopher, ed. (1989) *The Hungry Voice: The Poetry of the Irish Famine* (Dublin: Irish Academic Press).

Morash, Christopher (1995) *Writing the Irish Famine* (Oxford: Clarendon Press).

Morton, Timothy, ed. (2004) *Cultures of Taste, Theories of Appetite: Eating Romanticism* (London: Palgrave Macmillan).

Moss, Sarah (2009) *Spilling the Beans: Eating, Cooking, Reading and Writing in British Women's Fiction* (Manchester: Manchester University Press).

Nesbit, E. (1980) *The Phoenix and the Carpet* (Harmondsworth: Penguin).

Neuhaus, Jessamyn (1999) 'The Way to a Man's Heart: Gender Roles, Domestic Ideology, and Cookbooks in the 1950s', *Journal of Social History* 32 (3): 529–55.

Neuhaus, Jessamyn (2003) *Manly Meals and Mom's Home Cooking: Cookbooks and Gender in Modern America* (Baltimore: Johns Hopkins University Press).

Newnham-Davis, Liet.-Col. and Algernon Bastard (1903) *Gourmet's Guide to Europe* (London: G. Richards).

Nicolson, Mervyn (1987) 'Food and Power: Homer, Carroll, Atwood and Others', *Mosaic* 20 (3): 37–55.

Nicolson, Mervyn (1994) 'The Scene of Eating and the Semiosis of the Invisible', *Recherches semiotiqie/Semiotic Inquiry* 14 (1–2): 285–302.

Nikolajeva, Maria (2000) *From Mythic to Linear: Time in Children's Literature* (Lanham, MD: Scarecrow).

Nodelman, Perry (1996) *The Pleasures of Children's Literature* (New York: Longman).

Norton, Mary (1972) *The Borrowers* (Harmondsworth: Penguin).

Norton, Mary (1998) *The Borrowers Afield* (Orlando: Harcourt).

Novero, Cecilia (2010) *Antidiets of the Avant-garde: From Futurist Cuisine to Eat Art* (Minneapolis: University of Minnesota Press).

Oaten, M., R. J. Stevenson and T. I. Case (2009) 'Disgust as a Disease-Avoidance Mechanism' *Psychological Bulletin* 135 (2): 303–21.

Ó Gráda, Cormac (2006) *Ireland's Great Famine: Interdisciplinary Perspectives* (Dublin: Dublin Press).

Orwell, George (1968) 'Oysters and Brown Stout', in *The Collected Essays, Journalism and Letters of George Orwell* vol III, ed. Sonia Orwell (London: Martin Secker & Warburg).

Orwell, George (1989a) *The Road to Wigan Pier* (Harmondsworth: Penguin).

Orwell, George (1989b) *Keep the Aspidistra Flying* (Harmondsworth: Penguin).

Orwell, George (2013) *Down and Out in Paris and London* (Harmondsworth: Penguin).

Osgerby, Bill (2005) 'The Bachelor Pad as Cultural Icon: Masculinity, Consumption and Interior Design in American Men's Magazines, 1930–65', *Journal of Design History* 18 (1): 99–113.

Paster, Gail (1993) *The Body Embarrassed* (New York: Cornell University Press).

Pelletier, Yvonne Elizabeth (2009) 'Strawberries and Salt: Culinary Hazards and Moral Education in *Little Women*', in *Culinary Aesthetics and Practices in Nineteenth-Century American Literature*, ed. Moika Elbert and Marie Drews (New York: Palgrave Macmillan), 189–204.

Pennington, Fred (2000) *The Hungry Forties* (Leicester: Ulverscroft).

Perloff, Marjorie (1981) *The Poetics of Indeterminacy: Rimbaud to Cage* (Princeton: Princeton University Press).

Pierce, A. J. and J. A. Gauthier (2014) 'The Power and Politics of Disgust: Toward a Critical Theory of Food', *Social Philosophy Today* 131–46.

Plath, Sylvia (1981) *Collected Poems* (London: Faber).

Pollard, Scott, Kara Keeling (2002) 'In Search of His Father's Garden', in *Beatrix Potter's Peter Rabbit: A Children's Classic at 100*, ed. Margaret Mackey (Lanham, MD: Scarecrow).

Potter, Beatrix (1984) *The Complete Adventures of Peter Rabbit* (Harmondsworth: Puffin).

Potter, Beatrix (1989) *The Tale of Samuel Whiskers, or the Roly Poly Pudding* (London: Frederick Warne).

Powell, Julie (2009) *Julie & Julia: My Year of Cooking Dangerously* (Harmondsworth: Penguin).

Powell, Julie (n.d.) *The Julie/Julia Project*, https://web.archive.org/web/20021013043154/ and http://blogs.salon.com/0001399/2002/08/25.html.

Probyn, Elspeth (2000) *Carnal Appetites: Food Sex Identities* (London: Routledge).

Bibliography

Puckett, Kent (2008) *Bad Form: Social Mistakes and the Nineteenth-Century Novel* (Oxford: Oxford University Press).

'Quaglino' (1935) *The Complete Hostess* (London: Hamish Hamilton).

Quennell, Peter, ed. (1967) *Mayhew's Characters* (London: Spring Books).

Quennell, Peter, ed. (1969) *Mayhew's London* (London: Spring Books).

Randall, Margaret (1997) *Hunger's Table: Women, Food & Politics* (Watsonville, California: Papier-Mache Press).

Ransome, Arthur (2001) *Swallows and Amazons* (London: Random House).

Reichl, Ruth (1998) *Tender at the Bone* (London: Ebury Press).

Reynolds, Kimberley and Nicola Humble (1993) *Victorian Heroines* (London: Harvester/ Wheatsheaf).

Rich, Adrienne (1995) *Of Woman Born: Motherhood as Experience and Institution* (New York: W. W. Norton).

Richardson, Dorothy (1967) *Pointed Roofs*, in *Pilgrimage*, I (London: J. M. Dent & Sons).

Robbins, Bruce (1986) *The Servant's Hand: English Fiction from Below* (New York: Columbia University Press).

Roessel, David (2002) *In Byron's Shadow: Modern Greek and the English and American Imagination* (Oxford: Oxford University Press).

Roodhouse, Mark (2013) *Black Market Britain, 1939–1955* (Oxford: Oxford University Press).

Rose, Jacqueline (1984) *Peter Pan, or the Impossibility of Children's Literature* (London: Macmillan).

Rosner, Victoria (2005) *Modernism and the Architecture of Private Life* (New York: Columbia University Press).

Rothblum, Esther and Sondra Solovay, eds. (2009) *The Fat Studies Reader* (New York: New York University Press).

Roux, Albert and Michel Roux (1988) *At Home with the Roux Brothers* (London: Guild Publishers).

Rowling, J. K. (1997) *Harry Potter and the Philosopher's Stone* (London: Bloomsbury).

Roy, Parama (2010) *Alimentary Tracts: Appetites, Aversions, and the Postcolonial* (Durham: Duke University Press).

Rozin, Paul (1976) 'The Selection of Food by Rats, Humans, and Other Animals', in *Advances in the Study of Behaviour*, vol 6, ed. J. Rosenblatt, R. A. Hide, C. Beer and E. Shaw (New York: Academic Press).

Rozin, P., J. Haidt and C. McCauley (2008) 'Disgust', in *Handbook of Emotions*, 3rd edn, ed. M. Lewis, J. M. Haviland-Jones and L. F. Barrett (New York: Guildford Press).

Rushdy, Ashraf (1991) 'A New Emetics of Interpretation: Swift, His Critics and Alimentary Canal', *Mosaic* 24 (3–4): 1–32.

Russell, Sharman Apt (2005) *Hunger: An Unnatural History* (New York: Basic Books).

Rustin, Margaret and Michael (2001) *Narratives of Love and Loss: Studies in Modern Children's Fiction* (London: Karnac).

Ryan, Rachel and Margaret Ryan (1936) *Dinners for Beginners* (London: Hamish Hamilton).

Sceats, Sarah (2000) *Food, Consumption and the Body in Contemporary Women's Fiction* (Cambridge: Cambridge University Press).

Sceats, Sarah (2003) 'Regulation and Creativity: The Use of Recipes in Contemporary Fiction', in *The Recipe Reader*, ed. Janet Floyd and Laurel Forster (London: Ashgate).

Scholl, Lesa (2016) *Hunger Movements in Early Victorian Literature* (London: Routledge).

Scholl, Lesa (2017) 'The Rhetoric of Taste: Reform, Hunger and Consumption in Elizabeth Gaskell's Mary Barton', in *Food, Drink, and the Written Word in Britain, 1820–1945*, ed. Mary Addyman, Laura Wood and Christopher Yiannitsaros (London: Routledge).

Schor, Hilary (2013) *Women and the Trials of Realism* (Oxford: Oxford University Press).

Schor, Juliet B. and Douglas B. Holt, eds. (2000) *The Consumer Society Reader* (New York: The New Press).

Schwenger, Peter (2001) 'Words and the Murder of the Thing', *Critical Inquiry* 28 (1): 99–113.

Scieszka, Jon, and Lane Smith (1992) *The Stinky Cheese Man and Other Fairly Stupid Tales* (Harmondsworth: Penguin).

Sedgwick, Eve Kosofsky (2003) *Touching Feeling: Affect, Pedagogy, Performativity* (Durham: Duke University Press).

Selvon, Sam (2006) *The Lonely Londoners* (Harmondsworth: Penguin).

Shahani, Gitanjali G., ed. (2018) *Food and Literature* (Cambridge: Cambridge University Press).

Shapiro, Laura (1986) *Perfection Salad: Women and Cooking at the Turn of the Century* (New York: Henry Holt and Company).

Silva, E. (2000) 'The Cook, the Cooker and the Gendering of the Kitchen', *Sociological Review* 48 (4): 612–28.

Silver, Anna K. (2002) *Victorian Literature and the Anorexic Body* (Cambridge: Cambridge University Press).

Simon, Andre (1949) *Food* (London: Burke).

Sinclair, Catherine (1839) *Holiday House* (London: Ward, Lock & Co.).

Slater, Nigel (2003) *Toast: The Story of a Boy's Hunger* (London: Fourth Estate).

Slote, Sam (2010) 'Stuck in Translation: Beckett and Borges on Dante', *Journal of Beckett Studies* 19 (1): 15–28.

Slothower, Jodie and Jan Susina (2009) *Critical Approaches to Food in Children's Literature*, ed. Scott Pollard, Kara Keeling (London: Routledge).

Smart-Grosvenor, Vertamae (2011) *Vibration Cooking: Or, The Travel Notes of a Geechee Girl* (Athens, GA: The University of Georgia Press).

Smith, Joan (1996) *Hungry for You: From Cannibalism to Seduction: A Book of Food* (London: Chatto & Windus).

Snyder, Katherine (1999) *Bachelors, Manhood and the Novel, 1850–1925* (Cambridge: Cambridge University Press).

Spencer, Colin (2002) *British Food* (London: Grub Street).

Spry, Constance and Rosemary Hume (1961) *The Constance Spry Cookery Book* (London: J. M. Dent and Sons).

Stableford, Brian (2009) *The A to Z of Fantasy Literature* (Lanham, MD: Scarecrow Press).

Stallybrash, Peter and Allon White (1986) *The Politics and Poetics of Transgression* (Ithaca: Cornell University Press).

Stanton, Andy (2006) *You're a Bad Man, Mr Gum!* (London: Egmont).

Steere, Elizabeth (2013) *The Female Servant and Sensation Fiction: 'Kitchen Literature'* (London: Palgrave Macmillan).

Stein, Gertrude (1979) *Three Lives* (Harmondsworth: Penguin).

Stein, Gertrude (1983) *The Autobiography of Alice B. Toklas* (Harmondsworth: Penguin).

Stein, Gertrude (2003) *Tender Buttons* (London: Dover).

Stephens, Joseph Rayner (1838) *Northern Star*, 20 October.

Sullivan, Alexander M. (1877) *New Ireland: Political Sketches and Personal Reminiscences of Thirty Years of Irish Public Life* (Glasgow and London).

Sullivan, C. W. (2005) '"Chops … Cheese, New Bread, Great Swills of Beer": Food and Home in Kenneth Grahame's *The Wind in the Willows*', *Journal of the Fantastic in the Arts* 15 (2): 144–52.

Sutherland, John (2011) *Lives of the Novelists* (London: Profile Books).

Sutton, David (2001) *Remembrance of Repasts: An Anthropology of Food and Memory* (Oxford: Berg).

Symonds, James, ed. (2010) *Table Settings: The Material Culture and Social Context of Dining, 1700–1900* (Oxford: Oxbow Books).

Bibliography

Symons, Michael (2004) *A History of Cooks and Cooking* (Urbana: University of Illinois Press).

Tajiri, Yoshiki (2001) 'Beckett and Synaesthesia', *Samuel Beckett Today / Aujourd'hui*, 11: 178–85.

Tan, Shaun (2018) *Tales from the Inner City* (London: Walker Studio).

Thacker, Andrew (2004) 'Unrelated Beauty: Amy Lowell, Polyphonic Prose and the Imagist City', in *Amy Lowell, American Modern*, ed. Adrienne Munich and Melissa Bradshaw (New Brunswick: Rutgers University Press).

Thackeray, William Makepeace (1879) *The Book of Snobs*, in *The Works of William Makepeace Thackeray* (London: Smith, Elder & Co.).

Thackeray, William Makepeace (1985) *Vanity Fair* (Harmondsworth: Penguin).

Thackeray, William Makepeace (1993) 'A Dinner in the City', in *A Shabby Genteel Story and Other Writings* (London: Everyman).

Thirkell, Angela (1951) *Summer Half* (Harmondsworth: Penguin).

Thurer, Shari (1994) *The Myths of Motherhood: How Culture Reinvents the Good Mother* (New York: Penguin).

Tigner, Amy and Allison Carruth (2018) *Literature and Food Studies* (London: Routledge).

Toklas, Alice B. (1961) *The Alice B. Toklas Cook Book* (Harmondsworth: Penguin).

Tolkein, J. R. R. (1999) *The Hobbit* (London: HarperCollins).

Tomalin, Claire (1988) *Katherine Mansfield: A Secret Life* (Harmondsworth: Penguin).

Tompkins Kyla Wazana (2012) *Racial Indigestion: Eating Bodies in the Nineteenth Century* (New York: New York University Press).

Tompkins, Kyla Wazana (2013) 'Consider the Recipe, *J19: The Journal of Nineteenth-Century Americanists* 1 (2): 439–45.

Tromanhauser, Vicki (2011) 'Eating Well with the Ramsays: The Spirituality of Meat in *To the Lighthouse*', *Virginia Woolf Miscellany*, 14–16.

Trotter, David (2000) *Cooking with Mud: The Idea of Mess in Nineteenth Century Art and Fiction* (Oxford: Oxford University Press).

Truong, Monique (2004) *The Book of Salt* (London: Vintage).

Vallone, Lynne (2002) 'What Is the Meaning of All This Gluttony?': Edgeworth, the Victorians, C.S. Lewis and a Taste for Fantasy', *Papers: Explorations into Children's Literature* 12 (1): 47–54.

Vernon, James (2007) *Hunger: A Modern History* (Harvard: Harvard University Press).

Vester, Katharina (2015) *A Taste of Power: Food and American Identities* (Oakland: University of California Press).

Vike, Martina Plock (2010) *Joyce, Medicine and Modernity* (Gainesville: University Press of Florida).

Visser, Margaret (1989) *Much Depends on Dinner: The Extraordinary History and Mythology, Allure and Obsessions, Perils and Taboos, of an Ordinary Meal* (Harmondsworth: Penguin).

Visser, Margaret (1992) *The Rituals of Dinner: The Origins, Evolution, Eccentricities and Meaning of Table Manners* (Harmondsworth: Penguin).

Wallach, Jennifer Jensen (2014) 'How to Eat to Live: Black Nationalism and the Post-1964 Culinary Turn', Study the South, 2 July, http://southernstudies.olemiss.edu/study-the-south/how-to-eat-to-live.

'Walter' (1995) *My Secret Life*, Vol II (London: Wordsworth).

Warde, Alan (2014) 'After Taste: Culture, Consumption and Theories of Practice', *Journal of Consumer Culture* 14 (3): 279–303.

Warnes, Andrew (2004) *Hunger Overcome? Food and Resistance in Twentieth-Century-African American Literature* (Athens: University of Georgia Press).

Waugh, Evelyn (1980) *Brideshead Revisited* (Harmondsworth: Penguin).

Weir, David (1995) *Decadence and the Making of Modernism* (Amherst: University of Massachusetts Press).

Welch, Deschler (1896) *The Bachelor and the Chafing Dish* (New York: F. Tennyson Neely).

Westling, Louise, ed. (2014) *Cambridge Companion to Literature and the Environment* (Cambridge: Cambridge University Press).

Wharton, Edith (2012) *The House of Mirth* (Harmondsworth: Penguin).

Whelan, Irene (1995) 'The Stigma of Souperism', in *The Great Irish Famine*, ed. C. Poirtéir (Dublin: Mercier Press).

Whelan-Banks, Jane (2008) *Liam Goes Poo in the Toilet: A Story about Trouble with Toilet Training* (London: Jessica Kingsley).

White, Marco Pierre (1990) *White Heat* (London: Pyramid Books).

Wilder, Laura Ingalls (1964) *Little House on the Prairie* (Harmondsworth: Penguin).

Wilder, Laura Ingalls (2004) *Farmer Boy* (London: Harper).

Wilder, Laura Ingalls (2014) *Little House in the Big Woods* (London: Egmont).

Wilder, Laura Ingalls (2015) *These Happy Golden Years* (London: Egmont).

Williams-Forson, Psyche (2011) 'Foreword' to *Vibration Cooking* (Athens, GA: The University of Georgia Press).

Wilson, Bee (2002a) *New Statesman*, 19 August.

Wilson, Bee (2012) *Consider the Fork: A History of How We Cook and Eat* (London: Basic Books).

Wilson, Colin (2002b) *British Food – An Extraordinary Thousand Years of History* (London: Grub Street).

Wilson, A. N. (2005) *After the Victorians* (London: Hutchinson).

Witt, Doris (2004) *Black Hunger: Soul Food and America* (Minneapolis: University of Minnesota Press).

Woodham-Smith, Cecil (1991) *The Great Hunger: Ireland 1845–1849* (Harmondsworth: Penguin).

Woolf, Virginia (1966) 'Mr Bennett and Mrs Brown', in *Collected Essay of Virginia Woolf*, Vol I (London: Hogarth Press).

Woolf, Virginia (1980) *The Diary of Virginia Woolf, Vol III: 1925–1930*, ed. Anne Olivier Bell (London: The Hogarth Press).

Woolf, Virginia (1992a) *To the Lighthouse* (Oxford: Oxford University Press).

Woolf, Virginia (1992b) *A Room of One's Own* (Oxford: Oxford University Press).

Woolf, Virginia (1996) *Mrs Dalloway* (Harmondsworth: Penguin).

Woolf, Virginia (1999) *Jacob's Room* (Oxford: Oxford University Press).

Wynne Jones, Diana (1987) *A Tale of Time City* (London: Methuen).

Xu, Wenying (2008) *Eating Identities: Reading Food in Asian American Literature* (Honolulu: University of Hiwai'I Press, 2008).

Zafar, Rafia (1999) 'The Signifying Dish': Autobiography and History in Two Black Women's Cookbooks', *Feminist Studies* 25 (2): 449–69.

Zipes, Jack (2001) *Sticks and Stones: The Troublesome Success of Children's Literature from Slovenly Peter to Harry Potter* (London: Routledge).

Zlotnick, Susan (1996) 'Domesticating Imperialism: Curry and Cookbooks in Victorian England', *Frontiers* 16 (2/3): 51–68.

Zuckerman, Larry (2000) *The Potato* (London: Pan).

INDEX

Index

Index